THE ROMANCES OF CHRÉTIEN DE TROYES
A SYMPOSIUM

THE EDWARD C. ARMSTRONG MONOGRAPHS
ON MEDIEVAL LITERATURE

3

General Editor

KARL D. UITTI
Princeton University

For complete listing, see page 354

THE ROMANCES OF CHRÉTIEN DE TROYES
A SYMPOSIUM

EDITED BY
DOUGLAS KELLY

FRENCH FORUM, PUBLISHERS
LEXINGTON, KENTUCKY

Copyright © 1985 by French Forum, Publishers, Incorporated, P.O. Box 5108, Lexington, Kentucky 40505.

All rights reserved, including the right to reproduce this book, or parts thereof, in any form, except for the inclusion of brief quotations in reviews.

Library of Congress Catalog Card Number 85-70103

ISBN 0-917058-59-3

Printed in the United States of America

Jean Frappier
(1900-1974)

Eugène Vinaver
(1899-1981)

IN MEMORIAM

ACKNOWLEDGMENTS

I should like to recognize the material support provided this project by a number of agencies and individuals. A grant-in-aid from the American Council of Learned Societies (1979), typing, travel and other subsidies from Princeton University's Committee for Research in the Humanities and the Social Sciences, as well as assistance from the Editors of French Forum, Publishers, and from the Universities of Kentucky and Wisconsin, made it possible for the contributors to meet together and to defray typing and certain other expenses. A private benefaction made to the Edward C. Armstrong Monographs Fund, along with further support from Princeton University, has enabled us to meet publication costs. Our project as such was conceived during, and thanks to, a National Endowment for the Humanities Planning Grant (Research Division) awarded to me in 1975. Thanks, finally, must be expressed to Miss Linda Olson, of Madison, Wisconsin, who courageously undertook the final preparation of our joint typescript.

K.D.U.
Princeton, New Jersey
October 1982

TABLE OF CONTENTS

ACKNOWLEDGMENTS ... 7

PREFACE ... 11

DOUGLAS KELLY
Chrétien de Troyes: The Narrator and His Art ... 13

EDWARD J. BUCKBEE
Erec et Enide ... 48

MICHELLE A. FREEMAN
Cligés ... 89

MATILDA TOMARYN BRUCKNER
Le Chevalier de la Charrette (Lancelot) ... 132

KARL D. UITTI
Le Chevalier au Lion (Yvain) ... 182

RUPERT T. PICKENS
Le Conte du Graal (Perceval) ... 232

ALFRED FOULET
Appendix I. On Editing Chrétien's *Lancelot* ... 287

Appendix II. Chrétien's Indebtedness to the *Alexandre décasyllabique* ... 305

NOTES ... 311

SANDRA IHLE
Selected Bibliography ... 343

PREFACE

Chrétien's influence on romance was tremendous. The commanding position his works occupy in the tradition of medieval narrative and the excellence of his own production argue forcefully that romance, perhaps the most original development in medieval literature, is largely Chrétien's own invention. His successors and imitators, no matter how fine their accomplishments, constitute the tradition of which he may fairly be called the origin and fountainhead. Chrétien's romance, and the long line of those who emulate and continue him, depends on an art of romance that is his heritage and which made the tradition possible even as the art evolved, or rather, realized its potential in various matters and shapes.

What we know about Chrétien's art derives in the first instance almost entirely from authorial interventions in the prologues to his romances. It is our purpose to investigate that art as Chrétien sets it forth there. Of course, we shall examine and use the critical vocabulary scholarship tends to adopt to interpret romances: *matière, san* and *sens, conjointure, antancion,* and so forth. But we shall attempt as well to clarify and deepen that vocabulary on the basis of a historically demonstrable feature of art in Chrétien's time: a common technique for invention. The *trouvère,* like any other skilled *faber*—maker or craftsman—seeks his material in order to realize a certain intention through artifice. Every art, no matter how humble or exalted, in Chrétien's time, practiced invention. The application to specific works—romance composition, tapestry, mixing a potion—uncovers major features of the technique and facilitates the interpretation of discrete romances.

An important adjunct to Chrétien's art is his appreciation of the art of other narrators—including the narrators personified in his own romances. This means that the modern notion of intertextuality looms large in his art. Intertextual analysis is a more nearly historically accurate notion for traditional source study, the dominant concern of Chrétien scholarship for most of its early and middle years. But intertextuality takes into account authorial reflection on and adaptation of sources—and even a deliberate juxtaposition of source and adaptation in the text.

The text itself is problematic. There are no authoritative critical editions of Chrétien's romances. We are using the C.F.M.A. editions because of their ready availability. But the student is advised: there is no autograph manuscript of Chrétien, and, therefore, his text is a composite of variants pointing to a more or less faithful attempt to recover what Chrétien originally wrote. Our citations will sometimes contain changes on Roques's texts, changes which will be duly noted and justified to the extent necessary.

There are today a number of important comprehensive studies of Chrétien. There are the general surveys like Frappier's and Topsfield's,[1] as well as those that focus on an important problem, like Lacy's or Brandt's.[2] And, of course, there are more or less specialized studies in monograph and article form dealing with some, or even only one, of his romances. These studies are given due emphasis in this volume, although we do not intend a complete survey of scholarship. Such surveys already exist (see Bibliography below, pp. 342-53).

Nor do we promise complete unity of approach or interpretation, although there are no fundamental differences from one chapter to the other. This volume does constitute a whole—less, perhaps, because of uniformity of presentation from one chapter to another than from a common attempt to identify new, but historically valid and critically useful, perspectives on Chrétien the narrator and on the separate romances. Since, as a rule, general studies of Chrétien's works have tended to emphasize what is common, we have taken advantage of our multiplicity, our common interests, but diverse emphases, to explore the diversity of Chrétien. Thus, we can examine the narrator and his art in the major works, using suggestions explicit or implicit in the romances themselves. At the center of concern have been the authorial statements about romance art, about *san* and *matière*, *painne* and *antancion*, as these come together in romance *conjointure*. Infra- and intertextual references—the results of *conjointure*—suggest investigations into the significance of *jointures*, at beginning, middle and end, and in mirror-like reflections and refractions of one part of the narrative in another. The presuppositions common to all arts in the Middle Ages point to useful comparisons between Chrétien's and the practice of other arts described in the narrative. The modern tendency to fragment the narrator into various types, from the historical author to the self-referential text—a range of points of view in the text exploited by "Chrétien" himself —finds in these romances interesting, even exciting illustration. The diversity of Chrétien is evident whether he is observed from the angle of literary history or literary sociology, or in editing and discovering his sources, critical interpretation, or in the light of modern critical theory. This volume is meant to recognize and to encourage such approaches, whenever the romance texts seem to justify them.

D.K.

Douglas Kelly

Chrétien de Troyes: The Narrator and His Art

Chrétien de Troyes—the name evokes several figures, all of them candidates for what we may understand by narrator. But what is a narrator? This fundamental question lies at the heart of the diverse critical and historical evaluations and appreciations of Chrétien's romances, from the Middle Ages to the present. To begin the study of his romances, then, we may fairly attempt to disentangle the critical problems and identify the "Chrétien" who wrote the romances ascribed to him. This will not allow us to reconstruct his biography, as is possible for such late medieval authors as Charles d'Orléans and Villon. There is too little for such an enterprise in his works, and nothing in the archives. But we may observe the narrators Chrétien represents in his romances. From them we may better approach the art of romance, and, finally, study the romances in the light of that art.

Successive schools of scholarship and criticism[1] can be distinguished by the relative importance each accords to *matière*, *sens* or *conjointure*, words in Chrétien's prologues that refer to the basic features of his art. Scholarship at the turn of the last century stressed the establishment of critical editions as well as inquiry into Chrétien's language, dialect and biography, and the identification of his sources among real or putative Celtic, French and Latin antecedents. An immense amount of labor was spent on such investigations; today, however, these voluminous contributions are largely ignored. A sobering prospect! Nevertheless, the work of these scholars did raise important questions about romance invention, even if their answers are often vitiated by neglect of the artistic presuppositions by which the romance "was a means of giving shape to amorphous matter and thought."[2] Overemphasis on *matière* as source led to a failure to grasp the place of *sens* and *conjointure* in Chrétien's romances, and thus distinguish between what he may have borrowed and what he did with what he borrowed. Source study today is ground left largely fallow as far as Chrétien scholarship is concerned, although some relatively recent research—adumbrated, if not inspired, by Loomis' own studies[3]—has been clarifying the manner of oral tradition in ways useful for a just appreciation of the kind of *matière* Chrétien may have known. Hence we may speak, with Jean Fourquet, of two levels of coherence in a given romance, the one determined by the *merveilleux* retained from the sources, the other by the integrity of authorial conception of the work.[4] Thus we restore Chrétien's own balance of *matière* and *san* in *conjointure*.

The interest of Chrétien's romances as historical documentation has not been ignored. But it has until recently[5] been less his representation of feudal institutions and mentalities than his conception of love and marriage that has provoked discussion, debate and even perplexity. And even here, there was little of the serious investigation required to understand and appreciate medieval conceptions of marriage.[6] Chrétien's alleged glorification of conjugal affection in *Erec* and *Yvain* was once contrasted with his presumed displeasure with the adulterous love of Lancelot and Guenevere in the *Charrette*. Chrétien was even represented as being blessed with a "bourgeois" mentality, an alien in an aristocratic world (albeit to be "bourgeois" in the latter half of the twelfth century did not suggest the modern notion—it could even have been construed as revolutionary). What Chrétien studies need is a better appreciation of the aristocratic mentality as historians are beginning to understand it today. He and his fellow romancers assumed that mentality in their audiences, a fact evident in their choice and praise of patrons.[7] The need for a better understanding of the institutions and ideals in Chrétien's world has led to a reevaluation of literary history as literary sociology.[8] Corollary to this development is the recent effort to read Chrétien's romances as allegories of Christian theological and moral concerns.[9] The wide semantic range of *san/sens* in Old French has at least superficially accommodated such diverse and divergent readings.

The validity of both source studies and of historical evaluations of Chrétien's romances as documents requires an appreciation of his art.[10] It makes a difference whether his romances are perceived as works of literary art or as more or less successful conglomerations of earlier *contes*, whether they express a coherent conception or intention, or are mere entertainment, the *romans-feuilletons* of the twelfth century. This is the problem of *conjointure*, of the presumptive *bele conjointure* of each romance. *Conjointure* has not always been convincingly defined as a literary term. More often than not, it has been allowed to take on the meaning that fits a particular scholar's interpretation of a romance or group of romances. And since, unlike *san*, the word is a virtual hapax in French as a literary term, definitions are not easily controlled by divergent usage of the word outside the *Erec* Prologue; even its equation with *roman* does not clarify its meaning for Chrétien. Thus, the elucidation of *conjointure* has ranged from "figuring out" what is "going on" through historical investigations of its Latin background to identification of *conjointure* with the modern critical term *écriture,* the latter equally broad or precise, and thus controversial, in its applications.

It is impossible to summarize here the multifarious *conjointures* perceived over the years in Chrétien's romances; some will, of course, be discussed in the following chapters. It may be said, however, that many attempts to identify the *conjointure* of a given romance are not remarkable for clarity, consistency or even honest thoroughness. The primacy of Classical unity as a touchstone to esthetic appreciation and artistry; the assumption of a single archetype and of the *précellence* of the earlier, even lost version of a tale over later versions; the need to know the source in order to understand the derivative work; the study of the author's biography and reconstructed "philosophy" in order to appreciate presumed authorial self-expression in the work have all colored Chrétien interpretations.[11] Our real ignorance of, or great uncertainty about, influences artistic and otherwise on the composition of romance has inspired the current reaction, which is the critical displacement of the author in favor of the narrator and, indeed, the self-referential text—the *liber auctor.*

The divergency between the medieval and the modern esthetics has become of late a critical postulate and, indeed, a potential means of access to the medieval work. Alterity, as Hans Robert Jauss defines it, is "a reflection of its [the medieval work's] surprising aspects . . . , an activity which methodologically entails the reconstruction of the horizon of expectation of the addressees for whom the text was originally composed."[12] The strangeness of the medieval text for modern readers establishes a dialectics whose synthesis rests on both sympathetic appreciation of the work's "otherness" and accommodation of its artistic presuppositions to present-day esthetic expectations. This entails not only a serious evaluation of the work's esthetic and artistic orientation; it requires as well an attempt to know the art according to which the work was written.[13]

In his romances, that art is expressed by Chrétien de Troyes. Chrétien is the narrator, and he assumes a variety of narrator roles: the historical author; the person writing, reading or telling the romance story; the interpreter, even critic of that story. These narrator's voices, or, in Wayne Booth's terminology,[14] "implied authors," are our best and safest guides to the art of Chrétien's romances. Let us listen to what they say, and try to interpret their words in the milieu from which they, as Chrétien, speak.

The Historical Author

Recent Chrétien criticism has tended to neglect the author; at times, one even seems to hear the validity of historical or biographical allusions in the prologues questioned. Such skepticism comes close to denying the validity of historical evidence at the very times historians have been learning how to use such evidence to reconstruct and interpret medieval histories.[15] At the very least, Chrétien's personal or contemporary allusions introduce what may be called the "historical author" of his romances, and that author may have a voice which tells us of the world he wrote in and about. The historical author is a narrator whose voice informs us of the life, thought and avowed intentions of the once living Chrétien de Troyes.

Chrétien de Troyes lived and wrote in the second half of the twelfth century; he had died before the end of the century, probably not long after 1191.[16] His fame survived him, spreading over Western Europe as his works were copied, translated, adapted and no doubt discussed and even debated for several centuries after his death. All we know about the author himself comes from his romances. He must have begun to write about 1155 or 1160. The titles of his early production, almost entirely lost, are contained in the Prologue to *Cligés*, his second major romance. They include adaptations into French of three stories from Ovid's *Metamorphoses*, one of which, *Philomena*, probably survives incorporated into the fourteenth-century *Ovide moralisé*, and a version of the Tristan legend which Chrétien designates as "Del roi Marc et d'Ysalt la blonde" (l. 5) (About King Mark and the Blond Iseut). It has also been argued that he wrote *Guillaume d'Angleterre*, a kind of hagiographic adventure romance. The romances which gave shape to the European Arthurian legend are, in probable chronological order: *Erec et Enide*; *Cligés*; the *Chevalier de la Charrette* or *Lancelot*; *Yvain* or the *Chevalier au Lion*, which he wrote about the same time as the *Charrette*; and *Perceval* or the *Conte du Graal*. The *Perceval* is incomplete, probably because Chrétien died before completing it. And the last 1000 lines of the *Charrette* were written for Chrétien by Godefroi de Leigni, an otherwise unknown writer. Finally, there survive two or more of his courtly *chansons*.[17]

The extant romances provide a whole informed by themes that were to characterize Arthurian subjects throughout the rest of the Middle Ages: a dialectics between prowess in arms and noble, or "Arthurian" love,[18] a secular dichotomy occasionally darkened by conflicts like those between love and tournaments in *Erec* and *Yvain*. The quest is the motif usually employed to frame and show forth these themes, although combat, hospitality and the stages in the development of love are just as prominent.[19] Forces like fate and nemesis, chance and adventure, as well as the problem of the love between Tristan and Iseut—in whatever versions Chrétien may have known that legend—constantly surface in these writings as factors in the evaluation of love and prowess.

Chrétien says he wrote two of his romances, the *Charrette* and *Perceval*, at the behest of members of the high nobility. Marie de Champagne gave Chrétien the idea for the *Charrette*. She was a prominent figure in her time; not only Chrétien, but also Andreas Capellanus, the trouvère Conon de Béthune and others refer to her.[20] Marie belonged to an illustrious family whose influence on the spread of courtly literature and thought was broad and lasting.[21] Her great-grandfather was the earliest known troubadour, William Duke of Aquitaine and Count of Poitiers. Her mother was Eleanor of Aquitaine, her father Louis VII of France. Members of that family bore the courtly and chivalric ideals, as well as their forms of expression, throughout the Occident, implanting a brilliant new culture everywhere they went and thus fostering centers of artistic radiation within the European nobility.

Philippe de Flandre et d'Alsace, who Chrétien says gave him the book on which he based the *Perceval*, also figures prominently in the aristocracy of the later twelfth century.[22] Both Marie and Philippe are part of the royalty and high aristocracy that encouraged the emergence of courtly romance: the English court of the Plantagenets, the courts of the counts of Champagne, of Alsace-Flanders, of Blois and of the southwestern France of the *langue d'oc*. Chrétien's writings suggest that he may have moved about rather widely in this world. Besides the references to Philippe and Marie, he alludes in *Cligés* to the library of St. Peter's at Beauvais; and he may have visited England.

Chrétien's romances come from a world where public reception was quite different from what it is today. The aristocracy which he wrote for was characterized by a mentality that is hardly understood, let alone taken seriously, by the modern reader. The aristocrat determined—dictated would probably be too strong—and the author interpreted. This is clear from the *Charrette* and *Perceval* Prologues. Such deference recalls Erec's decision to ask the Queen to provide Enide with fine clothing, since such dress would be superior to what the count her uncle could provide for her stay at court. Erec was a king's son, and only royalty was fit to provide for his fiancée. Such gestures are founded on a trust in order and precedence, a deep sense of public rank and inborn worth. The author as authority expresses that view of the world in which the aristocratic ideal supersedes other prerogatives, sometimes even religious prerogatives.[23] Hence Chrétien's deference to Marie de Champagne and Philippe de Flandre in the composition of the romances they had him write. He hardly thought he erred in doing so. In fact, the works they proposed to him, dealing with Lancelot and Guenevere and with the grail, are the two most remarkable *matières* in his romances.

Chrétien's larger public probably embraced the entire aristocracy, including the less favored members of the lower nobility who may have found his idealization of the Arthurian world expressive of their own uncertain aspirations.[24] Women, too, may have taken a special interest in romances that deal so extensively with the lady, her feudal obligations and amorous propensities, especially since the literate aristocracy was probably composed primarily of women.[25] Chrétien's patrons are, insofar as his prologues indicate, of the very highest nobility. His principal characters occupy corresponding places in the romance world. For the most part the heroes are the sons of kings, emperors or the high aristocracy. The heroines represent a wider range of social origins, from imperial families to impoverished or dispossessed nobility. For all of them, love and marriage are means to maintain or restore rightful status. Such a feudal and chivalric élite served as an inspiration, a rallying point for good order in society.[26] Even the less fortunate or less well-born nobility enjoyed, through the bond of brothers-in-arms or *compagnonnage*, a place and a promise in the social order. These concerns permeate and inform the narrative in Chrétien's romances.

Neither the clergy nor the bourgeoisie and people play any prominent role in the romance narratives except in service to the knights and ladies. There is no textual foundation for the hypothesis that the villein in *Yvain*, as a man—"il me dist qu'il ert uns hom" (l. 328)—evokes a humanistic or democratic idealism. The villein, described as a kind of giant freak, elicits no pity, but only astonishment and some fright in those who meet him. He no more understands what knightly adventure is than the knight himself comprehends what kind of man—"Quiex hom ies tu?" (l. 329)—the gigantic, filthy and long-eared creature may be. The pity evoked in the same romance for the maidens forced to work for the devils is not based on sympathy for the working class, but only on distaste at base treatment of noble maidens forced to do the people's work.

Now, the French aristocracy was by no means a cohesive, orderly community in Chrétien's time. He alludes in *Yvain*—and he was not the first to do so—to the decline among his contemporaries from the ideals of courtesy and love essential to any civilization founded on *chevalerie* and *clergie*. For these two ideals are handed down from past civilizations to the present. This commonplace notion—the so-called *translatio studii et imperii*[27]—was adapted by Chrétien to a new order, that of knighthood. But knighthood, as is now known, was more of a profession than a class in Chrétien's time.[28] Yet he helped raise it from an art to a calling by his romances.[29] Furthermore, by the notion of *clergie* Chrétien confirmed the aristocracy's newfound appropriation of Latin learning as its own in romance and lyric.[30]

The union of knight and cleric is apparent from the romances, and *chevalerie* and *clergie* express the abstraction and idealization of those callings.[31] In addition, Chrétien fixes love as a source of inspiration in both spheres by the emphases of all his romances, even *Perceval*—love which had evolved and refined itself from the kinds of sexual or sensual passion that propels lovers in epic, early romance and Béroul's *Tristan*, to a *fin' amors* based on choice, quality of sentiment, will and even reason.[32] These ideas Chrétien expressed against the historical and social backdrop of a knighthood that, by distinguishing itself as a class, was becoming consolidated in order to represent and defend itself and its ideals. It is striking that, by emphasizing the knight and the cleric, rather than, say, the king, emperor or great leaders, or the ecclesiastical princes like bishops or archbishops, Chrétien is including all members of the noble classes in a common order—the order of knighthood and of clergy.

Such exclusiveness was not without its problems. Erich Köhler has detailed the difficulties in integrating a poor but new class of knights into an old, established and wealthy—but also small—landed aristocracy whose origins go back to Carolingian times and even earlier. How could integration of one's poor relatives, as it were, be usefully effected? On the more private level, what was to become of younger sons and daughters when the paternal estates fell to the eldest? And what of those dispossessed by war, famine, intrigue? The *Erec* was something of an answer, a partial one which, however, insisted on the need for unity of purpose and mutual esteem and even love among members of the same class.

These were surely great and immediate concerns in the second half of the twelfth century. The responsibility of the worthy was great, and largesse figures as a primary virtue in Chrétien's romances, as in many of those of his successors.[33] Equally important was the fact that the wealthy were too few to defend all that fell to their prerogatives, domains and responsibilities. As *cavaliers* became *chevaliers* and the feudal system emerged and spread, those newly admitted to the aristocracy began to show their mettle, that is, to demonstrate their nobility, before Chrétien started to write. An ordered hierarchy in which suzerain and vassal worked together for the common and collective good of their people, through the triumph of courtesy and civilization over villainy as well as the enhancement of prowess and love, fostered faith in the *preudome* as the bulwark against recalcitrant forces within and outside the nobility. The robber barons, the ignoble lords and scheming ladies—like Galoain and Oringle de Limors, Meleagant and the elder daughter of the Sire de la Noire Espine—had to be corrected or eliminated. Chrétien's romances show the struggle, and they provide the example by the Round Table of service to a higher cause that everyone might imitate, from dukes and counts to impoverished barons and landless knights. It is remarkable, in fact, how many royal sons and daughters hold to Arthur's court rather than their own: Gauvain and his brothers, children of King Lot; Erec, son of King Lac; Yvain, son of King Urien; Perceval, of the family of the Fisher King; probably Lancelot; Alixandre and Cligés, from the line of the Byzantine emperors. Indeed, Alixandre refuses accession to the throne in favor of achieving renown there where it is greatest:

> Nus ne m'an porroit retorner,
> Par proiere ne par losange,
> Que je n'aille an la terre estrange
> Veoir le roi et ses barons,
> De cui si granz est li renons
> De corteisie et de proesce.
> (*Cligés*, ll. 146-51)

(No one could dissuade me by entreaty or flattery from going to that foreign land to see the King and his lords whose fame for courtesy and prowess is so great.)

If such figures paid respect to honor and courtesy by serving at another's court, what could lesser, less fortunate figures do but imitate them? And what could their betters rightly do but encourage and sustain their noble inferiors by largesse and by example?

Now, nobility of blood has always been compared to nobility of mind. *Honor* in the twelfth century derives from the notion of lands and possessions, but it also extends to comprehend inner worth. The exemplar may achieve nearly perfect representation in figures who, at first blush, appear unworthy of the court, like Enide and Perceval. Shame and farce color hidden worth, while a *pucele*'s smile betokens Perceval's unique excellence in *chevalerie* (*Perceval*, ll. 1057-60 [1059-62]). Those possessing the qualities, the capacity to appreciate honor, will bring it to the fore and set it out, adorning it in fitting manner and gesture. Enide's father waited for someone noble enough to appreciate her qualities, and he found a prince and a crown for her in Erec. Erec raised Enide to Arthur's court, and all marveled at and acquiesced in homage to her wondrous self, a veritable exemplar of noble beauty. The perception and the ability to represent such excellence is the hallmark of the true artist, as Chrétien explains in the *Erec* Prologue. Like Erec looking at Enide in her tattered dress and unkempt appearance, Chrétien perceived in the diverse and incomplete *contes* related in the courts of his time the *molt bele conjointure* that became the first Arthurian romance, *Erec et Enide*.

The Art of Romance: The Narrator's Voices

Chrétien's predecessors, notably Wace and, probably, Geffrei Gaimar, adapting Geoffrey of Monmouth's *Historia regum Britanniæ* into French, hold mostly to the syntagmatic sequence and the dynastic emphases typical of chronicler and annalistic histories. The early French adaptations of Latin epic and legend (ca. 1160-1185) claim to be faithful renditions of the original sequence of events, despite interpretive amplifications like those on love and knighthood in the *Thèbes* and *Eneas* adaptations of, respectively, Statius and Virgil, as well as in the ambitious *Roman de Troie*, in which Benoît de Sainte-Maure rendered in French verse the accounts of the siege of Troy by the pseudo-Dares and Dictys:

> Le latin sivrai e la letre,
> Nule autre rien n'i voudrai metre,
> S'ensi non com jol truis escrit.
> Ne di mie qu'aucun bon dit
> N'i mete, se faire le sai,
> Mais la matire en ensivrai.
> (*Troie*, ll. 139-44)[34]

(I shall follow the Latin source exactly, nor shall I try to relate anything other than in the way I find it written. I don't say that I won't include some amplificatory flourishes, if I can; nevertheless, I will follow my source.)

Chrétien distinguishes his romances from these works by insisting on discriminate selection and combination of source material in a new, more artistically satisfying arrangement which he calls a *bele conjointure* (*Erec*, l. 14). The "beauty" of such a *conjointure* is the beauty of romance design itself. Therefore, in his subsequent writings Chrétien began to use the word *roman*—modern "romance"—in place of *conjointure*: "De la fu li contes estrez / Don cest romanz fist Crestïens" (*Cligés*, l. 22 and var. [p. 208]) (The story from which Chrétien made this romance was taken from there). The *roman* as *conjointure* became established among Chrétien's successors, as the Prologue to Renaut de Beaujeu's *Bel Inconnu* indicates towards the end of the twelfth century: "veul un roumant estraire / D'un molt biel conte d'aventure" (ll. 4-5)[35] (I want to draw a romance from a very beautiful tale of adventure). The fashioning of romance, or a *bele conjointure*, from disparate sources follows on the amalgamation of *matière* and *san*. Chrétien wrote that, when Marie de Champagne requested the composition of the *Charrette*, she provided him with both *matière* and *san*. He in turn applied his own *sans* and *painne*, or, as he expresses it in the same place, his *painne* and *antancion* to following her commands. The Prologue to the

Charrette makes clear that the artist as Chrétien conceives of him receives the *matière* and *san* as givens, which he or she then applies to the composition of the actual romance. The *matière*, then, is a source. It may be written or oral; Chrétien says he used a book for *Cligés* and *Perceval*, and tales of storytellers or jongleurs for *Erec et Enide*. His effort, or *painne*, transforms the sources into romance. *Painne* implies specifically the practice of his art as narrator and author.

It is generally agreed that Chrétien underwent the influence of the instruction on writing given in twelfth-century schools, where he probably learned the art he applied in his romances.[36] Despite the difficulty of achieving precise definitions for Chrétien's terminology, his words do express the artistic goal of authorial elucidation and adaptation of a given matter. Adaptation, indeed intertextual commentary, is pervasive in medieval French literature.[37] Attentive application to the elucidation of earlier writing draws forth and clarifies what the new author deemed implicit in his or her less perfect, or more obscure, predecessors. Chrétien's great contemporary, Marie de France, writing, probably in England for Henry II Plantagenet, sets forth the technique in the important Prologue to her *Lais*. The ancients, she announces—and for the Middle Ages almost any predecessor could be seen as an ancient[38]—wrote books which seem obscure, and they did so

> Pur ceus ki a venir esteient
> E ki aprendre les deveient,
> K'i peüssent gloser la lettre
> E de leur sen le surplus mettre.
> (ll. 13-16)[39]

(So that those who were to come after them and who would have to learn what they wrote might gloss the literal text and add to it what had been left unsaid.)

Here we recover a more precise sense of Benoît de Sainte-Maure's *bon dit*, the additions he permitted himself while carefully following his sources. Similarly, the *Eneas* author expanded upon the love not only of Dido and Eneas, but, even more extensively, upon that of Eneas and Lavine in Italy, a love story which Virgil could be said to have neglected. These narrative additions and amplifications entailed an appreciation of "obscurities" in Virgil—human affection—into which the new author read the chivalric and Ovidian language which his time adopted and thus took seriously. This, too, is an amalgam of *matière* and *san* in a new invention. These earlier writings provided Marie with the art employed in her own composition (*Lais* Prol., ll. 28-42).

Daniel Poirion has defined the *Eneas* esthetic as an *écart* between two world views brought into juxtaposition; two *cultes*, as he terms them, must therefore be conjoined in an elegant, but necessarily diverse amalgam.[40] In the case of the *romans d'antiquité*, there was the conflict between Classical pagan *matière* and Christian and aristocratic mentalities. The *concors discordia* in the romance that combines the two has its counterpart in the two *niveaux de cohérence* Jean Fourquet postulated for Chrétien's romances: the level of *matière*, Celtic and marvelous, and that of *san*, courtly and scholastic. Like Marie, Chrétien began with adaptations from Latin, as his *Cligés* Prologue states; he then applied the skills learned thereby to the new Celtic *matière* that had attracted her. His accomplishments are remarkable. He established romance form and narrative. He invented in his *matière* the questing knight, the love of Lancelot and Guenevere, and the grail. That is, he proposed an exemplary image in the three realms which, for Dante, yield the finest ideas—the *san*—of vernacular literature: prowess in arms, noble love and rectitude.[41] And he did so by the elucidation of obscurities in humble matter. Before Chrétien, the *graal* was a dish, a low-bottomed bowl equivalent elsewhere to the bowl (*escuele*) shared by guests at the medieval table.[42] Yet even if the word would not have seemed strange to his contemporaries, Chrétien's treatment of it was new and wonderful. He made the grail into an object of mystery, and medieval writers, fascinated from his time on by that mystery, probed its hidden potential for new significance. Their discovery is not dissimilar to late antiquity's realization that the humble language of the Bible contained wonderful and inexhaustible sources of mystery. It was the word of God. Just so, the word grail designated a sacred object after Chrétien.

Chrétien's Romances in the Middle Ages

How did Chrétien's contemporaries perceive his accomplishments? There seem to have been two responses, one immediate, explicit and laudatory, the other delayed, indirect and finally rejective. Judgments pertain to Chrétien's artistry and to the presuppositions of the world view expressed in and through his romances. His art, his language, especially his skill at amplificatory expression enjoyed general approbation. For Huon de Méry, "onques bouche de crestien / Ne dist si bien"[43] (never did Christian mouth speak more eloquently): Chrétien took "Le bel françois trestot a plein" (*Torneimenz*, l. 1339) (the full measure of beautiful French), leaving nothing to glean for those who followed him. His versification, we now know, was original, even daring; it broke the staid conformity and monotony of earlier octosyllabic couplets, where middle breaks were rare and probably disallowed in practice.[44] But he was also admired for his choice of matter, for the manner by which he represented the Arthurian world, its problems and ideals, in the modern, immediately accessible and significant contexts of feudal obligation, courteous sentiment and chivalric duty.

Yet Chrétien seems aware that he was vulnerable to criticism and interference. Godefroi de Leigni's Epilogue to the *Charrette* emphasizes the perfect balance between context and arrangement of *matière* in the work completed with Chrétien's approval (II. 7106-07). Chrétien intended the *Charrette* to be neither *depeciee* nor *corronpue*. In the *Yvain*, closely linked to the *Charrette*, Chrétien emphasizes the integral wholeness and veracity of the work (II. 6804-08). Such completeness is achieved by the *conjointure*.

The art of *conjointure*—invention—subsumes both contextual and narrative coherence. That is, the elaboration of the authorial conception of *matière* in the work provides a context within which the reader may understand and interpret the *récit*. Still, however *bele* the romance *conjointure* may be, the choice of context could make it appear vain, empty of redeeming value, even dangerous, if that context promoted ideas and principles of conduct in conflict with established authorities. It even invited censure:

> Dame, de ce n'avez vos cure:
> De mençonge qui cuers oscure,
> Corrompant la clarté de l'ame,
> N'en aiez cure, douce dame.
> Leissiez Cligés et Perceval,
> Qui les cuers tue et met a mal,
> Et les romanz de vanité.
> (*Vies des peres*, II. 29-35)[45]

(Lady, don't bother with such matters. Don't concern yourself, dear lady, with lies that darken the heart, contaminating the light of the soul. Put aside Cligés and Perceval, and romances on vain subjects, works that slay and corrupt the heart.)

Such censure fixes on areas of belief and moral hierarchies that Chrétien's romances often seem to ignore, or even to upset and implicitly question—for example, the sanctity of marriage.

Thus, the apparently original, if controlled mores that one finds in Chrétien's works were inimical to moral authority, and his idealism could hardly be sustained even by the aristocracy in the time of the early Inquisition.[46]

The Church had finally begun to bring the notion of knighthood under its moral and ideological sway, and this would not fail to affect the romantic idealization of love and its beneficial influence on prowess. This, combined with the inevitable discrepancies between ideal and reality, had deleterious effects. Abstract ideas were becoming vain, ultimately empty words.[47] One of the last appeals to the Arthurian ideal as opposed to, yet exemplary for, contemporary reality occurs in *Claris et Laris*, a long verse romance composed about a century after Chrétien's death. But like Chrétien in *Yvain*, the *Claris* author laments a vision lost in the contemporary reality. Arthurian verse romance as Chrétien invented it was moribund by then, and had virtually died by the end of the thirteenth century, except for recopying and occasional adaptations.[48] Chrétien's idealism survived only in the lyric and allegorical images of the fourteenth century. But Chrétien passes to these works through the prism of the *Roman de la Rose*.[49]

The *Rose* offers a dual evaluation of love and courtesy, both laudatory and censorious, lifting the courtly ideal to wondrous planes in Guillaume de Lorris, then reducing it to seduction, conquest, perhaps even rape in Jean de Meung.[50] Chrétien's Arthurian romances and their ideals also underwent reevaluation in the great French prose cycles that dominate romance production from the thirteenth century on. The grail and Christian religious and moral rigorism not only overshadowed, they overwhelmed the courtly presuppositions pervasive in Chrétien. Human conduct was meaningless when the great quests were inspired by purposes other than God's; in some cases predestination rendered human choice and innocence problematical.[51]

Problem Romances and Chrétien's Critical Vocabulary

Eugène Vinaver has described in Chrétien's works what we may call "problem romances."[52] This formula replaces the earlier notion of the *Thesenroman*, the *roman à thèse*, that promulgates a specific doctrine, code or philosophy.[53] We have observed that Chrétien's own emphases and those in the history of scholarship tend to locate the problems under one or the other head *matière*, *sens* and *conjointure*. Ideally, of course, the problems Chrétien raises would be treated, and resolved or elucidated, under all three heads. But this has seldom been the case. Critical emphases, even biases, have isolated or concentrated on one feature of his art of romance to the exclusion of others that are equally pertinent; and this has given rise to some ill-defined, even false problems. The following discussion will attempt to identify and analyze the most important problems in the light of Chrétien's own statements about them. It will thus anticipate and lay the groundwork for the ensuing critical readings of the romances.

Despite the relatively clear general conception of literary art expressed in Chrétien's authorial interventions, there is considerable uncertainty regarding the precise signification of his terminology and critical commentary. This is in part because some of his language is very broad; the referents for words like *matière* and *san/sens* and their traditions have not always been understood. Now, since medieval terminology, even in philosophy and the sciences (especially before the thirteenth century), is notoriously diversified, identification of Chrétien's artistic presuppositions requires both knowledge of the traditions to which he belongs and which he exploits, and careful interpretation of his romances as they reflect those traditions. Such historical emphases recognize "alterity" as a factor in interpretation. Alterity is in fact a necessary philological prolegomenon to translation of Chrétien's art into modern language.

Chrétien refers explicitly to the traditions that most affected his romances: the popular *conteur* tradition (*Erec* Prologue), the Classical tradition handed down through the monasteries and schools to the High Middle Ages (*Cligés* Prologue), Christian world view and doctrine (*Perceval* Prologue), aristocratic world views and class presuppositions (Prologues to *Cligés* and the *Charrette* and the opening statement in *Yvain*), and a "noble" conception of love between man and woman inspired by troubadour and Ovidian sources (*Yvain* opening statement). These traditions raise certain interpretive problems regarding the *matière*, *san/sens* and *conjointure* of Chrétien's romances.

Matière: Reception and Adaptation

A major problem in Chrétien studies is the lack of a good critical edition of his romances. No holographs survive. And the manuscripts themselves show sometimes remarkable divergencies. The two complete editions we have—Foerster's and Roques's—were established on editorial principles generally considered unsatisfactory today.[54] Furthermore, the differences between the romances as Chrétien wrote them and the results of deliberate scribal interventions are sometimes obscure. Chrétien seems to have construed his romances as strictly delimited in content (*Yvain*, ll. 6806-08). This concern is evident as well in the 1000-line conclusion which Godefroi de Leigni wrote for the *Charrette,* a conclusion which, Godefroi alleges, conforms to Chrétien's own plan for the romance (*Charrette*, ll. 7098-7112). But there are "unauthorized" scribal additions in some romances. These may well illustrate Vinaver's view that each scribe, each succeeding reader could elaborate on what seemed implicit or too brief—or even too prolix—in the original. The manuscript tradition for each romance contains evidence of such scribal tinkering; the incomplete *Perceval* is a veritable laboratory case of additions, interpolations and continuations. Such *mouvance,* the term Paul Zumthor uses to describe such phenomena, may indeed be an accepted feature of the art of romance.[55]

Mouvance also comprehends Chrétien's own reception and adaptation of sources. Nothing specific has survived from the *conteurs'* repertories or of the "books" which Chrétien claims to have mined for narrative material. Therefore, we cannot know his *matière* for the *Charrette*, for example, as we do know Chrétien's romance and can therefore appreciate its adaptation in the thirteenth-century prose *Lancelot*. Inquiry into the ways of oral and literary transmission—the process of *translatio*—does, however, yield some general information about what kinds of sources Chrétien may have known, and this in turn permits some generalizations about the kinds of changes he may have made on them.

To Chrétien the most obvious feature of the transmitted material was its strangeness, its alterity. The Grail book of Philippe de Flandre is wondrous, unlike any other; the *Erec matière* of the jongleurs appears outlandish and extraordinary. Yet it was precisely the extraordinary that provided romance *merveilles*. The referents for *merveille* in romance are of every color and description, extending from supernatural enchantment and sacred miracle to the merely uncommon or unusual. "Le moyen âge s'étonne aussi facilement qu'il croit," remarks a contemporary historian.[56] And Chrétien appropriated some of the most remarkable examples of such extraordinary phenomena from his sources.

Although the Middle Ages perceived the universe, and the order of the created world, as ultimately comprehensible, at least to God, such transcendent intelligibility was quite beyond the grasp of the secular aristocracy. In the twelfth century illiteracy was general except for those in the Church and some privileged members of the nobility. Knowledge was largely a matter of oral transmission. Such knowledge could indeed be complex, corresponding to a real social and economic order; it was at once concrete and spiritual, traditional and practical. Nonetheless, even here the intrusion of the unknown or the unexpected—that is, of the extraordinary—was a source of anxiety and fascination; marvelous phenomena elicited attempts to integrate the unknown into the known world or to eliminate it as a threat to peace and order. Forays into the unknown, into the *merveilleux,* exposed one to uncertain adventures; knowing or comprehending the *merveille* was its achievement by integration or dissipation. This could also lead to one's own destruction or impotence. Or so Chrétien's romances suggest.

Chrétien discovered in his sources the *merveilles* of his Arthurian vision: the Round Table, the Queen and her lover, the grail, the questing knight, certain adventures that recur throughout his romances and those of his successors, like the Perilous Ford, the evil dwarf and the midget knight, the lone maiden in the forest, the enchanted castle, the hospitable host.

Some of these recurrent adventures acquired special prominence in a single romance: the Flaming Lance, the Sword Bridge, Mabonagrain's garden of the *Joie de la cour*, the Magic Fountain, the Fisher King in the Grail Castle.

In order to weave together into a coherent narrative such obtrusive *merveilles*, Chrétien utilized the motifs of quest and encounter (*aventure*). His design is a fascinating skein of *aventures* and *merveilles*, often with no more cognitive significance than one finds in fairy tales. To Chrétien the *contes* he discovered certainly lacked what for him was coherent sequence and meaningful context. They were mysterious, obscure, yet fascinating. Chrétien adapted these elements from his sources in narratives that elucidate the mysterious by confrontation—confrontation between the orderly, or at least meaningful, defended by the questing knight, and the *aventure merveilleuse* that became a touchstone not only of his purpose and significance, but, by the encounter, of those of the romance itself.

It is useful in this context to recall that *matière* has two important senses in Chrétien's time: first, that of raw material or the source, as the author finds it; second, that of the material he chooses to incorporate into his romance. The contents of the given romances emerge from the winnowing and sifting, the shaping and polishing of its sources.

"Celticity," or the supernatural, is not essential to *merveilles* and the *émerveillement* they provoke. The *romans antiques* and later adventure romances demonstrate as much. *Cligés* has no quests and no adventures of the usual Arthurian kind. But it does have marvelous events and objects, like the cup Alixandre wins after the siege of Windsor or Jehan's tower into which escape Cligés and Fenice. The marvel of such settings is love itself. As in the *Charrette*, a romance characterized perhaps more than any other by marvelous and mysterious forests and adventures, the carnal union of Lancelot and Guenevere is the central *merveille*—a *merveille* as unspeakable for Chrétien as the grail:

> ... il lor avint sanz mantir
> une joie et une mervoille
> tel c'onques ancor sa paroille
> ne fu oïe ne seüe;
> mes toz jorz iert par moi teüe,
> qu'an conte ne doit estre dite.
> (*Charrette*, ll. 4676-81)

(In truth there overcame them a joy and a marvel such that never before was its like heard or known. But I will never utter it, for it is something that stories must not relate.)

Here, as in *Cligés*, the extraordinary quality of the *merveille* is translated through hyperbole and the topic of inexpressibility. A *merveille* evokes *émerveillement*, not definitions and analytic descriptions. It is astonishment, wonder turning to curiosity, as in the Old French verbal form which is a virtual question: "je me merveil . . . ."

Questioning inquiry is fundamental to invention. Such invention serves to situate the *merveille* in a context that makes it, or its function, meaningful within the narrative economy. Extensive monologues, dialogues and descriptions illuminate and translate the significance of the *merveilles* achieved in quest of adventure, love and truth.

San/sans: *Conception and Signification*

The semantic range of the word pair *san/sans* in medieval French, even in its literary application, is very broad.[57] The word is applicable to a number of techniques and faculties not contained in the modern word: invention, signification, context, intertextuality, the mental as well as sensory faculties, audience mentality and reception. The lack of a precise terminology in twelfth-century French makes it essential to exercise great caution in fixing usage and meanings in any particular instance. The most notable instance of the lexicographical problem is in the *Charrette* Prologue. Marie de Champagne, we are told, provided the *matière* and *san* for the romance; Chrétien contributed his *painne* and *sans* which, he protests, are less effective in the composition of the romance than are Marie's contributions. He clarifies his contribution by the word pair *painne* and *antancion*. *Antancion* is a learned term, familiar in school exercises as authorial purpose (*intentio*). Together with *materia*, it is the most common object of literary analysis.[58] In the *Charrette* Prologue, although the lines of demarcation are hazy, the general import of Chrétien's words seems clear: Marie de Champagne provided the idea, the *esprit*,[59] the conception of the romance, while Chrétien's effort realized the conflation of her *matière* and *san* through his purposeful amalgamation and elaboration of them in the completed work. Hers was the genius, his was the art. *San/sans* embraces both of these meanings.

The best manuscripts suggest that Chrétien's distinction in the *Charrette* Prologue between Marie de Champagne's *san* and his own *sans* is also a terminological one; and even if subsequent scribes corrected or corrupted the text to read only *sans* in both instances, their alteration does not eliminate the distinction Chrétien implied between the two.[60] That distinction has now been shown to be not etymological, that is, based on a putative Germanic etymon for *san* and a Latin etymon for *sans*. Rather, the distinction is technical and terminological.[61]

What Marie de Champagne and Chrétien cooperated in was called invention in the Middle Ages. Invention is the technique whereby a *trouvère*—an inventor—conceives and devises a work of art. It includes the elaboration of subject matter, that is, the amalgamation of *matière* and *san*, and it subtends the selection of what in the sources and the author's own construal of the *matière* may be utilized in the new work. The achievement of that work is the result of the author's artistry and purpose, his *painne* and *sans/antancion*. It entailed the elaboration of the source *matière* so as to show forth the original *san* through the character, actions, thoughts and sentiments of the principal narrative figures. The technique for such elaboration in Chrétien's time was topical invention—the invention of topoi that elucidate the extraordinary and seemingly incomprehensible, obscure *merveilles* in that *matière*.[62]

Topical invention identifies and elucidates mysteries and obscurities in the *matière* by exemplifying certain places in it so as to make persons, words and actions fit a proposed context (*san*). Mystery—*misterium*—is, in medieval parlance, not only modern "mystery," but also "significance." *Misterium incarnationis* describes the conception of Christ. The grail and the love of Lancelot and Guenevere are mysteries, as are the sparrow hawk, the white stag and the garden of joy in *Erec*, the lion and the magic fountain in *Yvain*. Such "mysteries" or *merveilles* may be elucidated, their obscurities illuminated, if, as Marie de France puts it in the Prologue to her *Lais*, the author can draw out of the *matière* the significance buried darkly in it—a *surplus de sen* (Prol., l. 16) elicited by the application of authorial *sens* (l. 20). If the source *matière* was obscure or incomplete, these *lieux* (*loci*, *topoi*) required the inset of elucidations conforming to authorial understanding (*antancion*). Such explanatory additions were then amplified so as to make of the *matière* and *san* a meaningful amalgam:

> Bien poez antendre et gloser,
> vos qui avez fet autretel,
> que por la gent de son ostel
> se fet las et se fet couchier;
> mes n'ot mie son lit tant chier
> que por rien il n'i reposast,
> n'il ne poïst ne il n'osast,
> ne il ne volsist pas avoir
> le hardemant ne le pooir.
> (*Charrette*, ll. 4550-58)

(Those of you who have done the same thing may well understand and gloss that he pretends to be tired and goes to bed because of the people with whom he was staying. But his bed was not so dear to him, nor would he have reposed in it for anything—he could not, nor would he have dared, nor would he even have wanted either the courage or the strength to do so.)

Topical amplifications are less didactic or learned disquisitions than they are qualifiers, perhaps explicit, perhaps implicit, within the recognizable context and circumstances ("Vos qui avez fet autretel"). In this sense, we can see how Marie de Champagne indicated to Chrétien her understanding (*san*) of the *matière* she furnished him with for the romance, then left him with the task of completing the narrative within the context as she perceived it. That is, she left him with the *painne* and *antancion*, just as Philippe de Flandre left to him the *antandre* and *gloser* in *Perceval*—and Chrétien implied the same activity in the *Charrette* public.

Chrétien's distinction in the *Charrette* between the experienced and the inexperienced lover implies audiences composed both of connoisseurs and amateurs, and of the ignorant, undiscriminating and unworthy. Such distinctions among audiences anticipate a more fundamental difference, which is not only or merely social, between the noble and the ignoble, those possessed not only of birth, but also of the distinctive quality of mind—the mentality—able to comprehend certain ideals and modes of conduct, and those lacking such distinction and discrimination. Authorial *san/sans* thus implies a corresponding audience *sans*, just as Marie's *sen* required a sympathetic author and public.[63] Original invention presupposes a knowledgeable and perceptive audience. It flourishes as the concern for gesture and rank peculiar to aristocracies, a concern Chrétien insists on by the rehabilitation of Enide's family through marriage and lands.

Here, there intrudes a problem that has bedeviled Chrétien studies from their beginnings: his presumed attitude towards love, especially adulterous love and conjugal love. The debate turns on the notion of courtly love, an expression taken up or rejected today with an often alarming *désinvolture*. Equated sometimes only with adultery, at others it describes marital affection. And it is generally associated with aristocratic figures. The most common medieval expressions for noble or ideal love are *fin' amors* and *amor par amors*. *Fin' amors* is characterized by finesse, the very perspicacity (*sans*) that, in an artist, is essential to original, effective invention.[64] Such a notion of love and loving precludes the established "code of love" or rules of love, the etiquette commonly associated with the notion of "courtly love" today. There were no codes of love as such in Chrétien's day. But there were reflection, discussion and debate about the notion, as it was evaluated and adapted to diverse circumstances and situations, notably situations characterized by given social, familial or religious restrictions—to the different orders in society.[65] All this is evident in Chrétien's works.

Consensus on conduct as an etiquette or even a code is a late medieval or even Renaissance phenomenon. Andreas Capellanus' famous treatise on love, the *De Amore*, dating from the end of the twelfth or the beginning of the thirteenth century, is not a code of love. It is an anatomy and illustration of love in varied social orders and levels: it relies on debate, diversity of opinion and eloquent persuasion.[66] The famous pronouncement allegedly handed down by Marie de Champagne, that love is impossible in marriage, is only a terminological problem. It neither denies marital affection nor enjoys absolute authority in the *De Amore* itself. Indeed, what the *De Amore* shows more than anything else is the adaptation of love to immediate social, moral and even political circumstances; it emphasizes above all quality of sentiment and rational, even sober-minded cultivation of affection. And as noble love, it manifests itself by eloquence, by postures and gestures suitable to the nobility.

In fact, Chrétien de Troyes and Andreas Capellanus express compatible views on love. Chrétien makes distinctions, sometimes radical distinctions, between the quality and properties of different kinds of love:

> Onques du buvrage ne bui
> Dont Tristan fu enpoisonnez;
> Mes plus me fet amer que lui
> Fins cuers et bone volentez.
> Bien en doit estre miens li grez,
> Qu'ainz de riens efforciez n'en fui,
> Fors que tant que mes euz en crui,
> Par cui sui en la voie entrez
> Donc ja n'istrai n'ainc n'en recrui.[67]

(Never did I drink of the potion that poisoned Tristan's existence; rather, a heart attuned to what is fine and a will set on what is good make me love more than he did. I ought to be appreciated for this, for I was never compelled to love; I merely trusted what my eyes showed me, and through them I have entered on the way from which I shall never stray; nor was I ever remiss in my duty to love.)

And he adapts the representation of his principal figures to the circumstances they find themselves in. In *Cligés* Guenevere counsels the marriage of Alixandre and Soredamor, marriage, she opines, being the safest way to preserve a happy love (ll. 2266-72). Marriage for love is made out to be more stable and satisfying; in the twelfth century this was certainly a more original idea than the usual feudal alliance confirmed by marriage.[68] Yet if love created a love triangle, divorce was hardly a ready solution. Here, too, circumstances determined conduct. In the case of Cligés and Fenice, love is frustrated by Fenice's marriage to Alis. But hers is not a marriage of love; it is a feudal contract between the Holy Roman Empire and the Byzantine Empire (ll. 2611-33). However, Fenice does not want to reproduce what she deems the incontinence of the Tristan-Mark-Iseut triangle. She and Cligés resolve the matter and do marry in the end, but only after considerable reflection and debate on appropriate conduct, after a hidden adultery and the death of Alis. In the *Charrette*, written after *Cligés*, Guenevere and Lancelot's love is adulterous. But their circumstances are different from those in the Cligés-Fenice-Alis triangle. And the one implied comparison with Tristan and Iseut in the *Charrette*—the blood on the sheets—does not betray Lancelot and Guenevere, who hide their love even more successfully than Fenice and Cligés, but, apparently, without Fenice's rejection of the conjugal duty.

These examples illustrate the "problematic" side of Chrétien's romances. In Chrétien love is not only passion or self-abandon, as in Lancelot's love trances:

> Et ses pansers est de tel guise
> que lui meïsmes en oblie,
> ne set s'il est, ou s'il n'est mie,
> ne ne li manbre de son non,
> ne set s'il est armez ou non,
> ne set ou va, ne set don vient;
> de rien nule ne li sovient
> fors d'une seule, et por celi
> a mis les autres en obli;
> a cele seule panse tant
> qu'il n'ot, ne voit, ne rien n'antant.
> (*Charrette*, ll. 714-24)

(And his thoughts are such that he forgets who he is; he doesn't know whether he exists or not, he forgets his name, he doesn't know whether or not he is armed, where he is going or coming from. He remembers no one but one single person, and for her he has forgotten all the others. He is so absorbed by thoughts about her that he hears, sees, notices nothing.)

It may be the self-control and conscious will of a Fenice or a Guenevere:

> Por ce reisons anferme et lie
> son fol cuer, et son fol pansé;
> si l'a un petit racenssé
> et a mis la chose an respit
> jusque tant que voie et espit
> un boen leu et un plus privé,
> ou il soient mialz arivé
> que il or ne sont a ceste ore.
> (*Charrette*, ll. 6846-53)

(Therefore, reason encloses and binds her mad heart and wild thoughts. And she restrained herself until she might see and espy an opportune place, one that is more private, where they could come together more conveniently than now.)

Passion, as Andreas Capellanus defines it, is a kind of sickness: *Amor est passio quædam*. Chrétien shows how that sickness may be overcome in ways beneficial to the lovers, but without destroying them, as it did Tristan and Iseut; and, indeed, in ways that would render their love beneficial to court society and established social and feudal values. Thus, Lancelot's love for Guenevere endows him with the prowess needed to liberate Arthur's subjects from imprisonment in another land. And Cligés' winning of Fenice rights a wrong committed by Alis when the latter married her in violation of a contract made with his brother, a contract meant to guarantee Cligés' accession to the throne on Alis' death. Love, for Chrétien, is potentially volatile. It can destroy the lovers physically and morally and undermine the social order, as in the Tristan legend, in the *Philomena* attributed to Chrétien, in many instances in the earlier *romans d'antiquité*, and as it nearly does in his own *Erec* and *Yvain*. But it can also make the bond between persons conducive to good order and understanding:

>Li autre parloient d'Amors,
>des angoisses et des dolors
>et des granz biens qu'orent sovant
>li deciple de son covant,
>qui lors estoit molt dolz et buens.
>(*Yvain*, ll. 13-17)

(The others spoke of Love, of its anguish and grief, and of the great good that often came to the disciples in his order, which was at that time most gentle and noble.)

For Chrétien the decline or debasement of good love, of *fin' amors*, is a serious threat to aristocratic civilization and its historical survival. This is not to say that Chrétien had a program, much less that he even reflected a mentatlity radically opposed to apparent aristocratic propensities to idealize extramarital liaisons. Such views of older scholarship are reductionist and, indeed, have no real foundation in Chrétien's works. Rather, what those works suggest is an aristocratic vision of Arthurian marvels wherein authorial invention is able, through topical elaboration, to set forth a variety of intrigues readily comprehensible to all levels of an aristocracy discriminating in its vernacular entertainment, yet worldly, or at least secular, in its tastes kept within the circumference of aristocratic exclusivity.

>Or s'en tesent de cest mestier,
>se ne sont clerc ou chevalier,
>car ausi pueent escouter
>conme li asnes a harper.
>Ne parlerai de peletiers
>ne de vilains ne de bouchiers,
>mes des deus freres parleré
>et leur geste raconteré.
>(*Thèbes*, ll. 13-20)[69]

(Let everyone keep silent, except clerics and knights, for anyone else can listen with about as much understanding as an ass would to a harp. I'll not speak of furriers, villeins or butchers, but of the two brothers whose knightly deeds I shall relate.)

So the anonymous author of the *Roman de Thèbes* about 1160, in one of the first romances. But there was still room for the critical evaluation of discrepancies, contradictions, shortcomings. The vision was not always whole, the somber and the ridiculous are not lacking. The very evocation of Arthurian perfection at the outset of *Yvain* recedes in the face of social and personal boorishness and strife (see below, pp. 202-04). Yet topical invention is precisely the evocation of possibilities for good or evil in any matter at hand. And there is good evidence that in Chrétien's time the aristocracy was aware of the grave threat of its decline in authority and in station, both from the king and from the rising bourgeoisie.[70]

The analysis of love and of the other values lauded in Chrétien's romances expresses the intention to curb that decline. The *antancion* does so by the elucidation of the *merveilles* found in his sources, the elucidation of adventures in quest, siege, single combat and palace intrigue. The qualities that such *aventures* bring out in the protagonists define their character and their characteristics. This makes the romances exemplary without reducing them to fables enunciating a specific moral or social truth, as in Marie de France's *Ysopet*. Rather, the narrative interplay of the diverse adventures and the homogeneous character of the different types of knights and ladies establishes what Erich Köhler has called the diversity and equality of the knights of the Round Table.[71] The same diversity in equality obtains among the lovers associated with that Table. The equality is, paradoxically, élitist. It is the identification of the unique excellence appropriate to each knight and lady as exemplars of a potentially ideal courtly and aristocratic civilization:

> Mes tant estoient bel andui,
> Antre la pucele et celui,
> C'uns rais de lor biauté issoit,
> Don li palés resplandissoit
> Tot autresi con li solauz
> Qui nest molt clers et molt vermauz.
> (*Cligés*, ll. 2715-20)

(But he and the maid were both so beautiful that a stream of light poured forth from their beauty and brightened the palace, just as the sun rises a bright incarnadine at morn.)

Their fairness flashes forth on all around them. Radiant beauty elucidates the narrative by coloring the *matière*, thus discovering what we see and how we see it. Such descriptive coloring, or highlight, is everywhere in Chrétien's romances. However, that elucidation is not expository. It reveals, as light shining from bright features rather than shaping them. The nobility of prowess and of love are the principal contexts. They irradiate and infuse the material data of the story. When Huon de Méry extolled Chrétien's eloquence, he was referring to his master's art of amplificatory display. Amplification serves to express Chrétien's *antancion* as it shines forth from his brilliant matter as *ceo k'i ert—merveilles* and *san*.

Conjointure: The Articulation of Romance

The recent equation of Chrétien's notion of *conjointure* with the modern concept of *écriture*[72] is not entirely anachronistic. *Ecriture* adapts principles of syntax to narrative disposition as a "narrative grammar." Just so, *conjointure* is, in the twelfth century, the extension of principles underlying Latin syntax to narrative disposition. Latin syntax—and that is the only syntax that an educated French writer would have studied in Chrétien's time—is flectional. Flection allows for freer arrangement and interlacing of parts of speech than is normally possible in modern French and English. Such articulation provides for the disposition and conjunction of source and topical amplifications in a meaningful whole. That whole is the narrative. In Latin, *coniunctura* and *iunctura* were used to describe both sentence and narrative composition.[73] In French, Chrétien's use of it quickly gave way to *roman*, or romance. Romance as *conjointure* is, thus, the elegant—*bele—conjointure*, or composition, of often disparate elements —the *merveilles* from antecedent sources. The arrangement is made coherent by the author's topical elaboration of the context he construes for and amplifies from the sources. Such arrangement focuses on one or more *merveilles* that lend fascination and appeal to the narrative; authorial conception makes that appeal comprehensible and morally and socially enlightening. All Chrétien's romances illustrate this correlation of narrative and conceptual coherence, this amalgam of meaning and wonder, without slipping into excessive didacticism or hazy mystery. The happy balance of potentially conflicting elements—a *concors discordia*—is a *bele conjointure*. The only potentially problematical romance in this respect is the *Conte du Graal*; but, though incomplete, it reveals elements of coherence and organization that allow us to understand Chrétien's intent in this narrative torso. Moreover, it is noteworthy that no grail romance succeeded in making the grail and its mysteries totally comprehensible, in effect dissipating its numinosity once and for all. The grail, humble as the strange platter or bowl may have been, was shown to be of *matière* too rich to be exhausted. That is already apparent in the version that Chrétien left us.

The grail, like Guenevere, the Magic Fountain, Joy, is a goal. The goal is achieved, in most of Chrétien's narratives, by a quest. The quest motif implies a series of displacements interspersed episodically with *aventures*. The *aventure* usually appears fortuitous, although it may have an at first hidden rationale or cause which becomes explicit in the course of the adventure or at some later point in the narrative. The movement from beginning of quest to achievement of the goal fixes a narrative beginning and end. The middle, structurally a fixed midpoint of major significance for the *san,* connects multiple and diverse adventures and episodes that reveal the qualities of the questing knight and his lady. The focus on the goal of the quest thus gives the narrative a beginning, middle and end.

But *conjointure,* like Latin sentence composition, allows for interlace. In narrative, this is the interlace of source and topical material. The interlace may be based on the way source material is combined, as when two *vers* or *contes,* that of the White Stag and that of the Sparrow Hawk, are intertwined in the first part of *Erec et Enide* and then conjoined by the person of Enide; or they may be narrative parallels juxtaposed in order to provide diversity and hierarchies, to make fundamental, but complementary distinctions among types or to offer specific statements pertinent to the meaning of the romance or to authorial intention. One example of a parallel is Calogrenant's and Yvain's adventures leading to the Magic Fountain; another is the parallel quests of Lancelot and Gauvain in the *Charrette*; and a third is the at least potential multiplication of quests— Perceval, Gauvain and many others—in the second half of the *Conte du Graal.* This romance is especially intriguing because of its use of abandoned, but sequential quests never completed, at least in the fragment Chrétien has left: Perceval's aborted quest of his mother does not lead to his promised return to Blancheflor or even to the burial of the mother as he earlier vowed; and Gauvain seems to wander off into never-never-land in quest of the Bleeding Lance, after a series of mishaps that abruptly set aside the indented defense of his honor impugned by Guiromelant.

The quest is, of course, not the only motif used in Chrétien's romances, as the *Cligés* demonstrates. *Cligés* makes clear the importance of commonplace motifs like siege, combat and hospitality, as narrative frames for topical amplifications on love, prowess and the more immediate concerns of the supernumeraries.[74] Appropriate sources of intertextual commentary— explicit and implicit Ovidian and Tristan reminiscences—introduce original, acute statements by suitable positioning in narrative. In fact, *Cligés,* through the commonplace motifs, effects an amalgam of the Tristan and Ovidian material with such subtlety and ingenuity that the marvel of Tristan and Iseut becomes the sensible and noble love, first of Alixandre and Soredamor, second of Cligés and Fenice.

Collocation of sources and of topical amplifications is essential to Chrétien's art. Proper linking or joining makes for continuity and coherence in the midst of narrative variety and diversity, surprise and suspense. Thus, by the end of the twelfth century, as we noted, largely through Chrétien's influence, the word *roman* has extended in meaning from the vernacular, or Romance, language to include a new kind of narrative composition.

Conjointure has undergone a similar broadening and deepening, extending principles of sentence composition to narrative composition. The result is medieval romance narrative articulation of marvelous *matière* and chivalric *san*.

Romance Invention

Enide's beauty was such that Nature could never again fashion her likes; indeed, God Himself could not improve on her features. For Enide is an *essanplaire* that can be imitated (*contrefaire*, ll. 418-20), as Chrétien does, but not reproduced in its perfection:

> Que diroie de sa biauté?
> Ce fu cele por verité
> qui fu fete por esgarder,
> qu'an se poïst an li mirer
> ausi com an un mireor.
> (*Erec*, ll. 437-41)

(What could I say about her beauty? She was in truth made to be gazed upon, for one could look on her as into a mirror.)

The laudation is hyperbolic. Enide appears before the reader as the representative of a stereotype so perfect that one could lose oneself in contemplation of her: she was made to be seen. And Erec gazed upon her.

But Enide returned Erec's gaze. For Erec and Enide, as mirrors of one another,

> ... estoient d'une meniere,
> d'unes mors et d'une matiere,
> que nus qui le voir volsist dire
> n'an poïst le meillor eslire
> ne le plus bel ne le plus sage.
> (ll. 1487-91)

(were of one kind, one conduct, one stuff, so that no one could truly select the better, the more lovely or the more sensible.)

Their union is perfect, they constitute in fact a *bele conjointure*.

In Old French a *conjointure* is as much a marriage, an architectural marvel, a combat, as it is a romance. The beauty of such unions is their exemplarity. An exemplar for Chrétien, as the description of Erec and Enide shows, determines kind (*maniere*) as the quality or character of a thing. The representation of such an exemplar is, in medieval parlance, an image. Erec and Enide are, accordingly, *beles ymages*: "onques deus si beles ymages / n'asanbla lois ne mariages" (ll. 1495-96) (never did religion or marriage unite two such beautiful images).

An image conjoins matter, shaping and embellishing it so that a new and beautiful object appears. That is why Chrétien adapts the composite assemblage of human parts that medieval writing used to describe beautiful persons.[75] A combination of features also makes splendid the cup Arthur awards Alixandre in *Cligés*. Alixandre's cup, a product of craftsmanship, illustrates a conception of *faire* that imitates the skills of God and Nature, conjoining the best of their productions as in a *bele ymage*. God is the master artisan, the true creator; His art Nature emulates in her own works, and the artist's representations emulate the best and, thus, most representative in nature.

Such emulation was condemned to failure. God created; the artist, like Nature, could only imitate: "opus Dei est, quod non erat creare.... opus naturæ, quod latuit ad actum producere.... opus artificis est disgregata coniungere vel coniuncta segregare" (the work of God is to create that which was not...; the work of nature is to bring forth into actuality that which lay hidden...; the work of the artificer is to put together things disjoined or to disjoin those put together).[76] Still, imagination is analogous to creation. God, Nature and the artist alike begin with an "idea." That idea in God's mind is an exemplar, and as such His thought brings it into existence, that is, creates it. Nature takes His idea, as it were, out into the open by impressing the exemplar into matter and producing thereby the different kinds of things in the world. Thus, each particular is a more or less nearly perfect expression in matter of God's exemplar, as formless stuff becomes an image representative of the exemplar. When Chrétien asserts that the quality of Erec and Enide is such that they shine as exemplars for Nature, he implies that this perfection is such that God alone could conceive of such consummate beauty. Their *maniere* thus shows forth exactly God's exemplar of human beauty. Not even Iseut can reflect that beauty which shines forth resplendent and pristine in Enide (ll. 424-26).

The notion of the analogous activities of God, Nature and the artist was widespread by Chrétien's time, especially through the influence of Neoplatonic thought.[77] The movement associated with Chartres—the so-called school of Chartres—took seriously the implications of the analogy and applied it to the art of poetry.[78] There arose from this application an important body of medieval Latin literature dealing with creation and the forces at work in creation. The image of Nature figured prominently in this literature as God's agent for the adornment of the universe with the kinds and particulars whose exemplars or archetypes God created in His own mind. In the twelfth century Bernard Silvester and Alain de Lille composed remarkable philosophical poems in which Nature functions in this role;[79] later, towards the end of the thirteenth century, Jean de Meung would be adapting their personification of Nature to his own representation of creation.[80] The instruction on creation achieved the status of an art, to be set down in a number of important handbooks on the poetic craft written in the twelfth and thirteenth centuries. Chrétien appears to have learned to write under the influence of this conception of composition; it clearly comes to the fore in the description of Erec and Enide, as it does elsewhere in his romances.

The arts of poetry rely on traditional instruction in the trivium and the quadrivium to work out the analogy between creation and imitation for the artist. The trivium offered instruction in correct, eloquent and convincing discourse; the quadrivium provided the fundamental knowledge necessary to understand and explore the physical universe. Chrétien was not unaware of the value of such instruction: he describes Erec's coronation robe as adorned with personifications of the four arts of the quadrivium, geometry, arithmetic, music and astronomy (*Erec*, II. 6684-6731), thus harking back to Macrobius and Martianus Capella.[81] But the most important arts for composition were grammar and rhetoric. Together with dialectics they make up the "logical" arts—the arts of *logos*, or speech. Grammar provided instruction and training in correct Latin and in the reading and interpretation of good literature. Rhetoric taught how to use language eloquently, how to move the listener or reader to appreciate as well as to understand one's words. All this was applied to poetic composition.

Rhetoric provided instruction in the invention, disposition and embellishment of the work. Invention is the art of identifying matter for the work, including the topical ideas that the work will express and amplify, an amalgam[82] of matter and ideas in subject matter. This is the process of conjunction and disjunction which epitomized for Hugh of Saint Victor the artist's craft. It is here that the exemplar imposed on matter in the analogous works of Nature and the artist becomes comprehensible. Invention is the human art which, being analogous to God's act of creation, amalgamates *matière* and *san* as matter and idea in the work. For that reason, Marie de Champagne provided Chrétien with all he required to exercise his art in the *Charrette* when she furnished him with its *matière* and *san*. Since hers is the conception of the work, Chrétien could concede Marie's "primordial" role in the composition of the *Charrette* (II. 21-23). Like God's priority to Nature, so is her antecedence in relation to Chrétien in the realization of the *Charrette*. She invented it. His own *sans* or *antancion* and *painne* permitted him to achieve, however imperfectly, the work she had conceived.

The *Perceval* Prologue betrays a similar scheme, except that Philippe de Flandre seems to have provided only the *matière*, a *livre*, not the *san* (unless the "book" already contained that *san*). But here, too, Chrétien brought his *painne* and *antancion*—"Crestïens, qui antant et peinne" (l. 62 [ibid.]) —to the task of rhyming ". . . le meillor conte, / par le comandement le conte, / qui soit contez an cort real" (ll. 63-65 [ibid.]) (at the Count's command, the best story ever told in royal court).

The grail, like Alixandre's cup in *Cligés*, is characterized by its material, its art and its embellishment:

> de fin or esmeré estoit;
> pierres precïeuses avoit
> el graal de maintes menieres,
> des plus riches et des plus chieres.
> (ll. 3221-24 [3233-36])

(it was of the purest gold; there were many kinds of precious stones, noble and dear, in the grail.)

All this is a great marvel to Perceval, a *merveille* at once the source of wonder and of questions, the questions Perceval fails to ask about the grail itself and about the bleeding lance that precedes it in procession before his astonished eyes. As such, the grail constitutes a mystery. Mystery, in its medieval sense of *misterium*, is, we have noted, a blend of mystery and signification, a secret whose sense is hidden in its matter, but which illuminates that matter and shines forth from it on all round about, eliciting fascination and inquiry.[83] As with the radiant beauty of Cligés and Fenice when they first appear, so with the grail:

> une si granz clartez an vint,
> ausi perdirent les chandoiles
> lor clarté come les estoiles
> qant li solaux lieve, et la lune.
> (ll. 3214-17 [3226-29])

(there came from it such a great brightness that the candles lost their brilliance, as do the stars and the moon when the sun rises.)

Perceval's failure is a failure to ask significant questions, to inquire into the grail and the lance he fixes in rapt gaze. The combination of grail, bleeding lance and maimed Fisher King is indeed an incongruous, but obviously not fortuitous, juxtaposition; it is a "diversity" that demands explanation. The questions Perceval should have asked, and which are partly answered in a very matter-of-fact way later by his uncle the hermit, are indeed the romancer's own questions. For Chrétien's invention of the *Conte du Graal* entails the interrogation, the mining of his mysterious *matière* for the hidden ore, which he may articulate as a *bele conjointure* that would be, like the *Cligés* cup, an exemplar of its kind.

Chrétien's contemporary, Marie de France, describes the invention of truth in mystery in the Prologues to her *Lais* and to her *Ysopet*. She derives her notion of invention from late Classical grammar, notably from Priscian's assertion that the "ancients" were obscure in their writings in order that those who were to come after them might become more perceptive as time passed, might study their works and glean from them what had been obscure heretofore. Implied here is a gradual elucidation of mystery, an inventive transmission that is apparent in the successive versions of the grail story in the Middle Ages from Chrétien through the *Perceval* Continuations of his *Conte du Graal*, the great prose romances that center on the grail in the thirteenth century—the prose *Lancelot*, the prose *Tristan*, the post-Vulgate *Grail* and others—until the time of Thomas Malory in the mid-fifteenth century.

At this juncture we may return to Enide to observe how Chrétien reveals hidden qualities.

Chrétien's description of Enide raises perplexing questions: why is such a beautiful maiden so poorly, indeed so shabbily dressed? Why does Erec insist that she remain so until her arrival at Arthur's court? These intriguing questions draw the audience into the romance, just as they elicited from Chrétien an adaptation and elucidation of his sources that included the perplexing description of the maiden Erec falls in love with and, indeed, continues to love in ways that, in the narration and to the reader, are little less than astonishing. Yet mystery always leads to elucidation, illumination of *ceo k'i ert*. Although an exemplar of human beauty, Enide's beauty was concealed: the sad plight of her impoverished father obscured her splendor. She wore a dress torn and full of holes. But beneath the torn outer garment she could still be seen to be beautiful: "Povre estoit la robe dehors, / mes desoz estoit biax li cors" (ll. 409-10) (poor was the robe outside, but under it her body was beautiful). Enide is unadorned. Yet only the best will suit such an exemplar of beauty, and so her father waits for the right person to deck her out in a way that most becomes that beauty. Erec himself refuses to accept anything less than a queen's crown and a queen's dress. Marriage provides her with the crown, and Guenevere the gown, "une bele robe avenant" (l. 1561) (a beautiful, becoming robe). The adornment agrees —"avenant"—with the quality if Enide's beauty, just as the precious stones complement the gold in Alixandre's cup and in the grail. The quality of the substance is made evident by the most precious ornament.

The art of embellishment as practiced in medieval classrooms and as perfected in French by romancers like Chrétien and Marie de France, was the invention of suitable adornment for a given *matière*. The technique for such adornment was well known to anyone who went to medieval schools.[84] It derived from Marie de France's professed mentor, the Byzantine Latin grammarian Priscian. It was topical invention. As such, it was an interpretive technique, intended to bring out the qualities hidden in obscure matter.

God and Nature adorn the world with all varieties of things. These things reveal the handiwork and mystery of God through their natures or species, that is, their inherent and special qualities (*maniere*). Similarly, the fashioning of the work's *matière* fit it to authorial conception, or *san*. In the *Charrette* this art comprehends a *san* and a *sans*: Marie de Champagne's invention and Chrétien de Troyes's expression, her idea and his ornament. When *matière* was scrutinized, within a context the author deemed appropriate, it was found to contain—like Enide's robe—gaps and tears, the *depecier* and *corronpre* of Chrétien's *conte d'avanture* in *Erec*. Such faults could be eliminated, the rent fabric made whole, by the intelligent elaboration of the conception as context in the given *matière*. This is the *niveau de cohérence courtoise* elucidated by Jean Fourquet. The *matière*, beautiful in itself, fascinating and marvelous, was dressed up anew and more brilliantly. Such embellishment enhances and explains the work's qualities, just as Enide's crown and Guenevere's robe state and adorn Enide's own exemplary beauty. By identifying topoi or *loci*, the "common" places, that is, "empty" places in the *matière*, the author fashions "arguments" that close or, more accurately, complete those places and elucidate the matter. The expression of the *uevre*, as Chrétien calls it in describing Alixandre's cup, is the precious adornment of the work, the artistic amplifications that perfect the topical embellishments and render the work beautiful.

Enide's beauty is not only a physical beauty:

> Molt est bele, mes mialz asez
> vaut ses savoirs que sa biautez:
> onques Dex ne fist rien tant saige
> ne qui tant soit de franc coraige.
> (ll. 537-40)

(She is beautiful, but her mind is much more precious than her beauty. Never did God fashion anyone more sensible and noble in heart.)

Enide's *savoir* and *sagesse*, her breeding and gentility, the quality of her mind, adumbrated by her physical and vestmental beauty, become an important factor in the quest that transpires in the second part of the romance, during her quarrel with Erec. For there she and Erec, so alike before as to be a perfect and complementary pair, are divided and brought into confrontation—a *discors concordia*, a *segregare*—by a disagreement that calls upon the wisdom, prudence and perspicacity of both husband and wife to achieve anew a harmonious union of opposites—*conçors discordia*, a *coniungere*.

Inventive adaptation was a probing of *matière* for its latent meaning. Such probing required some idea of what one might find: every miner knows what he is looking for and where he is likely to find it. We have noted that the great ideas of Chrétien's, and indeed of medieval, romance, those which most commonly provide context and, thus, narrative *maniere*, were set forth in retrospect by Dante at the end of the thirteenth century: prowess in arms, love and rectitude. Dante saw these subjects as "most excellent" and, therefore, suitable for the best vernacular writing, including Arthurian romance. Chrétien used the diverse situations presented in his *matière* to elaborate upon a given situation's potential for the expression of knightly prowess, noble love and moral resolve. Conflict was the theme that permitted him to confront different notions and to work towards a satisfactory narrative and thematic articulation of the idea. In such disputes a final decisive answer is less important than a reconciliation of opposites suitable for the persons and their circumstances with which the narrative was constructed and by which it was amplified.[85]

It is clear, then, that the persistent, but insoluble problem of Chrétien's opinion of, or attitude towards, conjugal love and extramarital or adulterous love is a false problem. It is false, and insoluble, because Chrétien's romance statements are determined by the circumstances of each romance. The conflict between the respective demands of prowess and love in *Erec et Enide* and in *Yvain* is developed in diverse ways, dependent in part on Chrétien's *matières*, in part on the qualities and character given to his protagonists. Thus, both Erec and Yvain adhere to the firm resolve to persevere in doing what is proper without suppressing personal affection. Reconciliation is the conclusion to each, astonishing and even humorous in *Yvain*, romantic and tender in *Erec*. For reconciliation reconciles differences in mutual understanding and common resolve. Chrétien makes that understanding the foundation of love. If Erec knew Enide's worth when he first admired her exemplary beauty, at the end of the romance he understands her love for him and can no longer mistake the import of her silence—her anxious fear for his life.

The two *conjointures* of *Erec*—the first and second part of the romance—culminate in sexual *conjointures* of husband and wife. The first, passionate, unbridled, consummates their marriage and is celebrated in a vigorous, but rough tournament, followed by the newlyweds' departure from court. The second also culminates in a sexual *conjointure*, the tender conclusion to the quest which reunites and reconciles husband and wife. This second union is celebrated both by the Joy of the Court and the great and joyous solemnity of coronation. It is noteworthy that precisely the opposite movements—first to court, then to the private castle—conclude the two parts of

Yvain. And the tenderness of the union of Laudine and Yvain contrasts with the violence of the stories that effect their reconciliation. These two stories of love, marriage and sexual union recall the reversed images in mirrors.

Other circumstances require different arrangements. In *Cligés* Alixandre and Soredamor tremble before each other while standing firm against their enemies in combat and affairs of the heart. Guenevere brings them to confess their mutual love, then finds in marriage the most satisfactory condition for a permanent and happy love. Such a solution is not immediately possible for Cligés and Fenice or for Lancelot and Guenevere herself in the *Charrette*. But conflicts are also worked out in accordance with social, moral and personal expectations and necessities ultimately resolved in a love at once *fin* and sexual. The understanding of that love is various; no idea is, in fact, susceptible to being reduced to a single definition for all times, places and purposes. Andreas Capellanus' debates on love show as much, by representing diverse types, situations and solutions to problems. Chrétien's artistic achievement is the invention of representative narratives through which his audience could appreciate, understand and even identify sympathetically with the circumstances and decisions of the principal actors.

Another great contemporary of Chrétien, Thomas d'Angleterre, expanded upon the character of cathartic identification with the figures that inspired his vision of the legend of Tristan and Iseut:

> Pur essample issi ai fait
> Pur l'estorie embelir,
> Que as amanz deive plaisir,
> E que par lieus poissent trover
> Choses u se puissent recorder:
> Aveir em poissent grant confort,
> Encuntre change, encuntre tort,
> Encuntre paine, encuntre dolur,
> Encuntre tuiz engins d'amur!
> (Sn², ll. 831-39)[86]

(I have written it as an example to embellish the story, which should please those who love, that they might find places in it that recall their own experiences. May they draw great comfort from it in the face of mutability, wrong, pain, grief and all the wiles of love.)

His "example" is, thus, an *essemplaire*, a *bele ymage*, for lovers to identify with.[87] Such identification is the awareness of common experience: the trials, the uncertainties, the joys and sorrows of each particular individual's own experience reflected in the proposed exemplars of the experience, Tristan and Iseut. There is a correlation between the idea of love in the lover and that expressed through Thomas' inventions, just as there may be opposition. Chrétien, too, sought to relate his audience's experience with the exemplary figures he invented. There is in this at one and the same time recognition and imitation. The audience recognizes itself in the common ideals, thoughts and sentiments, the trials and grief, of the figures in narrative romance. And it came to know and understand those ideals, thoughts and sentiments, to attempt to imitate and incorporate them in order to explain and influence conduct. The extraordinary excellence, the exemplary quality of such exemplars as Enide made for sharp representation of gestures and demonstrated nobility, essential to aristocratic appreciation. Vision of self thus merges in the eye with vision of one's better self: "Car es ialz se fiert la luiserne / Ou li cuers se remire, et voit / L'uevre defors" (*Cligés*, ll. 726-28) (For the light strikes the eyes, wherein the heart is reflected, and perceives the work outside of them). The light of beauty, whether of the grail or of heroes and heroines, is thus meant to meet the inner vision rising up to join it in the mind's eye. Such imitation, in the medieval sense, is the realization of oneself and thus, in an artifact, of a mental conception of what one perceives as the exemplar, and thus the truth, of the object of vision, and what would be appropriate to it in the diverse interplay of action and purpose. And as many of Chrétien's descriptions and digressions demonstrate, that interplay was founded on intertextual correlation and contrasts among his own romances, and among his works and contemporary and earlier writing, notably the Tristan legend and courtly lyric.

Now, the audience Chrétien envisages appears to have been a very self-conscious one, élitist and idealistic to the core, dominated by a common sense of mission and inherent worth. That audience was the aristocracy, the lords and ladies, knights and clerics alone capable of appreciating and usefully realizing the exemplars of the romances written for it. They alone could judge. For such audiences Chrétien proposed an ideal founded on an élite not unlike that still envisaged by Corneille almost five centuries later: "C'est aux rois, c'est aux grands, c'est aux esprits bien faits / A voir la vertu pleine en ses moindres effets" (*Horace*, ll. 1717-18). He acknowledges this in receiving from Philippe de Flandre and from Marie de Champagne the *matière* of two romances, and indeed of the two destined to have the most profound and enduring impact: the romance of the love of Lancelot and the Queen, and that of the Grail. One may, therefore, add to the *san* that was Chrétien's inspiration and the *sans* of his own inventive genius the *san* of the audience capable of appreciating his romances.

For the noble man and woman, the knight and the lady, as well as for the romancer, the realization of a work was the art of invention. This was the legacy which Chrétien sought to pass on to succeeding generations, as Gornemant handed knighthood on to Perceval. Gornemant's legacy, "la plus haute ordre avoec l'espee / que Dex a fete et comandee" (*Perceval*, ll. 1633-34 [1635-36]) (the highest sword-bearing order that God has made and commanded to be), was given to Perceval, destined to become the exemplar of knights:

> Car il li venoit de nature;
> et quant nature li aprant
> et li cuers del tot i antant,
> ne li puet estre riens grevainne
> la ou nature et cuers se painne.
>   (ll. 1476-80 [1480-84])

(For it was natural to him; and when Nature instructs him and his heart is set on it, nothing can be grievous to him in whom Nature and heart strive for accomplishment.)

Nature instructs the artist as well. For Chrétien *chevalerie* and *clergie* constitute a legacy so potent, yet so fragile, that it could survive in France "tant con durra crestïantez" (*Erec*, l. 25) (as long as Christianity endures) only if there were enough of the nobility who, like Alixandre and Lancelot, were willing to strive after the best in all things. To this end Chrétien, too, applied his art.

Edward J. Buckbee

Erec et Enide

Introduction

By all accounts *Erec et Enide*[1] is the first Arthurian romance of Chrétien de Troyes and may be dated at about 1170. Its position in the chronology of Chrétien's œuvre is indicated most directly by its conspicuous heading of the list of works by Chrétien with which his *Cligés* (ca. 1176) begins. Moreover, *Erec*'s long descriptive passages, because they resemble ostentatious displays of learning, appear to show the romance's debt to earlier, non-Arthurian narratives. Thus, P.-Y. Badel observes: "le goût de tels morceaux de bravoure est passé assez vite. Chrétien de Troyes, après *Erec*, renonce à eux ou du moins se soucie de mieux les intégrer au récit."[2] The romance seems to be the work of one new to the poetic craft, or at least of one who is opening a new direction through his art; this is supported by those who claim that *Erec*'s clarity distinguishes it from Chrétien's later, more ironic and ambiguous romances. E. Peter Nolan emphasizes the straightforward, systematic and non-critical way in which *Erec* identifies and utilizes traditional motifs, symbols and themes. According to Nolan, the romance devotes its first section to "a paradigm of the Arthurian quest romance itself" and elaborates that paradigm faithfully in the entire romance.[3] For Nolan, "all the evidence indicates that Chrétien never wrote with this degree of literary innocence again."[4] Chrétien uses his first Arthurian romance, then, to measure himself against the most successful efforts in narrative of his day, the *contes d'aventure* so popular in courts. The success of that effort will permit him to move on to realism, irony and criticism.

The traditional character of *Erec et Enide* has long been the object of scholarly elucidation. The story itself seems grounded in Celtic lore, and Chrétien may even have modeled his invention directly on a now lost Celtic version of the story.[5] Standard works in the scholastic curricula of the day, Latin Virgilian or philosophical allegories, biblical commentaries and the like, seem to have resonances in *Erec,* thereby suggesting the influence of contemporary educational and cultural canons.[6] References to the Tristan story, thematic and stylistic links with Wace and descriptions based on modes found in the *romans antiques* reveal his special debt to contemporary vernacular narrative poetry.[7] The broad learnedness of *Erec* shows that Chrétien was well educated and well read; the audience he addressed must have been civilized enough to understand and appreciate it. The learnedness alone is no key to the romancer's achievement, however. This entertaining and expressive narrative offers fast-paced action, intriguing characterization and glittering tableaux. The technical brilliance of its organization is matched by a remarkable diction which deftly commands a broad gamut of details and nuances. Such narrative quality marks an auspicious and potentially trend-setting beginning for Chrétien's production of Arthurian romances. Problems arise, however, when one endeavors to gain a purchase analytically on the compositional values at the heart of that narrative quality.

Much of the scholarly writing on *Erec* has concentrated on its major themes, variously identified as love, marriage, adventure, chivalry, courtliness and kingship.[8] The primacy of these themes has led many students of the romance to infer that it has relevance not only to considerations of human nature, but also to conceptions of a viable society. One finds consensus among scholars that the isolated themes are genuinely recognizable only when one engages in what might be called accurate reading. That is, the themes themselves are not mysterious, but they are presented indirectly or at least with great economy in *Erec* and so must be brought to light through a critical and imaginative engagement with the text. According to Jean Frappier, Chrétien is by no means obscure: "à le lire avec assez d'attention, aucune obscurité foncière ne subsiste dans la conduite de ses personnages . . . ."[9] Norris Lacy expresses a commonly held view that the presence of foreshadowing and recapitulation gives the work "a thematic unity which replaces the logical unity sometimes lacking in episodic romances."[10] Appreciation of the romance's structural configurations will, in this view, yield a clear perception of what A.R. Press terms "une démonstration objective d'un phénomène abstrait."[11] While not the only approach possible to an understanding of *Erec,* structural analysis of this variety best represents the prevailing critical emphasis: this romance calls upon its public to engage actively in the discovery of its fundamental meaning, what Chrétien refers to in the *Charrette* as *san.*[12]

It is perhaps surprising, then, that scholars differ as much as they do on what *Erec* means. It must be emphasized that differences of opinion tend to concern not the major themes themselves, but how they are related to one another. Erec and Enide are certainly in love. Their marriage is based on traditional roles of husband and wife. Adventure is a form of testing. Erec performs in the manner of a chivalrous knight. Arthur's world is a model of courtly society. Arthur illustrates the attributes of kingship. Few dispute such thematic generalizations. But how indeed are the themes to be related? Does marriage perfect love? Can marriage and adventure coexist? Does chivalry need adventure? How does the chivalrous knight function in courtly society? Does courtliness nurture feudal perceptions of kingship?

Disagreements on thematic evaluation stem in part from different approaches to the commonly perceived coherence of the romance. For example, different views of how scenes and episodes are articulated or how episodic details reverberate thematically in different parts of the romance can influence decisively one's perception of "objective" results. Do details in the narrative itself have such importance that "rien n'est purement fortuit, rien n'est simple ornement, ni fantaisie gratuite du poète"?[13] Or must we weigh carefully what is implied by the likelihood that, at performances of *Erec,* its public "n'avait pas le loisir d'interrompre le lecteur à tout moment et de revenir à tel endroit incompris afin de l'éclaircir par un examen plus attentif"?[14] What most consider to be the high compositional quality of Chrétien's romance seems to occasion and justify very different views of its thematic coherence.

This study will operate in largely familiar thematic territory. One of its major critical precepts, however, is that in *Erec* such notions as love, marriage, adventure, chivalry, courtliness and kingship are themselves hypothetical and experimental notions, fraught with paradox and ambiguity within shifting contextual emphases. What those notions mean is as much open to examination as the relations among them. What is the nature of the love between Erec and Enide? What does adventure involve? What kind of king is Arthur? Such questions as these presume that the evaluation of a theme in *Erec* cannot be taken for granted. The richness of its narrative has bearing on its key concepts, in themselves. Their special meanings will influence their relations. The romance's "wisdom" is itself a reflection of coherent contextual features. By characteristically shaping its themes, it seems to qualify narrative *sen* within a network of subtle implications. Which is not to say that such implications do not exist. The student of *Erec* must take to heart the observation of Jean Frappier: the poetic universe of Chrétien brings "la vérité humaine" into intimate and absolute association with "une gratuité romanesque inséparable de tout sujet arthurien."[15]

The Prologue

An inquiry into the composition of *Erec et Enide* may profitably begin with an analysis of the romance's important Prologue (ll. 1-26). In the *Erec* Prologue Chrétien discusses in detail and with some authority the considerations which have brought him to his task, the compositional quality of the narrative and the lasting interest of his work. These introductory considerations offer helpful guidelines for critical appreciation of the romance and so merit careful examination:

> Li vilains dit an son respit
> que tel chose a l'an an despit
> qui molt valt mialz que l'an ne cuide;
> por ce fet bien qui son estuide
> atorne a bien quel que il l'ait;
> car qui son estuide antrelait,
> tost i puet tel chose teisir
> qui molt vandroit puis a pleisir.
> Por ce dist Crestïens de Troies
> que reisons est que totevoies
> doit chascuns panser et antandre
> a bien dire et a bien aprandre;
> et tret d'un conte d'avanture
> une molt bele conjointure
> par qu'an puet prover et savoir
> que cil ne fit mie savoir
> qui s'escïence n'abandone
> tant con Dex la grasce l'an done:
> d'Erec, le fil Lac, est li contes,
> que devant rois et devant contes
> depecier et corronpre suelent
> cil qui de conter vivre vuelent.
> Des or comancerai l'estoire
> qui toz jorz mes iert an mimoire
> tant con durra crestïantez;
> de ce s'est Crestïens vantez.
>   (ll. 1-26)

(The commoner says in his proverb that one disdains that which is worth much more than one thinks; for that reason he does well who directs his endeavor to whatever good he may be able to impart, for he who neglects his endeavor may well keep silent something which would eventually produce much pleasure. For that reason Chrétien de Troyes says that it is right that each person continually think and strive to speak well and teach well; thus he draws from an adventure story a very beautiful composition by which one can prove and know that he does not act wisely who does not publish his knowledge as long as God gives him the grace to do so. About Erec, the son of Lac, is the story which those who are wont to live by telling stories customarily tear apart and ruin when reciting them before kings and counts. At this point I will begin the narrative account which will always be remembered as long as Christianity lasts; Chrétien has prided himself on that.)

The Prologue to *Erec et Enide* presents a meticulously arranged and persuasive argument. It begins with proverbial wisdom: a thing disdained may be more valuable than one thinks (ll. 1-3). The proverb's popular origin is signified by the figure of the *vilains*, though the relative clause introducing ll. 2-3 implies that the proverb is not quoted verbatim, but rephrased to reveal its wisdom. The conjunctive transition *por ce* in l. 4 announces that a second truth is linked to the first: we must do justice to what we undertake. *Despit* arises not just from some *chose* we probably do not know much about; it can occur in the course or exercise of *estuide*. Getting involved in some serious endeavor, having a certain commitment or devotion to it, can lead to disdain. Whatever that endeavor, one must bring it to a successful conclusion. Value, it is implied, will then be no problem. Endeavor takes on a more verbal connotation in ll. 6-8. Disdain is still a concern, though the world of the *vilains* seems far behind. The meaning of *atorne(r) a bien* is developed to clarify the relationship between *chose* and *estuide*, that is, the work and the endeavor. The danger is that something able to please may be left unsaid because one gives up. The argument, we see, has moved carefully from aphorism to a kind of pedagogy, from folk wisdom to a sense of literate culture. The austerity of the first maxim is matched by the sobriety of its successive reformulations. What may surprise in this exposition is the key positioning of *pleisir*. What is meant by this word? And how usual is its association with *estuide*?

In ll. 9-12 the narrator replaces the authority, elucidated by him, of a collective individual with that of a named individual, Chrétien de Troyes. An ever more studied rhetorical organization, evident in the use of the pairs *panser/antandre* and *a bien dire/a bien aprandre*, casts "pleasure" in the venerable form of pleasing instruction. Pleasure stems from no mere diversion. Indeed, the modest posture urged by the avoidance of *teisir* in l. 7 is replaced by a kind of moral fervor. Volition and quality of effort (*bien*) are emphasized; we are each and every one enjoined to share a dutiful and vital commitment to education. This goes beyond the initial modest view of what the individual (*l'an*) contributes. Reason is behind this appeal, not proverbial wisdom. The indirect sense of the value of *reisons* as speech makes eloquence the key; the fearsome world of *teisir* is replaced by *bien dire*. What is more, for the first time there is an admonition to teach. As with *pleisir* in l. 8, the full meaning of *aprandre* in l. 12 is revealed by what follows the word.

Thus far, the Prologue has had little to say about the object of one's *estuide*. Making the best of one's own resources seems to suffice. But ll. 13-

18 illustrate concretely the principle of speaking well and teaching well by the example of Chrétien's version of an adventure story. With *conte d'avanture* we are thrown back into the world of the *vilains*. Pleasing instruction derives from the transformation of a *conte* into a *conjointure*. Emphasized here is the orderly and effective arrangement of narrative material, the fabrication of an expressive network of coherence from an admittedly common subject.[16] For the *conjointure* is *molt bele*. *Molt* appears at key moments in the Prologue, first to stress value (l. 3), then pleasure (l. 8). Here modifying *bele*, it reveals not only that a *conjointure* is possible (might there not be several?), but also that one, at least, is very beautiful indeed. This Chrétien, an authority on eloquent teaching, now expresses that ideal in poetic composition. *Pleisir* now radiates from an artful construction. However, the use of a *conte d'avanture* picks up the Prologue's first motif of disdain. This subject matter is worth more than one might have first thought, and so it is pursued. This sense of test case is developed in ll. 15-18, such that the subject's worth is not really of its own making. The transformation of a *conte d'avanture* testifies (l. 15) what can be accomplished when one's *escïence* is given full expression. And *escïence* would seem to comprise the knowledge one acquires—from books, experience, even God Himself.[17] So, as *une molt bele conjointure*, this *Erec et Enide* becomes the third authority invoked in the Prologue. And l. 18 expresses a sense of one's responsibility in God's creation, a statement worlds removed from the almost utilitarian sense of enterprise seen in ll. 1-3. The realization of a beautiful composition wrested from the challenge of common materials reveals what human life must accomplish. One's candle is not to be hidden under a bushel.

The story is identified in l. 19. It is already known to the nobility through other storytellers. However, their performances for liberal remuneration have been destructive. Are not these performers guilty of that disdain before a common endeavor to which the *vilains* refers in l. 1? Unable to work with deceptive appearances, they cannot achieve the special beauty which comes from artfully conjoined material. Whether they lack *estuide* or fail to do it justice, we cannot tell. Success can be no guarantee of art.

As "endeavor" takes on increasingly concrete application in the Prologue, its prominence grows even more. There is the possibility that one text—this one—can represent the fullest use of God's gifts. Just as this expression of significance is enunciated, the narrator at last speaks for himself alone. It is as though in l. 23 he is just taking up his pen; we are to follow closely his redaction. He is our fourth authority. Standing somewhat apart from that historical Chrétien we met in l. 9, he reveals himself in the context of *une molt bele conjointure* which has, we now realize, already begun. And this exclusive identification leads to what is surely one of the most provocative puns in medieval literature, as Chrétien proclaims that the durability of his endeavor coincides with that of his own and his Christian faith. The contrast between this narrative and the others' hack work joins with the Prologue's recurrent meditation on time and effort. To preeminent achievement goes the ultimate accolade. *Estoire* stands here for a stabilized narrative account, a text. Durability and celebrity come from its being *une molt bele conjointure*. Public performers will not destroy this version of the story of Erec. In the realm of human culture, a sort of experimental progress has been made. The bravura of these lines has risen slowly from the dry wisdom of ll. 1-3 by conjunctive elements and recurrent ideas. The final line, l. 26, seals the development. The return to third-person address and the first use of the present perfect tense provide closure in a double sense, the name tagging all previous voices, the tense signaling a completed speech act. The referential span of *ce* being ambiguous, this demonstrative refers to "all of the above," the entire passage, the Prologue as such, the world of time and space that rings with the "Christian" name. Only with this accomplishment does the persona of the narrator identify himself as author, as the "real" Chrétien.

The Prologue verses of *Erec et Enide* reward careful reading. Their complexity and coherence illustrate the very principle of *conjointure*, which, it might be argued, they discuss as idea from beginning to end. Indeed, the Prologue, like any section of the romance, must measure up to the romance's claim to immortal excellence. Such narrative excellence stems from an informed application of *escïence*, seen in part as literary culture in all its richness. We must, however, be careful to avoid the tendency to focus our experience of the text on technical virtuosity alone. Chrétien does not set out simply to impress the fashionable literary circles of his or any day. The Prologue's first concern is with a general problem: what is the relationship between human effort and genuine excellence? How may we do justice to experience? What are our human resources and what are we to do with them? The problem is referred by the Prologue's narrator to attitude, endeavor, pleasing instruction and what might be called productive understanding. *Erec et Enide* is a kind of solution to the problem. It gives a direction to human experience. This narrative account will endure because it is beautiful and because it has application; it is pleasing instruction of the very highest order. Indeed, this Prologue goes so far as to confer a species of self-sufficiency on itself as a monument to genuine human effort. *Erec et Enide* intends that its audience be formed by the special experience it has to offer.[18]

Characterization and Inference

The Prologue's authoritative pronouncements converge on the subject of Erec himself. But although specifying that this romance's adventures will concern a character named Erec, the Prologue gives no hints as to what will be told about him. This brief mention may mean that his story was well known to Chrétien's public; after all, he asserts, court performers often related it. But strictly speaking, and since the narrator affirms the perennial value of Erec's story, the Prologue alerts us to the fact that Erec constitutes a subject matter lending itself to an attractive and meaningful *conjointure*.

Erec's first portrait, broadly sketched by the narrator when he first appears (ll. 83-93), highlights his several attributes. Esteemed, most handsome, possessing excellent knightly qualities, Erec stands out at Arthur's court, then on a global scale, then for all time (in his age bracket!) and finally beyond the very power of language itself. It is fair to say, of course, that such praise is standard for romance heroes. The elaboration and progression of common ideals, however, gives a kind of substance to Erec's otherwise hyperbolic perfection. To understand the intent of such conventional praise, we must examine what the narrative does to expand on the terms of this initial thumbnail sketch.

In the romance's first section a number of scenes show forth Erec's prowess. Though poorly armed, he seeks to avenge the shameful assault on himself and Guenevere's maid. He vigorously challenges his adversary and triumphs after the bitter struggle for the sparrow hawk. He produces Enide's perfect beauty at Arthur's court and settles the explosive conflict there regarding the most beautiful woman at court. And in the tourney following his marriage Erec outdoes a distinguished field. Understandably, then, Arthur is reluctant to give him leave to return home. To the king's mind, only his dear nephew Gauvain is "plus vaillant, plus hardi, plus preu" (l. 2231) (more valiant, more intrepid, more worthy).

The first section also shows that Erec is capable of deep personal affection. Soon after first seeing Enide, he succeeds in making her his own. Her love and beauty inspire him and explain his victory over Yder. Erec sends word to Arthur's court of Enide's matchless excellence and delights himself in the spectacle of her perfection. He insists that Queen Guenevere dress Enide fittingly. And her beauty increases immeasurably his desire to consummate their union.

There is yet a third side to Erec. As announced by the use of *genz* (l. 89) and *bontez* (l. 93) in the initial sketch, Erec is a man of noble character.

He lives by certain standards, even displays tenacity in defending them. Spurning better lodging and certain gifts, Erec honors fittingly the hospitality and convictions of Enide's father. The young knight explains to Guenevere the implications of the material poverty in Enide's family. His very first act after Arthur kisses Enide, sealing the observance of the White Stag Custom, is to make good his promises to Enide's parents. And one finds generally in the romance that Erec keeps religious observances, is mindful of social conventions, provides for others and brings joy to the various communities in his path. The narrative shifts focus from one attribute to another, but Erec is ever the same—valiant, affectionate, principled. A composite and nuanced portrait results, helping to explain and thoroughly justify his reputation. In fact, the narrative seems to reveal an Erec who surpasses his local reputation.

But the text's verification of Erec's excellence also leaves him opaque in some respects. Accounted for, often in detail, are his *immediate* intentions and actions, but we do not usually know what Erec thinks about before and after his decisions and deeds. He does not even seek advice. We are at a loss, then, to account for the feelings and cogitations which would constitute the motivations for Erec's performance. (Enide is different in this respect, as will be seen later in this study.) His very tangible magnificence, then, is not matched by a palpable inner plasticity. A brief illustration will suggest what the narrative gains from such restricted portrayal.

Enide appears in a lengthy description (ll. 402-41) that turns to a blush as she sees for the first time the unknown, but handsome knight Erec. As for him, only his immediate reaction, the possible makings of a *coup de foudre*, is recounted: "Erec d'autre part s'esbahi, / quant an li si grant biauté vit" (ll. 448-49) (Erec for his part was spellbound when he saw such great beauty in her). But Enide's father, a good host, breaks the enchantment, sending Enide off to care for Erec's horse. Later Erec asks his host three questions in the presence of Enide: why he does not better dress his beautiful and capable daughter, why all the knights are gathered in town, who the knight is, armed in blue and gold and accompanied by a young lady and a dwarf. The vavasor responds freely to each question. Erec reacts to the information only to say that he dislikes that knight and would challenge him, asking only for arms and that Enide be his *pucele* in the sparrowhawk contest. To support this request, he at last reveals to the father his identity and offers to take Enide home as wife and queen over ten cities. The vavasor literally hands her over to him.

During this sequence Erec's affection for Enide appears conjoined to his earlier project—revenge on Yder. But we are certain of his feelings only when his questions and requests announce that his heart and mind are set on what must be done. When does he decide on Enide? At first sight? As Enide looks after his horse? When she takes his hand? As they sit quietly before the fire? Must we postulate words which the narrative does not record? And, after all, since Chrétien does not mention love as such, what kind of affection is it? These unanswered questions point to a general feature of the romance: <u>the inner workings of Erec's powerful character are not displayed</u>.

One becomes acutely aware of such restricted portraiture at moments of suspense, usually when Erec announces a new initiative. He acts swiftly and decisively, as though grounded on firm convictions and motivations; only, they are not explained or revealed. In effect, we see little more of what moves Erec than do the individuals about him. This is not to say that he is inscrutable; no one would doubt his attraction to Enide. It is simply that our knowledge of Erec must be constructed primarily from inference. Succeeding speeches, actions and accounts amplify the characterization within the framework of the original brief description. As observed by Alfred Adler, "The event that comes later in time may be interpreted as a gloss, an elucidation of an earlier event. There is really no *earlier* and no *later*: there is one truth only, first revealed in prefigurations, and then, though still the self-same truth, more fully revealed through glosses to these prefigurations."[19] Descriptions and events foreshadow or echo. The full meaning of an occurrence is apparent only when one has traced its reverberations and connections throughout the narrative. Yet the inference of meanings cannot but carry with it a sense of mystery. To repeat: Erec always remains somewhat opaque.

The backdrop to Erec's excellence in the first section is the world of King Arthur. Erec is one of its stars. We expect his performance to illustrate Arthurian values, and few would deny that it does so. The paradox is that his performance also alerts one to incongruities in Arthur's world. That is, the narrative's demonstration of Erec comes at the court's expense. However, the comparison is not overtly made by characters themselves or the narrator. Inference is still the basic procedure. The narrative's organization guides one to perceive that Erec embarks on adventures which show him to outshine the very world that is the scene of his distinction.

In the first scene (ll. 27-76) Arthur sets about reviving the Custom of the White Stag, notwithstanding Gauvain's fears. The King puts emphasis on what will be marvelous and adventurous about the hunt. When it begins, the narrative changes scene. The hunt is scarcely described. Rather, we watch Guenevere and her lady companion start on a ride. Erec joins them and they encounter Yder and his companions. A scene change returns to Arthur. His attempt at adventure only proves Gauvain right: the hunt's success does not keep the knights from potential violence when the most beautiful woman is to be chosen. Thus, the narrative begins with two sequences, both of which end in failure. Only Guenevere seeks to remedy the frustration: "metez cest beisier an respit / jusqu'a tierz jor qu'Erec revaingne" (ll. 338-39) (postpone this kiss until the third day, when Erec returns). All agree to await his resolution of the dilemma, although it is hard to imagine how Erec could overcome the division at court. The other knights are unyielding in defense of their respective ladies' beauty. In effect, after separate adventures the court chooses to hold the custom in suspension while an individual pursues the defense of his and Guenevere's honor. No one seeks to help him.

The narrative is cast so as to distinguish Erec from the world of Arthur around him. He has nothing to do with the hunt. He obeys Guenevere once, then unequivocally asserts his determination to pursue his own enemies. The failures at adventure by Arthur and his Queen suggest limitations in the court's world as Erec moves forth to achievement. But the text offers no explicit comment on such limitations or on Erec's already separate initiative. His particular adventure, which culminates in the Sparrow-Hawk Custom, also rescues Arthur's promotion of the White Stag Custom. The presentation of Enide dramatically reunites the Arthurian world in a way no one there could have foreseen. Generally speaking, Erec's full demonstration of prowess, affection and principle while abroad outshines and brings together again the efforts of those at court.

The romance's first section, while filling out the initial portrait of Erec, also traces his progressive domination of the Arthurian scene. While always something of an outsider, he moves from a virtual absence when Arthur promotes the hunt to virtually complete domination of the tourney which follows his marriage. But just as our inferential knowledge of what moves Erec leaves room for ambiguity about him, so, too, what we are able to learn about his distinctive participation in Arthur's court or the latter's apparent difficulties leaves much unclear. That ambiguity has played no small role in the romance's critical and historical appeal as its readers have tried to pierce its mysteries.

After the Prologue's vituperation of those who are wont to *depecier* and *corronpre* the *conte* about Erec, one is surprised to find that the narrative presents so many mysterious features. After all, the opening succession of authoritative statements seems to establish a reliable narrator persona who is anxious to give explanations and formulate meanings. Yet his presence in the first section is subdued. He keeps his essential function, to be sure: he recounts what has been said and done. His accounts are generally detailed, and characters are quoted at length. Yet the narrator perpetuates ambiguities by limiting his information to what takes place in the field of action or by commenting only on what has directly transpired. An omniscient view is rare, so that at crucial moments the perspective on events belongs to just one of the participants, though one does not necessarily know that participant's feelings or share his judgment of what is in view. Consider the scene of Yder's arrival at Caradigan, where he is to report on Erec's victory over him (ll. 1090-1166). That arrival is recounted, described and in a sense reenacted through the words of those in the Arthurian galleries who observe it. The limitation in perspective serves less to trace an event briefly than to dramatize how Arthur's court responds to an anticipated occurrence of great importance. Their protracted and repetitious exchanges —their apparent fascination with conjecture—leave the narrator almost invisible. Arthur's court reveals itself as its members narrate to one another Yder's arrival. This is a technique applied with great subtlety elsewhere, as when Erec sees Enide the first time. Obscure motivation and causation are a feature of Chrétien's first Arthurian romance. It will return in others as well.

But the narrator is not always so self-effacing. When Erec first appears, the action stops briefly for background information and evaluation. This description is authoritative information, and we have seen that the narrative often corroborates it. There results a somewhat unpredictable shifting of the narrator's stance: he can move out of range or he can be truly prominent. Nowhere is this shift better seen than in the portrait of Enide. Just before she appears with her mother from a workroom, the narrator confesses: "ne sai quel oevre i feisoient" (l. 400) (I do not know what work they were doing there). He goes on to describe objectively her bedraggled appearance (ll. 401-10); then, to talk about her hidden physical beauty, he expatiates on Nature's handiwork, at one point comparing her to Iseut (ll. 411-41). This passage will be discussed later in some detail, but enough has been said to show that the narrator shifts his stance subtly and frequently, a profession of ignorance on a fairly minor point giving way to objective details, then to descriptive hyperbole at its most authoritative and literary. The problem with this procedure is consistency. The narrator at times is absent or mute on matters of much interest. At other times, he is the narrator of the Prologue—all assurance and information.

One approach to this problem is to examine closely the narrator's famous allusion to the *premiers vers*. It occurs at the successful completion of the Custom of the White Stag, a climactic and spectacular scene (ll. 1707-95). It seems that Arthur has recovered his leadership as the community about him judges Enide the most beautiful of all. So the narrator concludes:

> Li rois, par itele avanture,
> randi l'usage et la droiture
> qu'a sa cort devoit le blans cers:
> ici fenist li premiers vers.
> (ll. 1793-96)

(The king, by means of such an adventure, reestablished the Custom and the privilege that the White Stag used to have at his court: here ends the first "verse.")

What is meant by *li premiers vers*? It seems to refer to the matter of the white stag custom with which the romance begins, for indeed at l. 1795 that matter is closed. The narrator simply announces the completion of that portion of the *conte d'avanture*. We have noted that the scenes concerning the White Stag Custom alternate with scenes concerning other matters, notably the Sparrow-Hawk contest. Indeed, the latter receive more attention, to the point where Erec, never really concerned with the White Stag, both achieves his adventure and, tangentially, saves Arthur's court by successfully fulfilling the Custom of the White Stag. The Custom quickly gets involved in a larger development, much as Erec's pursuit of vengeance gets subordinated to his affection for Enide. These complications so embed the proclaimed *premiers vers* in the adventure of Erec and Enide that there is no real narrative pause at this point, other than that invented by the narrator himself in l. 1796.

If *li premiers vers* does harken back to the *conte d'avanture*, then it would serve as a reminder that this organization of scenes is distinctive and, so to speak, original. If this be the purpose of l. 1796, however, one must bear in mind that the very nature of this one-line insertion does not put a steady spotlight on the narrator persona and his dexterity. The text merely continues to relate Erec's actions after the Custom's completion. Now, transitions of scene in this romance tend to be accomplished with great delicacy. Consider the change which imperils the newlyweds. When Erec and Enide gain his father's lodging at Carnant, presents are showered on Erec by everyone, but Enide is the real prize (ll. 2397-99). Her beauty and nobility of character are admired. We see her on a quilt surrounded by other women, but surpassing them and all other women in beauty. There then occurs a remarkable shift from the account of her unsurpassed personal qualities to the fact that through experience:

> ... nus de li ne mesdisoit,
> car nus n'an pooit rien mesdire:
> el rëaume ne an l'empire
> n'ot dame de si boenes mors.
> (ll. 2426-29)

(... no one said bad things about her, for no one could say anything bad: in the realm or in the empire there was no lady of such good comportment.)

In the space of a few lines one shifts from a general description to an evaluation more specific to her life at Carnant seen in an undetermined habitual past. With astonishing yet subtle rapidity we move from a genuine apotheosis of Erec and Enide—they have claimed their own world, at least—to a problem of unknown dimensions. A microscopic shift occurs as the passage just quoted is followed by: "Mes tant l'ama Erec d'amors, / que d'armes mes ne li chaloit" (ll. 2430-31) (But Erec loved her with such love that arms no longer mattered to him). The danger implied in these lines is then developed from court rumor to Enide's tears and Erec's anger. As elsewhere, the delicacy of the shift from one matter to the next is quietly impressive.

The present discussion of characterization was facilitated by having the romance's "first section" end when the couple leaves Arthur for Carnant. But that division, it is now clear, has no more *textual* basis than does the narrator's *premiers vers*. Both designations, though convenient, do not, in fact, describe the actual articulation of scenes and episodes in the narrative. What this means for characterization is that the narrator in this romance behaves much as other characters do. At times we are very much aware of him, at other times not at all. Similarly, it is not always clear what he wants to achieve; he, too, has a certain opacity. Conversely, and this will be developed below when the matter of description is taken up, the narrator's knowledge, when he chooses to comment and not just describe, becomes a kind of exploit in his text, where exploits are not predictably successful. Thematic and technical control does not appear to reside solely in the narrator's hand.

Characterization presents the reader with interesting, admirable, if somewhat mysterious or ambiguous personages. How they are presented implies an intelligence or will that is not fully at one with the interventions of the narrator. Motivation is not clear. What are, after all, the personal or psychological qualities that lie behind Erec's obvious chivalric excellence? The initial mention of *conjointure* suggests the need for a closer look at the romance's compositional features—a closer investigation into its textual workings—if one is to find the meanings addressed by the Prologue or come closer to the themes so often studied in this romance. The quest of Erec and Enide forms an ideal piece for such an examination.

The Quest

The romance's first section has qualities which might suffice for it to stand alone, as an independent narrative. A problem of some gravity at the Arthurian court is introduced and resolved, while in the process Erec completes his service there and returns home. More than living up to his reputation as a knight, he also seems to fill the one conspicuous lack in his life by gaining Enide's companionship. They are a perfect couple, if we may judge by the approval readily given on all sides and by the narrator's evaluation, according to which they are equal in courtliness, beauty, nobility and understanding (ll. 1484-96). Little hint is given of problems ahead. Once Yder is defeated, happiness prevails. In a sense, too, Erec has gained our confidence: he is apt to take initiative in new situations and make the most of any opportunity according to his own lights. He seems not only reliable, but also perceptive and knowledgeable. Of course, his entirely adequate performance is shrouded in the mystery surrounding his feelings and motivations. The delicate compositional artfulness of the narrative whole—its *conjointure*—seems to counterbalance the mystery, however, engaging one in the interplay of inferred meanings.

The first section of the romance is followed by the quest, a substantial sequence of adventures which dominates the whole. But why should there be a second section? One obvious new feature is that performance now concerns both Erec and Enide. They face together a string of unforeseen, diverse adventures, while the world of Arthur, save in one notable episode, recedes from view. Some time after the couple's joyous installation at Carnant, Erec loses interest in arms and tournaments; he devotes all his time to loving Enide. Though still enjoying his liberality and sponsorship, his companions express displeasure at his conduct (ll. 2455-58). Such a knight as Erec should bear arms. Enide hears their criticism and is made unhappy, but does not reveal her concern to Erec, fearing that he may take offense. Yet Enide does finally open herself up to Erec (ll. 2470-2581), rehearsing general opinion fully and with spirit (ll. 2536-71); she even overstates somewhat the narrator's initial view of the problem. She expresses regret over Erec's loss of esteem, emphasizes her displeasure at being blamed and urges that he seek to recover his reputation. Enide's anguish makes her side with the general opinion that Erec's way of loving has compromised his chivalric reputation. Erec's response is immediate and to the point: Enide was right to express sorrow over his condition, as were all who blamed him (ll. 2572-73). Then, strangely, he orders her to put on her most beautiful dress and prepare to ride (ll. 2574-79). Sad and shocked, Enide does as she is told.

This is a remarkable scene. For the first time we learn Enide's thoughts, words and actions in some detail. Moreover, this is the first instance in the narrative where she and Erec have a genuine conversation. Enide, we now see, is sensitive to court gossip, fearful of displeasing her husband, yet anxious to be helpful. Erec, on the other hand, continues to display a decisiveness of character, a tendency to take charge (as he did with Guenevere) when confronting an unpleasant surprise. But that is all we see of Erec in this episode. While accepting criticism, or the right of others to criticize, he initiates a project without revealing its nature or purpose. The narrator, who has revealed the cause of Enide's unhappiness before she speaks, is strangely silent on what moves Erec. In preparing to leave, the knight displays unwavering firmness in dealing with his wife, his father and his companions. It is even difficult to tell whether or not he is wrathful. Impatient to be off, perhaps, Erec nonetheless makes sure that his father will look after Enide if necessary and will continue providing for the knights at court. And as he orders his wife to ride on ahead of him and not to speak to him, Erec assures her that she will be safe (l. 2771). Enide is convinced that he now hates her (ll. 2786-88), but the narrator reports only that "Erec s'en va, sa fame an moinne, / ne set out, mes en avanture" (ll. 2762-63) (Erec goes off, taking his wife with him, he knows not where, save on adventure).

What does Erec intend beyond seeking adventure? Enide may be right about his anger, but she may be exaggerating; in any case, Erec does not give vent to wrath. As in the first section, his conduct is mysterious. Once again, events urge one to examine the subsequent adventures in search of signs explaining Erec's project. Deeds may reveal where words fail. The project clearly concerns not just his honor, as when he pursued Yder, but his relationship with Enide. There is a parallel, certainly, with the first section, if prowess and exploits are at issue again; but this new section of the romance has an added ingredient—the disagreement of a couple that seemed made in heaven.

The two initial episodes of the quest form a pattern. Enide, riding in front, spots adversaries. After much hesitation, she breaks her vow of silence to reveal the danger. After chiding her, Erec proceeds to the encounter and emerges victorious. This sequence happens first against three robbers (ll. 2792-2920), then against five (ll. 2921-3079); and each time Erec reprimands Enide for doubting his prowess. The third version of the pattern (ll. 3080-3652) is more elaborate in that it involves a camp-out in the woods, a picnic with a squire, hospitality with a count who attempts to seduce Enide, her warning to Erec, the couple's hasty early-morning departure and the count's pursuit. After all this Enide announces the count's impending attack, and Erec again blames and threatens her. The final version occurs as the couple encounters Guivret (ll. 3653-3910). This episode follows the pattern more closely than its predecessor, except that, when Guivret submits, Enide virtually disappears from the main plane of the action. Erec says nothing to her as they leave Guivret, and she says nothing to him before the encounter with Keu.

What might be served by the narrative's variations on this pattern of silence followed by *parole*? For one thing, it facilitates one's perceptions of Erec's increasing level of achievement: he dispatches first three highwaymen, then five; proceeds to overcome a count leading a large band; and finally wears down a dwarfish king who, riding a tremendous horse, seeks chivalric combat one-to-one with any knight happening by his castle. Erec's adversaries are ever more fearful, yet from each combat he emerges victorious. The progression demonstrates Erec's prowess. And this fact is not lost on Enide. After the first combat she renews her promise not to speak again unless spoken to. After the second she says nothing when Erec renews that demand, but she does insist upon standing nightwatch. That night she repents again of the ill-chosen words that led to their quest, for it is clear that there is no better knight than Erec: "Bien le savoie. Or le sai mialz; / car ge l'ai veü a mes ialz, / car trois ne cinc armez ne dote" (ll. 3107-09) (I knew it then, now I know it better; for I have seen it with my own eyes, for he fears neither three armed men nor five).

Made more vivid in this sequence than Enide's renewed respect for Erec's prowess, however, is his own renewed sense of her respect and love. The counterpoint to his achievements, after all, is his requirement that no matter what, she ride on ahead and say nothing. The first time she warns him of danger ahead, Erec is angered that she has violated his order (ll. 2845-52). In the next encounter Enide, after more hesitation, warns Erec, whereupon he condemns this second violation of her imposed silence: "... tres bien savoie / que gueres ne me priseiez" (ll. 2996-97) (... I knew well all along that you did not esteem me at all). In this second encounter Erec is shown testing Enide. His wrath seems to be growing; having dispatched the five, he renews his standing order about silence (ll. 3074-76). Yet when she then insists upon standing watch, "Erec l'octroie, et bel li fu" (l. 3089) (Erec agrees to it, and that pleased him); and the next day he gladly accepts a squire's offer of food, bidding him to arrange their stopover at a nearby castle. Although Erec's words to Enide remain sharp, his conduct suggests less vigor in pursuing the quest, as if Enide's warnings are, after all, becoming meaningful to him. But as before, we are not told what goes on inside Erec.

Enide displays great presence of mind in dealing with the vain and passionate Count Galoain while assuring that her husband gets a second night's rest. When she wakes him, the narrator reveals: "Or ot Erec que bien se prueve / vers lui sa fame lëaumant" (ll. 3480-81) (Now Erec hears that his wife proves herself loyal towards him). Does this "proof" stem from the fact that Enide could have found such a count attractive or that at least her well-being was not in jeopardy as it had been before with the highwaymen? Nothing more is said on this point. Erec still admonishes Enide to refrain from speaking as they ride out of the castle to safety (ll. 3510-13), and she again ignores the admonition when the pursuing band appears. Once more he accuses her of not valuing him and threatens her as in the past. It is difficult to tell in this episode what tone Erec uses, let alone what he intends. And more than before his injunctions appear without foundation, unless a fine line is now being drawn between her obvious loyalty and the respect for his prowess which Erec requires through her silence when danger appears. Showing respect for prowess through silence seems an illegitimate requirement when the odds against Erec are overwhelming. When Guivret comes thundering forth and Enide, more terrified than ever before, cannot help but speak up again:

> Ele li dit; il la menace;
> mes n'a talant que mal li face,
> qu'il aparçoit et conuist bien
> qu'ele l'ainme sor tote rien,
> et il li tant que plus ne puet.
> (ll. 3751-55)

(She tells him; he threatens her; but he has no desire to harm her, for he perceives and knows well that she loves him more than anything, and he loves her so much that he could not love her more.)

Yet he threatens her. This is the last time he does so.

Erec defeats Guivret. We have every reason to expect the quest to end here, after the fourth use of the episodic pattern. After robbery attempts, a seduction scheme and a chivalric test, Enide has recognized her error, and Erec seems to have used the issue of chivalric respect in order to put Enide's love to the test. There is no tender reconciliation. What is most strange about this fourth episode is that, though as badly wounded as Guivret, Erec refuses medical attention and sets forth after getting bandaged on the site of the duel. Why? This determination is underscored in the subsequent episode, in which he rejects the determined efforts of the Arthurian court to care for him (ll. 3911-4279). He never retreats from the position he defends before Keu: "Ne savez mie mon besoing; / ancor m'estuet aler plus loing" (ll. 3991-92) (You do not know my mission; I must go yet farther). It is all the more difficult to understand this *besoing*, since the pattern of testing used by Erec for Enide no longer applies. His stratagem seems to have worked. Is Erec, even while grievously wounded, now questing more or less *à l'aventure*?

At each step in this quest Erec acts in ways that appear to shed light on his previous behavior, only to do something unexpected. *Events* justify him repeatedly, however. This is the case when he and Enide enter the forest, eventually to hear the cry of a damsel in distress. Fresh evidence is given of a change in rapport between Erec and his wife. He tells her what he hears, what it means, what he intends to do. Enide is to wait. In this episode Erec aids an unfortunate couple and tests his prowess against a fantastic, but brutal pair of giants. He requests only that Arthur's court be told of this achievement. Erec makes haste to rejoin Enide, fearing that someone may have borne her off. Enide, for her part, is convinced that he has abandoned her entirely. This episode reveals much about the quest's second half. Erec's demonstration of prowess, as such, continues. Moreover, its connection with the trial of Enide has broken down. This breakdown confuses the interpretation of his actions, although his performance is still impressive. But if Erec even remotely desires still to impress, he now directs word of his accomplishments to Arthur's court, rather than to Enide, who is not even present in the combat with the giants.

When Erec collapses from his wounds before Enide, she immediately moves to the forefront, in sharp contrast to her reserve when her husband defeated Guivret and spent a night at Arthur's court. Enide laments Erec's apparent death (ll. 4580-4631), feeling guilt for his misfortune, extolling his beauty, prowess and generosity, longing for her own death. She then firmly rejects the overtures and demands of the amorous Count Oringle, resisting his threats and violence, driving him to unworthy behavior by her obstinacy. It may be argued that, although Enide's performance is only verbal, it surpasses anything Erec has done. His successes, after all, have been chivalric ones, and not his first ones at that, whereas Enide responds with conviction and resourcefulness to a new threat. The *parole* which characterizes her performance from the beginning of the romance's second section receives its fullest and most efficacious display: up to this point her words have been private deliberations, warnings to Erec and a deception of the amorous count. Now they also repel an unwanted suitor and restore her unconscious husband. Erec has helped a damsel in distress, while Enide, also in distress, has helped herself against the unwanted help of another. This is her first combat alone. Even when Erec regains consciousness and dispatches the villain, this episode belongs to Enide. As they escape together riding the same horse, one infers that on the level of love, if not of chivalry, they are again equals.

No wonder, then, that at this point in the narrative (ll. 4879-4900) Erec addresses his wife and claims a full reconciliation with her:

>
> bien vos ai de tot essaiee.
> Or ne soiez plus esmaiee,
> c'or vos aim plus qu'ainz mes ne fis,
> et je resui certains et fis
> que vos m'amez parfitement.
> Or voel estre d'or en avant,
> ausi con j'estoie devant,
> tot a vostre comandemant;

> et se vos rien m'avez mesdit,
> je le vos pardoing tot et quit
> del forfet et de la parole.
> (ll. 4883-93)

(I have tested you well in everything. Now no longer be dismayed, for now I love you more than ever, and I am again certain and confident that you love me perfectly. Now I want to be henceforth just as I was before, entirely at your command; and if you have spoken anything amiss to me, I entirely absolve you of the crime and of the statement.)

This speech seems to reveal Erec's view of the quest as never before. He has been testing Enide and finds restored confidence in her love. Indeed, he is more devoted than ever. And he pardons her for her words, which he repeatedly blamed heretofore. We have no reason to doubt the sincerity of these words. And they provide a view of Erec's conduct which makes sense, agreeing in fact with Enide's interpretation all along. But Erec's conciliatory statement is also disturbing. This is not the first time that he has proof of her love, as we have seen. And it is Enide's remarkable performance that actually forces such a statement and the realization which lies behind it. Which is to say that *events* make it possible for Erec himself to understand what he was doing previously. Events are constituted and organized in such a way that Erec is brought to reconciliation. Indeed, his very appreciation of Enide at this point does not do justice to what she has achieved. She has more than proved her love, a fact which the narrative underscores by introducing yet one more adventure. Whatever Erec may think, his adventures are not yet over.

When Guivret strikes down the still-weak Erec, the latter is said to have acted wrongly by hiding his identity: "plus cuida fere qu'il ne pot" (l. 4974) (he thought he could do more than he was able). Temerity has its price. Enide, in turn, acts bravely and saves his life by grabbing Guivret's rein and lecturing him on striking the wounded. This action might be called her first chivalric exploit. It coincides with Erec's first defeat. For the first time he actually hears her extol his valor. And Guivret: ". . . Dame, ne tamez. / Bien voi que lëaument amez / vostre seignor, si vos an los" (ll. 5009-11) (My lady, do not be upset. I see clearly that you love your lord loyally, and I praise you for that). He gives his opinion before their identity is revealed to him. With Enide's exploit and his own defeat, Erec finally accepts medical help and rest. As Enide cares for him, Erec finds renewed assurance: "Or ne li set que reprochier / Erec, qui bien l'a esprovee: / vers li a grant amor trovee" (ll. 5096-98) (Now Erec, who has carefully tested her, does not know what to reproach her for: he has found a great love in her). When his wounds heal, Erec and Enide lie together for the first time since the morning she first referred to his *recreantise*:

> Tant ont eü mal et enui,
> il por li et ele por lui,
> c'or ont feite lor penitance.
> Li uns ancontre l'autre tance
> comant il li puise pleisir.
> (ll. 5203-07)

(They had so much suffering and vexation, he for her and she for him, that now they have done their penance. The one strives against the other as to how to please.)

This is true reconciliation, more effective than the verbal one earlier. Then, when Erec has embraced, comforted and reassured his wife, it is simply said that "Or n'est pas Enyde a maleise" (l. 4895) (Now is Enide not discomforted); the penance both make and their mutual effort to please suggest both reciprocity and unity. Events, not volition, have led Erec and Enide to this end to their quest. Events even give Erec, this most unique of knights, a knightly companionship he has consistently refused: Guivret's offer of friendship is accepted (l. 5240). As far as Erec is concerned, it is now time to return to his land by way of Arthur's court.

Viewed as a whole, the quest is a series of episodes which overlap through repetition. Erec's threats, his duels with Guivret, Enide's monologues, damsels in distress, amorous counts. At the same time there is progressive achievement, each exploit giving a new sense of what Erec and Enide are to and for each other, as well as what the couple makes possible in the love of man and woman. It cannot reasonably be claimed that Erec and Enide change because of their adventures. Whatever his thoughts and feelings, Erec remains determined, reasonable, lucid, seemingly mindful of some undefined code of behavior. Enide certainly becomes more active during the quest, but everything she does stems from her devotion to her husband. Their relationship is reaffirmed by what happens, but that reaffirmation involves removing some misapprehensions without changing their hearts. They are always in love. What must be kept in mind, however, is that events in the quest go beyond what either character has in mind, beyond even the problem they seem to face when the quest begins. Robbers are punished, a vain count admits the error of his passion, another couple is liberated from monstrous persecution, a brave knight meets his match and finds a friend, and a violent passion is punished. Many are touched by this private matter. It has increasing resonance. Yet Erec and Enide remain focused on the immediate problem of their love.

A further point bears emphasis: Erec's successes come about because from the outset he seeks *avanture*. We recall that as the couple leaves Carnant Erec has no idea where he and Enide are going, only that they are off on adventure. Erec persists in his determination to pursue adventure wherever adventure is. Hence his refusal to stay with Guivret after their first duel or with Arthur's court, whatever his wounds, as well as his refusal to accept companionship or pass by a possible adventure. It may be, in fact, that events instill in Erec a belief in the possibilities of adventure, which must continue as long as success does. One must keep going to the end. Erec never expresses that belief, but events justify something of the sort by yielding a repeated and comprehensive assurance that he and Enide are in love. That this pursuit of adventure matters greatly in the world of romance is confirmed by the episode which proves to be the last and the greatest in the quest—the so-called Joie de la Cort episode.

This adventure occurs despite the objections of Guivret, who would protect his new friend from such danger. Erec is first impressed by the prosperity of King Evrain's Brandigan and would like to visit it (ll. 5367-70). Guivret warns of the terrible adventure, but Erec cannot be dissuaded once he hears that its name is Joie de la Cort: "Rien ne me porroit retenir / que je n'aille querre la Joie" (ll. 5424-25) (Nothing could deter me from going in search of this Joy). Nothing does deter him, neither the concern of street crowds nor Evrain's warnings nor Enide's fears. The odds against success seem formidable, yet there is no hesitation, no worry, no fear. He expresses no desire to advance his reputation by succeeding where so many have failed or to release Evrain's community from the depressing spectacle of knights continually slain. The narrator summarizes Erec's attitude thus: "con plus granz est la mervoille / et l'avanture plus grevainne, / plus la covoite et plus s'an painne" (ll. 5596-98) (the greater the marvel and the more difficult the adventure, the more he covets it and strives for it). He is impatient to know what the fuss is all about. Once the adventure begins, moreover, Erec displays composure and valor. His adversary frightens him not in the least. Even more interestingly, when the defeated Mabonagrain relates in detail the origin of this adventure (ll. 5998-6106), Erec has nothing more to say; his curiosity appears to have been satisfied.

The Joie de la Cort episode portrays Erec's espousal of *avanture*. Curiosity is grounds enough for taking on an apparently impossible task. This is the first "pure" adventure which Erec chooses to undertake in his quest. One may even assert that this is his greatest feat: it is against the most incredible opposition, requires the longest combat and has the clearest, most positive and most extensive ramifications for another couple and for an entire community. Moreover, as scholars have observed, Erec's feat makes it possible for Enide to defend her legitimate relationship with Erec against the selfish and harmful arrangement her cousin has required of Mabonagrain. The perfection of the questing couple is now seen against its widest background yet. Erec's motivation is not complicated. He wants adventure and he gets it. What is adventure for him, if not the satisfaction of curiosity and the acquisition, in achievement, of "Joy"?

This vital episode may, in fact, imply that from the quest's inception Erec has perceived, however dimly, the need for more knowledge and a sense of joy through achievement in his marriage with Enide. But events have perhaps taken Erec's grasp of knowledge and joy beyond that context. Or perhaps his full reconciliation with his wife has somehow opened up for him larger vistas of knowledge and joy. How much does he understand, in the end, about what must be done? How much does he intuit? Events, at least, set him apart in the romance and guarantee a favorable issue to his activities. It is not unreasonable to suggest that the romance bars access to Erec's feelings and motivations because, except in select instances and only to a limited degree, he himself normally does not reflect on what he feels and intends.

What meanings, then, may be attached to Erec's successful and heroic efforts? God, we are told, occasionally protects him and Enide, but divine agency is not constantly at work in the romance. Erec has received no unusual training and does not seem much given to introspection. A striving after knowledge and joy, we have seen, is not clearly a goal towards which he moves unswervingly. He is not alone in having royal birth. Perhaps the one thing in the narrative which does set him, and Enide, apart from the others is perfect beauty. Let us examine briefly the representation of the two characters.

When Erec first appears in the romance (ll. 81-104), the narrator names him, situates him at court, emphasizes his beauty, asserts his distinguished character and gives some details on his costume. His beauty, as we have seen, is unequaled anywhere. The narrator is much more lavish in discussing the perfect beauty of Enide: once having made her, it is said, Nature could not reproduce the unique result; references to Iseut, the lily, stars and God's handiwork only begin to depict her features; the narrator concludes his tableau in these terms:

> Que diroie de sa biauté?
> Ce fu cele por verité
> qui fu fete por esgarder,
> qu'an se poïst an li mirer
> ausi com an un mireor.
> (ll. 437-41)

(What would I say about her beauty? In truth, it was the sort that was made to look at, for one could look on her as into a mirror.)

The narrator brings together erudition and rhetoric to describe Enide's beauty. On the level of hyperbolic rhetoric alone, Erec and Enide are from the beginning made for one another. The text only gradually unfolds Erec's determination to possess her, however, and their compatibility is finally asserted by the narrator after Erec's triumph, as the couple proceeds to Arthur's court (ll. 1484-96). Their physical perfection unites them as of one kind. Beauty is a precondition and sign of their excellence.

The beauty of the principal characters does not always affect events in *Erec et Enide*, nor does it have a predictable effect when it does matter. Enide's mere presence makes possible the peaceful conclusion of the White Stag Custom (ll. 1777-84). The highwaymen seem more interested in loot than in Enide's charms, but her pulchritude drives two counts to distraction and violent excess. Guivret hardly acknowledges her presence until she proves a gifted nurse, whereupon he gives her a horse and riding gear. When the couple arrives in Brandigan, the crowd immediately laments the approaching demise of so handsome a knight while paying no attention to the equal, but strangely inconspicuous beauty of Enide (ll. 5448-93). In effect, at no time in their quest does anyone realize fully the import of this couple's appearance. Indeed, Enide's repeated expression of concern over their fate betrays a reluctance to believe in their obviously special status. Erec's taciturn self-assurance, on the other hand, goes well with that special status. All Brandigan fails to perceive that it is Erec's beauty which foretells his victory against a Mabonagrain whose beauty is marred by unnatural height. Beauty betokens effectiveness. During the quest Enide translates her initial perfection into a series of exploits which support her father's initial claim regarding her extraordinary beauty. If beauty does indeed betoken effectiveness, this truth does not seem apparent to the romance's characters.

Adventures generally do illustrate, however, the excellence of the couple. Their distinctiveness is difficult for any realm, perhaps even Arthur's, to grasp. Events favor their perfection as though it were mysteriously normative. In this respect, their superior reality finally justifies the rhetoric displayed by the narrator when Enide first appears. Circumstances seem to propel this beautiful couple through their quest according to what can only be termed a special law of Nature. The narrative need not dwell on characters' thoughts and motivations. The heroic is made interesting through different instances of its always successful performance. It becomes difficult to construe such heroic behavior as exemplary because the unique status of the couple is simply given at the outset and without reference to a larger scheme of values. Such perfection is difficult to emulate perfectly, since, although extremely effective, it is difficult to understand. The fact that Erec and Enide are married does not begin to account for their relationship and achievements. Successful performance by the central couple, then, does not in itself provide perfect understanding of what the Prologue really means when asserting that this romance offers pleasing instruction.

Description and Poetry

There is an abundance of descriptive passages in this romance. They concern clothes, armor, architecture and landscaping, marvelous objects and beings, even what might be termed local color—town activities and settings, ceremony, husbandry, medical science. But only the extraordinary, beautiful, productive or effective is recorded. Some descriptive passages promote the narrative economy of the romance by being placed to set scenes or heighten suspense. There are also major sections which appear to break the narrative's flow, and because of them the romance has been found dated or prolix in places. Yet these static tableaux may be just the means for seeing what is accomplished beyond the limits of characterization in *Erec et Enide*.

Major descriptive sections coincide with major resolutions of interest—ceremonial pauses—in the narratives. The first such passage comprises a description of the clothes given by Guenevere to Enide (ll. 1567-1652). Precise information gives the substance and trappings of a tunic and mantle. Gold and gems abound. The dressing of Enide, the preparation of her hair and the bestowal of a small crown and a necklace, are detailed. Thus transformed, Enide is brought before Arthur's court, there to be pronounced the most beautiful. A second major descriptive tableau concerns the horse and riding gear given by Guivret to Enide for her ride back to Arthur's court (ll. 5268-5305). Her new palfrey's markings are given; its gear is covered with emeralds, while the saddle bows (the work of a Breton carver) display a series of scenes from the story of Aeneas. A third tableau describes Erec's coronation robe (ll. 6673-6747). The work of four fairies, the garment weaves in portraits the figures of geometry, arithmetic, music and astronomy (the quadrivium), each portrait showing activities and objects typical of its figure. The robe's lining is made from the fur of a singular, multi-colored animal, while the mantle has costly gems. In each descriptive passage much is made of not just the unusual, costly materials involved, but also the handiwork—the artifice—that has produced the finished pieces. These pieces adorn the persons of Erec and Enide.

Why do these tableaux appear in the narrative? They are found in ceremonial interludes which follow major accomplishments of the couple: their triumphant arrival at Arthur's court after victory in the Sparrow-Hawk Custom, the apparent conclusion of the quest as Guivret joins Enide and Erec in setting off for Arthur's court, and the great coronation scene which seals the destiny of the happy couple. Tangible evidence of achievement underscores Erec and Enide's unique excellence. Description coincides with and marks the placement of the couple in a situation which requires only their presence, not their initiative. In a sense, they cease momentarily to exist as functioning characters as ceremony takes over their lives. Spectacular appearance, added to their natural beauty, marks their new distinction. If description concerns only the conferral of a foregone distinction, one may indeed question the narrative utility of this technique. When recounting adventure, the narrative tends to avoid commenting on events and only implies meanings. Characters do not generally deliver extended speeches. Occurrences tend to be suspenseful and fast-paced.

Description returns us to the narrator's presence in the romance. He points to his handiwork, as in the Prologue. Indeed, Chrétien, as narrator, uses his final tableau to underscore the erudition of his descriptive art. Just prior to the coronation of Erec and Enide at Nantes, Arthur and Erec sit on matching thrones. Erec is dressed in a fabric of fine wool. The narrator adds:

> Lisant trovomes an l'estoire
> la description de la robe,
> si an trai a garant Macrobe
> qui an l'estoire[20] mist s'antante,
> qui l'antendié, que je ne mante.
> Macrobe m'anseigne a descrivre,
> si con je l'ai trové el livre,
> l'uevre del drap et le portret.
>   (ll. 6674-81)

(Reading we find in the tale the description of the robe, and I take for authority Macrobius, who employs his industry in the tale, who understood it, may I not lie. Macrobius teaches me how to describe the work and the design of the cloth, as I have found it in the book.)

Serving as the narrator's introduction to the portraits of the quadrivium, the passage emphasizes erudition by reference to one of the most widely known scholastic authors of the Latin Middle Ages. What is more, Macrobius offers a textual model, a pattern for inventions worthy of what Macrobius himself would describe. It is not possible to produce a precise Macrobian text which supports this claim of indebtedness. If any, a likely source would be Martianus Capella or the *Anticlaudianus* of Alain de Lille, although the latter raises problems of chronology.[21] Its erudite implications aside (Chrétien might well be challenging the clerks in his audience), the reference to Macrobius does advertise the learnedness of this poetry. Notice is served to all that the figures of the quadrivium which follow are not casual ornamentation at all. In substance, they betoken a lively contemporary interest in traditional and contemporary Latin culture; in form, the passage betokens modes of rhetorical ecphrasis, in which pictures are rendered in words. The world of scholastic practice, through descriptive discourse, ornaments the world of Erec and Enide, and the narrator takes pride in making this possible.

Part of the riding gear given Enide by Guivret is studded with emeralds. The saddle bows have scenes from the story of Aeneas. Each scene is characterized by an episodic motif: Aeneas leaving Troy, Dido's reception at Carthage, his betrayal, her suicide, his conquest of Laurentum and all Lombardy. Together the scenes outline Virgil's story of Aeneas, but no mention is made of visual details. Since the description stresses the story of Dido, and since Enide in the preceding episode most fully realizes her role as helpmeet by staying Guivret's hand before the fallen Erec, we seem called upon to compare and contrast the adventures of these two women. The somber tragedy marking Dido's epic destiny freshly illuminates the remarkable new wholeness which reciprocal, conjugal love has found through a couple's quest. Erec and Enide appear to succeed where Aeneas and Dido failed. Fate—the collusion of events—is much kinder to the Arthurian pair. A thorough study of the two couples could take on major proportions.[22] What matters here is that the romance uses description in order to elicit intertextual speculation. It is by no means clear that such speculation is meant to yield "real" thematic meanings. If the reference to Macrobius serves in the end to adorn the Arthurian world, then perhaps the allusion to Virgil adorns the excellence of Erec and Enide. After all, they do succeed. *Their* destiny avoids the pathos of separation and destruction. Classical tragedy only ornaments by contrast the triumphant ride of Enide.

If there be any doubt as to the playful aspects of this allusiveness, one need but look at other allusions to the story of Aeneas in *Erec*. Of the horse Guivret gives to Enide, only its coloration is described. The body is golden, while, as for the head, one side is white and the other black, with a green stripe in between. The horse is not so exotic as its gear, but that green stripe is unusual. One familiar with the Old French *Eneas* may recall, however, that the warrior-maid Camille possesses a more obviously marvelous beast.[23] It is described when she first appears after a standardized hyperbolic portrait of her person and much technical information about what she is wearing. Her palfrey displays a white head, a black lock on top, red ears, a bay neck, a violet mane with green tufts, a blue-gray right shoulder and a black left, the feet of a wolf, brown sides, the belly of a leopard and a lion's rump, black under the saddle, tawny legs in front, blood-red in back, four white feet, a frizzy tail part black and part white, hollow hooves with flat legs—altogether a handsome and agile beast! The description is completed with an account of the riding gear, each piece a triumph in precious materials and workmanship. Of special interest is this notation: "la

sele ert bone, et li arçon / furent de l'ovre Salemon, / a entaille de blanc ivoire" (ll. 4075-77) (the saddle was good, and the saddle bows were the work of Solomon, chiseled of white ivory). The unnoted parallel of the two passages is as interesting as the contrast between Erec/Enide and Eneas/Dido. As opposed to the obscure or absent textual model of the quadrivium pieces, this equestrian parallel is rather plain to see, providing one knows the *Eneas*. And there are fascinating differences. Fanciful color combinations are absent: a strip of green alone announces the marvelous. Monstrous physical variation is altogether absent. The simple technical brilliance of Camille's gear can be compared with the storied details of Enide's, though it is not Solomon, but a Breton, who fashioned it in seven years. With great economy and subtlety the passage makes possible an appreciation of Enide with respect to two celebrated classical women—Dido the star-crossed lover and Camille the warrior-maid. And it could be said that Enide proves to be more successful than both. What matters is that the text also plays with a descriptive model that rewards one's familiarity with other texts and examples of stylization. In this fashion the narrator clearly takes pains to show the value of his text.

The range of allusion in *Erec et Enide* is impressive. It includes a venerable ancient authority like Macrobius, a contemporary version of Virgil's renowned epic and contemporary philosophical epic (when Enide is said to be the handiwork of Nature). There is also the intriguing network of references to the story of Tristan and Iseut. In Enide's very first portrait, the narrator observes: "Por voir vos di qu'Isolz la blonde / n'ot les crins tant sors ne luisanz / que a cesti ne fust neanz" (ll. 424-26) (Truly I tell you that the blond Iseut did not have hair so golden or shining as to be of any value compared with this one's). As regards the town scene after the Sparrow-Hawk combat, the narrator opines: "Onques, ce cuit, tel joie n'ot, / quant Tristanz ocist le Morhot, / qu'an l'isle Saint Sanson vainqui" (ll. 1241-43) (I believe there was never such joy when Tristan killed the Morholt, whom he vanquished on the isle of Saint Sanson). When Erec and Enide come together on their wedding night, the narrator interjects: "A cele premiere asanblee, / la ne fu pas Enyde anblee, / ne Brangiens an leu de li mise" (ll. 2021-23) (At that first union Enide was not taken away and Brangien put in her place). These comparisons are obviously to the advantage of the present narrative: Enide is more beautiful, Erec's exploit greater and their marital love genuinely consummated. Interestingly, these allusions all precede the quest and so also the possibly more ambitious allusions, first to Aeneas-Eneas, then to Macrobius. The text also makes a brief reference to medieval epic when it is said that the staked heads at Brandigan would frighten even the likes of such heroes as Tiebaux li Esclavons, Opiniax or Fernaguz (ll. 5724-29).

It is one thing to claim that one's text is better than other well-known works; it is quite another to parade one's knowledge of texts for its own sake. The sheer range of descriptive allusion calls attention to the narrator's learning itself as much as to the text as such or even to the superior qualities of Erec and Enide. An example of such display occurs during the ceremonial interlude which traces the couple's departure from Arthur and installation at the court of Erec's father. Upon their arrival in Carnant, a procession takes them to church, where Erec presents much silver and also a gold cross which once belonged to Constantine. Because it contains a piece of the True Cross, the narrator pauses momentarily over the meaning of Christ's death. The cross is adorned with carbuncles which suffice to light up the entire church. For her part, Enide offers a green silk cloth and a great chasuble. The latter, we learn, was the work of "Morgue la fee" in the Val Perilleus, who had intended the cloth not for a chasuble, but for a gift of clothing to her *ami*. Guenevere, however, cunningly obtained it from the emperor Gassa. It was she who made a chasuble of it and put it in her chapel for a long time, "por ce que boene estoit et bele" (l. 2372) (because it was good and beautiful). Guenevere gave the chasuble to Enide as a going-away present. It is reasonable to infer from the bestowal of the two gifts at Carnant that two very different worlds of textual lore—the biblical and the Arthurian—are being associated through a network of details which identifies valuable workmanship with rare materials. These allusions may suggest vast exegetical horizons for the seemingly private drama of Erec and Enide, although those horizons are vague and shifting, indeed inscrutable in this romance. One thing appears certain: the matter of other stories counterpoints the account of this couple's distinction. Borrowing illuminates the special aspirations of a romance which is determined to be other than an ordinary *conte d'avanture*.

As the network of allusions broadens the scope of Erec and Enide's achievement and the text's own claim to distinction, the narrator intrudes more and more in the narrative, his descriptions and comments amplifying upon the action and the couple's destiny, from the Joie de la Cort to the end of the romance. When King Evrain welcomes the couple to his chamber, the narrator interrupts himself:

> Mes por coi vos deviseroie
> la pointure des draps de soie,
> don la chanbre estoit anbelie?
> Le tans gasteroie an folie,
> et ge nel vuel mie haster;[24]
> einçois me voel un po haster,
> que qui tost va par droite voie

> celui passe qui se desvoie:
> por ce ne m'i voel arester.
> (ll. 5523-31)

(But why should I describe to you the embroidery of the silk fabrics with which the chamber was embellished? I would waste time foolishly, and I do not at all want to hurry it; rather I want to hurry along, for he who goes rapidly along the right path passes by the one who loses the way: thus, I do not want to stop here.)

Thus the narrator, anxious to be brief, resists describing something. His reasons vary: he wants to get on with the action, a full account could never be given, he does not want to repeat what has already been told, he wants to finish, he does not know enough. But he will also describe something worth the effort, as when the mysterious and forbidding orchard at Brandigan comes into view:

> Mes ne fet pas a trespasser,
> por lengue debatre et lasser,
> que del vergier ne vos retraie
> lonc l'estoire chose veraie.
> (ll. 5685-88)

(But even at the risk of fatiguing and wearing out my tongue, I must not neglect telling you the truth about the orchard according to the story.)

The narrator can be humble yet resolute before a difficult task, as when he prepares to describe the coronation:

> Or ne porroit lengue ne boche
> de nul home, tant seüst d'art,
> deviser le tierz ne le quart
> ne le quint de l'atornemant
> qui fu a son coronemant.
> Donc voel ge grant folie anprandre,
> qui au descrivre voel antandre;
> mes des que feire le m'estuet,
> et c'est chose qu'an feire puet,
> ne leirai pas que ge n'an die
> selonc mon san une partie.
> (ll. 6640-50)

(No tongue or mouth of any man, no matter how well he mastered his art, could describe a third or a fourth or a fifth of the display which was at his coronation. So I want to undertake a great foolishness, I who want to attempt to describe it; but since I must do it, and it is a thing one can do, I will not refrain from saying a part of it according to my understanding.)

And we have seen that the narrator did turn to Macrobius for guidance in fabricating descriptive discourse (ll. 6674-81). Through such editorial insertions the narrator dramatizes his control of the narrative at a time when the couple's present and future are assured. Attention is centered fully on the quality of the narration itself. By drawing attention to the artifice of exotic details, to other texts and forms of discourse and to the narrator's powers of composition, description establishes a broad context for *Erec et Enide*. Characterization and thematics within the private world of the couple do not begin to account for the total romance. The characters care about the exotic or the marvelous only as these betoken prestige: they do not react to symbolic implications. Such details reveal best the narrator's hand.

Appellation is a major factor in description. When the couple arrives at Arthur's court for the first time, no names have been given to the place or principals in the Sparrow-Hawk world, save that of Yder after his defeat. It is only at the moment of the marriage that Enide's name is revealed:

> Quand Erec sa feme reçut
> par son droit non nomer l'estut,
> qu'altremant n'est fame esposee,
> se par son droit non n'est nomee.
> Ancor ne savoit l'an son non,
> mes ore primes le set l'on:
> Enyde ot non au baptestire.
> (ll. 1973-79)

(When Erec took his wife, it was necessary to call her by her real name, for otherwise a woman is not married, if she is not called by her real name. They still did not know her name, but now for the first time they know it: she received the name Enide at her baptism.)

Much later, when Erec finds out about Mabonagrain, the latter makes a curious observation about his name:

> Maboagrains sui apelez,
> mes ne sui mes point coneüz,
> an leu ou j'aie esté veüz,
> par remanbrance de cest non,
> s'an cest païs solemant non;
> car onques tant con vaslez fui,
> mon non ne dis ne ne conui.
> (ll. 6082-88)

(I am called Mabonagrain, but I am not at all known, in any place where I have been seen, by this name, except in this land; for as long as I was a young man I never said or revealed my name.)

And in the grand finale of the coronation mass Tarsenesyde and Licoranz, Enide's parents, are first identified (ll. 6830-34). Such deferred and restricted naming occurs in the special world of the principal characters and in the account of what actually takes place. It parallels descriptive allusiveness. Onomastic economy matches the economy of the action, whereas the narrator's penchant for long lists of knights attending major ceremonies (ll. 1662-1706, 1882-1959) goes with his love of description and allusion. The lists of names help to establish scenic ambience and the narrator's learnedness,[25] but the knights themselves contribute little to the narrative: their names are amplifications conducive to splendid ornament.

Description seems to replace the psychological and thematic commentary in *Erec*. The special destiny of the romance couple makes description possible by deflecting narrative suspense and making way for ceremonial pauses in the narrative. The couple's physical perfection, besides marking its destiny, establishes the adequacy of appearances in that reality. Appearances, as such, celebrate the triumph of Erec and Enide. Descriptive discourse permits the romance to reveal its own special workings. We can now see the wisdom behind the choice of subject matter announced in the Prologue. Besides being common and familiar, a *conte d'avanture* become *conjointure* produces transparent compositional art, audacious narrator interventions and learned allusion. A transmogrification of simple substance by narrative technique is in itself a way of teaching well. A text which disregards plausibility can become the vehicle for knowledge through topical artifice. *Erec et Enide* diverts while also defining the means and possibilities of diversion. Chrétien is convinced that such poetic beauty, grounded in the very possibilities of narrative discourse, will not be forgotten (ll. 23-26).

Arthur's Court and Conjointure

The court of King Arthur figures prominently at important narrative junctures in *Erec et Enide*. The narrative opens with a great Easter gathering at Caradigan and concludes with a spectacular coronation, devised by Arthur for Erec and Enide, at Christmas at Nantes. Events at court alternate, albeit more infrequently, with the activities of Erec. Knights go hunting. Yder, an unknown knight, is warmly welcomed, listened to and asked to join the court. The traditional Custom of the White Stag is celebrated. The marriage of Erec and Enide takes place. A major tournament is convened after it. Aid is offered during the quest to Erec in apparent distress, but his eventual return to the court is met with warm enthusiasm. The couple's coronation is produced with éclat. These activities sketch out a composite tableau of Arthur's court. This tableau is specific to the romance of *Erec et Enide*. Its special features set off the remarkable accomplishments of the main characters and by doing so articulate indirectly general meanings of the romance itself.

It would appear that Arthur actually has two courts. One is his residence at Caradigan. The other is the larger feudal community to which Arthur is central and which he gathers together at important narrative junctures. We observe the smaller community when Erec and Enide happen across Arthur's hunting party in the forest. Only Arthur, Guenevere, Keu and Gauvain are mentioned. Another view of this narrower world appears when Erec and Enide, together with Guivret and his entourage, end their adventures and return to Caradigan. There a despondent Arthur has about him only five hundred nobles of his household:

> onques mes an nule seison
> ne fu trovez li rois si seus,
> si an estoit molt angoisseus
> que plus n'avoit gent a sa cort.
> (ll. 6368-71)

(never in any season was the king so alone, and he was highly distraught at not having more people at his court.)

The larger feudal community, the one in the midst of which Arthur seems happiest, convenes regularly on feast days and for tourneys, marriages and coronations. Those present, if we take the opening Easter court as a model, include valorous knights and rich, well-born women, the feudal elite of Arthur's realm (ll. 1874-78).

Why does Arthur gather this festive community together? What purposes are served by the court's celebrations? Arthur expresses a particular conception of kingship: he wants to be honest, moderate and equitable, maintaining the rule of custom and right, truth, faith and justice (ll. 1749-70). Moreover:

> ... je ne voel pas que remaigne
> la costume ne li usages
> que siaut maintenir mes lignages.
> De ce vos devroit il peser,
> se ge vos voloie alever
> autre costume et autres lois
> que ne tint mes peres li rois.
> L'usage Pandragon, mon pere,
> qui rois estoit et emperere,
> voel je garder et maintenir,
> que que il m'an doie avenir.
> (ll. 1760-70)

(... I do not want to see end the Custom and the conventions that my family line traditionally upholds. It should grieve you if I wanted to establish another Custom and laws other than those my father the king held to. The practice of Pandragon, my father, who was king and emperor, I want to keep and maintain, whatever the consequences to me.)

In Arthur's view his function is to maintain established practices and time-honored custom. He prides himself on preserving continuity with the past. *Maintenir* is a key verb for Arthur. Courtly celebrations are traditional and so must be observed.[26]

What of the customs and usages themselves? What in fact takes place at the gatherings of Arthur's court? Arthur defends his determination to renew the White Stag Custom by anticipating the diversion, the adventure and the marvelous which await those who reestablish the Custom. At the reunions of Arthur's larger court we perceive his interest in what might be summarily characterized as *deduit*. For example, at the time of the wedding, Arthur expresses great joy at his newly gathered court by knighting a hundred youths, hiring numerous musicians, giving a feast for rich and poor alike, and lavishly paying the performers with furs, horses and money. When Erec and Enide come upon Arthur's hunting party in the forest, we are told that the king wants to remain there for a few days, "por lui deduire et deporter" (l. 3925) (to amuse himself and have fun). At the great concluding coronation scene, Arthur gathers notables from different countries and also dubs three hundred young men, showing a generosity heretofore unparalleled. Money is free for the taking by all. For the occasion Arthur provides remarkably ornate thrones, robes, crowns and a scepter. He seems to associate the observance of tradition with diverting activities and opulent spectacle, joy and solemnity. Tradition and entertainment preserve the community's unity and destiny. Indeed, the famous quadrivium figures on Erec's robe, the religious ceremony itself and the animal images which ornament Erec's royal scepter all suggest that Arthur is able to produce a ceremony having truly cosmic implications. The narrator assures us that at the coronation Arthur's generosity far surpassed that of Alexander, Caesar and all the kings named in story and epic (ll. 6611-20). Arthur's opulence, ceremony and entertainment confer distinction on an elite community.

Arthur's community is not inward-turning. It does not simply relish its genuine excellence. The king and his entourage are curious about the world about them. Guenevere is determined to meet an unfamiliar knight in the wood. Though sent by Erec to place himself in Guenevere's prison, Yder instead finds himself invited to join the court itself. When, in the forest, Gauvain informs Arthur that the court will have to relocate its hunting camp if the king desires to meet the best of knights—one who does not leave his path to seek lodging—the king immediately moves camp. Similarly, the king greets the returning Erec by inquiring about his adventures and welcoming Guivret to his court. Such hospitality goes beyond respect for feudal obligation and convention. It embraces the appreciation of chivalric excellence as such. Arthur wants distinguished newcomers to join his court.

Although there are many elements within *Erec et Enide* which form a positive image of Arthur's court, the fact remains that we do not see in this romance that Erec is entirely at one with that community. When he first appears, riding after Guenevere, the narrator announces that Erec is a member of the Round Table, that he is much praised at court, that he is its most handsome knight and that he has great prowess. For all his attributes, however, Erec keeps a certain distance from the court. He does not participate when Arthur renews the Custom of the White Stag. He leaves for his homeland after the marriage. He refuses to remain at Arthur's court for convalescence and sport during the quest. And the narrator does not divulge Erec's life at court during the two or three years between his return there and the coronation. During the final festivities we learn little about his thoughts, words and actions. The one occasion in which he does participate, that is, in the chivalric tourney which follows the wedding, his exploits set him apart from all others at court. This, his greatest triumph up to that point, is followed immediately by his request to leave (ll. 2197-2206).

We must be careful not to conclude that Erec rejects or criticizes Arthur's court. When first revealing his identity to Guivret, Erec says that Arthur alone has greater holdings than his own father, "car a lui nus ne s'aparoille" (l. 3867) (for no one is his equal). Erec's need to keep to his incomplete quest accounts for his stern reproach addressed to Keu and for the refusal to convalesce with Arthur's hunting party (ll. 3991-92). When he has rescued the unfortunate Cadoc from giants, Erec sends him to Arthur's court, as though anxious that news of his recent achievement be received there. And when the quest culminates in the renewal of love between Erec and Enide (ll. 5196-5211), Erec's first thought is to return to his *terre* by way of Arthur's court (ll. 5230-34). Brandigan will interrupt his return, but once at Arthur's court he accedes to the king's request to stay.

Erec is no rebel against Arthur. What he must accomplish simply does not involve the public world of Arthur's communal *deduit*. And as his destiny would have it, Erec's exploits matter to the court, even though such service is not his intention. Thus, while concerned about avenging his shame, Erec produces Enide at court, thereby providing an occasion for the court to resolve its differences over the kiss and end the Custom of the White Stag. Without apparently trying or caring, he has important influence. Similarly, Erec triumphantly appears with Enide, Guivret and a considerable entourage at a time when Arthur is anxious about how few notables are at court. The wedding and the coronation themselves elaborate upon the court's distinction through Arthur's considerable efforts. And it is King Arthur who bestows wife and scepter on Erec.

Nonetheless, Erec's relative detachment from activities at Arthur's court, compared to his achievements elsewhere, might well suggest certain deficiencies in that world of ceremony and convention. The very first scene, after all, implies that there are serious potential problems at court. Gauvain warns Arthur that through the renewal of the Custom of the White Stag, "Maus an puet avenir molt granz" (l. 49) (Great evil can come of it). The potential for divisive conflict emerges clearly once the stag is taken:

> Chascuns vialt par chevalerie
> desresnier que la soe amie
> est la plus bele de la sale;
> molt est ceste parole male.
> (ll. 295-98)

(Each one wants to prove through feats of arms that his beloved is the most beautiful in the hall; this outcry is very bad.)

Each knight's regard for his lady's excellence threatens the peace and harmony of the court, despite, indeed because of, Arthur's otherwise laudable desire to uphold established traditions. This community does not seem altogether healthy.

The restive knights themselves are not alone to blame for the problems at court. Arthur's performance itself is disturbing. He chooses to ignore the dangers inherent in renewing the custom by failing to heed Gauvain's warning. Yet when trouble breaks out, Arthur quickly appeals to his nephew for guidance (ll. 308-10). Before a council can meet to advise him, Guenevere returns to court with news of the altercation in the forest and Erec's departure for revenge. Arthur joins the others present in deferring the customary kiss for three days, when Erec is to return. Here, as elsewhere, the king does not seem to be a decisive leader when it comes to situations other than *deduit*. This is not to say that the court is ripe for revolution or that Arthur is a bad leader. If there is, as Badel claims, a conflict "entre l'orgueil de l'individu noble et la solidarité de classe,"[27] it turns out to be a momentary and circumstantial conflict. All those who owe Arthur fealty respond faithfully when he orders them to gather at court, as we plainly see not only at the beginning and end of the romance, but especially at the wedding (ll. 1879-81). All the court's festivities are successful except, at least at first view, the renewal of the Custom. That renewal itself does transpire peacefully, though in a way no one could have foreseen. Arthur cannot really take credit for the peaceful conferral of the kiss on Enide. Her very beauty confounds all opposition.

Besides successfully producing traditional celebrations, Arthur is most interested either in observing what is beautiful or in learning about adventures. Beauty and prowess are forms of distinction. When Erec and Enide first arrive together at court, Arthur devotes himself to the beautiful Enide while Erec and Guenevere concern themselves with Erec's achievement. Is Arthur simply preoccupied with using Enide's beauty to resolve the impasse at court regarding the customary kiss? Perhaps, but the final coronation episode suggests that Arthur has little interest in matters other than beauty, tradition and knightly distinction. At that coronation Enide's parents are presented to Arthur, and Erec points out that the vavasor is his famous host and friend:

> Einz qu'il me coneüst de rien,
> me herberja et bel et bien,
> quanque il ot m'abandona,
> neïs sa fille me dona
> sanz los et sanz consoil d'autrui.
> (ll. 6545-49)

(Before he knew me at all, he lodged me very well, put at my disposal everything he had, even gave me his daughter, without the advice and consent of others.)

Arthur does not respond immediately to Erec's appreciation of his father-in-law's trust. The king prefers to question Erec about the vavasor's lady. Told that she is Enide's mother, he praises her, then both parents:

> Bele est Enyde, et bele doit
> estre, par reison et par droit,
> que bele dame est molt sa mere,
> biau chevalier a en son pere.
> (ll. 6561-64)

(Enide is beautiful, and she must be beautiful, properly so, for her mother is very beautiful, and one sees a very fine knight in her father.)

Arthur sets greatest store, on every occasion, by the conventions associated with harmonious social intercourse. Very much a public figure, Arthur presides over and fosters a gracious and elegant courtly world, yet it is certainly one in which private expression at its most serious can take place. This civilization has room in itself for confidences, not to mention occasional, circumstantial disruptions, even those that arise in the name of what the court honors: beauty, prowess, ceremony. It is, after all, a great court. What might initially seem imperfections in performance by king and subjects alike works out to the satisfaction, and even to the benefit, of all concerned.

The fact remains, as I have said, that during the course of the romance Erec maintains a certain distance from the Arthurian world. He does not seem to be of the domain of that court's *deduit*, though his standing would certainly suggest that he might have been prior to events recounted in the romance. A useful approach to the problem of his relatively separate status and also to the problem of his dominant role in the narrative itself requires recognition of what might be termed a secondary community in this romance, a community composed of aspirants to adventure. Perhaps the most obvious example is the vavasor. When asked by Erec why his daughter is dressed poorly, the vavasor blames losses in war, but also acknowledges his refusal to let a local count, her uncle, clothe her. Nor will he marry her to a local man of distinction:

> Mes j'atant ancor meillor point,
> que Dex greignor enor li doint,
> que avanture li amaint
> ou roi ou conte qui l'an maint.
> (ll. 529-32)

(But I am waiting for something better, that God give her greater honor, that adventure bring to her a king or count to marry.)

Moreover, he even relegates, as Arthur would not, Enide's unequaled beauty to a position second to her mental gifts and accomplishments:

> Molt est bele, mes mialz asez
> vaut ses savoirs que sa biautez:
> onques Dex ne fist rien tant saige
> ne qui tant soit de franc coraige.
> (ll. 537-40)

(She is very beautiful, but her mental acquirements are worth much more than her beauty: God never made anyone so wise and prudent or whose heart is so noble.)

Adventure rewards the vavasor in the person of Erec, and Erec himself takes to heart the vavasor's view, as when he pointedly refuses the local count's hospitality or when he introduces Enide's parents to Arthur. Enide deserves better.

It may be said that Guivret, too, is an aspirant to adventure. When the questing Erec and Enide pass by his high tower, Guivret quickly arms and rides forth (ll. 3676-80). We are told that Guivret has no companions. To test his mettle, he fights alone against whoever passes by. His forte is duels, not tourneys. He will accept what comes. Guivret proves eventually to be Erec's determined and devoted friend.

Guenevere also seems to pursue adventure. While not involved in the Custom of the White Stag, she takes the initiative of riding with two companions into the forest to observe the hunt. She is anxious to make the acquaintance of the unknown trio crossing her path. She brings to a halt the court's deliberations on the Custom by relating the adventure that befell her and Erec in the woods. Actually, it is more or less through Guenevere that Erec makes himself felt at court during the romance. He avoids the initial hunt to be with her. He dispatches the defeated Yder into Guenevere's custody. The Queen explains to Arthur the bearing of Erec's achievements on the observance of the renewed Custom. Erec takes pains that Guenevere see Enide in poor clothes, then dress her better. He explains to the Queen his love for Enide. While Arthur conducts the public events surrounding the marriage, it is Guenevere who prepares the private world of the wedding night. Her *congé* is the last event before the newlyweds' departure for Carnant. Her joy exceeds that of all when the couple finally returns to the court.

Erec has a special fondness for Guenevere, Guivret and Enide's father. These people help him, test him, approve of his activities, or at least let him have his way. They understand him better than anyone else at court seems to. And they prepare the way for the special relationship which Erec and Enide realize during their adventures together. Erec's unique destiny is worked out through *avanture*. It may be argued that by Erec's decision to follow Guenevere and not the white stag he has made a commitment to his own adventure. After all, he is quick to seize the opportunity to make Enide his own by winning for her the sparrow-hawk. Might he have a special intuition about adventure? When he and Enide leave Carnant for the quest, he knows only that he is going off on adventure with his wife (ll. 2762-63). Does Erec know or learn through experience both when to keep going and when to return to Arthur's court? As we have seen, during that return he experiences his purest adventure, the Joie de la Cort.

Why are the vavasor, Guivret, Guenevere and Erec himself able to aspire to, even rely upon, adventure? Each stands apart from the immediate social environs. Each has a special reason for being different—poverty, small size, queenship, a special combination of beauty and prowess. Certainly, each is rewarded differently—a daughter well married and an end to poverty, a friend, satisfaction at the achievements of a friend, a wife and a crown. But the reasons for their separate status are never openly developed.

The secondary community formed by these pursuers of adventure is thoughtful, active and productive. And we know that adventure lies only just outside the Arthurian court. Is this to say that the court is unproductive, unsuccessful, even fatuous in its predilection for the various forms of *deduit* shaped by convention? The romance begins and ends with an Arthurian gathering. Erec leaves the intimate inner circle of Arthur, but eventually returns to it, stays there and leaves only with the court's blessings. Erec does not criticize the world of Arthur. To consider only the context of this specific romance, one gathers that the Arthurian world is able to produce adventurous individuals of the highest order. Yet it is not the only world to produce the adventurous: witness Guivret. Nor is it the only community in the romance to display some inner difficulties: consider the world of Brandigan. What Arthur can produce is an Erec. And Erec does not forget his special connection with, his debt to, Arthur's court. Indeed, the final coronation scene shows the absorption, so to speak, of all those pursuing adventure by the Arthurian world. That integration could be said to make for their highest achievement. Not only does Arthur produce and welcome those who venture into the forest, but he displays an active interest in their achievements, is anxious for news, will take special pains to intercept someone of distinction, and even acquiesces when the best of knights firmly refuses what Arthur most prides himself in offering—hospitality. Charles Foulon has shown that Gauvain represents an Arthurian model of comportment that is highlighted by the typical rudeness of Keu.[28] For Arthur's cherished nephew is not simply courteous, eloquent and adaptable; he also displays "connaissance des hommes et sympathie intelligente," a sensitive and active appreciation of others.[29] Indeed, Foulon finds important thematic implications in Gauvain's ability to succeed where Keu fails to get Erec to stay, if only briefly, with the Arthurian party in the wood: "Là où la force était bafouée, le 'grand sens' triomphait en souriant. Ce n'était ni charme magique, ni puissance surnaturelle. Chez Chrétien, c'est finesse, courtoisie, mais surtout clairvoyance agissante."[30] Such humane perspicacity is shown by the romance to be the best response to a world of adventure.

Arthur sees a natural connection between *deduit* and *avanture*. Each seems to produce and nurture the other. Individuals bridge the gap between the civilization of the court and the mysterious forest of unforeseen encounters. Convention coexists with surprises. Arthur does not fear adventure; it seems to be the crowning distinction, the *raison d'être* of his community.[31] In T.A. Shippey's view, "the resolution of risk and conservatism is indeed the poem's main thematic connexion. Customs must not only be established, but also maintained; Erec, having won his wife once, has to prove himself to her continually to keep their love intact. In each case the principle of good, whether it is love or sovereignty, has to go into danger in order to return from it refreshed."[32] The process of "refreshment" is open and continual. Hence, on the level of episodes *Erec* seems forever on the verge of ending, but in a sense never does so, its narrative breaking off rather abruptly in the middle of the coronation festivities with the narrator observing: "il m'estuet a el antendre" (l. 6878) (I must apply myself to something else).

We must not forget that, as far as the text permits us to see, it is precisely Arthur's apparently bullheaded effort to renew a Custom which sets in motion events that lead to the greatest court event of all: the coronation of Erec and Enide. No doubt beyond his expectations or sense of history, the diverting and marvelous hunt for the white stag in the adventure-filled forest brings new distinction and harmony to his world. The production of *deduit* can indeed be creative in the context of a romance where events mysteriously favor the productivity attending genteel entertainment. Indeed, that productivity touches other communities in beneficial ways. Good is spread to other communities in the forests of adventure. Thus, adventure brings about the spread of Arthurian civilization. Through the coronation Arthur becomes a kind of ancestor—a kind of Pandragon—to Erec.

Erec et Enide offers an accommodation of chivalric activity and community values. And it would appear that the romance acquired relevance to conditions in the feudal world of Chrétien's day by dramatizing a paradigmatic reconciliation between "an emerging chivalric individualism and the older, feudal idea of communal effort directed toward the suzerain."[33] The Prologue's articulation of the notion of pleasing instruction finds its final embodiment—perhaps its necessary implication—in the cultural dynamics at the heart of this romance's action. What Arthur and Chrétien have in common is this: both support the association of refined culture and worldly achievement. Understanding and delight can support the conquest of the unknown. This vision of civilization and its developing, spreading character presumes the existence of an elite, a group of the *cognoscenti*, a special kingdom—those willing to find the new by way of conventional observance and delight.

Chrétien's elaborate *conjointure*, we now see, conveys a powerfully suggestive notion of viable feudal or aristocratic community. His use of characterization, the quest sequence and description also calls attention to the intrinsic excellence of this narrative. The artful interplay of such themes as love, marriage, friendship, adventure and community associates with the narrator's erudition and contrivances to remind us of the Prologue's theorizing. Suggestiveness and complexity assure that a work like *Erec*, neither hermetic nor didactic, is a source of delight and edification. Chrétien takes justifiable pride in the ambitious and challenging artistry of his first major Arthurian work.

Michelle A. Freeman

Cligés

It is particularly difficult to describe Chrétien's *Cligés* in a linear fashion, since this text creates other spaces within itself, referring to other texts at virtually every point. Before describing a scene, a character, a motif or a theme in *Cligés*, one has to introduce into the discussion other scenes, other characters, other motifs, other themes from other works or from other moments of the poem. This romance cannot fully make sense in any other way, in my opinion, for it is a narrative that dwells on the activity of romance composition, as intertextual transposition, to the point that it constitutes a veritable demonstration of Chrétien's understanding of romance poetics. Consequently, the following essay on Chrétien's *Cligés* will not be a straightforward presentation of the episodes of that romance in a way that parallels the narrative sequence.

All the roads down which the reader can travel in the romance world of *Cligés* lead him to a meditation on the workings of an intertextual sort of romance discourse. The subject is metamorphosis exercised within a complex lineage, that is, within a set of textual possibilities that are related to one another in new combinations. Though I will try to keep a discussion of other texts to a minimum in the following pages, such texts cannot be excluded. Parts of the literary experience of Chrétien's audience have to be introduced and emphasized for a modern reader of *Cligés*, so that the meaning and poetry of the romance will not be sacrificed or overlooked. My essay will consequently stress the intertextual relationships elaborated in the *Cligés* and will do so in such a way as to circumscribe the poetic meaning of *translatio studii*[1] as this is made relevant to the romance.

The following aspects will be examined in turn: (1) the intertextual relationship of the Prologue to the body of the romance, (2) the structural transpositions of the *Tristan* corpus achieved by Chrétien throughout his text, and (3) the transformations of Part One—or the story of the hero's parents—rendered by Part Two of the narrative. Of course, none of these considerations can be viewed in a completely isolated fashion; they all involve a relationship to and with one another. Our three considerations will lead us in turn to a final reading of an intertextual nature, perhaps the most profound and the most original contribution Chrétien makes through his *Cligés* to the romance tradition: the transformation the text performs upon itself while itself performing. This is perhaps the single most characteristic element of the text that distinguishes it from the rest of Chrétien's *œuvre*, even though, as we shall see, it is by no means entirely divorced from that *œuvre*.

I offer these few remarks as an introduction to a chapter that in its methodology might seem somewhat out of keeping with the other studies of Chrétien presented in this volume. I wish to alert the reader at the outset that *Cligés* does in a sense stand apart from the remainder of Chrétien's work. It does stand apart because through it Chrétien takes a look at his own poetic activity within a tradition of similar activity. In *Cligés* he sends his readers outside the mainstream of his *œuvre*, just as in this work he sends them outside the mainstream of his own text, in order that they may better find their way through the layers, shifts and transformations of the romances as they return to them by means of the byways of such a textual *avanture*.[2]

The Prologue and Its Implications

I find it useful to borrow, for the purposes of analogy, an example from the architectural design of a medieval church pointed out by Otto von Simson in his *The Gothic Cathedral*: "With but a single basic dimension given, the Gothic architect developed all other magnitudes of his ground plan and elevation by strictly geometrical means, using as modules certain regular polygons, above all the square."[3] The prologue of a romance is comparable to this "basic dimension" from which the scope and heights of the work can be derived, or amplified, by means of the principles of grammar and rhetoric, or of literary topics, in the place of geometry. Or again, if we think about a cathedral analogically not only from the perspective of the architect, but this time from that of the congregation as it enters the cathedral, we might draw a comparison between the audience as it enters the romance text and the congregation. The representations of the life of Christ, of the Virgin, of a saint's legend, of historical figures, vices, virtues, Classical authors, and the like, that might find themselves sculpted on a given portal, their proportions and their spatial relationships to one another influence the one entering, creating his state of mind anew, preparing it as a framework of reference and relationships in which to set a "reading" of what is arranged from a multiplicity of perspectives inside the building and around it. Similarly, the references to values, heroes, *auctores,* and so forth, often mentioned by a prologue and the structural and rhetorical amplifications of them in relation to the other components of the opening statement also shape the mind of the reader/listener of a romance, creating for him the appropriate mental attitude for reordering and interpreting what follows the prologue.

A close reading of the *Cligés* Prologue is necessary in order to search out and take into account what is poetically relevant to the romance by understanding the basic dimension for the structure and essential configurations of the entire work that is presented in the Prologue's opening signals. The first seven lines present a list of titles. They are the names of poems composed by an author who styles himself here as our poet and as our narrator. Chrétien has selected these particular titles, grouped them together and spoken them before anything else to his audience. Names of poems, in a sequence, placed together as one *œuvre,* demand of the audience that it recognize the speaker as one who has traveled through his own series of poetic adventures, conjoined in his experience, though partaking of a pluralistic tradition. Certain characteristics of a formal *exordium* or prologue have been altered.[4] A *sententia* like the proverb which opens *Erec et Enide* is foregone for the opening of this romance, unless one considers the texts brought forth by our poet-narrator as exemplary clerkly deeds. An act of obeisance to a patron who bids the artist to compose a certain work according to his or her demands—such as those remarks concerning Marie de Champagne in the *Lancelot* or Philippe de Flandre in the *Graal*—is also absent, unless once more we choose to see the *comandemanz d'Ovide* in a light analogous to the *comandemanz* of either Marie or the Count. It would seem that a boastful Chrétien at first glance neglects his clerkly training; but upon further consideration, we might surmise that on the contrary Chrétien substitutes a specific modern *auctor,* namely, himself, for those princely authorizations one often finds at the genesis of a poetic work of this nature. The categories are fulfilled, but not obviously so; both a patron and a model of behavior are invoked, but they are each poets, *magister Naso* (i.e., Ovid) and *mestre Crestïens,* respectively.

The familiar concern for *conjointure* and for the *Tristan* material, implied in the list of titles, will surface at other times in the romance. But the other titles, the Latin ones, are Ovidian. "Le mors de l'espaule" (l. 4) and "de la hupe et de l'aronde / Et del rossignol la muance" (ll. 6-7) refer to Pelops and to Philomela respectively, two stories worked by Ovid into Book VI of his *Metamorphoses.* Since in *Cligés* these titles are chosen to play a significant role *in a prologue,* it is useful to investigate their own context as constituted by Ovid's introduction to that particular book. This story of the competition between Pallas and Arachne is one of two major studies not explicitly cited by Chrétien to be found in Book VI (the other is Niobe's grievous loss of all her children).

In the first story, the goddess and the maid each weave a tapestry made up of colored threads laid next to golden ones. Each represents a composite of examples taken from ancient stories. Those of Pallas' choosing exemplify the punishments in metamorphosis suffered at the hands of the gods by those men and women who in the past dared consider themselves as their equals. Arachne, in similar spirit, depicts those legendary human beings victimized by deities not through an exercise of divine power, but, to their shame, by various deployments of deceit and disguise. Perhaps unknowingly, each contestant mirrors in her work the sort of drama the two weavers are themselves reenacting. Their own example will become part of the corpus of stories told about the gods who punish mortals guilty of blasphemy and about exemplary individuals victimized by gods in disguise who act out of jealousy. Ovid, therefore, conjoins the subject matter of both tapestries in his own narrative.

In a final movement of pity towards Arachne, Pallas saves her from death, applies a poison to her body, transforming her into a spider, adding a curse that condemns her race to a similar fate. Ovid prefaces the descriptions of the two tapestries with a presentation of the techniques deployed by the two women. He includes the way they set up their looms along with the terminology and stages of the weaving. The presentation is somewhat technical in nature and detailed in its first lines before shifting to a description of the colors and their provenance. The relationship of the colors to one another *as they are combined* is compared to the colors of a rainbow in that, although a thousand colors shine within the spectrum, the *transitions* between each one are undetectable: "Transitus ipse tamen spectantia lumina fallit; / usque adeo quod tangit idem est; tamen ultima distant" (ll. 66-67) (Nevertheless the passage itself [from one color to the next] is indiscernible to the watchful eye, to the point that what touches looks the same, although the most distant colors differ greatly from each other).[5]

Ovid has described two artisans who equal one another in their craft and whose works complement each other, even though these are exercised in a spirit of competition. In his presentation he has stressed concrete technique, named some of the elements chosen, pointed out the deft masking of the places of transition and called attention to the dark purple colors mixed in together with gold threads. This technique and these motifs comprise, when combined, the pictures themselves; at the same time they provide the narrator with an opportunity to design his own reproductions of mythology conjoined to an analysis of his "historical source," the display of craft by Pallas and Arachne. His own text invites the reader to do the same with respect to it, for Ovid counterbalances, or mirrors, the art of weaving with a display of his own art of description.

A doubling, or squaring, process takes place in this first story, where ancient stories are used to display craft, first that of weaving and then that of poetry. References to certain mythological narratives provide the basis for the reenactment of another mythological narrative which, subsequently, is encased in the narrator's controlled framework description. The *exempla* of the gods versus men are transposed, placed in the context of a weaving contest; the story of the contest renews and adds to the preliminary corpus. It in turn is transposed, placed within a display of descriptive fiction. Ovid's example modifies, or at the least clarifies, an attitude to mythology, so that here it is important *as narrative* and consequently as material fit to be transposed and rewoven into other textual designs.

This example, then, offers two illustrations of intertextuality. They operate both within a hierarchy and within a chronology, ultimately serving Ovid's discourse, which is set in a direct line of texts. The transitions between these texts are no more readily apparent to the reader—though the distinctions between the starting point and the final product are great—than were the rainbow transitions between one hue and the next in the colors of the tapestry.

This particular example from the *Metamorphoses* displays a number of textual transformations. It suggests that a description presented by a poet-narrator can be a fitting device for the display of such transformations and of the way these call attention to his own craft. Translations of texts that place previous examples in new contexts so that their rearticulation in the new setting becomes an original focal point, suggesting another translation, provide for the celebration of one art in terms of another. These matters will prove to be relevant to the poetics of *Cligés*, particularly when we consider the modalities of certain of its descriptions.

One specific analogy may yet be singled out between Arachne and our Prologue's narrator. We noted that Chrétien describes himself only in terms relevant to his craft; he is known to us through the titles of poetic works, and their implications, exclusively. He thus avoided the practice of Latin rhetorical tradition (passed on to the Middle Ages) that counseled winning the audience's confidence by stressing the author's hereditary or social connections of an influential sort.[6] Similarly, Arachne has achieved prominence in her community by means of her art alone: "Non illa loco nec origine gentis / Clara, sed arte fuit" (ll. 6-7) (She was not famous because of her status or because of the origins of her people, but because of her art or skill).

These concerns for artifice and intertextuality introduce Ovid's *Meta-*

morphoses, Book VI, from which two selections constitute the framework for the story of "Marc" and "Ysalt." A son sacrificed, served at a banquet and resurrected, plus the transformations of the three principals in a love triangle, encase the Celtic myth. These three in turn follow upon Ovid's general prescriptions and his manual on love. All the texts mentioned find themselves locked in the still larger framework of the *Erec et Enide* of l. 1 and the untitled *Cligés* of l. 8. *Tristan* is inserted within the context of the *Metamorphoses,* itself understood in light of Ovid's treatises on love, all of which is controlled by the romance poetics of Chrétien. A chain that builds upon successive contexts by which one work is brought into the context of another, controlled finally by his most recent exercise in poetic articulation, is sketched out in the opening lines of *Cligés* as well as in those of Ovid's Book VI.

The story of Philomela has in common with the first story of Book VI a central device: the weaving of a tapestry. For Arachne and Pallas the tapestry serves to retell ancient stories for the display of craft in another medium; in Philomela's case, the tapestry tells the artist's own story in order to seek vengeance and liberation. All the stories woven into the two tapestries depict victimizations caused by crime or deception. *Pelops* and *Philomela* share the theme of the sacrifice of a child who is prepared as food. In both cases, a banquet is the place for deceit and revelation; in the first instance, in order to show off a culinary talent and impress the invited guests; in the second, in order to implement the plan of revenge begun by the tapestry. The story has a happy ending in *Pelops* ("le mors de l'espaule"): the gods put the child back together again, replacing the missing bone with an ivory shard. In *Philomela* there is no resurrection for Itys. The distinction persists, perhaps because the sacrifice or murder in Pelops' case was gratuitous, whereas Philomela's punishment, if not completely justifiable, is understandable. Furthermore, the two stories are themselves connected by Ovid in that the first, no more than an eight-line digression, serves as a transition and immediate introduction to the over 260 lines of *Philomela.*

The Ovidian examples and teachings may be filtered through the theme of resurrection, of putting something back together again (as emblematized by Pelops)—an art displayed in *Erec et Enide*—in order to introduce *Tristan* material. The latter may be resurrected, put together anew, substituting in the process an artificial device for the natural piece left out, as in Pelops' body. Tragedy may be overturned and a happy resolution made to mark the new ending. The interchangeable themes of deceit and artifice of the original Tristan legend resurface in *Cligés.* Artifice is first emblematized in those rewards—the shirt, the goblet—bestowed upon Alixandre, who combats those who willfully deceive the King, Angrés and his followers; and, second, it is deployed, in the story of Fenice and Cligés, in order to justify deception as punishment for neglecting an oath—Alis' promise not to marry. All three of the Ovidian examples we have touched upon share a specific interest in the translation of an event, either from the immediate past or from antiquity, into a new medium. Artifice, re-doing, communicating or leaving a lasting mark in some other medium or language is shared by the three tales from Book VI. They resurface in Chrétien's *Cligés* in a way that also permits us to glance into the mirror of Chrétien's own art, which they reflect in a way similar to Ovid's mirroring of tales in his own *Metamorphoses*. The situation in the Ovidian examples seems to be reversed, however, in that, in Chrétien's descriptions, stories are not depicted in the object, as was done by the Ovidian tapestries at the same time that the narrator focused on technique. In Chrétien's examples technique is the matter contained or displayed by the object in question, whereas stories or narrative episodes, as we shall see, suggest themselves as a result of the narrator's descriptions.

In the first seven lines of *Cligés*, then, the narrator provides his self-portrait in terms of his past achievements, in terms of an abbreviated history of his own works. He amplifies upon this first model to provide a number of summary histories in the remaining sections of his Prologue. In the next ten lines (ll. 8-17) the audience is treated to a brief synopsis of the histories of Alixandre and Cligés, although the two are not named. Cligés is identified particularly in terms of lineage: he is Greek, he is of the line of King Arthur, and he is his father's son. The history that will be told in chronological order is in fact presented backwards, out of sequence. The reference to the manscript of the source *Cligés* found in the Beauvais library follows in the next seven lines (ll. 18-24). Once more we cannot be sure that we can accept this reference at face value. The implications may be multiple. Referring to a written source for one's text is a topic of authority. This tongue-in-cheek practice applies, of course, whether a source did or did not exist for *Cligés* as such. In addition, the topos suggests that Chrétien is translating into Romance, that is, into a vernacular tongue, another text which relates the story of a Greek. This relationship reinforces other similar relationships in the Prologue's matrix. Ovid adapted Greek mythology in Latin; Ovid is now being translated from Latin into Romance. Could the original, perhaps Latin, text of *Cligés* be itself a translation from a Greek original?

So far the narrator has appeared intent on origins, lineage and changing contexts. *Marc et Ysalt* now finds itself situated in the context of the *Metamorphoses*; Alixandre finds himself transplanted to England; the history of father and son is located now in the library of Saint-Pierre *et Beauvais*, now in the text before us. All of which brings us round to the principal theme of the Prologue, to the art of *translater,* the act of carrying over from one place to another, from one generation to another, from one language to another, from one context to another. This phenomenon can be considered from two sides: a thing can travel to one or more places, so that the background varies, so to speak, or a variety of things can pass through the same place, so that the series of occupants changes. For example, the context of an *exemplum* has been maintained in this Prologue, but it has been renewed by placing something unexpected *into* it. The exemplary model is not a Solomon or an Alexander or an Arthur, but a poet and a translator. Unless such a model was implied because of the *physical* space or context it traditionally occupies, the reader might not posit the new role Chrétien assigns to himself as exemplary. The two sides of the coin might be labeled, respectively, the syntagmatic and the paradigmatic aspects of the ways literature, seen in its tradition and in its structurings, has to renew itself. The motif of *translater,* which has run implicitly through the first 24 lines, is finally articulated in an explicit and somewhat traditional manner in the last eighteen lines. These recall the *translatio studii* and *translatio imperii* topics, here alluded to in the corresponding terms of *clergie* and *chevalerie.*

Chrétien explains that Greece enjoyed first the glory of *clergie* and *chevalerie,* which then came to Rome. He does not say that Rome inherited or continued specific traditions. Rather, he personifies *chevalerie* in particular by saying "Puis vint chevalerie a Rome" (l. 31) (Then came chivalry to Rome), as if a person had made the journey. (This personification recalls the earlier lines that stated that the father went from Greece to England.) In his abbreviated style, Chrétien does not make explicit that anything more than a horizontal transfer from one place to another occurred. No reasons are given for the change, no inference of improvement or of transcendence is adduced for the shift in locale. In contrast, a move for the better is implied in the transfer from Rome to France, since the narrator hopes that nothing will make it necessary for further transfer.

Chrétien recalls: "Puis vint chevalerie a Rome / Et de la clergie la some, / Qui or est an France venue" (ll. 31-33) (Then came chivalry to Rome and the sum total of learning, which now has/have come to France). The verb Chrétien selects to describe the arrival of *chevalerie* and *clergie* in France is in the singular: *est venue.* A singular verb agreeing with a composite subject is not uncommon in Old French,[7] so it is possible that Chrétien wants his audience to understand that both *studium* (*clergie*) and *imperium* (*chevalerie*) continue in France. However, he may be exploiting the ambiguity of this grammatical feature to imply that *only* "la some de la clergie" made it to France. If so, what happened to *chevalerie* is not clear. But if the latter is represented by the Germans or by the Empire in the East at Constantinople, then one wonders to what extent it can be admired when facile or less than satisfactory heroes such as the Duke of Saxony, Alixandre and Cligés represent it. The ambiguity implied by the singular verb is further underscored by the next line "Dex doint qu'ele i soit maintenue" (God grant that it be maintained there)—which continues with a singular subject pronoun and a singular verb. If indeed there does exist some tension between *clergie* and *chevalerie*, the possibility of rivalry between Germany and Greece, on the one hand, and France, on the other, is suggested. But matters are even more complicated.

In the romance, we do not find French heroes getting the better of German or Greek knights. We see Germans falling at the hands of a Greek/Breton hero or a Greek helping to restore a Breton kingdom. In addition to the expression of the *translatio studii* and *translatio imperii* topics, and similar to them in articulation since placenames are involved, we have the outline of a hero's past, a hero who traveled from Greece to England. The starting point for *chevalerie* is correct, but the point of arrival does not correspond to the topic. What has happened here appears to be the mix-up of the *translatio* topics with the myth of the Trojan origins of the British, a myth espoused and propagated by the Anglo-Normans,[8] notably at the court of Henry II of England by Wace and Geoffrey of Monmouth. Aeneas fled Troy and arrived in Italy, where he founded a new line in the original land of his ancestors. His descendant Brutus, himself exiled from Rome to Greece, eventually made it to England, where he founded the British race. So England could be considered as a legitimate new Rome, and *chevalerie* seems to be "factually" established in *Bretaigne*.

On the other hand, no chivalric deeds in this poem take place in France. France, in the Prologue, can be connected only with Chrétien, who in *Erec* is Chrétien de Troyes. (This Christian poet from "Troy," *in France* and not England, could only be aligned with the *translatio studii*, though he bears the placename from which the British line originated.) Since in this romance we do not see French *knights* getting the better of British, Greek or German rivals, but rather a French *poet* who makes light of them all as representatives of *chevalerie*, then it is *clergie* and *clergie* alone that can be seen as having migrated to *France*. It is the exercise of this *clergie*—in French—that is the ultimate ideal to be cherished and preserved and which this romance ultimately celebrates. The one who exercises *clergie* in France, the one who lives up to the final topic as articulated by the Prologue, is in fact our poet-narrator who writes about Greeks, Germans and the British in a style derived directly from what is Roman, from Ovid. He would remind the *chevaliers* of his own country, no doubt, that history is written by *clercs*, that heroes are made and remembered only through the activity of those who keep names alive and meaningful by keeping books alive and meaningful.

The opposition between the two *translatio* topics provides for a structure of alternating themes throughout the lines of the introduction: *clergie* (ll. 1-8), *chevalerie* (ll. 9-17), *clergie* (ll. 18-24), *chevalerie* and then *clergie* in combination (ll. 25-31) and finally *clergie* (ll. 32-42). To the theme of *clergie* the narrator devotes both the first and last words of the Prologue. The origins of Chrétien's romance, the specific lineage of *Cligés* as text or book are sketched at the midpoint of the passage (ll. 20-22). Its place of origin—its "country" or *locus* of provenance in a metaphorical sense—is "l'aumaire / Mon seignor saint Pere a Biauvez" (the library of my lord St. Peter at Beauvais), the name, included at the center of our narrator's introduction, that completes his litany of placenames. The midpoint of the Prologue sets its sights on the story as book—on "livres" and "contes"—and depicts the poet's role as one of *estrere*, of drawing out or extracting a book from one language into another: *translatio* once again.

Cligés *and* Tristan

The relationship of Chrétien's *Cligés* to the body of the Tristan material is at the heart of Chrétien's second romance. It is by far the thorniest problem to sort out when dealing with this narrative because it is a relationship that is complex, difficult to isolate, at times tedious to articulate, always subject to hypothesis, and one which has been argued and reargued for close to a century.[9] Critics have asked themselves: Did Chrétien imitate Thomas or was it the other way around? Did Chrétien know Béroul's *Tristan* or only some other example of the so-called *version commune*? And what precisely did Chrétien react to in the texts he did know?

We have only fragments of Thomas' and Béroul's texts in Old French, in addition to the two *Folie Tristan* adaptations, and some foreign adaptations, notably the medieval German versions by Eilhart von Oberg and Gottfried von Strassburg. Therefore, we can discern only with difficulty the relationships of the *Cligés* to complete Old French versions of the *Tristan*. But another problem surfaces. To what end did Chrétien write a romance so obviously connected with the *Tristan* corpus? Some have wondered whether the "immorality" of the love triangle in the Tristan legend shocked him, and if so, whether he wished to "correct" it. Did he wish to complete Thomas? Did he intend to write an *Anti-Tristan*, a *Neo-Tristan* or a *Super-Tristan*?

These questions will in all likelihood never be settled. Some of them have become irrelevant or uninteresting. They will no doubt remain a matter of opinion and conjecture, at least to some degree. My own particular bias is to avoid ascribing a label, whether Anti, Neo or Super, to *Cligés*, although I do agree with those scholars, like Anthime Fourrier (*Le Courant*, 111-78), who see Chrétien's romance as a reaction to both Thomas' poem and to some text of the *version commune*, which for purposes of concrete discussion I shall consider as represented by Béroul.[10] Pinpointing exact relationships between *Cligés* and Thomas, or between *Cligés* and a Béroul-like text, is a detailed and exhausting project. Fourrier has attempted this kind of analysis, arguing the case for Thomas' anteriority with respect to Chrétien's romance. He presents meticulous documentation and convincing arguments in order to show that Chrétien transposes material from each of the two *Tristan* compositions. In order to provide the reader with some idea of the sorts of borrowings possible, I will describe a few typical examples, partly overlapping in my demonstrations with the work done by Fourrier. My examples will not come close to constituting a complete listing of the transformations Chrétien performed on various versions of the *Tristan*. They will, I hope, be significant enough to provide a basis for discussion of the problems of method and artistic motivation that shaped *Cligés* and gave it direction.

The configuration most fundamental to the Tristan story is the love triangle Mark-Iseut-Tristan, a relationship brought about by the love potion. The potion was originally intended for Mark and Iseut on their wedding night, but was consumed inadvertently on board ship, prior to the arrival of Iseut at Mark's court, by Tristan and Iseut. In Béroul's poem the potion has only temporary effects—it lasts three years; in Thomas the potion's power is life-long.[11]

At the root of the relationship between *Cligés* and *Tristan* is Fenice's objection to the life led by Iseut. Though her heart belonged to one man, Iseut shared her body with two. Consequently, the triangle threatened her life and reputation as well as her lover's, their social position, the happiness of all involved and the security of the kingdom. In *Cligés* Fenice resorts to a potion to avoid dangers such as these, and she does so consciously, not by accident. She orders Thessala, her nurse and a magician of merit, to prepare a device that allows her to pretend to submit to her husband, though in fact such is not the case, in order that she may remain faithful to her husband's nephew Cligés in both body and spirit, thereby avoiding any disturbance of the status quo. The potion is consumed by the husband alone. Its effects are permanent; Alis will possess his wife only in his dreams. At a later date, Fenice asks Thessala for a second potion. The effects of this potion are short-lived. They are applied this time to the wife. The potion brings about the appearance of death, so that Fenice can be buried, then removed to an underground palace, where she lives secretly and comfortably with her lover. How do these givens of *Cligés* square with Chrétien's borrowings from the *Tristans*?

First, there are two potions: one long-lived, the other of temporary duration. Chrétien therefore has incorporated into his poem both the potion of Thomas *and* that of Béroul; in this instance, he has put two versions of *Tristan* into the account of Fenice and Cligés. And by combining two versions into one (technically, into only the second part of his narrative, where he treats the potion device), he has doubled the number of potions.

Second, the first potion is drunk exclusively by the husband, not by the lovers. The situation is reversed exactly when compared with the circumstances that prevailed in Béroul's composition. Third, the first potion creates an illusion of physical love; no other sort of love is brought about by the potion. One of the original properties of the *Tristan* potion has, therefore, been eliminated. Another has been reversed: the potion drunk by Alis creates illusion, not reality. One could add that the very areas disturbed by Béroul's potion—politics and morality—are in fact the ones safeguarded in Chrétien's romance by Thessala's device. The cause of the disturbances in Béroul or Thomas, that is, the adulterous love between the King's nephew and the Queen, is brought about by means of the love-drink, whereas the love that exists between Fenice and Cligés exists without regard to a potion. Thessala's is a brew that keeps politics and morality from coming into conflict with the love between the Empress and the Emperor's nephew.

Fourth, the two properties of the *Tristan* potion, namely, that it carries with it love and death, have again been separated out in Chrétien's poem. A second potion is called for to bring death, but, like the first potion, it creates illusion, effecting only the appearances of death.

The procedure of inventing parallels or doubling not only applies to the *Tristan*, but also functions with respect to Chrétien's own givens. A technique applied intertextually between Chrétien's romance and another (or others) is internalized and applied self-referentially also to itself. Just as two potions are necessary to construct, first, the illusion of love and, second, the illusion of death, so Chrétien introduces a second artist in order to build two containers, that is, two tombs for Fenice. One serves to further the appearances of death, in part, but more importantly furnishes the means for Fenice's resurrection and transition into her new life. This is the sepulchre that Jehan builds and inside which Fenice may lie and yet not suffocate while awaiting the arrival of her liberators. Obvious light-hearted plays on the paradigm of Christ's passion, death and resurrection promote the comic character of this irreverent intertextual drama. The other "tomb,"

Jehan's tower, insures Fenice and Cligés of comfort and safety while enjoying a fully shared love (a counterpart to the Forest of Morois in the Tristan legend). For this reason Jehan gives over to the couple the inner sanctum in the underground recesses of his tower. Once more the fact of parallels and of doublings is apparent.

Other *Tristan* borrowings appear in these segments. When Tristan lay dying, he sent for Iseut to come heal him. In our poem, it is not the counterpart to Tristan who is dying, but rather the counterpart to Iseut who feigns death—yet another inversion. Reality is changed to illusion, while Chrétien also reverses the roles of the principal characters. In Thomas' poem Iseut was to arrive in the person of a doctor (l. 1287). When Iseut arrived, Tristan was already dead and the sounds of the people mourning greeted her as she stepped off the boat. Similarly, once Fenice is pronounced dead and the people of Constantinople mourn her in the streets, three doctors from Salerno appear and ask to see the body. They rightly suspect Fenice's death; it reminds them of Solomon's wife who betrayed her husband in like manner. To an outsider to this world Fenice's plan is not realistic; it is patterned too obviously on another fiction. Neither "Doctor" Iseut nor the good doctors of Salerno resuscitate their respective "patients," and those who come to rescue the dead die in their turn—Iseut tragically, tugging at the audience's heart; the doctors comically, with a pratfall out the window.

Parallels, reversals and switches are put into operation in order to stress the role of the potion as a device that can be detected and tested, but not undone. These procedures are also employed in order to reveal the episode of Fenice's false death as one that, in contrast to the *Tristan* model, is quite explicitly fictional and highly comic in its machinations, which work, almost fail and then just barely succeed. Many segments of the *Tristan* system operate in a similar manner. A plan succeeds for a time, is found out, fails temporarily, then is put back on track with another ploy, and so on.

The tombs Jehan prepares also evoke a number of *Tristan* resonances. By means of the second potion, Fenice is bodily removed from court and Cligés, unsuspected, remains by his uncle's side. In Béroul's poem, a letter, not a potion, was composed by the hermit Ogrin in order to bring Iseut back into Mark's good graces, whereas Tristan had as a result to go into exile. He did not reside at court any longer, but he did not leave the country either. Instead, he sought the company of a friend, the forester Orri, and hid away in his underground cellar. Two reversals are hereby effected: the opposite counterpart (Tristan) is removed from the court to live underground, where all his needs are provided for by a servant. And the order of the two tombs in *Cligés* has been altered as well, since the underground palace in which Fenice hides away parallels, in an obverse fashion, the Morois Forest before Tristan is banished from court to hide in Orri's underground habitat. The chronological order of the corresponding events has been juggled in *Cligés*.

The Morois Forest as described in Béroul was primitive and wild. The couple wandered through the woods, constantly on the run, never spending more than one night at a time in the same place. Their clothes became rags, their food came only from hunting. Iseut turned pale and thin. Both hero and heroine longed for home, for their former social positions and for luxurious comforts. The symbol of their stay in the Morois is, of course, the *feuillée*, the hut or lean-to they constructed out of branches and leaves woven together. There they were discovered by a hunter who recognized and betrayed them to the King. Mark went to the spot unaccompanied and found the couple asleep together, but dressed and not embracing. Tristan's sword lay between them. The King, suddenly convinced of their innocence, did not rouse them, but exchanged rings with the sleeping Iseut and swords with Tristan, in order to alert them symbolically to his change of heart. These signs are, however, misread by the couple as a threat, and they consequently decide to take flight once more.

Chrétien has turned all the particulars of the Morois Forest upside-down. Fenice lives in Jehan's tower, which is a wonder of architecture, engineering, sculpture and painting. She lacks none of the comforts of her former palace apartments: Jehan has even installed hot and cold running water! In fact, her only complaint, after fifteen months of residence, is that she does not see enough of the sun and the moon, sights which Tristan and Iseut certainly did not feel deprived of. When the couple is at last discovered, they are lying in nude embrace under a pear tree, the branches of which reach down to the ground in a bower that blocks out all rays of sunlight, an obvious avatar of, and improvement on, the Morois *feuillée*, which did not keep the harsh sun from striking the sleeping Iseut's cheek.

There are, thus, no mitigating circumstances that argue for their innocence, no signs of hardship that can sway the reader's sympathy and mask the facts. The hunter who discovers them can scarcely believe his eyes—like Mark. Not until a pear falls, grazing Fenice's head (the tree has a similar flaw after all!) and thus awakening her, does she exclaim that they have been discovered. This changes the reader's evaluation of the scene. Tristan and Iseut, we recall, went on sleeping; their surprise could not betray their guilt, their silence was more convincing. The hunter runs to fetch Alis, who neither returns alone nor finds the lovers still in the garden. He finds at the tower only Jehan, who confesses the workings of both potions and the betrayals worked by the Emperor's wife and nephew. It is Alis who conveniently dies, not the lovers. Fenice and Cligés return to take the throne they should have occupied formerly. Fenice remains Empress and Cligés, as the son of Alis' elder brother Alixandre, resumes his rightful role as the legitimate heir.

In addition to the fusion of two *Tristan* versions, Chrétien splits one *Tristan* element to make material for the two generations of heroes he describes. A good example of this procedure is afforded by the scene of declaration between Tristan and Iseut. The avowals there revolve around three homonyms: *amare/mare/amarum*, in Old French *l'amer* ("love")/*la mer* ("the ocean")/*l'amer*[*tume*] ("bitterness"). This word-play is missing in the *Tristan* fragments of Thomas as we have them now. They are present in Gottfried's poem, an adaptation of Thomas, where Tristan believes that Iseut complains of suffering from the sea and the bitter wind. He hesitates to grasp her true meaning. Iseut finally explains that she is not seasick, but lovesick: she suffers from *l'amer*, from love.[12]

Chrétien transposes this word-play into his romance when Alixandre and Soredamor are crossing the Channel together with Arthur's retinue. The two fall in love at first sight, without benefit of the potion. However, they, too, like Tristan, are too timid to declare their love. In Chrétien's narrative the play on words is not part of a dialogue between two lovers who are testing each other's feelings. The narrator has taken on this juggling of homonyms himself in order to explain Guenevere's confusion upon seeing the two turn pale. She is slow to understand the meaning of these signs, but gradually comes to recognize at a later stage the love between her niece and the Greek visitor, which feeling she helps them to articulate. Her counterpart in the second part of *Cligés* is Thessala, who inquires into Fenice's pallor because she suspects her ward of being under a spell. But the girl explains the real reason for her agitation without wasting any time.[13]

During Alixandre and Soredamor's crossing, then, the narrator explains that Guenevere

> ... garde s'an prant,
> Qui l'un et l'autre voit sovant
> Descolorer et anpalir;
> Ne set don ce puet avenir,
> Ne ne set por coi il le font
> Fors que por *la mer* ou il sont.
> Espoir bien s'an aparceüst,
> Se *la mers* ne la deceüst,
> Mes *la mers* l'angingne et deçoit
> Si qu'an *la mer* *l'amor* ne voit;
> An *la mer* sont, et d'*amer* vient,
> Et d'*amors* vient li max ques tient.
> Et de ces trois ne set blasmer
> La reïne fors que *la mer*,
> Car li dui le tierz li ancusent

> Et por le tierz li dui s'escusent
> Qui del forfet sont antechié.
> (ll. 533-49, my emphasis)

(The Queen takes notice of it, she who sees one and the other blush and pale repeatedly; she does not know whence this behavior can come, nor does she know why they blush, except because of the sea where they find themselves. But the sea tricks and deceives her, so that she does not see love at sea. They are at sea, and from bitterness and from love comes the illusion which holds them. And of these three the Queen knows not which to blame, except for the sea, for the two accuse the third to her, and by means of the third the other two escape detection, the two which are guilty of the crime.)

This kind of analysis, in which each facet of a problem is examined in its turn, is similar to the explanations and commentaries one often finds in Thomas' poem, either in the words of its narrator or in the words of Tristan.[14] This particular word-play could well have been inspired by Thomas' example. But did not Chrétien bungle the matter of transposition?

> Le poète introduit ses artificielles variations en les accrochant à la constatation d'une comparse, la reine, et sans les conduire à aucun résultat . . . ; et a maladroitement inversé le rapport de deux contre un (*mare-amarum* contre *amare*, les deux premiers étant seuls accusés par Tristan, alors que le vrai coupable est le dernier, —d'où progression ingénieuse) en un rapport de un contre deux (*mare* contre *amarum-amare*, où la gradation fait place à la confusion). (Fourrier, *Le Courant*, p. 126)

Fourrier also finds evidence here for Thomas' precedence over Chrétien, arguing that an author is more likely to imitate by breaking a coherent example apart than by devising a compact segment of narrative from something rather more disparate:

> Or, ici nous avons, d'une part un ressort décisif de l'intrigue, et d'autre part, une simple arabesque. La question, dès lors, est de savoir si le chemin le plus naturel conduit du principal à l'accessoire ou de l'accessoire au principal, c'est-à-dire s'il est plus facile, plus normal d'extraire des variations d'un thème plutôt qu'un thème des variations. Il paraît donc plus logique de croire à l'antériorité de Thomas. (ibid.)

Rather than judge Chrétien's version less successful, I would concentrate on what Fourrier terms an "arabesque." Chrétien's transposition of the Thomas example makes it into something gratuitous, into a flourish that seems extraneous to the plot's advancement. His transposition brings out the *Tristan* echo, emphasizing the fact of transposition *per se*. So with this example Chrétien underscores intertextuality, or, to use an equivalent medieval term, *translatio studii*. If the use of the motif appears halting when compared to the gracefulness and propriety of Thomas' execution— as Fourrier would have it—the "stumbling" nevertheless has its purpose. The *apparent* lack of grace achieves an association in the reader's mind between Chrétien and the pun on *amer*, that is, between the narrator and *translatio*, making the association a hallmark of Thomas' discourse turned to comic effect in Chrétien.

Nevertheless, Chrétien is not incapable of devising a word-game like that of Thomas in order to have characters admit gradually, even convolutedly, their love to one another. Chrétien postpones the expected traditional effect he *seemed* to have bungled when he borrowed Thomas' pun. He splits the word-play of *amer* in two, distinguishing between the material of the rhetorical figure—the pun itself—and the use to which it is put. The second side of the example that disappeared in the encounter between Alixandre and Soredamor resurfaces in a scene between Fenice and Cligés, thereby effecting a *conjointure* of two scenes otherwise unrelated. For this dialogue Chrétien also manages to entwine preciosity and avowals with yet another famous motif from Thomas, the dichotomy between *cors* and *cuers*.[15]

Upon his return to Germany Cligés explains to Fenice:

> Ausi com escorce sanz fust
> Fu mes cors sanz cuer an Bretaingne
> . . . .
> Ça fu mes cuers [après vos], et la mes cors.
> (ll. 5120-21, 5125)

(Like bark without wood was my body without a heart in England . . . here [following after you] was my heart, and there [in England] was my body.)

In contrast to the Thomas example, here it is not Fenice, the counterpart to Iseut, who starts off the figurative language, but Cligés, the counterpart to Tristan. Fenice apparently has no difficulty in perceiving the underlying message and does not miss a beat in the dialogue's tempo:

> En moi n'a mes fors que l'escorce,
> Car sanz cuer vif et sanz cuer sui.
> N'onques an Bretaigne ne fui,
> Si a mes cuers lonc sejor fet.
> (ll. 5144-47)

(There is nothing left in me but the bark, for I live without a heart and am without one; I have never been to England, and yet my heart spent a long time there.)

The paradox is unraveled as Cligés asks for details. When was her heart in England? While he was there? "Yes," answers Fenice. Whereupon Cligés laments, in language worthy of French Classical preciosity, his ignorance of this fact while he was there:

> Dex, je ne l'i soi, ne ne vi.
> Dex, que nel soi? Se le seüsse,

> Certes, dame, je li eüsse
> Boene conpaingnie porté.
> (ll. 5158-61)

(My God! I didn't know it there, nor did I see it. God! why didn't I know it? If I had, certainly, lady, I would have kept it good company.)

The exchange goes on as they explain that each possessed the other's heart, and in fact still does: "Dame, don sont ci avoec nos / Endui li cuer, si con vos dites; / Car li miens est vostres toz quites" (ll. 5170-72) (My lady, therefore here with us are both hearts, just as you have said, for mine is yours entirely). This reply echoes and completes the scene where Cligés bids Fenice adieu before his journey to England from Germany: "Mes droiz est qu'a vos congié praigne / Com a celi cui ge sui toz" (ll. 4282-83) (But it is right that I take my leave of you as of one to whom I belong completely). These ambiguous words occasion a full-fledged debate in the mind of an uncertain Fenice, who hesitates to take them at face value, though this is clearly what she would prefer. Here again it is the opposite counterpart who performs the analogous action: Fenice (not Cligés) is left to interpret an ambiguous avowal. As the narrator explains: "A li seule opose et respont, / Et fet tele oposition" (ll. 4364-65) (She objects to her own presentation and answers it herself, making the following argumentation). This speech parallels the similarly analytical disquisitions, or interior monologues, of Alixandre and Soredamor. There, we recall, each character pondered whether or not to love. In Fenice's case, she does not doubt that she is in love; she questions the words and feelings of the one she loves, trying to deduce from a standard phrase and demeanor whether or not she is truly adored. In each case a monologue takes on the characteristics of a dialogue wherein a character newly in love tries to discover logically—and therefore comically—the truth about himself or of the beloved.

To recapitulate, the pun on *amer*, apparently derived from Thomas, splits into two separate strands: the words and their function. The pun itself is played out by the narrator in the first story, but, as Fourrier points out, to no effect; its function in the plot has been neutralized and its only effect is to comment on the relationship between different versions of the *Tristan*. Second, the function of the pun has been salvaged and worked out by Chrétien with another familiar *Tristan* motif, also found in Thomas: the *cors/cuers* dichotomy. The declarations of love that revolve around this opposition develop in turn an earlier leave-taking between the same two lovers. It had also occasioned an analysis using monologues in the form of dialogues on love and hesitation to make feelings known to one another. These are intertwined with the original pun on *amer* as used by the narrator. A borrowing dismantled into its component parts—which represents a kind of analysis on the poet's side, making what is normally singular into a plural or a duality, similar to the monologue-dialogue performed by the characters—is worked into the two narratives through parallels and echoes between various parts of the entire romance.

When Cligés departs, leaving Fenice to meditate on his ambiguous farewell, his parting phrase—like Soredamor's comely form which Alixandre likened to an arrow which passed through his eye to his heart—is described in an equally precious manner as a spice that she places on her tongue and finally locks away in her heart. The narrator thus prefaces her *explication de texte* with a description which compares the phrase to be analyzed to two things: to nourishment and to a treasure that cannot be stolen. Cligés' words, now become spice thanks to the narrator's metaphor, are her sustenance. The narrator uses, moreover, the word *bevrage*, informing us that Fenice's substitute for drink soothes all her ills; this could remind the audience ironically of the *Tristan beivre*, which, of course, was not metaphorical and which did not assuage.

In *Tristan* the pledge of love is always unambiguous where the lovers themselves are concerned; it is ambiguous only for those who overhear. Instead of an exchange of words, it is usually an exchange of gifts or love tokens, such as a ring, that takes place in the *Tristan*. Chrétien has reversed the *Tristan* situation completely, as usual. It is the lovers who are confused, not a spectator like King Mark up his tree spying on them. Words are left behind as a love token instead of a ring or a dog. The words are then described metaphorically by the narrator so that they are perceived as objects by the audience.

The second part of the metaphorical description shows the spice-words locked away in her heart like a treasure. But Fenice need not fear the threats of robbers, says the narrator:

> Car cist avoirs n'est mie mobles,
> Einz est ausi com edefiz
> Qui ne puet estre desconfiz
> Ne par deluge, ne par feu,
> Ne ja nel movera d'un leu.
> (ll. 4354-58)

(For this possession is not moveable, rather it is like an edifice which can be destroyed by neither flood nor fire, nor will it ever move from the spot.)

I wish to single out these comparisons not only because they show the narrator performing the metaphorical operation which changes words to objects so that what is exchanged between the parting lovers conforms to the *Tristan* paradigm (though trifling with it), but also because the particular points of comparison and transformation—*espece* and *edefiz*—are two fundamental motifs that will be developed quite concretely in the remainder of the story.

Upon Cligés' return, when this conversation is completed, Fenice reveals her fidelity to Cligés by means of Thessala's potion made of *spices*, drunk by Alis, and affecting his heart; they manage further to ensure their love by means of an *edifice*, Jehan's tower, that hides Cligés' treasure away. Reversals and play with specific *Tristan* motifs provide Chrétien with material upon which he can build segments of his romance, which themselves effect reversals on yet other *Tristan* elements.

As we have seen, Chrétien does not observe strict lines of demarcation in constructing his version of *Tristan*. Segments that have been split apart are recombined while spilling over into various parts of the narrative. For example, although there are two stories in this one romance treating respectively the history of the parents and then the history of their orphaned son —a structure that exactly parallels that of the *Tristan* story—motifs like the pun on *amer* that, strictly speaking, "belong" in the latter segment find themselves redone in the first part of the narrative. Similarly, the shirt given to Alixandre that contains two kinds of gold threads side by side and the marvelous cup that the hero wins after he captures Windsor Castle echo and amplify upon a cup and a comparison between two sorts of gold that appear near the end of Thomas' *Tristan*. (We will later have the occasion to return to this silk shirt sewn by Soredamor.)

From these examples we may observe that Chrétien carries the *Tristan* material over into his romance in ways that do not involve, strictly speaking, translation, but rather *translatio*, or structural transposition and transformation, in a dazzling variety of ways. These means involve doubling, fission, reversal, fusion, conflation, and the like, in any number of combinations that allow numerous complex patterns to emerge.

These transformations of the *Tristan* material are not the only ones to participate in an express intertextuality. Chrétien constructs parallels and echoes, reversals and doublings even with respect to his own text, that is, between the story of Alixandre and that of Cligés. Both Alixandre and Cligés travel to Arthur's court. One makes his identity known immediately, the other goes incognito. There are no potions at work in the love story of Soredamor and Alixandre; there are two potions in the story of Fenice and Cligés. Similarly, when the first two die, there are no tomb descriptions; in the following narrative, no one really dies (except for Alis, whose burial goes unmentioned), but two tombs are constructed and described. In the first account Alis splits or shares an emperorship with his brother, retaining the appearances of the office; in the second account, Alis shares a marriage with his brother's son, again in appearance only. No triangle affair pertains in the relationship of Alixandre and Soredamor, but one triangle is replaced by another for Fenice, when Alis/Fenice/Cligés replaces the Duke of Saxony /Fenice/Alis. The last arrangement represents a halving of triangles in Thomas' *Tristan*: (1) Cariado/Iseut/Mark, (2) Cariado/Iseut/Tristan, (3) Mark/Iseut/Tristan, and (4) Iseut/Tristan/Iseut aux Blanches Mains.

The Midpoint: The Potion

In the *Yvain* and the *Lancelot* there lies at the midpoint a scene that reveals the identity of the protagonist. The hero is named in a new and significant fashion which situates him in a relationship of service and rescue with another. In *Yvain* the knight takes on a new identity as Le Chevalier au Lion by saving the lion who becomes henceforth his companion. At the close of the romance this alternate identity becomes integrated with Yvain's original persona as a knight of the Round Table and as Laudine's husband and, consequently, her champion. Conversely, in Chrétien's *Lancelot* an unknown knight assumes early on a mysterious identity as Le Chevalier de la Charrette. At the midpoint the Knight of the Cart is identified by Guenevere herself as Lancelot du Lac, knight of the Round Table, engaged in her rescue as defender of Arthur's kingdom. With *Erec et Enide*, which seems to be arranged in three parts, or with the unfinished *Perceval*, it is difficult to settle on a given scene as a midpoint. However, Chrétien's *Cligés* contains such a scene, though no one is renamed therein. In fact, quite the opposite sort of character occupies the strategic narrative moment in this romance, even though this character is still a person acting to rescue a lady. The expectations of Chrétien's reader are thwarted and reoriented when the midpoint of *Cligés* focuses on a Greek woman, the sorceress Thessala, Fenice's servant and nurse.

At the midpoint episode of *Cligés* the poet-narrator interrupts the smooth flow of the narration to say:

> Que vos iroie tot contant?
> Lor afeire vont apruichant
> Li dui empereor ansanble,
> Que li mariages asanble,
> Et la joie el palés comance;
> Mes n'i voel feire demorance
> De parler de chascune chose;
> A Thessala qui ne repose
> Des poisons feire et atranprer
> Voel ma parole retorner.
> (ll. 3199-3208)

(Why should I go on telling you everything? Both Emperors whom the marriage brings together continue arranging matters, and the palace's celebration commences. But I do not want to dwell on every detail; I want to turn my attention towards Thessala, who does not rest from making and mixing her potions.)

This interruption emphasizes the narrator's presence for the audience in conjunction with his rejection of wedding festivities and political alliance as matters worthy of commemoration. He now chooses to describe the preparation of another kind of commingling and conjoining destined to undo the hopes and plans of the emperors. Thessala's exercise of her craft is mightier than the most powerful politics. Her interference in their assemblage will reorient the way the reader and Cligés' lineage will view it forevermore, as the Conclusion will show.

The description of Thessala, as she contrives her device of subterfuge, encompasses three scenes. The first takes place between Fenice and Thessala, the third concerns an exchange between Thessala and Cligés. The second scene, where her craft is concretely applied, mediates between the two lovers, serving, on the one hand, as an exchange of dialogue between the narrator and the audience, and, on the other, as the transfer and realization of Fenice's intention into the artifact that Thessala invents for Cligés, who transfers it yet again to his uncle the Emperor when he presents him with the potion.

Thessala is implicated in other modalities of transfer when we consider the genesis of her character, both within and without the framework of this romance. A poet conversant with Ovid and particularly with the *Metamorphoses* would readily recall a line of nurse figures or sorceresses to use as components for his own Thessala. These include Medea and Myrrha's nurse. Furthermore, this particular aspect of the Ovidian tradition is part of another transference. The *Roman d'Eneas* had already adapted it for two of its own scenes: one between Lavine and her mother, where the daughter haltingly reveals her love for Eneas, and one where Dido asks her sister to consult a non-existent sorceress (a metaphor for death) in order to remove her passion for Eneas. One could view the scene from *Cligés* as both a transference of the Ovidian tradition through the *Eneas* model and as a combination of the two episodes which perform the *translatio* of Ovid in it. Like the binary multiplications or divisions familiar from his handling of *Tristan* material, we find a similar treatment of the *Eneas* model.

Fenice tries to escape one potential love while promoting another more dangerous to achieve, with the help of Thessala. Chrétien introduces Thessala as an artisan figure involved with her own tradition. Her name is that of her native country, a country noted only—at least for the purposes of our text—for its tradition of witchcraft, a feminine tradition of long standing (ll. 2965-70). Chrétien translates the Classical tradition of magic and witchcraft appropriate to a Medea into the medium of a kind of school tradition. Thessala's identity stems from her involvement in and practice of the art which she carries with her from her country. Her identity, unlike those of Yvain or Lancelot, is adumbrated only as tradition and transfer of craft exercised in service of another person. Furthermore, her name does not change within the romance, though her craft—magic instead of medicine—is revealed. Her identity is not significant in terms of her personal history; we are only introduced to her. But as encompassed in the narrative sequence of *Cligés*, she does represent an alternate identity and a new name for a constant figure of the text: the poet-narrator of the Prologue. Thessala, in her permutation of the *Tristan* potion, reveals in a novel and significant fashion his identity in relation to the text and in his service to the audience.

Just as Yvain and Le Chevalier au Lion or Lancelot and Le Chevalier de la Charrette are each one and the same person, though seen at different times and in different perspectives, so can "Chrétien" and Thessala be considered as the same presence seen at different times and in different lights. They are indeed similar and are similarly presented in the narrative. Chrétien is introduced in the Prologue, associated with a country—France—and with a tradition and the exercise of a particular craft, and he considers himself, like Thessala, to have a Classical model whom he imitates and surpasses! Chrétien supplies the audience with a self-portrait of his own poet-narrator persona in the Prologue, referring in the first line indirectly to the one provided by the Prologue of *Erec et Enide*. Similarly, he describes the person of Thessala, preparing the way for her own self-portrait as she describes herself to Fenice. Both characters are similar in their attributes, functions and presentations, but with the distinct difference that one is the performer of the discourse, whereas the other is an actor in the drama. With this play of similarity and difference in mind, we can see Thessala as a transformation of the figure of Chrétien's poet-narrator persona and as a projection of that persona from the outskirts of the fiction into its center, so that Chrétien's relationship to the text becomes implicit in the drama of the narrative. To complete the analogy, the description of Thessala's potion reveals in part the workings of Chrétien's own romance process.

The preparation of the potion in *Cligés* is described twice: once by the poet-narrator and once by Thessala herself. The first description places the poet-narrator in a relation of service to Thessala and associates him with an object or symbol—like the cart or the lion—namely, with the preparation of a crafted product, the potion that responds imaginatively to the *Tristan* potion. The narrator describes his artisan blending her spices into a clear, sweet potion:

> Thessala tranpre sa poison,
> Espices i met a foison
> Por adolcir et atranprer;
> Bien les fet batre et destranprer,
> Et cole tant que toz est clers
> Ne rien n'i est aigres n'amers;
> Car les espices qui i sont
> Dolces et de boene oldor sont.
> (ll. 3209-16)

(Thessala mixes her potion, she puts an abundance of spices into it in order to sweeten and lighten it. She beats them and grinds them up well, straining it until everything is clear. Nothing in it is sour or bitter, for the spices included are sweet and fragrant.)

Thessala ambiguously describes the value of the beverage to Cligés, persuading—duping—him to serve, and his uncle to drink, the magic potion:

> Je cuit que molt amer le doive,
> C'onques de si boen ne gosta,
> Ne nus boivres tant ne costa.
>
> . . . .
>
> Que ja ne sache dom il vint,
> Fors que par aventure avint
> Qu'antre les presanz le trovastes,
> Et por ce que vos esprovastes
> Et santistes au vant de l'air
> Des boenes espices le flair,
> Et por ce que cler le veïstes,
> Le vin an sa coupe meïstes;
>
> . . . .
> (ll. 3244-46, 3251-58)

(I think that he will like it a great deal, for he never tasted any so good, nor did any drink ever cost so much . . . . may he never know where it came from, except that by chance you happened on it among the gifts, and because you smelled the aroma of the good spices wafting through the air, and because you saw that it was clear, you poured the wine into his cup.)

The verb *tranprer* and its variations *atranprer* and *destranprer* receive emphasis in the first description, since they occur in part in rhyme position and participate in an *annominatio*. Alliterations are frequent throughout the descriptions as well as repetitions of certain key sounds, notably those that make up Thessala's own name: /t/, /a/ and /s/. Furthermore, Chrétien has not stinted, any more than did Thessala with her spices, on rich rhymes. Though certainly not an uncommon characteristic of Chrétien's prosody, they are, nevertheless, quite consistent within these particular lines. Chrétien has in fact renewed the pun imported from Thomas to reecho in these descriptions the words *amer* ("to love") and *amer*[s] ("bitter"), omitting the third compenent, *la mer*—which was opposed to the first two originally —for obvious reasons. The element of liquid inherent in the missing component is, of course, a characteristic of this drink as it is of all others; this common denominator allows Alis to be deceived as the sea allowed the Queen to be in the earlier scene.

The narrator qualifies Thessala's activity as *tranprer*, "to mix, to temper," and then goes on to define it more specifically as made up of three steps: the adding of an abundance of sweet spices, the beating and grinding up of these ingredients and the repeated straining of the mixture. The end product is characterized as sweet, or rather as not bitter or sour, and as clear. The narrator goes a bit farther than simply naming the steps; he also explains in part why they are followed. There are direct correlations between the sweetening and lightening of the potion and the grinding up of the spices, and between the straining or filtering process and the clarity of the liquid. None of the individual spices is mentioned by name; neither their proportion nor the order of their addition is given. The reader is not caught up in a realistic or mimetic representation of the activity, but in the activity as a concatenation of devices tending to specific purposes within a particular context. In short, the description is not a recipe or formula that someone else—some witch not trained in the school of Thessaly—could apply mechanically to obtain the same results. Rather, the narrator reveals only that Thessala resorts to expensive, imported, sweet material.

This description is analogous to Chrétien's own procedures in putting together his *Cligés*. He, too, uses a number of rich imported materials, such as the *Tristan* corpus, the *Roman d'Eneas* and Ovid. Chrétien also mixes and "grinds up" his material, as in his handling of elements taken from these texts. Just as Thessala makes her mixture of imported ingredients clear, so does Chrétien have the audience recognize the clarity of his recombination of a number of textual transferences.

What is the filtering or straining process he uses? First, the audience senses, no doubt somewhat the way Cligés or anyone else would, the sweet fragrance of Thessala's *boivre*, the sweet fragrance of what is pleasing and diverting about a *Tristan* delivered in Chrétien's uniquely devised Byzantine trappings. We recognize certain *Tristan* motifs, overtones and relationships without being able to isolate absolutely a particular element in the mixture. But beyond these hints at other texts that make up *Cligés*, another implement is applied to the narrative that allows it to appear clear despite the abundance of the ingredients. The audience is not lost when reading or hearing *Cligés* because it is guided by the poet-narrator, by such interruptions as the preface to the description of the potion and by analogues present in descriptions, such as this one with Thessala found at the midpoint.

The transformation of Chrétien, poet-narrator/artisan figure of the Prologue, into Thessala, the artisan figure of the midpoint and actor in the drama of Fenice's love affair, is one of a series of such encounters between the audience and the poet-narrator. It takes place as part of a mediation of similar transformations and analogous descriptions. For example, the couple of Soredamor and an unknown artisan are responsible for two artifacts like the potion. Soredamor fashions a shirt and an artisan produces a gold cup, both of which are bestowed upon Alixandre, the one by the Queen and the other by the King. In the second part of the romance, another couple prevails: Thessala and Jehan, the servants and confidants to Fenice and Cligés. Thessala prepares two potions, Jehan prepares two tombs for the living Fenice. The notion of a *conjointure* of artisans is maintained, the number of artifacts is doubled, just as Chrétien himself writes a double romance.

The midpoint of Chrétien's *Cligés* fits the more prevalent pattern for midpoints in the corpus of Chrétien's romances, though at first it seems to present a departure from the usage characteristic of them. The processes in the development of the romance itself, of the relationship between the artisan and his invention as begun in the Prologue, are renamed and revealed in the description of Thessala and her potion. When temporarily considered in isolation, as the narrator's interruption and the solitude of Thessala in her secret activity condition us to see the scene, the midpoint sets the description apart from the plot and the adventures of Fenice and Cligés. The narrator's intervention also opposes his presentation of Thessala to that part which he edits out of his translation: the glorious conjoining of two empires. In this way Chrétien also makes the midpoint and what Thessala represents work for the enhancement of *clergie*, in distinct opposition to *chevalerie*, a distinction, we remember, already suggested in the Prologue. Consequently, the framework and inner workings of the narrative both work towards the same ends, a point which argues for an even stronger *conjointure* of the couple Chrétien and Thessala in their joint venture of putting together the story of Cligés.

Chrétien spoke, very appropriately, of his familiarity with Ovid's *Metamorphoses* in the Prologue. His own persona is metamorphosed in the person of Thessala, who serves to reveal the character of his invention, while, if the argument for the historical veracity of this account can be admitted, Chrétien serves in his clerkly fashion to translate into words the original genesis of the couple Fenice and Cligés which Thessala makes possible, and so brings to light her secret alternate identity as sorceress. The relationship of these two characters brings into play a duality in the way we designate the chronology of the genesis of Fenice and Cligés and the direction of the service appropriated to the narrative. The duality is repeated in the techniques of invention outlined by the description. The process that comprises *tranprer, mettre a foison, atranprer* and *destranprer* manifestly is one of introducing a number of imported foreign elements that are recombined in a pleasant way to be enjoyed by one person and benefited from by another, while the elements of the scene are informed by an intertextual context that itself results from the importation of a number of elements from outside this narrative's world. These are recombined, or conjoined, in new and intricate ways so as to cut or temper the force of the sources drawn from. The creative process described by the narration simultaneously reveals and renames poetically the fictional process of which it partakes. A look at other similar moments in *Cligés* will demonstrate that the midpoint's revelation is not an isolated phenomenon in this romance, but rather part of a *conjointure* of similar moments. They divert our attention away from the lives of the characters to what they represent, to what they reveal of the text, which in turn points to its reworking of other texts. These moments, then, serve to show that, though involved with the demonstration of the history of Cligés as well as with a literary history, the text makes use of both sides of this duality to focus attention back on itself.

Description and Translatio Studii*: Towards an Intertextual Reading*

Along with the couple Chrétien/Thessala, another couple emerges in the story of Fenice and Cligés. This couple is formed once again in part by Thessala—in this sense she can be seen as a kind of pivot for the pairing off of artisan figures—and Jehan. The presentation of Jehan and his introduction into the narrative closely resemble the techniques of the midpoint episode. He is a craftsman in the confidence of his master, and he helps the young lovers by means of two singular devices, Fenice's sepulchre and the tower. Both devices seem to be one thing while actually performing quite a different function. Both were made prior to their being deployed to an end different from the original one they were intended to serve. Conversely, Thessala's two potions were brewed for the unique purposes to which they are put. Fenice's sepulchre is real enough to fool the throng of mourners, but it is equipped inside for her comfort. It allows her to breathe while lying in the cemetery until Cligés rescues her. The second mausoleum, the tower, appears to be an ordinary dwelling, but proves to be instead quite extraordinary. Jehan takes Cligés on a tour of this out-of-the-way place in order to introduce him to the underground sanctum replete with palatial luxuries. Here is Jehan's place of retreat, here he exercises his craft in private. Jehan introduces himself and his recondite talents as he addresses Cligés. Thus, like Thessala, he describes his work to the one who will benefit from his ability to camouflage reality with artfully contrived appearances. Jehan's description of his tower is, then, pertinent as an extension of the revelation of Chrétien's art signified at the midpoint.

While Jehan explains his work to Cligés (ll. 5487-5570), we hear a concatenation of voices—Jehan's, the narrator's and Cligés'—a conflation of possibilities that were left separate in the Thessala example. Multi-levels, a guided tour and a return visit figure prominently in the description of Jehan's tower. First, we are told that the construction is situated south of, or below, the city in an out-of-the-way spot. Second, Jehan takes Cligés throughout the many-storied tower, upstairs and down. Third, we and Cligés are finally introduced to the hidden underground recesses of the tower. The rooms Fenice will eventually occupy are below that part of the tower that is readily apparent, on a deeper level within an interior spatial relationship. The description of Jehan's tower, like the description of Thessala's potion, occupies a narrative space that is to one side of the mainstream of events and that allows the skill of a secondary character, a servant, to shine. Similarly, the description marks a pause in the narrative, a digression on the poet-narrator's part. He chooses to set off this tower and its description in detail rather than have Cligés report briefly about it to Fenice, or rather than describe it as a background to Fenice's arrival. Instead, he describes it as something quite apart from the action, emphasizing Jehan's *san* and *painne* ("molt ot pené") in its construction as a revelation to Cligés; in counterdistinction to the potions, this artifact is fully explained to him before its narrative deployment.

The description of the potion at the midpoint of the romance, we saw, could be read in two ways, or on two levels of the poet-narrator's discourse, namely, as part of the plot and as a metaphor for the text's own process. This sort of alternate reading is also applicable to the tower description. The literal description of the tower rooms provides a similar mirror. These lower rooms perform two functions. They become relevant to the characters and their history when Fenice occupies them, and as well they are the place where Jehan works, where he invents. Just as the description of the tower, like that of the potion, could occupy one spot in the narrative, so in its metaphorical meaning the description shows the reader where Chrétien works, where he invents the artifices of romance narrative.

The entrance to the lower regions of the tower, where the secret and private making of art and of love takes place, is hidden to the naked eye. The door to the connecting staircase is hidden in a painted wall. Even when Jehan pauses in front and leans against it, Cligés discerns no *jointure* (ll. 5530-47), no specific place where the door and the painted wall come together. He cannot see how anyone could pass through without damaging the wall in some way, just as he cannot imagine how to gain access to the hidden lower regions where human creation occurs, without incurring damage, physical and otherwise, to his own beloved.

To enter in order to attain access to an inner sanctum or chamber of love without harming the exterior is an image that the reader has encountered once before in this romance. The impossible entrance to another world, crossed without apparent violence to an exterior structure, occurring in this last of Chrétien's metaphorical descriptions, stands in symmetrical relation to the arrow that passes through Alixandre's eye into his heart. (We recall that this image incorporated as well the metaphor of candlelight passing through a lantern, although the glass is not broken—an image traditionally used to symbolize the Incarnation. The sexual overtones continue to obtain.) Just as the door image is explained by a male character in lieu of the poet-narrator himself, so the arrow image is evoked by a male character in the initial description (ll. 687-745), where Alixandre in the midst of his *granz conplainte* explains to himself in a typical monologue as self-dialogue how he fell in love with Soredamor. Soredamor is likened to an arrow which Cupid, or Love, shot at the unsuspecting Alixandre; her beautiful image struck his eye without harming it or visibly wounding it, and then passed through this mirror to his heart, filling him with lovesickness.

An Ovidian cliché, a topic from the traditional romance love casuistry, is here extensively amplified. The first stage of the amplification develops the eye-to-heart imagery; there ensues the representation of the eye as the mirror of the heart, which leads to a meditation on the eye as the glass plate of a lantern in which the heart, like a burning candle, is placed. The development culminates in the lengthy metaphor of Soredamor and the arrow. Through this monologue/dialogue with himself, Alixandre analyzes and becomes fully aware of falling in love. The tirade begins the first love story of the romance, initiating both plot and descriptions. Here a figure of speech and an image of Soredamor are presented as literal explanations of a change in a character's psychology, leading to self-knowledge. The protagonist engages in a dialogue with himself such that the creator of the image of the eye struck by the arrow/love at first sight must explain its significance in a special event by both literal and figurative language.

In the description of the tower, a literal image—the painted wall—becomes something else: an entrance which is not harmed or broken when Cligés and Jehan pass through it to an inner sanctum where love is experienced. Even the rhyme words that express the essence of the dilemma— *trespasse/quasse*—recur in both descriptions (ll. 705-06, 5539-40, and

5547-48). Furthermore, each passage mirrors the other in a complex *conjointure*. The poet-narrator does not do the explaining, but instead has a male character, with whom the image originates, take on the task; also, the two passages occur in roughly similar places with respect to the proportions of the narrative, approximately one quarter of the way from the narrative limits, one occurring at the beginning of the romance, the other near the end. Whereas the first description elaborates a metaphorical description explained by the protagonist alone in a way that appears comical to the reader, the description of the tower presents fresh material and an image that is shared in its presentation by both the poet-narrator and the image-maker himself, so that something is revealed to the character in love, while something else is revealed to the reader, which is not the case with Alixandre's description (though critics have remarked on the conflation of voices of the character and the poet-narrator in this passage, perhaps a prelude to further developments). What was previously merely comical and diverting has now provided a methodology for description deepened and widened in scope when the technique is displayed for the last time. The method can finally be attributed to the poet-narrator's monologue, which, like Alixandre's, also functions as a dialogue, affording the reader an exegesis of the image in the text.

That the image, designed to afford entrance into a more intimate world, is a painting, full of colors—a motif also underscored in the Alixandre monologue (ll. 728-33)—illuminated and containing figures, makes the point about description as exegesis that much more explicit. Jehan leads Cligés to a painting, pauses there, even leans on it, before showing that it hides a door. Similarly, the narrator leads the reader to descriptions, then pauses to linger over them until he shows him that they afford a way into the deeper recesses of the text, to the secret places where he works and where the reader can find new delights. Just as Jehan insists that Cligés is dependent upon him to guide him through his house, and particularly to show him the way into the hidden places that are most precious, so the reader of Chrétien's romance is dependent upon the figure of the poet-narrator and his avatars in the text to point to the relevance of these descriptions and the more delightful places of the poem. The insistence on the guided tour, where the observer is, as it were, led by the hand, is not accidental. It points out that our perspective on the text, and on the descriptions in particular, must be that of the person who invented them. That we must not lose sight of it or of him as we procede through the rooms of his house is central.

One additional intertextual reference is appropriate to our interpretation of this description as a metaphor applicable to Chrétien's romance poetics. Geoffrey of Vinsauf's "comparison of poetic composition with architectural planning, analogous to Horace's comparison of the work of the poet and painter, is a commonplace before Geoffrey, and in a variety of contexts. Conrad of Hirsau likens Donatus' grammatical writings to the foundation of the house of learning upon which subsequent stories are built."[16] This commonplace metaphor argues, I think, for an interpretation of the tower description, which is the work of an architect and a painter, as a metaphorical commentary on poetic composition within the same tradition; it can be even more pertinently applied to the romance *Cligés* and, thus, viewed as a poetically conceived art of poetry, conceived, that is, through deed and example.

The Reading and the Misreading of Signs: The "Semiotics" of Cligés

One of the famous motifs of the Tristan legend is the single strand of golden blond hair carried by a swallow to Mark, who decides to marry the woman from whom it was removed, provided that she can be found. This vow prompts Tristan to seek her out and to bring her on the fateful voyage to her husband-to-be. Thomas apparently excludes this detail.[17] Chrétien puts it back into his text, but he introduces it through many twists and turns.

Soredamor, Gauvain's sister and lady-in-waiting to Guenevere, made a shirt out of fine white silk; she sewed the seams and attached the collar and cuffs with gold threads. She also wove into the stitching strands of her own golden blond hair together with the golden threads, as a test. She hopes to identify the knight who will notice this artifice, discern the comparison, detect the origin of the second thread and, by judging the two components simultaneously, prefer her naturally golden hair. Consequently, the shirt as shirt, though delicate and beautiful—sufficiently so as to be chosen by the Queen as a fitting gift to mark the occasion of Alixandre's being dubbed a knight by Arthur—is not interesting primarily as an example of the perfect *chemise* (*Cligés*, ll. 1139-75). These secondary characteristics, presented as only superficially primary, permit the garment to figure in the story, to take its place among the descriptions that tie the characters together. Just as the finest gift Guenevere could locate from among the contents of her coffers, though meant as a token of homage to *chevalerie*, finally plays a key role in the very different domain of love, so the text Chrétien "found" in the library at Beauvais—where he was presumably looking for his subject (*inventio*)—starts out as a salute to chivalrous ancestors, only to finish by serving quite a different purpose, the praise of *clergie*.

Alixandre flunks the test. He notices only the superficial elegance of the Queen's gift and fails to recognize its deeper significance for him. Only later, when the Queen recalls by chance that it was Soredamor who made the shirt, does this fact become important to him. She has Soredamor describe her handiwork to Alixandre, once it is clear that the two are in love. In this way the Queen becomes a reader of the signals of the shirt, though not through an original discovery. Rather, she reads through memory, through an accidentally perceived relationship, an intertextual one because what she recalls becomes functional in a new narrative context. In this instance the shirt serves to initiate a process of mediation whereby the slow, but nevertheless observant Guenevere, in two separate stages, prompts the young lovers to tie the knot. By doing so, the string of events the silk shirt triggers intersects with the equally famous *Tristan* motif of the golden strand.

When Guenevere notices the lovers turning pale before her, Alixandre wearing his new silk finery and Soredamor sitting shyly next to him, it dawns on her that they alternately blush and turn pale because they are in love. This recognition makes up for her previous failure to ascribe to love the same symptoms she noted before during the Channel crossing. Guenevere fails to read the *Tristan* intertext into the first episode; the audience, of course, cannot fail to seize the opportunity, since Chrétien repeats the pun on *l'amer, la mer* and *l'amer*. In this fashion, a *conjointure* of stellar *Tristan* motifs occurs wherein resemblances and what they mask have been dissociated and rearranged in order to show off their components and their roles in the composition, or "text-ure."

The audience, in a sense, also fails to pass Soredamor's test, or rather it is not given the opportunity to do so, since it never "sees" the shirt except through the explanatory description akin to the one Soredamor eventually gives to Alixandre, but which the audience never expressly hears. The narrator's description jumps the gun on what Soredamor will reveal and undercuts its possible significance for the audience, dissociating its reactions thereby from those of the principal characters. But the narrator's description parallels Soredamor's in another way, and justly preempts it, since it enables him to comment *par moz coverz* on his own creative devices in the suturing of the intertextual plays in his own text, so as to test those who gaze upon his handiwork, as received, perhaps, through the hands not of Guenevere, but of Marie de Champagne. In this way the seemingly gratuitous description of the shirt, performed, as it were, out of sequence, serves two purposes at once. It introduces an object that will act in conjunction with its mate, the cup bestowed by Arthur, to bring the first story to a close; and, by playing on *Tristan* patterns and motifs, it functions as a self-referential commentary on the unfolding poetic discourse.

Additional relationships to the *Tristan* are involved in the reworking of the strands of hair motif. These plays hinge on Chrétien's connecting the motif to a comparison: the metaphorical value of Iseut's hair—hair of spun gold—which is exploited quite literally through the metonymic comparison between the types of gold, one inferior, one superior. Comparison between the two objects made of gold(s) of differing qualities becomes a device whereby two levels of discourse are carried on simultaneously, thanks to disguise and thanks to an object functioning as a sign of something other than itself, that is, thanks to its semiotic and poetic value. The object in question can do these things since it has developed a secondary meaning by its role in a history—in a sequence of events lived by Tristan and Iseut, unbeknownst to Mark—that leads to the scene between Iseut and Tristan's messenger. In other words, a previous narrative context is introduced into a seemingly banal and unrelated context, where no other meaning for the object or the words spoken would rightfully be suspected unless the item is recalled and recognized in terms of its previous history. Consequently, the natural—or conventional—in *Tristan* can become a vehicle for staged artifice, for a hidden dialogue: the given scene depends on a built-in intertextuality in order to function successfully and completely. Its intertextuality seems to originate with the characters, although demonstrated consistently to the audience by the narrator and revealed only gradually to some of the characters and never to others, thus providing the romance with its dramatic irony. The drama of *Tristan* depends on both factors. Chrétien imitates this, while going it one better by transposing the audience's interest away from a character's reading of the object to the reading of the object in a dialogue between the reader and the poet-narrator, a level of reading that was omitted, or at least deliberately camouflaged, in the *Tristan*.

At the end of Thomas' poem, Kaherdin makes the trip from Brittany to Cornwall, from Tristan to Iseut, in order to fetch Iseut, who alone can minister to the dying Tristan. These circumstances invert, near the close of the narrative, those that brought about the beginning of the love triangle: here Iseut is accompanied away from her husband across a body of water to Tristan by the return to her of an object of gold that was originally hers. This inversion makes the *Cligés* scene that much more interesting, since it plays upon the original golden strand of hair. Kaherdin appears upon Tristan's instigation as a merchant who sells rich silks and the like at Mark's court (Thomas, Douce Fragment, ll. 1309-14). He gives the King a cup as a present and as a free sample of his wares. And he encourages the Queen to purchase a gold brooch (ibid., ll. 1409-21). In order to extol the merits of these ornaments, he pulls out his own ring so as to show, by comparison, the superiority of the gold worked into the brooch. But the ring is actually Iseut's own, the very one she gave Tristan when they parted. Upon seeing the ring, Iseut recognizes Kaherdin, discovers the plot and arranges secretly to make the return journey to Tristan. Once Iseut recalls an object out of its present context and in its former one, she sees through the disguise, the persona, of the individual addressing her, perceiving his more deeply pertinent identity for her. She then returns to the one who devised the disguise, to the one who introduced the device that triggered the intertextual reading of the scene.

Chrétien combined and inverted many elements in *Cligés*. First, the cup and the gold comparison no longer figure at the end of the story, but in the first part of the romance. They are no longer together; rather, they have been split up so as to figure in separate scenes that orient the two separate strands of the themes of *chevalerie* and *amour*: arms and love. They do not preface the *dénouement* of the romance and the death of the protagonists; instead, they serve to introduce the birth of its principal protagonist, Cligés himself. Second, Chrétien has borrowed the silks and the comparison of golds (which functioned merely as props, or distractions, in the *Tristan* setting) and made of them integral parts of the objects he describes. He also transposes the technique of extolling the merits of the object, not by invoking a comparison that camouflages, as in the *Tristan* model, but in order to point out a comparison that itself was artfully camouflaged and, consequently, difficult to see. It is as if the givens that went into the staging of this penultimate *Tristan* scene are rendered into abstractions in such a way that they operate metaphorically and intertextually with reference to the creative processes of that particular scene. What was metonymic and compared in the one scene served to introduce a third function, the alternate identity, or semiotic function, of the ring. I repeat: metonymy in the *Tristan* example serves as a camouflage, as a vehicle for the introduction of functional intertextuality and for the reorientation of Iseut's reading of the signs placed before her. The second scene, the one which concerns the shirt in *Cligés*, which is not so clearly metonymic and blatantly comparative, takes on a metaphorical value when finally revealed as such. The scene uses the intertext of *Tristan*, borrowing and blending motifs that were originally distinct there, and but latently metonymic, in order to create a new kind of intertextuality—a translation of itself by means of this digression into a description read, finally, as metaphor.

What is more, the effect, in a *Tristan* of Thomas or Béroul, of this kind of scene is that the reader is propelled into the workings of these art objects as signs operating among certain characters and then, in turn, into the effects of such workings on the outcome of the plot. In *Cligés* this obvious interest focused upon by the *Tristan* scenes of the Kaherdin-Iseut sort quite blatantly does *not* work when the characters try them out, and, furthermore, they have virtually no consequences for the outcome of the plot.

However, what is camouflaged in another respect in the *Tristan* scene outlined above is the author's role in constructing the semiotic operations on the level of the plot. The related *Cligés* scene serves to unmask this indifference or apparent irresponsibility in favor of some kind of involvement on the part of the reader in a narrative that masquerades as historiography. Chrétien also focuses his scenes on precious objects of well-wrought craftsmanship and describes them in a way that attracts the reader's attention away from the possible semiotic value these objects have for the protagonists and their entanglements, and towards the semiotic value they hold for a dialogue between the author—or, more exactly, the poet-narrator—and the reader.

In the Kaherdin-Iseut scene of Thomas' poem, the audience witnesses Tristan planning the scene as he invents and directs the characters, their stage props and their actions; Kaherdin will stand in for Tristan, acting like him and for him by meeting Iseut in the open, but in disguise. In *Cligés* Soredamor functions as a stand-in for, or as a transposed projection of, the poet-narrator, acting for him and like him in the romance as she devises the text of the shirt. The shirt's natural, or obvious, meaning is accepted by Alixandre just as Mark accepts the comparison of the ring and the brooch at face value. The alternate connotation, the device as sign, is apprehended by Iseut, on the one hand, and by the audience, on the other; the audience, like Iseut, is brought back to the one who devised the system initially, that is, to Tristan in Thomas and to the poet-narrator, or "Crestïens," in *Cligés*. In this fashion Chrétien manages to provide in his description both narrative and commentary simultaneously.

Chrétien is able to communicate in this dual manner in part because the use to which he puts description has a history similar to that which he developed in his first romance, *Erec et Enide*. An explicit intertextual example is afforded there in the description of the saddle given to Enide after she and her husband have become reconciled (ll. 5289-5305). The saddle portrays, in ivory and gold (the same color motif as in Soredamor's shirt, we recall), the exemplary figures of Dido and Aeneas on one side, and, presumably, on the other it depicts the triumph of Lavinia and the hero.[18] The twelfth-century *Roman d'Eneas* is a tripartite romance, organized around three female characters, Dido, Camille and Lavine. I subscribe to the argument that Enide represents in her development a composite of these three women.[19] By the time we see her seated on the elaborate saddle atop her new palfrey, she has already progressed from a situation reminiscent of Dido's when, in the first third of the text, the love, or *joie*, she and Erec enjoy together poses a threat to their reputations. But Erec does not deceive or abandon Enide. They proceed together into the second section of the romance to *avantures*. In this section *Enide* rides first into danger.

She does battle within herself, deciding over and over again whether to disobey her husband's strictures of imposed silence as punishment—or as a possible challenge—or to break her silence, choosing each time to speak out and thereby to protect her husband. In the last two encounters in this middle section Enide even becomes somewhat involved in the actual battles, picking up the lance as Erec takes up his shield when they rush into the middle of the Count of Limors' court after Erec revives, or running up to the as yet unrecognized Guivret after Erec faints from his wounds, tugging at the attacker's reins and defending her companion both physically and verbally. In these ways Enide reflects the kind of zeal in battle for which her counterpart, the *bellatrix* Camille, was famous in the *Eneas*. Lastly, the third and last section of the romance, which begins with the Joie de la Cort, redeems a couple in which the wife is compared explicitly to Lavine in the *Eneas* (*Erec et Enide*, ll. 5840-43), an encounter which is followed by the coronation. In the saddle description the evocation of the Dido and Lavine episodes of the *Eneas* serves to call our attention directly to the reworking of that romance and, specifically, of the three women in the one character who passes through three important stages of development in Chrétien's poem. Camille, who is not mentioned at the last note of the middle section, is, nevertheless, present by implication; she comes to mind as we see Enide astride the palfrey that is a marvelous animal decorated exotically, similar to the horse in the magnificent description of Camille as she enters the *Eneas* poem on her steed.

This explicit intertextual reference emblematizes the various stages through which the development of the romance's single couple takes place, introducing an intertextual note into the narrative—once more in a kind of digression—just as the workmanship of the saddle introduces another kind of artistry, of a representational sort, into its display. But the saddle description in *Erec et Enide* affords a commentary on the themes, characterizations and events narrated. A final description in that romance proceeds further along these lines before this particular function to which description is put in Chrétien's romances is amplified upon in *Cligés*.

The feast at Erec and Enide's coronation is so sumptuous and so plentiful that it defies description. Nevertheless, the narrator tells us he will attempt *folie* and describe at least a part of the festivities (ll. 6645-50). This remark immediately prefaces Chrétien's description of the two identical ivory thrones which Erec and Enide will occupy at the moment of their coronation (ll. 6651-70). Then he presents us with the challenge to look the thrones over in order to tell them apart. This recalls another challenge, the one, pronounced explicitly to a second-person interlocutor as well, by Jehan when he dares Cligés to seek as best he can for an entrance to the underground chambers of the tower. Chrétien praises the craftsman of the two folding stools for his ingenuity and cleverness, no doubt reflecting upon his own similar qualities as he contrives this subtle description. The thrones are unique and draw the narrator's praise because they are identical, intricately carved and made once again of precious gold and fine ivory. The observer would be incapable of telling them apart; similarly, Erec and Enide both possess qualities such that nothing of beauty or wisdom present in the one is lacking in the other. It is fitting that such a couple should occupy such splendid seats. But it is also fitting that the thrones should be designed for use on this day, since in the first third of the romance the narrator described Enide as a mirror into which Erec looks, so that by implication the two would appear to be the identical reflection of one another (ll. 437-41). Also, we recall, he had described the couple on their way to Arthur's court after the sparrow-hawk episode in the following manner:

> molt estoient igal et per
> de corteisie et de biauté
> et de grant debonereté.
> Si estoient d'une meniere,
> d'unes mors et d'une matiere,
> que nus qui le voir volsist dire
> n'an poïst le meillor eslire
> ne le plus bel ne le plus sage.
> Molt estoient d'igal corage
> et molt avenoient ansanble;
> li uns a l'autre son cuer anble;
> onques deus si beles ymages
> n'asanbla lois ne mariages.
> (ll. 1484-96)

(they were indeed equal and on a par with one another in courtliness, beauty and graciousness. They were of one kind, of one nature and of the same substance, so much so that anyone who would want to tell the truth could not choose the better of the two or the more handsome or the wiser. They were indeed of the same disposition and went well together. Each one steals the other's heart away. Never were two such pretty pictures ever joined together by religion or marriage.)

The description of the throne, associated with the couple through metonymy, echoes the description of them as they ride away from Enide's home every bit as much as the scene of Erec's revival "ausi come hom qui s'esvoille" (l. 4817) (just like a man who awakens) directly echoes his first awakening to the sound of Enide's voice ("de la parole s'esveilla" [l. 2507] [he awoke at her words]), or as the description of Jehan's doorway echoes Alixandre's description of the eye struck by the arrow of love. The portrayal of the couple, which used language fit for the description of pictures or statues (*ymages*), has now been transferred to portray two identical art objects, applying the common denominator first to what has been created by Nature and then to what has been forged by art.

Furthermore, when Enide was initially presented as the product of Nature's handiwork, the narrator explained how Nature marveled at the perfect exemplar she had fashioned. Enide is an original. Nature is incapable, try as she might, of reproducing what she fashioned so well that one time. Interestingly, what Nature is incapable of, art can in part supply. Nature cannot replicate her triumph, whereas the clever artisan who carved the two ivory thrones was capable of duplicating his work exactly in order to afford ultimately, through the mediators Arthur and Guenevere, a vehicle, and a place of celebration and display, for the perfectly matched pair of lovers and rulers.

Chrétien, before launching into this presentation of the thrones, does utter the word *descrivre* (l. 6646), a term he repeats before describing Erec's marvelous cloak or robe (l. 6679). According to Lewis and Short,[20] in Classical Latin the term *describo*, besides the obvious meaning we still ascribe to the word, also meant, and had as its first meaning, "*to copy off, transcribe* any thing from an original (freq. in Cicero)[21] . . . so, *to write down, write out* . . . in carved letters . . . and far more frequently, II. *To sketch off, to describe in painting, writing*, etc." The meaning of "to copy off from an original" is particularly revealing since Chrétien's narrator is engaged in describing something that is itself a copy of an original, displayed with the original so that the copy and the example cannot be told apart. It is even more interesting that the chairs are carved not in letters, but in animal figures, and that the narrator is also delineating something in writing. In other words, all three definitions are present at once. Could we understand the notion of description, defined as the activity of rewriting, of writing again in a new place, as also the activity Chrétien is engaged in both in *Erec et Enide* and in *Cligés*, namely, the reworking of an original text, including the reworking—in a written, textual form—of a different passage of his own text, in the way that the artisan has duplicated his own artifact? In this case, the description of the thrones, which in its own way is redoing, or rewriting, the original description of the couple (ll. 1484-96), would be the first place in Chrétien's *œuvre* where a description of an object, in the usual sense of the word, is also a place where a reworking of a related passage takes place and where a commentary on the procedure the romance is employing surfaces even while the commentary is taking place. Such an application of description is still appropriate in yet another dimension when it occurs for the first time in the throne description, since in the high Middle Ages carved thrones that incorporated scenes of some sort were apparently intended to be used not as real seats, but rather to display books, notably the Gospels or the Bible.[22] In *Erec et Enide*, if the description of the thrones is understood as a reworking—as a copy—and as a commentary on the procedure of reworking a previous text so that both texts are placed side by side for comparison in the reader's mind, then they can be seen, in the light of the tradition of art history, as a fitting locus of display not only for Erec and Enide the characters, but for *Erec et Enide* the book as well.[23]

In the *Cligés* example the intertextuality is less obvious than the saddle description in *Erec et Enide*. Names are not mentioned, the story of *Tristan* is not retold, not even briefly, though *Tristan* motifs decidedly are everywhere present. However, the commentary in the shirt's description/digression on workmanship in the art of romance is like the description of the thrones. Chrétien can proceed with this sort of description-metaphor in *Cligés* and amplify upon it to the point where it becomes a constant in the text, because in *Erec et Enide* he has prepared his audience for description as intertextual commentary. It is first applied to another text and then to his own, always entirely anchored within the confines of the narrative.

The description of the *chemise*, understood in the context of self-referential commentary, begins a pattern of similar descriptions to which the audience becomes progressively more attuned, thus assuring a new orientation in its reaction to the poet-narrator's discourse. The characters in *Cligés* try at times to duplicate similar arrangements; they try to emulate the brilliant deceptions of a Tristan and an Iseut, but their efforts usually backfire or are at least less than totally successful. Alixandre, for example, gains admittance into the traitor's castle by disguising himself as one of the enemy. His ruse succeeds; he defeats the enemy, taking them by surprise, and so wins back Windsor Castle for Arthur. However, he succeeds at the expense of a fair amount of grief and despair on the part of his companions and in particular on the part of his lady love, Soredamor. They have not been informed of his plan and, therefore, do not read the signs of deception properly, any differently or any more correctly than those who are deliberately deceived. Similarly, Fenice pretends to be dead and fools her husband and the entire court, so that she might eventually escape to a secret hide-away with her lover, but not without first fooling him as well. Fenice and Thessala somehow overlook informing Cligés about the second potion—or the first one, for that matter—for some time (ll. 6139-43). Therefore, he, too, can read the signs of feigned death, of disguise, in only one way. Cligés believes Fenice to be truly beyond his grasp and is on the verge of a *Pyramus and Thisbe* death scene from which he is spared only in the nick of time.

The backfiring of Fenice's plan is brought about by the interference of a third party, in fact by a trio of third parties who read the signs *correctly*, who are aware of the ruse of duping one's husband by playing dead. Fenice's plan comes close to utter failure when she and Cligés almost suffer the tragic fate of Tristan and Iseut, albeit played out in reverse with Fenice at death's door and Cligés ready to expire over her corpse, because three learned doctors of Salerno stroll unexpectedly onto the scene. Because they perceive the scene intertextually when it is retold to them *as a narrative* by the townspeople, they immediately grasp the double significance of the signs before them. Their interpretation serves to underscore rather amusingly the way the romance calls attention to itself at every turn in the mosaic-like composition it derived from various textual sources like the *Tristan*. But this exercise of intertextual reading is clearly performed within the story—not, then, as a digression, but rather as an integral part of the plot. The kind of activity so far suited to the system of commentary communicated by the poet-narrator to the audience that takes place on a level distinct from narrative events is with this episode located right at the heart of the romance. The metalanguage that operated so well between Tristan and Iseut, and which was transferred from their counterparts in *Cligés* in order to be conferred on the dialogue between poet-narrator and audience, has now, with the doctors of Salerno episode, been restored to work among characters, but only accidentally and not between the right ones.

If the audience should succumb to the fictional argument that Chrétien is transmitting an historical account concerning the Greek grand-nephew of Arthur, then the Salerno doctors' intertextual exercise, performed, of course, with the story of Solomon's wife as intertext, is history; on the other hand, such a reading practice constitutes the underpinnings of Chrétien's fiction. Whereas Tristan's staging of events—which deliberately calls for intertextual perceptions—is portrayed as historical fact and, therefore, as authorization of the document that bears witness to the couple, a similar application of causality in *Cligés*, though apparently practiced, leads to absurdities. Fenice, in trying to avoid a repetition of Iseut's example (ll. 3105-23), thereby basing her conduct on intertextual decisions of her own, does not escape becoming a notorious example in her own right. The narrator informs the audience, at the close of his tale, that as a result of her subterfuge and its eventual coming to light, forever after—even, presumably, up to the present day of Chrétien's writing—emperors of Constantinople have kept close watch over their wives, making of them prisoners guarded by eunuchs. An exotic, but bizarre custom is, as it were, explained by this lengthy romance, apparently as if it were the point of the whole story, the way an explanation of the origin of the flower seems to be the point of Ovid's presentation of Narcissus. It would seem that the text of *Cligés* itself is authorized and validated by Fenice's decision and example, and is, therefore, based in turn on the example of Tristan and Iseut—thus providing us with a third lineage for Cligés!—since her story has been told and kept alive through the ages, presumably in texts like the one Chrétien "found" at Beauvais and which he "translates" for us. Chrétien imitates the pattern that underlies the verisimilitude of a *Tristan*, as portrayed, for example, by Béroul, in imitation of epic and hagiography, in a way that makes that delicately laid plan look foolish in a romance, though, to be sure, interesting and amusing as a contrivance. The principle of an intertextual reading is not, on the other hand, portrayed as a principle of authorization when we find it in the central episode. Rather, this principle that has controlled the reader up to this point finds a blatant confirmation at the same time that it affords a source of comedy when transposed from a technique of composition to a narrative event.

There continues to be, therefore, a structural inversion in *Cligés* of the *Tristan* events, inclusive of the principles that generate the latter text. This inversion is designed in such a way as to confuse what is seemingly natural, but false with what is artificial, but real. Perhaps the most striking example of this reversal is suggested by Anthime Fourrier's presentation of the genuinely historical events of the twelfth century that Chrétien apparently drew upon in his text for purposes of parody (*Le Courant*, ch. 2). Unlike the *Tristan*, which portrays romance fiction as history, *Cligés* draws upon historical events, transforming them into fictional material.

The *Tristan*, essentially constructed of multiple episodes, re-performs its principles of deception in virtually every scene. It recalls itself by re-performing these patterns of textual generation, and specifically by reechoing previous scenes and motifs in new settings (like the retelling of the couple's story, the ring, Husdent, meetings, bed scenes, spying scenes, and the like). The text is constantly repeating itself, in other words, deriving a margin of verisimilitude from repetition and reenactment not of a paradigm or model extraneous to it, but of itself. The *Tristan*, therefore, applies the principles of reenactment and variation within a tradition that allows epic and hagiography to evoke belief in the audience, and it has applied them to romance material, to a tangential episode in the history of Arthur and the kings of Britain. The attributes of the power of genres which serve exterior truths to a genre that serves an interior or poetic truth[24] is the genius of the *Tristan*.

Chrétien's *Cligés* has demonstrated the *Tristan*'s ability to cloak artifice under the cover of conventionality. Ultimately, the *Cligés* transforms the creative process of intertextuality as it applied in the *Tristan* so that the text no longer echoes or repeats itself, but rather translates itself within the context of a canon of texts including the *Tristan*. It thus initiates a novel dialogue of intertextual commentary, claiming, in opposition to the *Tristan* example (which it has absorbed and transposed), this very commentary as a new path for subsequent romance composition.

Closing Remarks

My discussion of the Prologue to *Cligés* included an excursus into Ovid's story of Arachne and Pallas. The structural transpositions of texts exterior to *Cligés*—notably the *Tristan* intertext—described in the last four sections have served, I hope, to justify this departure.

Though not specifically cited by Chrétien in the list of titles that initiates the Prologne, "Arachne" suggested itself since that story introduced the two episodes from Ovid's *Metamorphoses* that themselves helped introduce *Cligés* to us. Consequently, it constitutes an allusion by means of contiguity and by structural analogy. Once investigated, it appears to offer a paradigm of possible narrative uses to which description can be put.

Though completed in competition, the Ovidian tapestries complement one another in that each presents a theme in counterpoint to the other. Similarly, *Cligés* and *Tristan*, displaying as they do inverted images of each other, might also be viewed as complementary patterns of romance narrative also woven—at least on Chrétien's part—in a spirit of competition. Chrétien might be compared to both rivals depicted in Ovid's account. On the one hand, like Arachne's work, his narrative mocks those in power as well as those successful poets who preceded him. On the other hand, though perhaps embarrassed by the "shameful truths" contained in the *Tristan*, or though possibly angered to a degree by the sly manipulation of the craft of fiction achieved by a rival poet, Chrétien, like Pallas, assures in his metamorphosis of the *Tristan* model that it and his competitive response to it will never be forgotten.

Just as the weavers themselves reenact a scene similar to the ones developing in the tapestries they produce, so a similar, though, of course, inverted, case ensues in the medieval work. The stories of Alixandre and Soredamor, of Cligés and Fenice, recall the two halves of the *Tristan* narrative, whereas the artifacts which appear in them multiply and/or separate elements from the original. In addition, there was forged a chain of mirror images from these pictures of selected events from ancient history. Each representation, in turn, served as material to illustrate the circumstances of each artificer in succession: from event to pictorial weaving to words of description. Each stage progressively fuses events that once were separate. Each of the tapestries depicts a group of events; each picture forms part of a diptych which holds the two groups in one moment of juxtaposition. It is the narrative which describes the juxtaposition and verbalizes the simultaneity as it also combines the two individual themes in its single presentation of the two rivals in one instance of competition. Each successive reworking of a previous drama serves, on the one hand, to recall the originator of the event—hero, weaver and narrator—and, on the other, to call attention to the medium that recreates that event: weaving, description, poetry.

Cligés imitates this chain by analogy. The objects devised to further its story summon up the devices in the *Tristan* model. Meanwhile, they underscore the descriptive devices of its own narration, so that the romance progresses from the objects that recall various *Tristan* motifs to their description and then to what these descriptions reflect of the poet's art. In addition, the trajectory of the romance also passes from fiction as history (the Béroul model, for example) to history as fiction (the story of Cligés) to the history of (a) romance fiction (the poetic commentary).

The transformation of Pallas from goddess to old-woman weaver and back again, and the metamorphosis of Arachne from artificial to natural weaver (maiden to spider), find their respective counterparts in the transformation undergone by Chrétien from the poet-narrator of the Prologue to those artificers who take part in the drama of the narrative, and in the lovers who at times play at Tristan-like disguises before finally reverting to their original roles.

The self-conscious poetic treatment of mythology as fiction in the *Metamorphoses* associated a number of disparate tales in one book, itself one in a group of books displaying poetic invention. Facets of this technique have found their way into Chrétien's *Cligés*. As its poet-narrator promised us, he found ways to illustrate the importance of books—specifically of *Erec et Enide*, *Tristan* and Ovidian tales—and then that of their intertextual weaving into a new book which, also through associations and by means of a chain of poetic transformations, offers another story of invention, of poetic invention in Old French romance.

Matilda Tomaryn Bruckner

Le Chevalier de la Charrette (*Lancelot*)

Prologue

In the very opening statement, the first sentence of his thirty-line Prologue, Chrétien has not only aligned his work with a whole literary tradition; he has introduced in essence all the problems that have for centuries enticed readers and critics of the *Chevalier de la Charrette*. It will take more than a single sentence to unravel those issues here and show how Chrétien uses the conventional rhetoric of prologues to develop his own particular introduction to the story of Lancelot and Guenevere.

All of Chrétien's prologues give ample evidence of his training in the use of *exordium* topics, the recommended formulas for beginning a literary work. His effort to "capture our goodwill" (*captatio benevolentiæ*) is two-pronged: while citing Marie de Champagne's commission as his "reason for writing" (*causa scribendi*), he at the same time exploits the humility topic to describe his own attentive service to her wishes. Both these topics are elaborated as the Prologue develops. But before pursuing their specific content, we should evaluate their use as a commentary on Chrétien's literary project.

The topics of the Prologue signal from the very start the conventional "agreements" shared by author and public. While all medieval literature operates within a traditional context that emphasizes conventionality, repetitions and variations in romance are particularly self-conscious. They signal explicitly its status as a collection of conventions to be (re)invented by the particular combinations of a given romance. Chrétien thus establishes his credentials for the courtly public—a public already alerted to romance potentials—by introducing recognizable elements: his choice of topics puts the *Chevalier de la Charrette* into a general framework that points, on the one hand, to other literary texts (e.g., contemporary romances) and, on the other, to an historical audience, the commissioners and consumers of courtly romances. Moreover, Chrétien's use of conventions inevitably marks his own text as the same as others and yet quite different, his own version of a common store. That difference already appears implicitly in l. 5, when Chrétien describes his service by negation: it will be accomplished with no flattery. A gap appears between himself and other writers, and we begin to suspect that others may have tarnished their literary service with flattery—of a sort that becomes immediately clear, as Chrétien elaborates the point with two examples:

> mes tex s'an poïst antremetre
> qui li volsist losenge metre,
> si deïst, et jel tesmoignasse,
> que ce est la dame qui passe
> totes celes qui sont vivanz,
> si con li funs passe les vanz
> qui vante en mai ou en avril.
> Par foi, je ne sui mie cil
> qui vuelle losangier sa dame;
> dirai je: "Tant com une jame
> vaut de pailes et de sardines,
> vaut la contesse de reïnes?"[1]
> Naie voir; je n'en dirai rien.
> (ll. 7-19)

(but another might undertake it who would like to flatter her. He would say—and I would stand witness for it—that she is the lady who surpasses all others living, just as the zephyr which blows in May or April surpasses all winds. Upon my honor, I am not at all he who would like to flatter his lady. Would I say: "The Countess is worth as many queens as a diamond is worth pearls and sards"? No truly, I'll say nothing of the kind.)

Chrétien makes reference here to another staple of prologue-writing: praise of one's patron(ess). He himself will begin *Perceval* with a long encomium of Philippe de Flandre as exemplifying the virtue of charity more perfectly than Alexander; other authors sing the praises of their benefactors with similar paeans. Hyperbole will ever be in the mouths of those who praise—and if one hyperbole is good, surely two are better. Chrétien's doubling thus illustrates how well he has mastered the techniques. He knows ("jel tesmoignasse") what others say and knows how to say it as well. Yet his doubling is more complex than simple repetition: he gives two examples only to demonstrate that he could do what others do—but he will not stoop to such flattery. Three times he qualifies that other approach as *losenge* (ll. 6, 8, 15); three times he insists on his own difference with all the force of his first-person voice, introduced in the negative or interrogative modes (ll. 14, 16, 19). All this self-conscious artfulness operates as a general reference—in reverse—to the common literary practice: Chrétien imitates the way someone else would flatter his lady—only to fault the other poet!

Chrétien's wit, however, does not stop there. The scorn turned on others ultimately catches up with him. He would not care to flatter his lady with such hyperbole, and yet "s'il est voirs maleoit gré mien" (l. 20) (it is true in spite of me). With this verse a whole new perspective opens: Chrétien's charges against flattery have previously implied a gap between reality and hyperbole—a gap into which his own service will rightly (self-righteously?) not fall. Now he is forced to admit in spite of himself—thus he emphasizes the paradoxical—that hyperbole does in this case coincide with truth. He has, moreover, phrased his subtle about-face in such a way as to play with the audience's ability to recognize within the general references to literary convention a possible gibe at another romancer's work. Chrétien's contemporary, Gautier d'Arras, begins his romance *Ille et Galeron* by praising his patroness Beatrix with a whole string of hyperboles.[2] Chrétien may very well have used Gautier's Prologue as the target of his humorous criticism, even inverting Gautier's "Et si est voirs si com je quit" (l. 88) (And it is certainly true as I believe it to be) to come up with his own paradoxical twist.[3] Chrétien's facetious play focuses here on a serious problem of romance: how can he say what others say (say, indeed, what Gautier said, if we consider the reference intentional and/or recognize it), how can he, in other words, observe the conventions of his medium and still say the truth?

Chrétien returns to this problem later when his narrator describes how difficult it is to speak the truth when that truth appears neither true nor credible. He expects to be taken for a liar or a fool when he tells us that Lancelot would not accept a whole market's worth of goods if it meant not finding the strands of golden hair he has discovered on Guenevere's comb, hair the brightness of which surpasses that of refined gold, just as the most beautiful day of summer outshines the night (ll. 1480-94). The obstacle to truth here as before is a rhetorical one. When confronted by a situation so extraordinary, the narrator needs hyperbole to speak truly. The accumulation of hyperboles brought into play (cf. the doubling of examples in the Prologue) suggests, in fact, a narrator easily seduced by the charms of his rhetorical tools, eager to display his art. Yet he clearly knows the dangers posed by hyperbole: the charges of flattery, the mistrust that grows when art appears mere artifice, deliberately removed from the reality behind it by hyperbolic distance. Briefly in the Prologue, more extensively elsewhere in the romance, the narrator introduces the question of truth, as if to anticipate and disarm our accusations: "My words only appear to lie because others have said the same thing or because reality is indescribable in its extreme forms. So believe my story: it is true."

But can we be sure Chrétien would like us to be completely persuaded? His irony, the playfulness of his wit, may undercut credibility. Are we not left with a sense of the problematic? The ambiguity of Chrétien's hyperbole makes his text perplexing, forces us to ask questions about truth and the appearances of truth. His rhetorical devices work as a strategy designed to make us interpret: the romance public cannot simply receive his story with passive ears;[4] it must attend to what the narrator reports, evaluating what it is told according to the way it is being narrated.

Having thus been put on our guard, we may return to Chrétien's opening remarks describing the relationship of patroness, author and work:

> Mes tant dirai ge que mialz oevre
> ses comandemanz an cest oevre
> que sans ne painne que g'i mete.
> Del *Chevalier de la Charrete*
> comance Crestïens son livre;
> matiere et san li done et livre
> la contesse, et il s'antremet
> de panser, que gueres n'i met
> fors sa painne et s'antancïon.
> (ll. 21-29)

(But this much I will say: her commandment works more effectively in this work than any sense or effort that I put into it. Chrétien begins his book on the *Knight of the Cart*. The Countess gives him matter and sense, and he undertakes to put them together, scarcely contributing anything except his effort and his intention.)

With these verses we reach one of the most controversial problems in *Charrette* criticism: what exactly does Chrétien mean when he attributes *matiere* and *san* to the Countess, *sans*, *painne* and *antancïon* to himself? One of the major functions served by romance prologues is the establishment of a text's authority by stating who authorizes or guarantees the truth of the work at hand. Chrétien furnishes here a number of guarantors for his romance: first he names the Countess of Champagne and gives her major responsibility for the project. Not only has she commissioned the poet's work, but she has also given him "matiere et san." Moreover, her contribution is more effective than the poet's own "sans ne painne." We can discern in these remarks how cleverly Chrétien has combined two exordial topics already evoked separately in his opening sentence, while at the same time referring obliquely to a third, the "humility" topic suggested by his service to Marie. This is now elaborated by his self-effacement before her command. Twice (ll. 21-23, 26-29) Chrétien chooses constructions that place Marie's contributions first and diminish his own ("mialz . . . que," "gueres . . . fors").

Yet if we consider the preceding dazzling display of hyperbolic praise, if we remember how ambiguously Chrétien played there with rhetoric and commonplaces, we may wonder just how seriously we should take his self-effacement—especially when the third topic touched on almost by inversion in l. 23 enjoins writers not to hide their light under a bushel: they are morally obliged to share their faculties and information with others.[5] Perhaps even more significantly, Chrétien gives two more authorities for his work, prominently displayed in the midst of his humble disavowals: "Del *Chevalier de la Charrete* / comance Crestïens son livre" (ll. 24-25). The narrational *je* is here identified and, in a sense, authenticated by the author's name. Later, in the Epilogue, Godefroi de Leigni will refer to Chrétien in almost the same words—"Crestïen, qui le comança" (l. 7107) (Chrétien, who began it)—to authorize his own continuation (an issue to be explored shortly). Having named himself, the author then repeats the content of ll. 21-25 in the variation of ll. 26-29: *je* has become *il*, paradoxically the "less personal" pronoun guarantees more. Though the third-person pronoun speaks to us less directly, from a greater distance than *je*, it confirms by objectifying.[6] That objectification puts author and work on the same plane: "son livre," his book, has a name, too, offered in conjunction with the author's own. His name is familiar to us, from earlier romances, notably *Erec, Cligés* and the entire list of books in the *Cligés* Prologue. In this conjunction of names in the *Charrette*, we may discern a note of pride not entirely in keeping with the self-effacing tone elsewhere in the Prologue. Finally, the third authority is the text itself. Written down, made into an object that can be passed on, the book represents the surest guarantee of historical continuity. As such, it authorizes truth and furnishes the means of transmitting it.[7] Furthermore, the Prologue promises quite explicitly to speak the truth: "s'est il voirs maleoit gré mien." Of course, Chrétien has already suggested how difficult it is to speak truthfully. His title indicates that the difficulty extends with equal force to praising one's patroness and to telling a story about Lancelot. Since knights are not normally associated with carts, such a paradoxical association promises much of the surprising and the unexpected—which, in turn, will raise many a question about the truth(s) to be associated with the *Chevalier de la Charrette*.

The way in which a romance establishes its authority may also furnish hints about how to read it. In order to pursue this possibility, we must return to those troubling terms Chrétien uses to describe his own and Marie's contributions. *Matiere* itself causes little difficulty: it refers to Chrétien's source(s), a story handed down by tradition—possibly a Celtic tale about the kidnapping of Guenhuhar, though scholars also argue for locating his source(s) in the classical and/or medieval Latin tradition.[8] But difficulties enough crop up as soon as we pass on to the second gift from Marie: what does *san* (l. 26) signify, especially in combination with *matiere*, and how does it relate to the poet's own *sans* (l. 23)? Though the four manuscripts containing the *Charrette* Prologue give us little help in unscrambling these two terms (*san, sen* and *sens* appear indiscriminately in them), their etymology and twelfth-century usage suggest that Chrétien was playing off against each other two related, but not quite synonymous terms: *sans* of l. 23 comes from the Latin *sensus* and generally means "understanding," "sense," "good sense"; *san* of l. 26 evolves from the Frankish **sin* (direction) and suggests the organizing idea of the romance.[9] While the validity of the etymological distinction has recently been put into question,[10] the possible play of different meanings for *san* and *sans* remains well established and of particular significance to this study. Sense and direction: those two fields of meaning are clearly marked out in twelfth-century usage, and yet they tend to merge at the same time, since both terms are frequently used as synonyms. Etymology can help us begin to understand the range of possibilities in Chrétien's usage, but it does not necessarily give us the "exact" sense used in a given context. Interpretation enters into the process of defining, once we try to follow the particularities of Chrétien's play. If Chrétien's *sans* (l. 23) seems fairly clearly to describe the author's own faculty for understanding, the combination of *matiere* and *san* in l. 26 suggests, rather, a distinction between a story and its interpretation.[11] Since Chrétien does not follow the model of fable or *fabliau*, genres where the moral is explicitly drawn out from the story, we are left to wonder what Marie's *san* may have been. This means that we must determine what effect the distinction of roles between patroness and poet has on our reading of the romance. Is Chrétien shackled by Marie's *san*, or does his own understanding lead to an interpretation of Marie's *matiere et san*?

Jean Frappier takes seriously the role attributed by Chrétien to the Countess. There is a change in tone at l. 21: Chrétien has finished his witty galantries and now passes on to objective information; though his compliments continue, we should recognize the historical truth behind the conventional appearance.[12] The quest for historical truth then leads Frappier (along with many others) to Andreas Capellanus' *De Amore*. There the Countess of Champagne is said to decide questions regarding courtly love. The most celebrated decision concerns the incompatibility of love and marriage.[13] Marie's *san* is, accordingly, interpreted as an apology for adulterous courtly love. But if this represents Marie's view on marriage and love, a further problem presents itself: Chrétien is generally seen as an apologist for love *in* marriage, as the plots of *Erec et Enide* and *Yvain* seem to suggest. If Marie commissioned Chrétien to write a poem on adulterous love, then the poet must have been unhappy with the subject assigned—hence Chrétien's abandonment of the poem's conclusion to Godefroi de Leigni. Even those critics who do not see Chrétien "travaillant la mort dans l'âme," in Frappier's expressive phrase,[14] tend to interpret the "unfinished" state of the *Charrette* as an expression of Chrétien's reluctance to endorse Marie's *san*, despite his pleasure in the creative work itself.[15]

Unfortunately, the problems of truth and perspective which we have already discovered operating within the romance also apply to their references outside the literary text. The traditional series of explanations about Chrétien's and Marie's intentions no longer seems assured once the historical objectivity of *De Amore* has been undermined. This is precisely what the most recent scholarship on Andreas seems to indicate. The treatise is properly understood, I believe, in an ironic perspective: the choice of Latin instead of the *romanz* of Marie's court reflects its character as school exercise or literary joke for fellow clerks.[16] While there may indeed be some historical referent behind Andreas' game, we cannot read his text directly as historical reportage. I have the impression that readers of the *Charrette* have been led to invent a romance about Chrétien and his patroness based on Chrétien's own romance about Lancelot and the Queen: the superior, even capricious lady who requires unquestioning obedience from her lover/servant.[17] In trying to understand the Prologue, we find ourselves enmeshed in the same activities of interpretation and judgment that will occupy us with Lancelot and Guenevere in the body of the *Charrette*. As with the hyperboles in the first part of his Prologue, the poet's strategy invites speculation at every step, without quite furnishing us with all the materials needed to resolve the ambiguities sown along our path.

Even if *De Amore* accurately reflects Marie's view of love and marriage, we cannot necessarily deduce from it what her *san* was in the *Charrette*, nor can we document any speculation about possible discord between patroness and poet.[18] Let us instead focus our effort to understand on the *Charrette* itself. *Matiere et san* may have been given to Chrétien before he set to work, but our perception of his romance's meaning can come only after study of the text. A specific answer to the question of what Marie's *san* or Chrétien's *sans* is must, therefore, be held in suspension until we explore the elaboration of the romance in its entirety.

As suggested above, one of the aims of a Prologue is to show us how to read the romance. We would do well to pursue this suggestion by searching out any other examples of reading included in the *Charrette*. These may help us learn how to interpret what we read. The cemetery episode immediately presents itself. There Lancelot reads the inscriptions on the tombstones, then proceeds to question the monk about what has been read:

> ... Et cil respont:
> "Vos avez les letres veües;
> *se vos les avez antendues,*
> don savez vos bien qu'eles dïent

> et que les tonbes *senefient*.
> —Et de cele plus grant me dites
> de qu'ele sert." . . .
> (ll. 1876-82, my emphasis)

(And the monk replies: You've seen the letters; *if you have understood them*, then you know what they say and what these tombs *signify*." "And about this bigger one, tell me what it is for.")

Up to this point we know that Lancelot has read the inscription on each of the tombstones except that on the biggest one. The message is in each case of the same type, quite unexceptional for tombstones until we notice the verb-tense shift from the customary present to the future: "Here will lie Gauvain, here Louis, and here Yvain" (ll. 1865-66). Given that tense shift, and despite the apparent clarity of the messages, Lancelot's question seems a not unreasonable test to establish their truthfulness.[19] While his tone suggests a certain impatience, the monk's reply confirms that the inscriptions do indeed mean what they say.

With that point established, Lancelot pursues his questioning by concentrating on the one special tombstone, not yet described except insofar as it stands out from all the others by its extraordinary size and beauty.[20] Any reticence on the part of the monk is now dissipated as he praises the tombstone's beauty with elaborate hyperbole. Having announced that the inside is even more beautiful than the outside, he dismisses Lancelot's interest: the stone is so heavy that only the combined effort of seven strong men can lift it—and yet, as the inscription indicates, that feat is reserved to one knight alone, the one who will liberate (note again the future tense) the prisoners from Logres retained in Gorre. The reader/listener may at this point be confused as to where this inscription is located. Nevertheless, we learn in a later conversation that the inscription is located on the outside of the tombstone. Lancelot may have already read it as he viewed the various tombstones in the cemetery before stopping before the largest. That reading must have motivated his desire to confirm the truthfulness of the inscriptions. We already know how important the inscription on the large tomb would be for this anonymous knight who is pursuing Meleagant and the Queen. In fact, as soon as the monk stops reciting the inscription, Lancelot goes over and easily lifts the tombstone.

The monk's astonishment, after his disparagement of Lancelot's interest in the large tombstone, indicates that he is an excellent reader of inscriptions, but a rather less competent reader of men. Accordingly, the scene's center of gravity now shifts as the monk himself eagerly inquires about Lancelot's identity. For the first time the anonymous knight endorses the narrator's own strategy of concealment by refusing to give his name.

Instead, he resumes his role as questioner: Who will lie in this tomb? The one who will deliver the prisoners (ll. 1932-36). With this last exchange their conversation comes full circle: we return to the initial reading of the tombstone inscriptions and the usual information to be found in them. The more typical message is apparently not written on the special tombstone; question and answer thus accent the difference between the two types of inscriptions. Despite the actual placement of the inscription on the outside of the tombstone, the message that applies to Lancelot has a quality of interiority about it that sets it off from the more accessible "outsidedness" of the other inscriptions. The distinction inside/outside applies not only to the knight elected for the special adventure as distinguished from all who would fail it, but also to those who can understand what they read in contrast to those who cannot.

The narrator himself refers later to a similar distinction when he describes Lancelot's feigned need of repose in anticipating his rendezvous with the Queen: "Bien poez antendre et gloser, / vos qui avez fet autretel" (ll. 4550-51): we who have done the same thing can understand and gloss Lancelot's action, penetrate the feint and discover his true motivation. We who know are the initiated: our activity, glossing—the technical term for explicating a text—pictures us as readers trained to interpret what we read, cautiously deciphering messages received on the basis of actions observed, whether Lancelot's or the author's.

Narrative strategy, with its use of selected, limited points of view and its careful ordering in the presentation of materials, plays a crucial role in this activity. In the cemetery scene the narrator unfolds his tale in installments, describing the action now from Lancelot's point of view, now from the monk's. At each stage his method, like the characters' questions and answers, partly reveals, partly conceals what is happening or what is going to happen; it introduces tension and suspense, allows questions about truth and meaning to surface. By following his manipulations, we begin to see how the whole issue of truth is inevitably tied to how and by whom a message is passed on. That feature of the narrative is apparent when the only witness to Lancelot's feat describes it first for the Immodest Damsel and then for the Father and Son. In those two conversations we see how information is disseminated and especially how it is commented upon and interpreted. The *pucele*, who has already witnessed for herself Lancelot's amazing capabilities, responds to the monk's account with her own confirmation of the singular Knight of the Cart:

> . . . une chose
> seürement dire li ose,
> qu'il n'a tel chevalier vivant

> tant con vantent les quatre vant.
> (ll. 1951-54)

(She dares to tell him one thing with certainty, that there is not such a knight living as far as the four winds blow.)

On the one hand, we notice here the necessity to buttress the message with an assurance of veracity (*seürement*); on the other, we discover a variation of the very hyperbole Chrétien would have used to describe Marie in the Prologue (ll. 12-13), if he could have used it to speak truthfully. The mechanism is the same in both cases: where the extraordinary is described, there hyperbole finds its place; where hyperbole seems incredible, there protestations of truthfulness are pressed forward. This reflex is even more apparent when the monk twice affirms the truth of his message. Though he has already promised to tell two knights following Lancelot "all the truth" (l. 1965), as soon as he wants to characterize Lancelot's singularity, he once again feels the need to vouchsafe the truth of his hyperbole (ll. 1978-80).

On the whole, the tombstone episode elaborates what we have already glimpsed in the Prologue: reading a message in romance is not a straightforward proposition, either for the participants within the action or for the public without.[21] Sometimes messages mean what they appear to say, but what they appear to say depends on who sends them and who receives them. It is important not only to be "on the inside," among "those who know"; even insiders must proceed cautiously: our knowledge of the truth will depend on how our interpretation is applied to the narrator's manner of telling his story.

If we transfer this lesson in reading back to the problems of the Prologue, it suggests that once Chrétien begins to execute his lady's commandment, once "il s'antremet / de panser," he cannot but fashion his own interpretation of Lancelot's story. His *antancïon*, or artistic effort directed towards a goal, endows the *matiere* with meaning, a *san* realized in the textual organization itself.[22] Though he underplays his poetic activity as a means of complimenting the Countess, he nevertheless makes sure that we fully recognize "sa painne et s'antancïon." The ambiguity of the poet's stance—he is at once humble in his courtly service to Marie and proud of his art—signals to the romance public that, however unclear the *Charrette*'s *san* may appear, it is there to be found if *we* are willing to strive after it.

This ambiguous stance establishes a significant comment on the two parallel couples, Chrétien and Marie, Lancelot and Guenevere.[23] The literary service of the poet mirrors and glosses Lancelot's knightly service—and vice versa. Just as *clergie* and *chevalerie* are coordinated in the *Cligés* Prologue, so literary and chivalric activities are inextricably combined in the course of the *Charrette*: each one involves paradox, invites interpretation.

We shall thus continue our study of Chrétien's own strategies by focusing more specifically on Lancelot's quest for his Lady and Queen. And if we would know who the quester is, we must move directly ahead to the midpoint of the romance, where the Knight of the Cart is revealed as none other than Lancelot.

Midpoint

While anonymous characters abound in romance without necssarily demanding any special attention from the critical audience, Lancelot's anonymity in the *Chevalier de la Charrette* deserves a full analysis of its mechanism and import. Unlike Perceval, who needs to discover his name,[24] Lancelot is fully aware of his—fully aware, that is, except when so lost in thoughts about his lady that he loses all sense of self (ll. 714-24). While the narrator clearly enjoys describing Lancelot's *pansers* in an elaborate series of anaphora,[25] he is at the same time teasing the romance public; we have not yet learned who this man is. Since the Prologue announced that this is a story about the "Chevalier de la Charrette," we are understandably curious to know his identity. He has appeared so far primarily as knight and lover, particularly characterized by his ride in the cart. Our curiosity is heightened not when the narrator withholds his name, but when the hero himself explicitly refuses to give his name even in the face of repeated appeals. When that revelation finally comes, its dramatic potential is fully exploited, both in its placement at the center (i.e., at l. 3660 in a romance 7112 lines long, within the central event of Lancelot's first big duel with Meleagant) and in the way we actually learn who he is. An analysis of that midpoint scene will clarify the parallels between the couples Lancelot/ Guenevere and Chrétien/Marie, and then lead into a more detailed discussion about Lancelot's identity in the context of the entire romance.

I have already suggested how important a role the romance public plays in its active reception of Chrétien's narrative. The public represented within the story, whether at Arthur's court or Bademagu's, plays an equally crucial role as spectators and commentators of Lancelot's knightly performance. Preparations for the encounter between Meleagant and Lancelot include the arrival in large numbers of citizens of Gorre and prisoners from Logres, all crowding into the open place before Bademagu's tower, the site of the projected duel. The Queen herself has requested a good view, so Bademagu has placed her at one of the tower windows, himself on her right at a second window, and with them yet another throng of knights, ladies and maidens, both natives of Gorre and foreigners. In the course of the fighting

Lancelot interacts as much with these witnesses (if less violently) as he does with Meleagant; in fact, he directs his own actions according to the cues he receives from certain members of the crowd.

The battle opens with great fury and continues so for some time (II. 3618-21). It then divides into distinct stages, depending on which of the two combatants prevails. Lancelot is the first to flag as a result of the wounds incurred during the Sword Bridge crossing. Amid the general dismay of those favoring Lancelot, one young lady guesses that Lancelot is acting for, and because of, the Queen. Since love conventionally inspires prowess, once Lancelot sees the Queen is watching him, he will certainly regain courage and strength (II. 3634-48). Before the *pucele* can intervene, however, she needs to know Lancelot's name, a piece of information the Queen herself supplies, since she can see no harm in the request (II. 3660-61). It is entirely fitting that we learn the hero's name precisely from the lady who has been the object of his quest and the object of his constant thought.[26] The formality of the Queen's reply, giving Lancelot his full title, reflects the importance of the revelation. She may be speaking privately to the *pucele* (who will in turn announce it publicly to the assembled crowd), but she also speaks here for the benefit of Chrétien's own public. The *pucele*'s happy relief mirrors our own satisfied curiosity, our release from the tension of suspended knowledge.

Once the *pucele* calls out to Lancelot, the drama of his naming produces action. She tells him to turn around and see who sees him. Her paraphrase (l. 3668) emphasizes the importance of observing and being observed. The sight of "the one person in the world he most desired to see" (II. 3672-73) transports Lancelot into ecstatic contemplation: rooted to the spot, his eyes riveted on the Queen, he no longer really fights at all, but merely defends himself from behind while Meleagant seizes his advantage with increased vigor.[27] Far from improving Lancelot's performance, as expected, the sight of Guenevere has actually made matters worse. But only temporarily. A second intervention of the *pucele* reminds Lancelot of his past prowess and suggests a strategy that allows him to see the Queen *and* fight Meleagant: "Torne toi, si que de ça soies / et que adés ceste tor voies, / que boen veoir et bel la fet" (II. 3701-03)[28] (Turn yourself around to be on the other side, so that you can see this tower, for it is good and fine to see). Lancelot's reaction indicates how sensitive he is to public observation and opinion. His shame here is particularly acute, since he knows everyone has seen him getting the worst of the battle. Now, with his effort redirected, he goes on the offensive: his blows maneuver Meleagant into a position between himself and the Queen, now pushing back, now forward, but never too far, his movement circumscribed within direct sight of the Queen.

The narrator at this point takes obvious pleasure in describing Lancelot's actions. The tools of his trade are much in evidence: the personifications of "Amors et haïne mortex" (l. 3725) (Love and mortal hatred), the standard metaphor of love as "cele flame si ardant" (l. 3752) (that so ardent flame) firing Lancelot's courage, Meleagant led about "come avugle et come eschacier" (l. 3756) (like a blind man and a cripple), manipulated in spite of himself.[29] All this maneuvering underlines the parallel between hero and author. In this midpoint scene we are at the heart of the romance not only in regard to Lancelot's story (in which Meleagant is literally and figuratively between the Queen and her knight), but also in terms of Chrétien's poetic activity: Lancelot's deliberate stationing of Meleagant serves as a metaphor for the arrangement of the romance itself.[30] Here at the midpoint the narrator joins the linear pattern of Lancelot's quest to the complex narrative patterns of the second part.

While the details of this strategy and its significance for interpreting the *Charrette* will be discussed later, we can already appreciate how the middle fuses what lies behind and what lies ahead simply by continuing to chart Lancelot's ups and downs in the combat with Meleagant. I have already noted two analogous phases in that process punctuated by Lancelot's naming and his ecstatic fixation on the Queen. In each of these stages Lancelot's prowess seems to lag behind his heroic promise. Thus, they recall earlier moments when the Knight of the Cart exhibited a similarly unintentional sloth in accomplishing his goal.[31] Each time, Lancelot finally rallies his energies and establishes complete control over his opponents. In this case, however, he does not move uninterruptedly towards victory. Motivated by obedience to the Queen, who agrees to Bademagu's request that his son be spared, Lancelot desists from all combat, despite Meleagant's frenzied onslaughts. If we look ahead to the episode of the tournament at Noauz, the same configuration of events recurs on a larger scale, with Lancelot fighting "as badly as possible" and "as well as possible" according to the Queen's instructions. Just as Chrétien willingly obeys Marie's commandment to write the *Charrette*, so Lancelot submits to all of Guenevere's commands with equal willingness to serve.[32] From another point of view, a diffferent parallel between author and character appears, since the way Guenevere maneuvers her knight's performance may also recall Chrétien arranging his *matiere*. It highlights as well the humor that accompanies such arrangements. We see explicitly within the text how the Queen has the last laugh: knights may joke at the "coward's" experience, maidens may swear to marry only the Red Knight who vanquishes all, but the Queen gleefully enjoys her own private knowledge that Lancelot would not marry even the best of them for all the gold of Araby (ll. 6007-11).

Similarly, we can imagine the smiles that Lancelot evokes in the romance public as he is pictured motionless, with Meleagant raining blows on his undefended head and shoulders. Indeed, the extremes of Lancelot's behavior make him an easy target for humorous jabs.[33] But we in the audience had better be mindful of the Queen's example—and of Chrétien's own, as he demonstrated with the paradoxes of the Prologue. While enjoying our view from the tower, we had best keep an eye on the fancy footwork of knight and poet.

If, as the midpoint scene suggests, Lancelot's love service can inspire both extreme passivity and extreme activity, then we should ask more questions about who Lancelot of the Lake is and especially what the revelation or concealment of his name implies. Lancelot's physical appearance is clearly of little importance for his identity in the *Charrette*.[34] What matters is the relation between his name—or the act of naming him—and his actions. The use of anonymity, as well as the perceptions of other characters, exerts a powerful influence on that relationship. They also suggest that Lancelot's identity is not static: though it contains certain givens—Lancelot's heroism is part of his character—it also reflects a process of discovery, both ours and the knight's. These factors provide us with guidelines for exploring Lancelot's identity.

To begin, we can say that Lancelot's name plus his actions equals one form of identity: his reputation—that is, identity as evaluated by the other members of an Arthurian society. Lancelot's accomplishments before the *Charrette* begins have already given him a reputation for excellence. We see that reflected in the comments of the *pucele* (ll. 3662-63) and the prisoners (ll. 3909-12) at the mere mention of Lancelot's name. That earlier reputation generates certain expectations regarding Lancelot, expectations that are at first frustrated by his *panser*, but then fulfilled by his success. In the absence of his name, however, Lancelot's actions during his quest generate two distinct sets of rumors, thus furnishing him with two additional and separate reputations: one as the Knight of the Cart, one as the savior of the captives. When those two rumors come together, Lancelot's hosts predict dire consequences for his reputation, already besmirched by the cart ride. Yet once Lancelot's name is associated with his actions during the quest, there is no mention of his shameful ride in the cart—except in the private domain of the knight and his lady. This divergence, along with Lancelot's ability to inspire differing and even incompatible reputations, suggests that we need to follow the construction of his identity through the differing perceptions of public and private eyes. We can do so most economically by focusing on the tournament episode, since it seems to crystallize all the issues surrounding Lancelot's identity.

This time the romance public is privy to all the tactics that conceal and reveal who the "Red Knight" is. We know Lancelot has purposely hidden his name by using another knight's arms and armor. A shield ordinarily functions as the appropriate sign of a knight's past actions and consequent reputation, as in the long list of combatants identified by their shields (ll. 5773-5822). Lancelot's borrowed shield generates no expectations: it is a blank upon which the unknown knight can inscribe only the actions of the moment. Yet Lancelot does not remain completely incognito at the tournament: two characters recognize him and add drama to his performance by recalling and testing his past reputation. Since it is precisely the herald's business to identify knights, the sight of an unknown shield serves for him as an invitation to investigate: when he sees Lancelot unarmed, he recognizes him immediately, but his role as public announcer is frustrated by Lancelot's threats. Hence, his repeated cry, "Or est venuz qui l'aunera!" (l. 5563, etc.) (Now he has come who will take the measure!), preserves Lancelot's incognito, yet at the same time refers to his previous actions by predicting great feats for him at the tournament.

What the herald seems to know about Lancelot is short-circuited when the second process of recognition occurs.[35] Confusion arises as we move from public reputation to private identity. As before, the Queen recognizes her knight, but while the tower scene dramatized the naming itself, the tournament episode concentrates on a two-staged verification of who Lancelot of the Lake is. The excellence of his chivalric performance immediately makes her suspect that the anonymous knight is Lancelot. Her first message to fight "au noauz" (l. 5645) (for the worst) confirms the initial perception. His actions correspond to what she expects her lover to do; he has properly read and acted upon her secret instructions. Her second message and Lancelot's continued willing submission to her commands confirm not only that he is Lancelot, but that Lancelot is as completely hers as she is his—that is, Lancelot of the Lake is not only knight *par excellence*, but knight and lover without peer. Yet this identity is not—cannot be—available to the entire tournament public. Though Lancelot's superiority stems from his actions in love *and* combat, public knowledge of him within the romance remains necessarily fragmented and confused. His actions at the tournament are in perfect accord with his identity, yet he appears now as the worst coward, now as the best champion, confounding the expectations of herald and crowd. Where does he belong, in the camp of *Malvestiez* or of *Proesce*? Lancelot certainly seems to be "the one who will measure," but it is not always clear whether as the best or the worst. Indeed, this uncertainty, sustained throughout the episode,[36] confirms one fact: Lancelot's actions are constantly viewed and evaluated by others in order to determine and rank who he is, but that determination can never be successful unless the observer can mediate between Lancelot's public and private conduct. The Queen's instructions play specifically on the gaps in perception: her joke is to reveal who Lancelot is by momentarily concealing his chivalric excellence. By obeying his lady's commands, the knight acts out his true identity right in the public forum, but only the Queen (and the romance public) can successfully integrate his disparate actions into a composite, but whole picture of Lancelot.

How do Guenevere's manipulations fit with Lancelot's own expression of his identity? If we consider how he himself uses anonymity, we can appreciate how similar their approaches are. Already in the first half of the romance, Lancelot shows himself willing to generate a number of separate identities for different publics. By withholding his name, he cuts off current actions from past reputation and prevents them, at least temporarily, from being added together under his own name. While he remains incognito, these anonymous actions are neither credited nor debited to his account: pride neither urges him to claim for himself his great feats in the cemetery or at the tournament nor requires him to protect himself from the scorn heaped upon the Knight of the Cart or the coward at Noauz.[37] While Lancelot's earlier accomplishments would surely have prevented such an accumulation of public shame, he shows no interest in relying on past laurels, nicely cooperating with the author who intends to spin out a plot with plenty of suspense and mystery. His anonymity removes from those who would interpret his actions the familiar points of reference furnished by a name, an established reputation. His orientation is forward: with each new action unencumbered by expectation, he (re)invents his identity as the single knight capable of saving the Queen. While he is content to bewilder others with fragmentary perceptions, however, Lancelot cannot ignore Guenevere's scorn. He wants her to see the complete knight and lover: she must understand that the Knight of the Cart serves her as much as the redeemer of the captives, precisely because of the love between them.

Here again we see the complexity of Lancelot's identity refracted through the different angles of public and private visions. That identity is not exclusively interior, nor does it operate only in the public forum under the observing eye of society: the Knight of the Cart exists in both dimensions. While Lancelot identifies himself to the monk at the cemetery as a knight of Arthur's kingdom,[38] his conduct, privately motivated by love for Guenevere, does not represent a pattern that all Arthurian knights can or should follow. The Queen can recognize him, occasional characters in particular circumstances can recognize him. Meleagant's sister, for example, reenacts a variation of the midpoint scene when she "names" Lancelot imprisoned in the tower and then helps him renew his battle with Meleagant. But most characters in the *Charrette* do not recognize him. This is true even of Gauvain: despite his repeated encounters with Lancelot during their quests, despite his enjoyment of Lancelot's chivalric performance at the tournament, Gauvain more frequently than not fails to recognize his friend.[39] We may take this to reflect not a hasty author's oversight, as some critics of Chrétien have charged, but rather as an indication that identifying Lancelot requires a more comprehensive point of view than Gauvain's own. Like Perceval, Lancelot is motivated by more than the ordinary conventions of knighthood. Significantly, the maidens who organized the tournament at Noauz continue to favor the Red Knight even when his conduct seems inexplicable to his fellow combatants. If we would benefit from our larger point of view outside the romance, Lancelot's relationship with Guenevere, and more generally with the many other women in the *Charrette*, suggests that we pursue his identity in the more private domain of love.

Hero and Women

Lancelot moves along a route marked by encounters with members of the opposite sex. He is not only of particular service to the unusually large number of *puceles* met during his quest, but he himself is greatly served by them. They provide him with information and arms, release him from prison, encourage his prowess and protect his weakness. In the course of his experiences with *dames* and *dameiseles*, Lancelot's relationships with these women reflect his relationship with the chosen lady of his ecstatic contemplation. Lancelot is above all a knight in the service of woman: his progress from hesitation to willingness to eagerness, illustrated in his successive dealings with the Immodest Damsel, the seneschal's wife and Meleagant's sister, mirrors the rising curve of his service to Guenevere[40]—and his service to the Queen, motivated by love, leads him to heights of chivalry and prowess attained by no other knight in the *Charrette*.

The Immodest Damsel is the first to comment explicitly on Lancelot's singularity, his desire and ability to do what no one else dares to undertake (ll. 1270-78). Her hospitality puts him through two tests: during the staged combat Lancelot demonstrates his unequaled strength and skill in arms, even against superior numbers; in the damsel's bed, which he is required to share by the terms of her hospitality offer, Lancelot shows an even greater strength of character. On the one hand, when he overcomes his disinclination to share her bed, Lancelot demonstrates that he keeps his word; on the other hand, the Immodest Damsel perceives Lancelot's total devotion to another lady when he remains untouched (both figuratively and literally) by his hostess' charms. Direct experience thus allows the damsel to perceive the connection between Lancelot's love and his courage.

The romance public is even more privileged during this scene, since the narrator explains to us in some detail that Lancelot is able to resist the maiden's considerable charms because of his love (ll. 1228-42). The separation of Lancelot's heart from his body whenever he and Guenevere are apart shows metaphorically that the lover's heart belongs to the Queen (e.g., ll. 3976-78, 4692-97). Even the seneschal's wife knows that when Lancelot promises her "all the love that he has," she has received nothing, since that love is in another's keeping (ll. 5484-88). The site of Lancelot's heart seems to be common knowledge, at least among the ladies of the Arthurian world.

As much as Meleagant is misguided and ultimately brought down by the passions of his *fol cuer* (l. 7084; cf. ll. 3166-67, 6309-10), Lancelot is singled out by a *boen cuer* (l. 6308) that knows humility in its service to Love. Indeed, Love has been so lavish in endowing Lancelot's heart that others seem miserably deprived by contrast (ll. 4664-68). The Knight of the Cart demonstrates by self-forgetful love meditation how defenselessly he submits to "Amors qui le justise" (l. 713) (Love, who governs him). Later, when rumor makes Lancelot believe his lady dead, Love leads him even to submit to "the justice of a strangling knot" (l. 4307)—though luckily he is spared such harsh punishment. In the lamentations that follow his suicide attempt, when he tries to understand the Queen's apparent anger, Lancelot echoes and elaborates the narrator's description of the lover's conduct (ll. 4356-96): anything he does at Love's commandment, anything performed for the sake of his *amie*, far from being blameworthy, actually improves the knight/lover. Those who blame such behavior reveal only their own ignorance of the customs of Love. Too fearful to submit to her commandments, they fail where the obedient lover succeeds. While his pride and courage may seem foolishness to others, Lancelot himself is no fool: he knows quite well that obedience to Love may give him the temporary appearance of *Malvestiez*, but that ultimately it leads him to the greatest triumphs—triumphs all the more striking because of previous eclipses. Love and prowess may indeed appear as opposites, as when Reason bids him to avoid stepping into the Cart, or when fighting "au noauz" evokes jeers and scorn. This opposition is, however, an optical distortion, a misunderstanding of reality. Love and prowess are both important systems of value, both generate appropriate actions, but their relationship is hierarchical: Lancelot's conduct demonstrates that Love's demands are superior to all others. Where a choice appears, he obeys Love first—and then discovers that any apparent conflict implied in the choice is finally dissipated by his extraordinary achievements.[41] Love's values do not eliminate those of chivalry: action inspired by love ultimately redounds to Lancelot's credit as knight.

Far from being insensitive to the problems of honor and shame, the knight/lover has a good deal to teach his fellows on that subject. When the prisoners in Gorre quarrel about who will lodge Lancelot for the night, he solves the conflict by directing their attention to the central issue—how to advance his mission—and by defining their desire to honor him as equivalent to the actual performance of service. Lancelot has a clear sense of where true shame and honor lie: if he is following Love's dictates, no one else's opinion (except the Queen's) sways him; if Love is not involved, he is his own severest critic—as when he blames himself for taking so long to defeat the Ford Knight. The same distinction operates when he realizes he tore his fingers while bending the bars to the Queen's bedroom: having acted for the sake of love and with the Queen's permission, he is neither dismayed nor angry, though he would have been so had he wounded himself for any other reason. Lancelot exhibits the same imperturbability when confronted by the Proud Son's boasting or the Orgueilleux's scornful reproaches: secure in the value of his own private motivations, confident of his strength and skill in arms, the knight/lover speaks with both reason and calm. His honor does not demand unnecessary demonstrations, but if an opponent insists, he will respond to the challenge with all due vigor.

Reasonable, assured, discriminating: these are Lancelot's characteristics as knight.[42] But what about the passionate excesses of the lover, the complete self-abandonment of his *panser*, the extravagant adoration of his lady? While Lancelot is moderate as knight, he appears quite immoderate as lover —at least by the standards of knighthood. By love's own standards, his conduct is entirely appropriate:[43] in the realm of Love, *folie* and *sagesse* often change places. As Chrétien writes in one of the two lyrics generally ascribed to him:[44]

> Nuls s'il n'est cortois et sages,
> Ne puet d'Amors riens aprendre;
> Mais tels en est li usages,
> Dont nulz ne se seit deffendre,
> Qu'ele vuet l'entrée vandre:
> Et quels en est li passages?
> Raison li covient despandre
> Et mettre mesure en gages.

(No one, if he is not courteous and level-headed, can learn anything about love. But such is love's custom, from which no one is exempt, that she demands payment for entry, and no matter what the passage costs, the lover must spend reason and pawn moderation.)

The paradox expressed here reappears in the characterization of Lancelot. In consonance with the demands of *corteisie*, he is polite, reasonable and well-mannered. But these are mere prerequisites for the courtly lover, who must abandon moderation when under the commandments of love.

This tension between love and *mesure* has both tragic and comic possibilities—and the author of the *Charrette* clearly prefers the latter.[45] Without robbing Lancelot of his extraordinary status as hero, Chrétien catches him more than once in a comic pose, the victim of his extreme passion. This is especially apt to happen when Lancelot's ecstatic concentration on the thought of Guenevere prevents him momentarily from dealing with the demands of reality. Thus, when he learns from the Immodest Damsel that the comb they have just found belongs to King Arthur's Queen, he swoons; slumped forward over his saddle, his color completely vanished, Lancelot nearly falls from his horse.[46]

Though Chrétien obviously has a good time showing the comic extremes to which Lancelot's love sometimes carries him, he never leaves his hero too long in such foolish postures. In fact, Lancelot always ends up demonstrating the heroic prowess his love inspires. In the episodes with the Immodest Damsel, for example, the comb scene is directly followed by the encounter with the Proud Son, the unwanted suitor of Lancelot's hostess. Acting in accord with the custom of Logres, the Proud Son claims the lady for himself and assumes that defeating her escort is as good as done, the matter of a moment's work. That combat never actually takes place—first because there is no room for it on the narrow forest path, later in the meadow, because the youth's father, the White-haired Knight, prevents it.[47] The entire incident emphasizes Lancelot's confident defense of the *pucele*, the almost magical sense of excellence that the wisest knights recognize in him even before he demonstrates his prowess.

In fact, Lancelot's experience with the Immodest Damsel and the custom of Logres offers an analogue to the quest and rescue of the Queen. The subplot contains the same triangular set of relationships as the main plot, though the direction and fulfillment of desires is quite different:

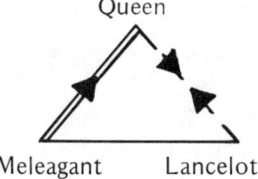
Queen

Meleagant   Lancelot

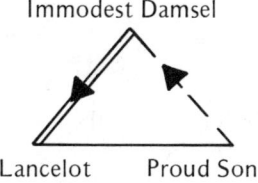
Immodest Damsel

Lancelot   Proud Son

In each case a lady is escorted (willingly or unwillingly) by one knight and desired (for various reasons) by another.[48] According to the custom of Logres, the challenger can do as he pleases with the lady "without incurring any shame or blame" (l. 1316), if he can win her by force of arms. This situation recalls the agreement offered by Meleagant in the opening scene: if one of Arthur's knights will escort the Queen into the forest, Meleagant will challenge him for possession of the lady. Thus, an earlier triangle can also be superimposed on the other two:[49]

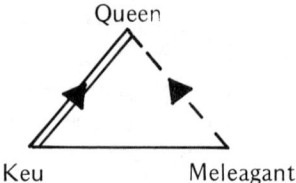

Queen

Keu   Meleagant

While Meleagant was the victor in that first combat, his father prevented him from enjoying the fruits of his success. This gave Lancelot the chance to replay the custom with even greater success, since his victory is duly celebrated by the lovers' consummation of their love.

Each of these triangles offers a set of repetitions and variations of a basic pattern. If we superimpose them, the parallels created open a rich field for critical inquiry. Many elements in the romance suggest and elaborate the analogy between Guenevere and the Immodest Damsel. Lancelot himself calls our attention to it when he compares his quest for Guenevere to the rescue of his hostess. His monologue shows him grappling with the same problems of honor and shame, delay and hesitation, that occupy him before the cart or in the first duel with Meleagant. The rape scene itself, apparently staged by the damsel, but puzzling by its unexpected violence, becomes more understandable if we view it, too, in terms of the other triangles of defense and desire:

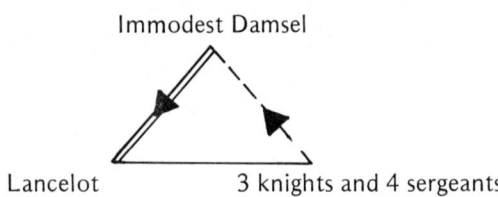

Immodest Damsel

Lancelot   3 knights and 4 sergeants

On the one hand, the attack allows Lancelot to demonstrate his valor in battle. On the other, by exposing the damsel "uncovered up to the navel"

(l. 1082), the attack mirrors the erotic implications of her hospitality. Finally, the obligation to "win" her by force of arms suggests a conflation of her proposition, the custom of Logres and Meleagant's own conditions for liberating the prisoners: the rape scene thus parallels—in an admittedly more blatant manner—the Queen's relation to Meleagant.

This flair for overstatement accords well with the Immodest Damsel's general forwardness. She takes the first step, offering Lancelot hospitality, making herself his *amie* (l. 1051), arranging the night's adventures and the following day's encounters. Her manipulations recall Guenevere's own talent for arranging Lancelot's service, as in the tournament at Noauz. Both ladies put Lancelot to the test as knight and lover, and both agree in their estimation of his excellence. But on the whole, Guenevere is a passive character by contrast with the Immodest Damsel. Both she and Lancelot participate in the custom of Logres and Meleagant's *covant* as an unavoidable response to the aggression of others. In the realm of love especially, the two ladies are at opposite poles: Guenevere, the object of Lancelot's noblest desire, his hostess completely unwanted even with all her charms exposed. The damsel is as blatant and fast-moving in her approach to love as the Queen is discreet and gradual.

The complexities of Guenevere's characterization, like Lancelot's, require a variety of situations to reveal themselves.[50] In the opening scene she appears as Arthur's wife and queen; she is as subject and obedient to his commandments as Lancelot is to those of love. More than one critic has commented on her victimization at the hands of Keu, Meleagant and Arthur, and on her consequent need of a champion like Lancelot to rescue her from their quite arbitrary manipulation. Appropriately, then, we next see the Queen refracted through Lancelot's *panser*, the object of total adoration and submission. Except for the extraordinary brightness of her golden hair, we have no description of her physical beauty. But we see the hyperbolic wonders of her beauty in its effect on her *ami*. Nor is her beauty just a physical attribute. Her moral and social virtues are readily apparent to the various knights attending the tournament at Noauz; most of them had come there for her sake alone (ll. 5512-20).

During the first meeting between Lancelot and the Queen we see another side of her character when she "fet sanblant de correciee" (l. 3940) (appears to be angry). But does appearance coincide with reality? Guenevere seems to be playing the role of the capricious lady of lyric, the haughty and superior *domna* whose cruelties furnish the subject of many a troubadour's lament. While the narrator fails to comment on or explain the Queen's behavior, neither Bademagu nor Keu nor Lancelot can understand why she acts with such surprising and apparently undeserved harshness. Later, in a monologue, when she thinks Lancelot has been killed, Guenevere herself severely criticizes that behavior: her cruelty was only acting ("a gas," l. 4205), but Lancelot's sincere love prevented him from appreciating her humor. The joke backfires and reveals yet another facet of the Queen's character: her own passionate desires:

> Ha! lasse! con fusse garie
> et com me fust granz reconforz
> se une foiz, ainz qu'il fust morz,
> l'eüsse antre mes braz tenu.
> Comant? Certes, tot nu a nu,
> par ce que plus an fusse a eise.
> (ll. 4224-29)

(Alas! How I would be relieved and what a great comfort it would be if, just once, before [Lancelot] died, I had held him in my arms. How? Skin to skin, of course, to enjoy him more fully.)

Beneath her public roles as Queen and *domna* we discover the inner woman and lover ready to punish her cruelty with a life of suffering, but returned to delight soon enough when she discovers, in news of Lancelot's unsuccessful suicide attempt, proof of his love for her. Given the opportunity to replay their first meeting, Guenevere receives her knight with all the generosity of her passion, if first discreetly in the public eye, when she gives him an explanation for her earlier coldness, yet unreservedly in the privacy of her bedroom, where they share the joys of a pleasure kept silent and hidden by the story (ll. 4680-84).

Of course, Guenevere does once again indulge her pleasure in games when she manipulates Lancelot's performance at the tournament and sets all the knights and ladies to speculating on his contrasting performances. She enacts with Lancelot another drama in which he can display his total obedience to her command and atone, as he requested, for his two-step hesitation before the cart. Yet when the narrator describes her reaction to Lancelot's unreserved obedience, we learn that the submission is mutual. She is completely his as he is hers (ll. 5873-75). Lancelot may adore and worship Guenevere as he would a saint, but her response to his desire makes them equal partners in love.[51] Equal partners? Well, not quite, since Lancelot's heart is such that, if Guenevere has a great love for him, his love for her is a hundred thousand times greater (ll. 4662-63). I noted earlier how generously Love endowed Lancelot's heart above all others. His uncontrollable ecstasies, the extent of his self-abandonment, as well as his extraordinary heights of prowess and general disregard for ordinary people's sense of shame, are all measures of his immeasurable love. The Queen, by contrast, seems far more able than Lancelot to observe the demands of moderation. Though we are repeatedly informed of the gap between her public composure and her private turmoil, despite the depth of her passion fully demonstrated in words and actions, she does not appear to have Lancelot's capacity for total self-abandonment. Her manner of receiving her messenger at Noauz is emblematic of her role as Queen:

> et la reïne s'est dreciee,
> se li est a l'ancontre alee;
> mes n'est mie jus avalee
> einz l'atant au chief del degré.
> (ll. 5900-03)

(and the Queen stood up and went to meet her. But she did not go down; instead, she waited for her at the top of the stairs.)

This particular notation, with its concern for the "petit fait vrai" so typical of Chrétien's art, contrasts noticeably with the description in the opening scene when, as ordered by her king and husband, "from as high as she was" (ll. 148-49), Guenevere fell at Keu's feet. The Queen's sense of her own dignity and responsibility, whether in the public domain of the court or the private realm of love, restricts her movement as heroine. Despite her superior station, despite her playful role as *domna*, she remains limited, an object of desire, whereas Lancelot is the desiring subject who transcends the boundaries she must observe.[52]

Since Lancelot's superiority is so clearly linked to his capacity for loving, we should close this section by focusing more particularly on the *Charrette*'s characterization of his love. In general, Lancelot's love appears as a sort of religion, the all-absorbing central force guiding his life. His humble and obedient service to his lady and his self-abnegating *panser* recall the mystic's ecstatic contemplation of and submission to God.[53] The narrator chooses language that explicitly elaborates the religious attributes of Lancelot's love: the lover has more faith in the few strands of Guenevere's hair than in St. Martin's or in St. James' aid (ll. 1476-78); he enters his lady's bedroom with the solemn adoration due a cult object, bowing and worshipping, and later suffers "grant martire" (l. 4691) when he must tear himself away. Lancelot earlier suffered a more physical martyrdom when crossing the Sword Bridge, the knife edge of which cuts into his hands, knees and feet. But Love sweetens and assuages his suffering. In general, Lancelot's quest for the Queen takes on messianic implications: his entrance into the "land from which no one returns" (l. 641) seems to echo Christ's Descent into Hell. Just as Christ unlocks the gates and redeems the sinners imprisoned within, so Lancelot liberates the citizens of Logres held captive in the country of Gorre.[54] Meleagant himself, with his unredeemable talent for evil-doing, his absolute and unceasing *desleauté*, strikes a devil-like pose,[55] beyond mercy, and is finally destroyed by Lancelot.

These sacred echoes in Lancelot's very secular heroism are not presented as either blasphemous or parodic. The esthetics of conventionality operating in medieval literature demands that typical elements—motifs, themes, figures, plots—be reused and reassembled as writers (re)invent new works.[56] Just as the manuscript illuminators borrowed their models for tournament scenes from representations of biblical battles or represented Tristan *jongleur* as indistinguishable, except by context, from King David playing his harp, so Chrétien may have used religious narrative models for his own secular elaboration. How better to suggest the extraordinary quality of Lancelot's heroism than to give him messianic trappings? Of course, such repetition does not preclude variation: Lancelot is not an allegory for Christ, even though he does have some Christ-like characteristics.

In the same fashion, Lancelot takes on the conventional pose of courtly lover, as Chrétien adapts for his romance materials from troubadour lyrics and Ovid's treatises on love. The problem of moderation and love, so prominent in Lancelot's characterization, also plagues Bernard de Ventadour, who exclaims in one place that "qui en amor quer sen, / cel non a sen ni mezura" (he who looks for [good] sense in love has neither sense nor moderation).[57] In Lancelot's *panser* we discover the same propensity for oblivion that Bernard himself describes when he is lost in the thoughts of his lady and the joy of his love: "del joi qu'eu ai, no vei ni au / ni no sai que·m dic ni que·m fau" (because of the joy that I have, I neither see nor hear; I know neither what I say nor what I do).[58] The well-known metaphor of love as flame appears in the *Charrette* as the narrator describes Lancelot's emotion rekindling his prowess (ll. 3750-55), while the convention of the lover dying for love receives a comic twist when Lancelot tries unheroically to strangle himself upon hearing the rumor of the Queen's death. In the set of parallel monologues in which Guenevere and Lancelot each laments the other's ostensible death, we can observe the author giving a full display of all the rhetorical skills he learned at school: exclamation, question and answer, personification, refining (repeating the same thing in different words), and so on—the very tools that permit him to "recycle" materials from a variety of traditions. Moreover, the lovers' dissection of motive and mores in love reflects Chrétien's own delight—shared with the troubadour poets—in exploring the art of courtly love, or the art of courtly behavior in general.

This is not to say that the *Charrette* illustrates or applies a doctrine of courtly love located outside Chrétien's text, whether in the poetry of the troubadours or the treatise of Andreas Capellanus. It does mean that Chrétien freely uses and recombines models for loving available in a variety of sources. That Lancelot and Guenevere's love is adulterous remains indisputable; that it is adulterous by doctrine, or that adultery *per se* is an issue in the *Charrette*, is not. When Guenevere's bloody sheets suggest adultery, Chrétien shields Lancelot by making Meleagant the accuser and Keu the mistaken culprit. The displacement signals a central problem in the romance, where the role of the Queen's defender shifts from Arthur to Keu to Lancelot. At the same time it obscures the adultery by deflecting it onto another issue: Meleagant's error. The question of guilt, which should have been determined by the judicial combat between Lancelot and Meleagant, remains in suspension, evaporates when Bademagu intervenes to postpone the duel, and at the same time returns us to the theme of the liberation of the prisoners in Gorre.

Though Lancelot and Guenevere's love is adulterous and must, therefore, remain hidden away in the private realm of the two lovers, it is not asocial like Tristan and Iseut's love.[59] Its values are secret, but operate in the service of Arthurian society: to rescue the Queen is to rescue all the captives of Gorre. The two feats are indissolubly tied together. Lancelot's service to Guenevere overflows into his service to all—and especially to all ladies. When Lancelot himself is liberated from prison by Meleagant's sister (the *gueredon* promised for his earlier service to her), he expresses his gratitude without reservation: "Por ce poez mon cuer, mon cors, / et mon servise, et mon avoir, / quant vos pleira, prandre et avoir" (ll. 6684-86) (For this you can, whenever it pleases you, take and have my heart, myself, my service and my possessions). We who are privy to Lancelot's private thoughts, who have witnessed (or at least almost) his passionate embraces with the Queen, and who keep in mind the bemused understanding of Lancelot's promise evinced by the seneschal's wife, will not risk misunderstanding his words here.[60] Lancelot's gratitude finds eloquent expression in his unbounded capacity for service. But we should not confuse such courtesy with love: his declaration to Meleagant's sister, as exuberant and polite as it is, actually introduces his request to leave for Arthur's court and finish his quarrel with her brother.

That final action guarantees the Queen's safety, in jeopardy since she first left Arthur's court. By serving Guenevere, Lancelot serves the entire Arthurian society: he redeems the captives and saves Arthur's Queen, not in spite of being an adulterous traitor, but because he is Guenevere's secret lover and, therefore, the best knight for the adventure.

Adventure

Adventure: the very word conjures up the knight errant who sets out to face the unknown in the apparently random events that happen along his route,[61] discovered by chance and yet each as if designated for a particular knight, marking him with its own special mystery. As Lancelot moves along the *droit chemin* to Gorre and the rescue of the Queen, he meets a series of adventures, marvelous tests in which his own unique excellence is confirmed, his own particular destiny revealed. Chance and necessity, activity and passivity combine in these encounters. Each adventure forms an episode; the juxtaposition of episodes structures the entire romance as Lancelot pursues his quest.

The scene with the Flaming Lance is particularly remarkable for its gratuity. While the tombstone episode, Lancelot's other major contact with the marvelous, foreshadows the successful completion of his quest and demonstrates the magic quality of his strength, the Flaming Lance episode has no later repercussions in the *Charrette* plot. The morning after the knight's adventure his hostess does not comment on his experience, despite her quarrelsome warnings the previous evening that he would regret daring the adventure. While this episode has no causal relationship to the chain of events, it does make a significant comment on Lancelot's character and on the character of his adventures. Let us read quickly through the specific events of the adventure itself and then turn to more general observations about them.

Though Lancelot is offered a bed just like Gauvain's, once he sees a larger one, longer and higher than the others by a "demie aune" (l. 505) (half an ell),[62] once he learns that it is reserved for the deserving, he immediately responds to the challenge and claims the adventure. Lancelot's own sense of himself and his worth is prominent here. He disdains the hostess' prohibition and insults by quick repartee (ll. 494-502). Lancelot's straightforward manner of speaking with no words minced, even while his tone remains calm and confident, reappears continually in his personal encounters. The Knight of the Cart has full confidence that he deserves a bed whose cover is fit for a king (ll. 510-11): the richness of the bed-clothes provides a metaphor for Lancelot's own excellence—an ironically apt metaphor, given his singularity as knight and lover![63] The complete absence of fear evinced by his words also describes Lancelot's conduct when the flaming lance suddenly falls, setting the bed and sheets afire. He puts out the flames, tosses the lance into the center of the room, then, without once having left his bed, falls back to sleep with the same confidence he demonstrated at the outset.

The hostess' predictions of disaster contained no indication about what precisely would happen if Lancelot slept in the bed. Even after Lancelot's experience, the meaning of the event remains puzzling. Why does the lance have a flaming pennant? Why does it just nick Lancelot on the side, when it was intended to impale him on the bed? Allegorical (and even psychoanalytic) interpretations jump readily to mind, but they lead off into the realm of unverifiable or anachronistic speculation, since the romance itself leaves such symbolism undeveloped.[64] We may be better served by considering the adventure as a pretext to elicit Lancelot's qualities: meaning or explanation lies not in the adventure itself, but rather in the knight who encounters it. If this is so, then the primary narrative significance of the Flaming Lance test seems to be that of pointing to Lancelot's singularity. For the characters within the romance, as well as for the still mystified romance public, it is surely paradoxical that a knight who has just been shamed by riding in a cart should demand to sleep in a bed where no one lies who has not deserved the honor. Curiosity as to who this knight is intensifies in the face of such paradox. Contact with the marvelous throws a revealing light on his identity, even if it does not yet bring total clarity.[65]

Erich Köhler has pointed out that the marvelous in romance introduces the realm of fairy tales into the Arthurian world of legend.[66] With its optimistic world view, the fairy tale promises meaning, ultimate harmony and final victory over all that is "other," foreign and menacing in legend. But only the hero participates directly in the benediction of universal harmony: the community benefits only through his mediation (p. 121). In a sense, then, Lancelot is already marked in the Flaming Lance episode as his community's representative, a role that will be explicitly confirmed in the cemetery adventure. There his achievement is appropriately designated as "mervoille" (ll. 1917 and 1968): contact with the marvelous reflects back on the knight who meets it. Even the "ordinary" dangers of knightly combat appear marvelous as executed by the hero: Lancelot's defeat of the sergeants at the Stone Passage becomes *mervoille* and *avanture* (ll. 2242, 2247).[67] Likewise, Lancelot's crossing of the Sword Bridge is dubbed marvelous both as technique (l. 3096) and as accomplishment (l. 3195): the feats performed for love also participate in the marvelous.[68]

The opposition between fairy tale and legend is not the only polarity operating in the knight's pursuit of adventure.[69] A whole series of binary oppositions is apparent: departure/return, court/forest, known/unknown (or foreign), order/disorder, good/evil, individual/community, and internal/external. What does this mean in romance terms? The knight elected to adventure leaves Arthur's court in an effort to save it from the intrusion of disorder, the menace of a hostile world.[70] Yet his departure itself isolates the knight-errant from his community. By accepting the test of adventure, he demonstrates a will to transcend the limits of ordinary experience, to go beyond the stable hierarchy of the social order. The effort towards reintegration—reintegration of the menaced society itself whose integrity is a guarantee of universal order, and reintegration of the knight within that ideal human organization—leads paradoxically to the separation of individual and community and a renewal of the cycle of adventures. Confronted by the gap between interior and exterior worlds, the uncertainty of a world filled with mysteries and contradictions, the knight-errant internalizes his adventures as a quest in which to define himself by realizing his potentiality. Adventure itself becomes an experience that cannot be completed: single adventures end, but the quest for identity remains open to be undertaken again and again in other adventures, other quests—whether those of Erec and Yvain in the two parts of their respective romances or those incipient multiple quests we encounter in the *Charrette* and *Perceval*, as well as in the prose cycles of the thirteenth century. We have already seen in an earlier discussion how the concern for identity preoccupies Lancelot as he moves between private and public values in an effort to coordinate their competing claims. The open-ended quality of Lancelot's adventures will be considered shortly, but before pursuing that subject, we need to focus on the way adventures are linked together, the predictabilities and unpredictabilities of their combinations.

Bademagu tells Meleagant that it was "avanture" (l. 3187) that brought them to a tower window just in time to witness Lancelot crossing the Sword Bridge. When Meleagant's sister sets out in search of Lancelot, with no directions to guide her, she takes the first road and follows it "par avanture" (l. 6398). Yet after she has wandered hither, thither and yon (see ll. 6410-25), Fortune finally leads her straight to Lancelot's tower (ll. 6437-38). Each of these statements conjures up the unexpected, the role of chance, the surprises and even the good fortune to be found in the romance world. The knight-errant in general faces into the future; Lancelot in particular, aware of the pressures of passing time, moves hurriedly into the unexpected on his way to the expected goal. The surprises for Lancelot, and for other characters as well, pop up at every stage in the romance: Lancelot and the Immodest Damsel are all alone in her castle, yet she is assaulted by a number of knights and sergeants. The entire court at Bath is as mystified by Lancelot's sudden disappearance as Arthur's court is delightfully shocked by his unexpected reappearance just in time to fight Meleagant.

Nor are the surprises limited to the participants in the romance plot. We in the audience are constantly manipulated by the narrator's skillful use of surprise and suspense. His technique seems to imitate the hero's own movement, letting the future happen without any apparent preparation,[71] allowing us to discover events as Lancelot himself does. The very opening scene of the romance has something of the non-sequitur, as we witness first Meleagant's astounding challenge and then the apparently unrelated, but equally shocking intervention from Keu. Such non-sequiturs, whether real or apparent, recur continually in the construction of episodes or in the conduct and characterization of episodic figures like the cart dwarf, who refuses to answer anyone's questions and then disappears himself altogether. Just as we expect an incident to take its natural course, the narrative veers off and we are left wondering "what's happening?" "what now?" Hence our surprise when Lancelot's expected victory over Meleagant twice escapes him or when his quest for Gauvain twice ends in disaster.[72] While we thus follow each twist in the narrator's tale, we are not always and completely in the dark before the lightning intrusions of chance. In fact, the narrator uses a variety of preview announcements, both short-term and long-term, as part of his play with the expected and the unexpected. He favors a type of foreshadowing that reveals and conceals at the same time. For example, we know immediately that Lancelot will regret his two steps of hesitation before the cart (ll. 362-64), but we must wait until much later, in his second interview with the Queen, to find out the reason for his regret (ll. 4484-89).[73] While the *pucele* at the crossroads tells us about the Sword Bridge that Lancelot will cross, and the cemetery episode guarantees that he will indeed cross it and liberate the captives according to the custom of Gorre, that same prediction makes us all the more anxious—along with the monk, the White-haired Knight, his Son and the Hospitable Damsel—to learn who this liberator is.

The characters Lancelot meets on his journeys are particularly prone to making predictions about what Lancelot will or will not accomplish: the first hostess' warnings about the bed, the Immodest Damsel's *covant*, the Proud Son's boasting, the herald's cry, etc. Unfortunately, a great many of these predictions backfire: they set up expectations for what might occur, but prove all too often to be false and misleading signs along Lancelot's *droit chemin*. Lancelot's two escorts are convinced that the Sword Bridge is unpassable: one can no more pass over it than return to the womb and be reborn, one could as easily hold the wind or forbid the birds to sing or dry the seas. Yet Lancelot does indeed cross over the Sword Bridge with the same relative ease with which he overcomes any of the other obstacles on his way (ll. 3094-3129).

Of course, some predictions are realized, but not always as announced. The series of *puceles* Lancelot meets in the course of his quest either ask for or promise a *guerredon*, a reward for service rendered. Most of these promises are never redeemed. But there is one exception: when the *pucele* who turns out to be Meleagant's sister releases Lancelot from his tower prison, she amply fulfills an earlier promise in the Orgueilleux episode to help him. Her thrice-repeated prediction about Lancelot's future need of and benefit from her service (ll. 2802-03, 2898-99, 2936-37), while completely without specification, contributes to the romance public's suspense regarding subsequent events. In her efforts to convince Lancelot that he should show the Orgueilleux no mercy, she makes another type of prediction: unless Lancelot cuts off the disloyal knight's head, his deceit will work once again to the hero's detriment. While the Orgueilleux himself does not have a chance to confirm the *pucele*'s prediction, it certainly does prefigure her own brother's subsequent, repeated treachery: Meleagant is throughout the romance the very incarnation of *desleauté*, spared, but unsparing, always instigating yet another deception. Expected unpredictability and the predictably unexpected thus keep open the road of adventure.

Open-endedness

"What happens next?" "How will it all end?" Surely storytellers have always expected and found such questions to be basic ingredients in their audience's response, whether they reflect the naïve interest of a rapt five-year-old caught up in the hair-raising adventures of Little Red Riding Hood or the sophisticated appreciation of a medieval public initiated into the playful pleasures of courtly romance. While both questions are intertwined in the composition of any narrative, the one focused on endings is especially problematic in romance, where events tend to proliferate at the expense of Aristotelian unity and any simple build-up to an unambiguous closure. Of course, Chrétien's romances remain quite manageable in size and distinctly separate in organization. *Erec et Enide, Cligés, Lancelot, Yvain, Perceval* all retain their individual status, without joining together, as in the prose romance cycles of the thirteenth century. Yet like all romances of the twelfth century, they operate in a context larger than the individual text with its own beginning, middle and end. This is true not only because conventional elements reappear from one romance to the next, but also because romances do not properly end—that is to say, they stop without quite concluding. They reach a point where "what happens next" is suspended, but the potential for continuation remains implicit in both story matter and formal structure. As Paul Zumthor suggests, the hero's quest may end a particular series of actions, but that ending (or rather interruption) does not exhaust the virtuality of his destiny.[74]

As Chrétien composes his romances, he seems to have more and more trouble with the endings—or rather, we should say that ending the action, the series of adventures generated by the plot, becomes more and more problematic for Chrétien's characters, for his narrator, and thus for his public. *Lancelot* marks an important stage in this development, a special case within Chrétien's work, one which identifies the problem of closure in romance narrative. This problem appears in the *Charrette* on a number of different levels. The Epilogue touches on one of these: the role played by Godefroi de Leigni in finishing Chrétien's romance (II. 7098-7112). Godefroi is no Jean de Meung, who continues Guillaume de Lorris' *Roman de la Rose* in order to redirect his predecessor's romance. Nor is he quite in the same category as the various continuators of the *Perceval*, since Godefroi assures us he is only bringing Chrétien's own plan to completion, with Chrétien's full consent. While the designated assistant is careful not to overstep his commission,[75] his explicit intervention itself introduces the possibility for continuations. Though we do not know precisely why or under what circumstances Chrétien asked Godefroi to finish *Lancelot*, the relay of tasks does emphasize how difficult it is to end this romance. Indeed, the debates that have occupied scholars over the years as they try to decipher the Epilogue's meaning demonstrate the problem. Godefroi's specific insistence on closure—"here ends the romance completely"—suggests a need to guard against unauthorized continuations. And with the hindsight of centuries we know how impossible it was, and still is, to enforce such a ban.

Perhaps we should see Godefroi's warning rather as an implicit acknowledgment of romance process, the tendency of romancers to continue the work of predecessors and contemporaries. The potential for continuations appears in the *Charrette* much earlier than the Epilogue in what may be characterized as a whole series of "loose ends": episodic characters like Guinable or the dwarf who appear and disappear with tantalizing prospects left open and unexplained by the narrator, mythic materials like the Flaming Lance and the cart itself whose significance remains enigmatic, rumors that fleet about with no apparent carriers, Lancelot's childhood, and so on. These "loose ends" have occasioned much harsh criticism of *Lancelot*'s incoherence and lack of logic, the confused multiplicity of its episodes. While Robert Guiette has responded to such charges quite convincingly with a defense of poetic mystery as part of the charm of Chrétien's story, a necessary ingredient of adventure and the marvelous,[76] it is equally important to see the value of these "loose ends" as signs pointing to the open-endedness of romance narrative.[77] Lancelot's story as told by Chrétien is embedded in a whole web of possible tales. The narrator may refer obliquely to these possibilities, as when he mentions Lancelot's childhood with the Lady of the Lake, but his story cannot include them all. Later romancers will include more and more of these other stories: the Vulgate Cycle of the thirteenth century, which presents Lancelot's Cart Adventure within the complete chronicle of Arthur's kingdom, from its establishment to its calamitous fall, grows by a process of additions that fill in the actions which precede and follow those recounted in Chrétien's romance. But Chrétien's art does not yet have that sense of *horror vacui*: he is quite content to suggest openings, to sketch only roughly spaces within and around his own work.

Godefroi's Epilogue indicates that Chrétien ended his part of the *Charrette* with Lancelot imprisoned in the tower. May we not read this as a comment, however wittily indirect, on romance endings as action suspended rather than finalized? Some critics, however, have interpreted Lancelot "enmurez" as an expression of Chrétien's personal distaste for adultery.[78] Others suggest a failure of authorial invention once Lancelot's initial quest has been (more or less) completed.[79] Although neither of these explanations is conclusive, each may be seen as pointing towards useful avenues of inquiry. While all romances combine themes of love and combat, the combination particular to *Lancelot* does involve an adulterous love. Since Arthur cannot be so conveniently disposed of as Alis in *Cligés*, a tidy ending like marriage in *Erec et Enide* seems impossible. The love relationship between Guenevere and Lancelot is explicitly held in suspension. After the night of love which consummates their union for the first time, the narrator tells us: "No date is set for another meeting. This weighs on Lancelot, but it cannot be helped" (ll. 4704-05). The possibility for a second private meeting between the lovers is again raised, only to be again postponed, in the closing scene. This time the narrator takes the Queen's point of view as he describes how public decorum prevents her from acting on the promptings of *fol amer* and *fol panser*, "foolish love" and "foolish thought." Instead of giving in to her desire to kiss Lancelot, she postpones the matter until a more private place can be found (ll. 6849-53). Both these passages suggest that the major "loose end" of the *Charrette* is precisely the future of Lancelot and Guenevere's love affair. Their story is decidedly not closed, cannot be closed, when Chrétien's romance ends.

How, then, does Godefroi end the romance for Chrétien? Such closure as there is centers on the story of Meleagant. And if that is so, we may question whether *Lancelot* ends as abruptly as some critics have charged.[80] Let us start by comparing the opening and closing scenes. What factors introduced by the first episode at Arthur's court need to be unraveled in the last one? Meleagant, two prisoners, an agreement concerning combat, a challenger and the safety of the Queen are at stake. In one sense, Meleagant's initial challenge to Arthur raises the specter of a story without any ending:

> Rois Artus, j'ai en ma prison,
> de ta terre et de ta meison,
> chevaliers, dames et puceles;
> mes ne t'an di pas les noveles

> por ce que jes te vuelle randre;
> ençois te voel dire et aprandre
> que tu n'as force ne avoir
> par quoi tu les puisses avoir;
> et saches bien qu'ainsi morras
> que ja aidier ne lor porras.
> (ll. 51-60)

(King Arthur, I have in my prison knights, ladies and damsels from your kingdom and from your household. But I'm not giving you news of them because I want to give them back to you. Rather, I want to tell you that you have neither force nor wealth by which you can have them back. And know well that you will die without being able to help them.)

Meleagant is kinder to Arthur when he proposes a possible issue to this predicament: double or nothing, the Queen for the prisoners, all pending on a duel between Meleagant and any champion the king appoints. The agreement, which Arthur is forced to accept without realizing it because of Keu's trick and the Rash Boon, means that each time Meleagant engages one of Arthur's knights in combat, we expect the *Charrette* to end shortly thereafter. Such an expectation is highlighted by Lancelot's oath before the second combat with Meleagant, which includes a promise to show no mercy (ll. 4977-84). That predictable ending is, however, delayed, as closure is evoked, postponed and finally confirmed by nearer and nearer repetitions of the opening scene at Arthur's court:

1. The opening scene at Arthur's court introduces the possibility of later combat. Those present include Arthur, the Queen, Keu, Meleagant and Gauvain. Lancelot is absent. Meleagant offers to fight any of Arthur's knights who will escort the Queen into the woods. Such is the agreement. At stake are the prisoners and the Queen.

2. Stage 2, the first displacement, is Keu's combat in the woods; the Queen, Keu and Meleagant are present. Those absent, but in pursuit, are Arthur's court, especially Gauvain, and Lancelot. The same challenge and risk are involved. No description of the encounter.

3. Stage 3, a further displacement, occurs when Lancelot fights with Meleagant, but is overpowered by superior numbers. There are no witnesses to this combat and no description of it. We learn of it only in retrospect, when Gauvain sees the traces left on the battle scene. Significant are Lancelot's presence and Gauvain's continued absence.

4. The fourth stage is located at Bademagu's court in Bath. With Gauvain still absent, combat between Lancelot and Meleagant takes place twice according to the initial agreement. The prisoners and Guenevere are liberated, but a new agreement prepares a repetition of the Lancelot-Meleagant duel at Arthur's court—with the Queen's safety once again at risk.

5. In the fifth stage Meleagant arrives at Arthur's court to initiate the second agreement. Lancelot is absent, and there is no news of his whereabouts. Meleagant accepts Gauvain as a substitute champion for Lancelot in a year's time.

6. The final stage at Arthur's court occurs when Meleagant returns to fulfill the agreement. The scene unfolds in two parts: (a) Gauvain substitutes for the absent Lancelot, (b) Lancelot arrives in time to defeat Meleagant. Meleagant's death eliminates all risk for the Queen and any future repetitions of the pattern.

Certain reverse parallels highlight the links between the opening and closing scenes. While one major constant throughout is the Queen herself— only she is present at all stages—her importance in the first scene, when Lancelot was absent, contrasts noticeably with her reduced role at the end, once Lancelot has arrived and the drive to end his combat with Meleagant takes precedence. The presentation of Guenevere's thoughts about Lancelot mirrors this play, as they are briefly evoked in his absence (Foerster, ll. 211-13), then more elaborately described in his presence (Roques, ll. 6820-53). In both scenes we know that Lancelot has been riding hard to arrive in time, though we learn this fact only after the initial episode at Arthur's court has been played out. Lancelot's failure to arrive in the first case is the significant variation (at least in retrospect) that allows the romance action to proceed, introducing Lancelot's quest and the repeated duels.

But why does the romance not end in the fourth stage, at Bath, with the defeat of Meleagant? What is Chrétien up to in the second half of the *Charrette*? In his discussion of bipartition as a typical pattern of medieval narrative structure, William Ryding describes the middle as the point of maximum logical discontinuity, the point where fictionality asserts itself because the author must invent the links that join the two parts of his narrative.[81] In his view, Lancelot's reversal of fortune, when the Queen refuses to speak to him, divides the romance into two parts: while the end is fixed from the very beginning, the uncharted middle stretches out, accordion-like, as that end is delayed. This particular description of *Lancelot*'s bipartite structure makes clear the minimal difference between those scholars who identify the *Charrette*'s structure as bipartite and those who designate it as tripartite. Douglas Kelly, for example, divides the work into

    1. Opening scene at Arthur's court
        a. Lancelot's quest
        b. Lancelot at Bath
        c. Lancelot's imprisonment
    2. Closing scene at Arthur's court[82]

Z.P. Zaddy first dissects the romance into six episodes, then groups them into three parts, the first of which serves as preface to the last two.[83] Each of these schemes demonstrates a concern for designating a midpoint dividing the linear organization of Lancelot's quest (during which episodes are juxtaposed along the "straight road" leading to Bademagu's castle) from the quite different arrangement of the later episodes, at once more circular in character (as indicated by the departures and returns to Bath and Arthur's court) and more logical in their use of cause and effect to combine events.

This difference in narrative structures is reflected in the time sequences indicated by the narrator as he unfolds his tale. In the quest section the alternation of days and nights is carefully indicated: Lancelot follows Meleagant and the Queen for six days, spending each night in a different lodging along his route. Even the canonical hours are frequently marked off as Lancelot progresses through each action-packed day (and night). Once he arrives at Bath, the narrator alternates between precise sequences of time and larger blocks of time that pass by with little or no specific chronology. Compare, for example, the carefully marked stages just before, during and after Lancelot's rendezvous with the Queen with the indefinite stretch of time spent at Bademagu's court waiting for news of Lancelot or with the length of Lancelot's imprisonment.

Having distinguished these two different types of narrative organization, we need to return again to the question of how and why Chrétien has combined them, how and why he exploits discontinuity to continue elaborating his romance. If, on the one hand, those "non-sequiturs" mentioned earlier lend a sense of openness and surprise to Lancelot's encounters on the *droit chemin*, his quest is, nevertheless, securely tied to a goal, a specific end: rescue Guenevere (and thus liberate the prisoners). By contrast to Erec's and Yvain's quests, Lancelot's is both more compressed in time and more specifically anchored to a particular course and destination. Yet, paradoxically, his is the longest unresolved.[84] It is as if Chrétien's narrative keeps duplicating the pattern of pursuit that recurs so frequently in his story: after an initial delay, Gauvain quickly sets out to follow Keu, the rest of Arthur's knights imitate his celerity in dashing after Gauvain, Lancelot rides his horse to death pursuing Meleagant, Gauvain hastens to catch up with Lancelot, and so on—each one rides at top speed, yet manages to lose sight, at least temporarily, of the object pursued. Just so, Chrétien's audience feels itself repeatedly hurtling towards a conclusion, only to find itself caught in the byways of delay as Chrétien unwinds his tale in the time-honored, long-winded fashion of yarn-spinners.

One might say, in fact, that delay is the mode of open-endedness most characteristic of the *Charrette*: delay operates at every level of Chrétien's narrative from motif through episode to overall structure, from Lancelot's characteristic hesitations to his relationship with the Queen, from the smallest units of verbal patterns to the largest problems of meaning and evaluation. If, for example, we consider how the two parts of the *Charrette* relate to each other through the middle section, it is clear that the entire development that follows upon Lancelot and Meleagant's first combat at Bath is a delay occasioned by Bademagu's intervention. With the Queen's consent, he stops their fight and sets up a new agreement between them (ll. 3877-83). The end of the present combat is delayed and a new period of delay is established. The very terms of the agreement play on the motif of delay like a set of Chinese boxes: Lancelot must respond "without any delay" (l. 3879) to a call for combat, yet that call will occur at an unspecified time in the future and then only after another year's delay (l. 3882).

The circularity in the narrative composition of the second half particularly enhances this sense of delay by its repeated pattern of departures and returns. Lancelot twice leaves in quest of Gauvain, but never does find him; subsequent repeated searches for Lancelot are equally fruitless. Lancelot leaves his place of imprisonment for the tournament, returns, and still no one at Arthur's court has any word about his detention. Meleagant twice goes to Arthur's court and each time finds Lancelot absent—until his sudden arrival just as Gauvain is about to take his place in the combat.

This final scene is especially suspenseful precisely because of the tension between delaying and not delaying. Meleagant accepts Gauvain as substitute defender and wants an immediate duel: "car plus ne vos en atandrai" (l. 6745) (I shall wait for you no longer). Gauvain himself responds "without delay" (ll. 6755, 6757, 6764). Yet the narrator takes his time in a leisurely thirty-line description of Gauvain's arming (ll. 6755-85), which enhances the building pressure of suspense. We already know that Lancelot is on his way to Arthur's court, but will he arrive in time? Even when Lancelot does appear just as Gauvain is about to take up his shield, the narrator delays the final combat somewhat more by describing the court's joyous welcome (including the Queen's private reaction) and Lancelot's explanation for his delay. Again we prepare to witness the final duel: Lancelot arms "tot sanz delai et sanz demore" (l. 6911) (completely without delay or hesitancy), while the narrator makes us privy to Meleagant's astonishment (including a monologue in direct discourse some 24 lines long, ll. 6920-64). Lancelot is now ready to attack, but this time Arthur keeps us waiting by selecting a site for combat below the tower on a beautiful plain. All the combatants and spectators reassemble there, while the narrator devotes eighteen more lines to a description of the place. Thus, the narrative teases us with its rhetorical pauses, while it claims to rush towards the end "without delay."

Nor are such tactics limited to the second half of the romance, despite the linearity of Lancelot's quest. Douglas Kelly has pointed out how Chrétien uses the technique of *entrelacement* to link episodes in an interlocking ABABA pattern.[85] In this way, for example, the encounters with the Proud Son and his father "interrupt" Lancelot's voyage with the Immodest Damsel, first after their discovery of the comb and again after the tomb adventure, at which point both the damsel and her would-be suitor leave off following the mysterious hero. A similar pattern of deferral occurs when Lancelot arrives at Bath,[86] and later when the narrative alternates between Lancelot and Guenevere during the first unsuccessful search for Gauvain.

Without enumerating all the recurrences of this pattern, we can already see that the tendency to defer endings is as basic to the construction of episodes as it is to the overall organization of Chrétien's romance. This is true not only for the narrator's art, but for the characters' actions as well. Consider the arrangement of the tournament at Noauz: an initial delay allows for news of it to circulate as widely as possible, while Lancelot's victory and disappearance lead to another delay when all the maidens decide not to marry within the year because they cannot have Lancelot. Lancelot's anonymity itself at the tournament and during his quest constitutes a delay, deferring knowledge of his identity, reserving it for a particular time or a particular person. In fact, the most critical event in the romance (as signaled by the title itself) is marked by delay: Lancelot delays entry into the cart by two steps. That delay in turn triggers a second one, since the Queen's unexpectedly cold reception temporarily defers any direct contact between the lovers. In fact, Lancelot's conduct shifts repeatedly between the extremes of delay and haste, or "no delay," as it is frequently noted by the text. His love-motivated *panser*, itself a kind of suspension of the self out of time, leads repeatedly to delayed action, as when he fails to return Meleagant's blows while he contemplates the Queen with ecstatic abandon. In the series of combats which mark his progress towards Bath, the narrator sets up a pattern of delay in finalizing Lancelot's victory, whether it be with the Ford Knight or the Orgueilleux de la Lande, with the men who threaten to violate his hostess[87] or with Meleagant himself.[88] On the other hand, Lancelot's promptness is equally characteristic.[89] Indeed, when offered hospitality at an inappropriately early hour, he replies with a "policy statement" on his need for haste, a need of which he is fully conscious—barring his moments of *panser*—though it surfaces with particular urgency at different junctures:

> Car malvés est qui se demore
> ne qui a eise se repose
> puis qu'il a enprise tel chose;

> et je ai tel afeire anpris
> qu'a piece n'iert mes ostex pris.
> (ll. 2268-72)

(For he's a coward who delays or stops over at his ease, once he's undertaken a great enterprise. And I have taken in charge such an affair that I won't take lodging for some time yet.)

Other characters perform similarly without delay, as when the Proud Son rides up to claim his lady or Meleagant's sister sets off in search of Lancelot. On the other hand, they may find their movement retarded for one reason or another, through their own actions or someone else's. Gauvain himself tells King Arthur that he failed to rescue the Queen because of his delay (l. 5326). Only Lancelot, however, lives out the paradox of one who, always pressed for time, constantly falls into the trap of deferred action.

Lancelot's problem with temporal delay needs, moreover, to be related to his problem with spatial delay—that is, his detention as Meleagant's prisoner—and this in turn should be considered together with the problem of the prisoners detained in the land of Gorre. In order to do so, I shall return once again to the romance's opening scene to examine how the themes of delay and detainment are coordinated from the very beginning.

The first part of Meleagant's speech stresses the open-ended nature of the prisoners' entrapment: there is no time limit to their detention; not even Arthur's death can introduce one. The second part of his speech, suggesting a possible issue to the initial impasse, introduces a sense of the "time until" (*tant que*) an action occurs: Meleagant will wait until a champion comes to meet him in the woods. This formulation does not yet suggest any pressure from a specific time limit. The offer might even go by unaccepted, since Arthur has already resigned himself to the fate of the prisoners. But that would be atypical of Arthur's court: such challenges often occasion reluctance and delay among Arthurian knights, but a champion—usually the as yet unrecognized hero, but here Keu, a sort of "antihero"—eventually requests the honor of meeting the challenger. Keu's action, however, as described by the narrator, cannot immediately be connected to Meleagant's challenge. It seems to introduce a second, parallel problem of delay and detention (or retention) when Keu threatens to leave Arthur's service (ll. 89-92). Keu's precipitous exit demands swift action:

> Seneschax, si con vos solez,
> soiez a cort, et sachiez bien
> que je n'ai en cest monde rien
> que je, por vostre *demorance*,
> ne vos doigne *sanz porloignance*.
> (ll. 106-10, my emphasis)

(Seneschal, stay at court as you are wont, and know that I have nothing in the world that I wouldn't give you without delay to keep you here.)

The rhyme words go to the crux of the problem (and not incidentally demonstrate the narrator's consummate ingenuity). *Demorance* here signifies Keu's "staying" at court, but its repeated use elsewhere in the romance to mean delay (whether as verb or noun)[90] pinpoints the connection between detaining and delaying. Arthur will detain his seneschal, that is, delay his departure, by promising to give *without delay* anything in exchange for Keu's deferral. When Keu refuses to accept the bargain offered, Guenevere is called upon to intervene by falling at Keu's feet. In a sense, her gesture dramatizes and refines the pattern already set up by Meleagant—action coerced by waiting or delay (here with a specific time limit): she will not rise from her place on the floor *until* Keu agrees to stay.

At this point, the court and Chrétien's public learn that Keu has set up this elaborate charade precisely in order to obtain a "Rash Boon" from King Arthur: the right to escort the Queen into the woods and encounter the waiting knight (a variation on his original intention to depart). The pressure of time first introduced by Keu's maneuver thus carries over to the bargain offered by Meleagant, since Keu's presumption and subsequent defeat trigger the somewhat delayed, but nevertheless hasty pursuit led by Gauvain in an effort to recover the Queen from her captor. As the plot develops, we learn that an important factor omitted in that opening scene was Lancelot's absence. That critical absence only barely surfaces in the Queen's mysterious whisper addressed to someone who would not have allowed her to be led off without resistance.[91] Though we never learn what detained Lancelot, we do come to realize that his delayed arrival was the *sine qua non* of Meleagant's successful detention of Guenevere and the captives.

The play between delay and detainment reappears throughout Chrétien's text. The custom of Gorre itself makes it a leitmotif. Those who are natives of Gorre may enter and exit with equal ease. Those who are natives of Logres find matters more difficult. There is a two-tier system operating: any ordinary man, woman or child of Logres may enter Gorre freely, but once inside may not leave until one person from Logres enters and exits from Gorre. For this person, or rather for her champion (since it turns out to be the Queen's), a special system operates: entrance is no longer so simple, but must be effected by way of one of two bridges, the *Ponz Evages* or the *Pont de l'Espee*, the Underwater Bridge or the Sword Bridge. According to the information given by the tomb inscription and elaborated by both the vavasor host and the narrator,[92] once this special champion enters by the requisite route and then leaves, all the citizens of Logres may leave Gorre with complete freedom. That seems simple enough. But when the Queen and the former prisoners return to Arthur's court, apparently in accordance with the custom of Gorre, a new prisoner remains behind —despite Lancelot's explicit identification earlier as a citizen of Logres (II. 1929-30). What has gone wrong?

The custom of Gorre sets up two formulas for the romance plot: exit = end, detain = delay (including delay of the ending). If all the captives leave Gorre after the first combat between Meleagant and Lancelot, then Chrétien has run out of story and his romance must end. If, on the other hand, someone can be retained prisoner, the plot remains open, the ending deferred. While Chrétien's collaborators in delay include at one time or another all the major characters of the *Charrette*, Meleagant in his essential disloyalty may be considered the prime mover in this respect. He is the one who initially misrepresents the custom of Gorre: first he implicitly denies its existence, since according to the conditions of the custom—and contrary to his opening remark—the story of the prisoners was always a story with a possible ending. Then he substitutes his own version of it by proposing a duel with one of Arthur's knights, winner take all: Queen and prisoners. His agreement thus seems to specify the manner by which the captives may exit "loyally," an issue left vague in the description of the custom offered by the vavasor host (ll. 2112-15).

I shall take up the problem of loyal action again shortly. In the meantime, we can follow a shift in the party for delay once Lancelot reaches Bath. At that point neither Meleagant nor Lancelot wants to put off immediate enactment of the agreement, despite the repeated entreaties of Bademagu to defer their combat.[93] While Bademagu does succeed in postponing the duel overnight, he would prefer to eliminate any combat between Lancelot and his son. Interestingly, his argument to dissuade Meleagant from fighting extends further the range of potential meaning to be developed within the themes of delay and detainment. In his speeches delay and peace are constantly associated—an association easily effected through the verb *detenir* (cf. our current use of *détente*): Bademagu, "qui tant con il puet les detient, / si se painne de la peis feire" (II. 3552-53)[94] (Bademagu, who holds them back as much as he can, works hard to make peace). In Bademagu's opinion, Lancelot's crossing the Sword Bridge has already shown him to be such an extraordinary champion that Meleagant should not simply defer their combat, but indeed defer to the unknown knight: honor him by returning the Queen without any combat before the knight even demands her return.[95] But Meleagant, the *desleal par excellence*, is deaf to any argument based on yielding to another's superiority. The combat will take place as determined by his original agreement. Meleagant wants his own ending.

Nevertheless, throughout this critical middle section Bademagu serves the narrator's desire to continue his story. Renewing his interventions to prevent what he considers Meleagant's imminent death, the king forces his son to suspend the combat. In spite of what everyone has witnessed, Meleagant insists that he was winning—as he was at one point, but only because Lancelot stopped fighting. However, once Meleagant has accepted the new agreement arranged by Bademagu, he cheats on his end of the bargain: his explicit denial of Lancelot's superiority may cover private feelings of inferiority. Lancelot's entrapment is designed to prevent him from completing the deferred combat. Finally, Meleagant's disloyalty explains why the custom of Gorre breaks down: his own agreements do not quite coincide with the terms of the custom, which demand respect for loyal action. Yet his disloyalty in detaining Lancelot is precisely what enables Chrétien to detain his public and prolong his story. Though the narrator constantly uses the motif "without delay" to describe not only his characters' actions, but also his own haste in sticking to his story and moving it along expeditiously (e.g., ll. 3181-84), that leitmotif is simply a mask for his deferred endings. The narrator's craft, like Meleagant's craftiness, involves games of deception.

If all the delays enumerated so far do retard the conclusion of Chrétien's romance while at the same time detaining his public's interest by the suspense they introduce, we might still wonder if a secret connivance links these delays and the romance's actual ending: are they contradictory or complementary—or perhaps a bit of both? In the middle section, for example, from Lancelot's rejection by the Queen to the trap engineered by Meleagant, the action of the romance seems to lose all forward momentum as we zigzag back and forth between Lancelot's aborted quests for Gauvain and the state of the Queen's mind and health while still at Bath. The hand of the narrator can be felt as he manipulates Fortune and Rumor to create a series of quick reversals. While Lancelot and Guenevere oscillate between life and death, suicidal sorrow and unexpected joy, the rhetorical character of their monologues, the doctrinal quality of their disquisitions on love, underline the narrator's play not so very far behind the scenes. In fact, one suspects a certain humorous twinkle in the narrator's eye when he describes how Lancelot wants to kill himself "sanz respit," then shows him give way to a long lament, generously elaborated through 22 lines. Yet the back-and-forth movement of the narrative does not simply return us to any fixed point of departure. In the course of those monologues, the narrator reveals his characters' thoughts to us—and to Lancelot and Guenevere themselves. The Queen certainly learns more about the intensity of her own love when she hears about Lancelot's death, and the rumors of his suicide attempt reveal—or confirm—the depth of his love for her. Lancelot's rescue from suicide further allows him to speculate on the Queen's motivation in rejecting him and thus to develop his own ideas on proper conduct in love. This series of revelations and speculations, occurring completely within the inner domain of thought, while effective action seems to be deferred, produces new passion, new action that leads to the night of love consummated. Narrative delay and narrative development work hand in hand. Just as the ladies who would like to detain Lancelot for themselves, whether amorous hostess or amicable jailor, only further his progress towards the Queen,[96] so narrative delay and narrative development work hand in hand.

The pattern of delay that recurs in Lancelot's encounters with the Ford Knight, the Orgueilleux and Meleagant may also appear from one angle as part of the strategy to hasten towards a conclusion. In those combats, where Lancelot perceives that the battle has gone on for an excessively long time, his consequent anger and shame—especially intensified by the presence of spectators—so fire his prowess that victory is quick (ll. 866-81, 2717-28, 3704-11). In those combats where the ending is deferred by a third party's intervention, an accelerated rhythm characterizes the movement from one fight to the next. Once Lancelot has established his superiority, his prowess quickens the pace to the end.[97]

Lancelot is the narrator's key tool for bringing his story to a close (even without complete closure). If the character of the *desleal* is an unceasing source of plots and deceptions, as Meleagant's sister indicates, Lancelot's *leauté* and *droiture* keep him—and the narrator, when he chooses to follow him—on the straight road ahead. Thus, it is Lancelot's impetus that sustains the linearity of his quest in the first half of the *Charrette*, his loyalty in keeping his word once an agreement has been established that drives him, and Chrétien's romance, to the final scene at Arthur's court. Yet Lancelot's virtue can also be exploited by the less virtuous. The second dwarf easily diverts a trusting Lancelot from his search for Gauvain by promising to lead him to a "very good place" (l. 5075). Later Meleagant knows that Lancelot will return as promised to the seneschal's wife; his circular movement of departure and return thus allows the *desleal* to continue practicing his own circuitous deceptions.

In fact, loyalty and disloyalty dovetail to structure the romance. Linearity and circularity appear in constant combination. This is true not only on the level of narrative structure, but on that of meaning as well. As mentioned earlier, Lancelot's paradoxical character often leads his forward haste into paths of delay, not only because of the machinations of Meleagant, but also because of his own virtues—or rather because of the paradoxical nature of the virtues themselves as they are combined in the ideal knight and lover. At the castle of the Immodest Damsel Lancelot hesitates repeatedly. Should he endanger his mission for the Queen by going to the aid of his hostess? Can he keep his agreement to share her bed and still remain faithful to his lady? Later, faced by the apparently incompatible demands of *largece* and *pitiez,* Lancelot stops again to debate the alternatives (l. 2831). Should he satisfy pity and spare the Orgueilleux, or should he ignore the defeated knight's cries for mercy and generously satisfy the damsel's request to cut off his head? Each one has a valid claim on his service. So Lancelot responds affirmatively to both appeals.

Nor is Lancelot the only character caught in a world of conflicting demands expressive of conflicting obligations. The repeated interventions of Bademagu on behalf of Meleagant pose the same sort of problem: the king's love for his son and the Queen's *corteisie* both cooperate to allow Meleagant's treachery continued play. While their filial and social virtues delay putting an end to Meleagant's vices, they also impede virtues like justice and loyalty. These paradoxical situations reveal a last twist in the theme of delay: choosing between different actions—that is, deciding to whom or to what to defer—may require deferring all action until the appropriate course can be determined (cf. the French verb *différer*). Furthermore, if these different actions, equally compelling and virtuous, derive from incompatible value systems, we may have to defer judgments altogether. An excellent illustration is the adultery of Lancelot and Guenevere itself. Thus, the open-endedness of romance extends into the domain of meaning and interpretation, as we no less than Chrétien's characters seek the *droit chemin,* the true narrative *san.*

San *(Romance World)*

Following the *Charrette*'s paradoxical lead, we shall take the *droit chemin* full circle in this final section by returning to an issue raised in Chrétien's Prologue. Now that we have explored the larger context of the entire romance, how should we understand Chrétien's *san*? Lancelot himself gives us a useful approach to that elusive term. At one point in his journey with the Immodest Damsel, he perceives that she has led him off the "droiz chemins batuz" (l. 1379) and insists that such a detour is inconsistent with his mission. Once he has started down the "beaten path leading straight ahead," "je ne tornerai autre *san*" (l. 1381, my emphasis). Of the various possibilities for translating *san,* this passage clearly refers to the "direction" Lancelot has chosen: "I will not turn in another direction." The narrator leads up to Lancelot's remark by repeating in a variety of formulations the motif of the "right road,"[98] reverting to it constantly to describe Lancelot's direction.[99] And to talk about his own direction as storyteller: "ne je ne la [ma matire] vuel boceier / ne corrronpre ne forceier, / mes mener boen chemin et droit" (ll. 6249-51)[100] (I do not want to disfigure or leave gaps in or twist [my matter], but lead it along a good and straight path). This road "straight ahead," whether for Lancelot or the narrator, obviously involves more than geographical or temporal orientation; its metaphorical overtones of rightness appear explicitly in the romance dialogue on more than one occasion. When, for example, Lancelot gives Gauvain first choice between the two bridges leading into Gorre, the latter replies with his customary courtesy: "... mes n'est pas *droiz* qu'an moi remaingne / quant parti m'an avez le geu" (ll. 694-95, my emphasis) (it's not *right* for me to hesitate, since you've given me the choice). Elsewhere the question of *droiture* is evoked by the first night's hostess (l. 575), by Lancelot himself (ll. 1600-01, 1707), by Bademagu (l. 3445) and even by Meleagant (ll. 4794, 4805, 4874, 4952), whose problematic connection to "rightness" will be considered shortly. With such associations operating, it is not surprising that Lancelot refuses to take those roundabout, easy paths that avoid the risks of the *droit chemin* or that more than once the straight road ahead is so narrow that only a single knight can pass through. These moral overtones may be introduced seriously with Lancelot at the stone passage or humorously with the Proud Son, so worried about turning his horse around without injury on the narrow path, but the symbolic value of the "right road" as a difficult journey, a series of tests that single out the hero (or distinguish the accomplished narrator), operates throughout the romance.

What, then, do we make of the associative string that moves from *san* to *droit chemin* to *droiture*? I would suggest that the meaning of the *Charrette* is the direction towards understanding, the search for significant values, be they ethical or artistic ones. Chrétien's romance outlines a direction to take, furnishes guidelines and necessary questions along the way to formulating truth, meaning and value. This formulation still requires further glossing. Does it permit us to explain that "courtly love" is the meaning of the *Charrette,* the *san* given by Marie de Champagne? That has been the main theme of critical argument on *Lancelot* ever since Gaston Paris coined the term "amour courtois" and used Andreas Capellanus' example to describe Chrétien's four-part "doctrine on love."[101] As I suggested earlier in the Prologue discussion, debate has centered primarily on whether Chrétien himself was "for" or "against" courtly love so defined and, consequently, in or out of agreement with his patroness. The analysis here confirms that love as an experience and as a mode of conduct in courtly society is a major concern in the *Charrette*. Regardless of whether "courtly love" existed as an historical phenomenon in French society of the twelfth century, it is indisputably a theme in this romance, as in other contemporary and subsequent medieval texts. I think we can even say that the *Charrette* shows Lancelot as knight and lover in as favorable a light as possible.[102] The narrator's ironic wit filters without obscuring the brilliance of Lancelot's heroic accomplishments, and these depend in large measure on the intensity of his passion for Guenevere.

But we should not mistake an important theme of Chrétien's romance for its meaning. The latter results not from the content of the story *per se*, but from the way that content is handled in the total organization of the text. In this larger perspective, we can discern the *Charrette*'s general preoccupation with social behavior in an ideal society. Love is not the only value system operating there. Customs, feudal hierarchy, chivalric courtesy, marvelous adventures and even private agreements between individuals—each tends to organize itself as a code of required and forbidden actions, desirable virtues and undesirable vices.[103] Unfortunately, one system's honorable exploit may be another's shameful crime. Lancelot and Guenevere's joy—is it adultery or treason?—is the most obvious, if understated, example in the romance. But it is only one of several implied conflicts. When Arthur observes the custom of the Rash Boon and allows Keu to lead Guenevere off to the woods, he chooses not to fulfill his feudal and family obligations to protect the Queen. Even within a single system of values, different virtues may compete with each other, as in Lancelot's debate between Pity and Largess before cutting off the Orgueilleux's head. Where conflicts and paradox abound, we must deduce from the solutions offered which values prevail, when they are to be observed and how they may be related. Lancelot's own solution is an interesting one. We saw earlier how he subordinates all competing claims to those of love. He does not eliminate the other values, but provides guidelines for choosing among them, at least when love is in question. To a certain extent, Lancelot's conduct is exemplary. He is "cil qui l'aunera," the one who will measure for us, setting a standard for what is better, what worse.[104] The extreme shifts in his own behavior indicate how important a particular context may be for determining correct action, appropriate value. Company is sometimes desirable, sometimes not. Certain situations require silence and calm, others a tongue ready with quick retort. But is it always so easy to know which response is appropriate or what a given action signifies in a particular situation? What should we think when Meleagant claims to speak for *droiture*—or when the narrator claims to avoid conventional flattery and yet such flattery is true? Lancelot's guidelines may not be adequate: his solution may not be transferable within or without the romance context. Time and again one character tries to interpret the actions of another and fails. The derision attached to Lancelot's conduct at the tournament, the speculations about cowardice and beginner's luck, all juxtaposed to the Queen's inside information and secret delight—that incident provides ample illustration of how mistaken Chrétien's characters can be. Nor is Lancelot exempt from human fallibility, as indicated by his misunderstanding of the Queen's cold reception. The hero's own hesitations and delays suggest how much the problem of interpretation moves into the very plot of the *Charrette*.

The general preoccupation with interpretation, especially as the interpretations themselves so often fall short of the truth, seduces the audience into taking up the activity and trying to improve on such manifest incompetence. With the aid of our superior vision, coached by the narrator's more encompassing view, we easily see how mistaken is Meleagant's accusation of Keu, how unfair Lancelot's indictment of Fortune. Chrétien's text thus constantly invites interpretation and judgment, yet warns us both seriously and comically against hasty conclusions. After all, Lancelot's horse, too, can follow the best and straightest road (ll. 726-27), but the horse's thirst leads straight to a good dousing for the hero and a shameful reversal to the Ford Knight's challenges. We should not forget that one of the meanings associated with *san* is "good sense": Chrétien's characters, as well as his audience, need plenty of good sense to know how to follow the guidelines of understanding, how to recognize the limits of knowledge and how to defer judgment until all the relevant data have been evaluated.

The problem of interpretation leads inevitably to the common romance theme of appearance and reality. These two planes are more often than not out of phase in the *Charrette*, where the title event itself leads to so much confusion. In particular, Lancelot's character and conduct require a kind of double vision that penetrates confusing appearances and discovers the reality of his singular heroism. Such penetration, as we have seen, is denied to most of Chrétien's characters. They see only a section of the truth and so misconstrue the whole. What is the reality that can put together and explain his inconsistent appearances? When do the fragmentary perceptions of Lancelot coalesce in a truly integrated vision? Where questions like these surface, the verb "to see" will obviously serve a critical function. Many scholars have pointed out how extensively the *Charrette* develops the visual aspect of experience, both what is seen and what is hidden from view.[105] Appearance and reality may or may not coincide, but we often arrive at the real by first interpreting what we see. As common sense dictates, "seeing is believing": visible signs often help clarify the truth. When Arthur's knights see Keu's horse emerging riderless from the forest, with broken and bloody saddle, they know that Meleagant has defeated him and now has control of the Queen. Later, confronted with Meleagant's apparently outrageous claim that Keu has betrayed his King by sharing the Queen's bed, Bademagu relies on his eyes for the facts (II. 4826-28). Those bloody sheets may be "ansaignes bien veraies" (I. 4774) (very true signs), but they do not unambiguously announce the truth to all who see them. Meleagant's interpretation seems logical enough: if the Queen's sheets are bloody and Keu's sheets are bloody, then there must be some relationship between them. While the charge of adultery may be entirely correct, we in the audience know as well as Lancelot and the Queen where the process of deduction has gone wrong. We can follow the subsequent course of events through Lancelot's "equivocal oath" and the judicial combat with special insight into the gaps in Meleagant's vision of the truth.

Chrétien seems to delight in multiplying the points of view available in his romance. The narrator, for example, frequently describes one character's actions as they are seen by another: Gauvain watches Lancelot approach the cart, the Immodest Damsel sees Lancelot nearly fall from his horse, spectators witness each of the duels fought by Lancelot, and so on. Different perceptions of the same scene are often included: the tournament as seen by Guenevere, the damsels and the knights; the joyous welcome given Lancelot at the end as public celebration of the court and private desire of the Queen. It is conceivable that such multiple views could add up to a fuller, "truer" picture of reality. Such is the expectation of the Cubist painter, who multiplies the angles of vision in order to catch a complex whole. But in Chrétien the different points of view more frequently demonstrate ironic distortions of the truth, a failure to achieve complete vision. By juxtaposing multiple perspectives, he demonstrates just how limited and subjective is the information they yield.

Even the narrator tells his story without a complete overview: Gauvain and the Dameisele de la Tor's private conversation, for example, remains closed to him (II. 548-49), as does the motivation of the masons who work for Meleagant (I. 6114). Such details are simply irrelevant to his *matière* and are set aside in the interests of moving along the straight road of his story without delay.[106] But occasionally the narrator actually suppresses knowledge he clearly possesses, either as a ploy to create suspense[107] or for the sake of modesty.[108] Each of these games in which the narrator denies or refuses information highlights the more general problem of limited and subjective perspectives. If we would evaluate Lancelot's behavior as knight or lover, we must follow the example set, however unwillingly, by the Proud Son: rather than relying on first impressions, we need to involve ourselves in a process of collecting and evaluating data, combining the partial views offered in an effort to reconstruct a whole picture. Visible signs like a man's appearance or his observed actions help guide us in that process of investigation, but good sense reminds us that they may be ambiguous and may require vigilant questioning before their truthfulness can be ascertained. Such is Lancelot's conduct when he questions the monk about the inscriptions he read on the tombstones. Such also is the caution shown by the Queen, who carefully tests the identity of the unknown knight at the tournament before trusting her impression that such a champion must be Lancelot. The possible ambiguity of messages, which Guenevere herself exploits with the instructions to fight *au noauz*, might help explain why she repeats her trial the second day, since only continued verification can avoid the pitfalls of "true signs" that somehow turn out to be false and deceiving.

The limitation implied in the narrator's use of the impossibility topic[109] reminds us also that just as the narrator cannot say everything, so the vision offered by the romance world cannot show everything. Its views remain partial, individual, humanly circumscribed. The series of problems just reviewed—competing social values in conflict, multiple and limited points of view, truth and the ambiguity of signs—together suggest that Chrétien's *Charrette* is not arranged to exemplify a single, unambiguous truth. It is not a romance recommending or condemning courtly love. If we are to find a message in Chrétien's entertainment, I think that *Lancelot* aims at a wider ethical problem, not the codification of a single value, but the contradictions of the human experience within the courtly secular ideal.[110] Chrétien seems to have organized his romance like the school exercises for clerkly debate.[111] The arguments for either side of a question are given, but the decision that would conclude or resolve the debate is left out.[112] In the process of its own elaboration, the *Charrette* gives directions for weighing values, invites interpretation and judgment, moves towards an ideal, even as it shows the conflicts that arise between ideals. In this case, moreover, resolution is not simply withheld for the sake of game or exercise. Within the perspective offered in Chrétien's romance, the contradictions are irreducible: Arthur's ideal secular society cannot solve them, even if an exceptional hero like Lancelot seems to achieve the impossible when he satisfies the conflicting demands placed on him.[113]

Lancelot's successful resolution recalls the poet's own accomplishments. His *conjointure*, the harmony and unity of his text, conceals its lack of closure beneath the polished surface of art. But if the romance conceals, it ultimately reveals the open-ended quest and contradictory ideals contained within it.[114] It does so by drawing us into itself, by emphasizing its own process of invention—thus, the parallels at every stage between the actions narrated and the act of narration itself. Chrétien already hints in that direction as he describes his role in the Prologue. Despite the modesty of his deference to Marie de Champagne, it is surely significant that *san(s)*, in whichever of its many guises, appears there to describe his activity as well as her gift. Even more significantly, the Prologue ends by evoking Chrétien's own craft as poet: "sa painne et s'antancïon" (l. 29). This shift to the poet's role as shaper of his story is even more noticeable in all the extant manuscripts except Roques's Guiot, since they include after l. 29 a transition to the romance that follows: "Des or comance sa raison" (Foerster, l. 30) (Now he begins his narrative). *Raison*, a word rich with varied meanings in Old French, may refer here to Chrétien's poetic composition both as narrative and narration, a story retold by the romancer. Such is the immediate context of *raison* in the Prologue, at the beginning of Chrétien's narrative. But the wider context of the entire *Charrette* leads us to recall other possible meanings of *raison*: our effort to understand the poet's *san(s)* has already invited us to associate his sensible, reasonable reflection to the *droit chemin* followed by both character and narrator in quest of the right way, the way towards rightness, *raison*. The human values[115] generated by Chrétien's romance thus remain embedded within its complex literary texture; the individuality of Lancelot's enterprise continues to mirror that of the poet's artistry and understanding.

Karl D. Uitti

Le Chevalier au Lion (*Yvain*)

Introductory Remarks (Date of Composition and Matters of Chronology)

Much scholarly controversy surrounds the issue as to when Chrétien de Troyes composed his *Chevalier au Lion* (Lion Knight), or *Yvain* (as it is frequently referred to today).[1] Conjectures and hypotheses abound, since so few facts, or certainties, are available to us. The problem merits summary here at the start of our study of the romance. As we shall see, the date of *Yvain* and the matter of its relative position within the whole of Chrétien's œuvre both have significant poetic implications.

Inasmuch as *Yvain* goes unmentioned in the list of titles provided in the Prologue to *Cligés*, most scholars agree that it is posterior to both that text and *Erec et Enide*. Also, it may be remarked, in *Cligés* and *Erec et Enide* the figure of King Arthur and the splendor of his court are presented as entirely positive values. There is no hint in these narratives pointing to the kind of Arthurian flaws we discover in *Yvain, Le Chevalier de la Charrette* (*Lancelot*) or in *Le Conte du Graal* (*Perceval*). Given the fact that the story of Arthur, as recounted by Geoffrey of Monmouth and Wace earlier in the twelfth century, tells the tale of Arthur's rise to glory and his subsequent decline (and death through betrayal), it would seem likely that *Yvain, Lancelot* and *Perceval* are posterior to *Erec et Enide* and *Cligés*. Meanwhile, it is generally accepted that *Le Conte du Graal* is the last of Chrétien's five romances of certain attribution. This text, it is believed, was composed, but left unfinished, some time before 1191, either because, presumably, of Chrétien's own death or because of that of his last patron, Philippe de Flandre, who died in that year. *Yvain* and *Lancelot* consequently remain to be allotted a place in Chrétien's chronology and, if at all possible, to be assigned a date within that chronology.

Since the late nineteenth century and until relatively recent times, majority opinion has held that because in *Yvain* there are three allusions to Queen Guenevere's abduction (and eventual deliverance)—the story of

Lancelot—Yvain must have been composed subsequently to *Lancelot*. These allusions refer (1) to Gauvain's absence from Arthur's court, where he is sorely needed in order to keep his sworn promise and defend the hapless Lunete against her accusers (II. 3696-3709), (2) once again to Gauvain's departure on the quest for the abducted Guenevere and, consequently, to his inability to rescue his own niece and nephews from the threatening giant, Harpin (II. 3908-14) (in both cases Yvain, now publicly known only as the "Lion Knight," must stand in for him), and (3) to the Queen's deliverance from captivity, as well as Lancelot's imprisonment, which permits Gauvain to take up the cause of the Lord of the Noire Espine's unjust elder daughter, whose younger sister Yvain—unbeknownst to Gauvain—will champion (II. 4734-39).

Gaston Paris maintained this reasoning most vigorously, objecting particularly to Wendelin Foerster's caution on the matter. For Foerster, it was merely possible that *Yvain* postdates *Lancelot*—indeed, he suggests, the two romances may have been composed more or less simultaneously.[2] Some three decades ago, however, Anthime Fourrier quite cogently demonstrated that certain details of the *Lancelot* make sense only when referred to *Yvain*, for example, II. 34-35: "Aprés mangier ne se remut / li rois d'antre ses conpaignons" (After dining the King did not abandon his companions), surely an amusing, and precise, allusion to Arthur's leaving his guests in the opening scene of *Yvain*.[3] To the evidence adduced by Fourrier the late Jean Frappier added that, in his view, Chrétien would hardly have depicted Arthur and Guenevere sharing the same bed had he previously told the story of her adulterous affair with Lancelot.[4] Fourrier concludes, and Frappier concurs, that in all probability Chrétien started *Yvain* first, interrupted it in order to commence work on *Lancelot*, finished *Yvain* and left the ending of *Lancelot* to Godefroi de Leigni.

The *Lancelot-Yvain* relationship—to which we shall shortly return—is further complicated by questions of dating. For some scholars, Keu's reference to "Loradin" (*Yvain*, l. 596), identifiable as the Sultan Nur-Eddin, a thorn in the side of Christian crusaders, who reigned until 1174, proves that *Yvain* must have been composed before that date. (Other manuscripts, however, give "Noiradin"—of which "Loradin" is a variant—and even "Saladin.") Also, Arthur's decision to arrive at the Magic Fountain on the eve of St. John's Day, "before a fortnight passes" (l. 666)—a decision uttered, we recall, on Whitsunday and which prompts Yvain precipitously to undertake the adventure that will lead to his marriage with Laudine, the Lady of the Fountain Castle—has set scholars scurrying to discover which years during the second half of the twelfth century saw Whitsunday and St. John's Day separated by only two weeks. Fourrier determined that only 1166 and

1177 fit the bill, and for him the latter year seemed more plausible than the former. Noting the presence in *Lancelot* (Roques, l. 5770) of the word *croisié*, "crusaders"—the only time the term ever appears in Chrétien's entire *œuvre*—Fourrier is led to associate the use of this term with the revival of an intense crusading spirit that took place, as of 1177, at the court of Champagne. Count Henri took the cross that year, and, Fourrier reasons, Chrétien's mentioning the presence of unarmed crusader knights viewing the tournament of Noauz is perfectly natural. Furthermore, the *croisié* reference in *Lancelot* and the allusion by Keu to Nur-Eddin in *Yvain* might be deemed to suggest, or reinforce, the idea of a close temporal relationship between the two romances; around 1177 crusading was on the mind of Chrétien's patrons and audience.

Nevertheless, as the late Jean Misrahi has warned us,[5] a too-literal reliance on such bits of textual evidence can hardly lead to ironclad certainty. Indeed, Keu's sarcastic mention of Nur-Eddin may be nothing more than a common proverb signifying idle boasting ("After a good meal, well washed down with wine, knights are wont to go off to kill Nur-Eddin," i.e., "take the cross"). For Misrahi, whose skepticism is absolute and, indeed, who describes himself as the "devil's advocate" in these matters of dating, our only certain date concerning Chrétien is 1191. He very convincingly questions 1164 as the year of the marriage of Marie, eldest daughter of Louis VII and Eleanor of Aquitaine, to the Count of Champagne; Marie de Champagne, we remember, was the "Lady" to whom Chrétien dedicated *Lancelot*.

By and large, however, scholars have tended to support the thrust of Fourrier's contentions, namely, that *Yvain* and *Lancelot* were composed at about the same time, perhaps even conjointly, probably no earlier than 1177 and no later, surely, than 1181 (the year of Count Henri's death upon his return home from the Crusade he had led forth in 1179), when, it is supposed, Chrétien passed into the service of Philippe de Flandre.[6] Thus, Philippe Ménard[7] has reacted strongly against Misrahi's—to him "unfair"—insistence on certainties, preferring, as he puts it, "probabilities": since certainties are not forthcoming in these matters, exclusive reliance on them simply cuts off all, even potentially fruitful, discussion. In defense of Fourrier, Ménard remarks that in order for St. John's Day (24 June) to occur before two Sundays had elapsed after Whitsunday (see *Yvain*, ll. 666-69), Easter—like Whitsunday a moveable feast—must have taken place between 23 and 25 April, "un cas rarissime" (p. 120). That was exactly what happened in 1177, when Easter fell on 24 April. Following Fourrier, Ménard contends that this remarkable event is not lightly to be set aside when one seeks to determine the date of *Yvain*. It is likely, especially given the fact that Chrétien's chronological specificity at the start of *Yvain* is precise to the point of uniqueness within the corpus of his five extant romances, that, consequently, he is deliberately drawing on his own (and his audience's) fresh memory, or experience, of this "rare" concatenation of dates. It is, therefore, probable that Chrétien undertook the composition of *Yvain* during the spring of 1177.

Although I am about to anticipate here arguments and analyses which will be developed later in the present study, I should like to state at this point my essential agreement, on grounds of poetic coherence, with the Fourrier-Ménard theory. As I hope eventually to demonstrate, *Yvain* displays a close correlation between a certain view of "clerkliness" (*clergie*, or writing) and "knightliness" (*chevalerie*): his hero, Yvain, and his "I"-saying, though anonymous, narrator "grow up" together. Each—*clerc* and *chevalier*, respectively and conjointly—learns, as it were, to master his craft and, in a sense, to fulfill himself in terms of his identity as clerk and knight. More than any other of Chrétien's narratives, *Yvain* is solidly rooted in the here-and-now, in reality experienced and observed (as opposed to arbitrary *a priori* categories). Consequently—and given Chrétien's own extraordinarily careful artistry (nothing is left to chance, everything has its purpose)— the highly unusual and exact attention he pays to the temporal coordinates (themselves reflecting a very peculiar, but, nevertheless, authentic set of circumstances, as Fourrier-Ménard show) must be significant poetically. The dates he gives, *in the precision of their relationship to one another*, signify a "real time," albeit an unusual one, locatable in terms of his own, and his public's, experience; and, by implication, they are opposed to what one might call the "standard," or vague, "romance-type" references to "Easter," "Whitsunday," "Ascension," etc., that one finds repeatedly in twelfth-century French narrative and which generally serve either to signal that what we are reading is a romance or, as in the case of the Good Friday and Easter of *Perceval*, some other iconological purpose. (It is liturgically entirely appropriate that Perceval comes to an awareness of his sinfulness on Good Friday and prepares to receive Holy Communion on the following Easter Sunday.)

In other words, then, the chronological allusions—Whitsunday, St. John's Eve, a fortnight (Arthur's *quinzaine*, l. 666)—we find in the opening scenes of *Yvain* do correspond to the typical romance temporal coordinates (at the start of *Lancelot* it is stated, vaguely, that King Arthur "had held court on *an* Ascension Day" [ll. 30-31]), but in their real, albeit exceptional, specificity, they tend to undermine the pure "romance-ness" which such coordinates normally are called upon to signal. In this manner, and in conjunction with the narrator's contrasting of the "good old" Arthurian times with the decadence of today (ll. 7-32), *Yvain* appears to be telling us that we are indeed on romance territory and in romance time. However, because of the precise specificity and the "real" memorableness of the *Yvain* dates, this territory and this time differ considerably from the conventional, or standard, romance world. We shall have occasion below to study this process of undermining in greater detail, but at the risk of some anticipation we can, nevertheless, call to mind the odd association contained in the rhyme words at ll. 5-6, where *Pantecoste* (Whitsunday) is identified as "cele feste qui tant *coste*" (that feast that *costs* so much) (my emphasis); an association of this sort, involving money, is very peculiar indeed—it jars the reader in his "normal" romance expectations.

It seems to me that, in great part thanks to the recognizable and, in all likelihood, *recognized* uniqueness of these "real-life," present-day chronological allusions, Chrétien is setting up a deliberate and nuanced complicity with his reader(s) and that, furthermore, this complicity is of a nature entirely opposed to that of the exaggeratedly courtly and hyperbolically expressed rapport we find outlined in the Prologue to *Lancelot*. In this latter text, we recall, "Crestïens" elaborately proclaims his (clerkly) devotion and service to "ma dame de Chanpaigne," a lady who was very much alive at the time *Lancelot* was composed and whose perfection is such that he will willingly undertake to fulfill her "comandemanz" and make the "romanz" on the basis of the "matiere et san" she has provided him (ll. 1-29). Nothing of this sort is to be found in *Yvain*—indeed, alone among Chrétien's romances, *Yvain* has no prologue-type forematter whatsoever. In structure as in plot, *Yvain* and *Lancelot* stand in utter—in systematic—contrast to one another.

This contrast, furthermore, is borne out in the attitudes expressed by the two romances in respect to both writing (*clergie*) and *chevalerie*. The poetics of *Lancelot* depends on an explicit literariness (clerk and patron, both named; topics of source and authority; romance thematics, as, for example, the adulterous, or "courtly," love of Lancelot and Guenevere, and an almost impossibly ideal "chivalric service"; identifiable "courtly" genres, such as the *alba*-like night of love experienced by Lancelot and Guenevere; etc.). Such "literariness," when found in *Yvain*, is either gently mocked (as during the scene of Yvain's falling in love with the widow of the man he has just killed) or otherwise made the butt of irony (e.g., Calogrenant's perfect romance-style narrative of his knightly... failure). In *Yvain* the poetics of explicit literariness finds itself replaced, so to speak, by an implicit literariness.

But let us not anticipate too fully our analysis of *Le Chevalier au Lion*. It is clear, however, that the chronological relationship between *Yvain* and *Lancelot* is poetically of the highest relevance. The two texts, I believe (and as Fourrier has suggested), were surely composed simultaneously; and this simultaneity enters into how we are to read them both.

By what I have just said I do not mean to imply that *Yvain* is a kind of "anti-*Lancelot*" any more than I believe *Cligés* to be an "anti-*Tristan*"; I mean, rather, that the two romances interpenetrate one another on virtually all levels and that they do so in a remarkably systematic manner. Based on a play of contrasts, reciprocal allusions and shared attributes, the system serves, I contend, to "pair off" *Yvain/Lancelot* against the mythopoetic and celebrative mode Chrétien had illustrated in the earlier romance pair of *Erec et Enide* and *Cligés*. Each in its own way, *Yvain* and *Lancelot* carry romance narrative to an extreme: *Lancelot* ostensibly exalts an Ideal, a kind of impossible romance dream, which, in turn, *Yvain*, with its emphasis on such intrusive everyday concerns as marriage and even social injustice, does not so much deflate as show how quintessentially romance-like that dream is. Without itself ceasing to be a romance—a romance of a most unique kind—*Yvain* up-ends romance.

Some concluding remarks on the *Yvain-Lancelot* relationship are necessary at this juncture.

I have already mentioned a number of the most obvious contrasts to be found in, and between, the two works. Others readily come to mind: love (and growth) in marriage (*Yvain*) vs. a static—that is, "given"—and, in a sense, hopeless adulterous love in *Lancelot*; a completed, or closed, narrative in *Yvain* vs. a far more open-ended narrative, perceived as such, in *Lancelot* (witness the many subsequent recastings of the Lancelot-Guenevere story; there will be no such development of an *Yvain* tradition); Yvain winds up departing, for good, from Arthur's court, while Lancelot, of course, is irrevocably tied to the court. These and the many other contrasts (too numerous to mention here) serve, on the deepest level, to link the two texts rather than definitively to oppose them; or rather, the oppositions are contained in and shaped by the above-named systematic play. I have already enumerated cases in which the two romances refer to each other on the level of plot and temporality. The story of *Lancelot* takes place, so to speak, after Gauvain's visit, with Arthur, to Laudine's castle following upon her marriage to Yvain and, to all intents and purposes, before Yvain's duel with Gauvain in the daughters of the Noire Espine episode. Yvain thus acquires a wife just before Arthur is about to lose his; in the one case, the husband *returns to* his wife, while, in the other, the wife *is returned to* her husband. Meanwhile, interestingly enough, Yvain is mentioned, along with Gauvain and a certain "Looys," as one of the knights whose names Lancelot deciphers on the tombs of the "future cemetery" reserved for the Round Table (*Charrette*, ll. 1865-66); "Gauvains" and

"Yvains" are in rhyme position, that is, linked in what the narrator chooses to record of Lancelot's observation. However, as scholars have noted, the embedding of the *Charrette* in *Yvain* is not complete; to be sure, Guenevere has been freed, but Lancelot himself remains imprisoned in a tower (*Charrette*, ll. 4738-39). Curiously, the two occasions on which, so to speak, Lancelot's and Yvain's personal adventures meet face to face involve, in the *Charrette*, Yvains's *future* demise (and prison-like resting place) and, in *Le Chevalier au Lion*, Lancelot's *present*, and incapacitating, tomb-like incarceration. Such facts as these have encouraged scholars to offer ingenious guesses as to how and when Chrétien composed the various episodes of the two romances, as well as with respect to the order in which they were read to his audience. For example, we recall, Fourrier's citing of *Lancelot*, ll. 34-35, where we are told that on this day Arthur did not abandon his dinner companions, suggests to him that Chrétien must have written the opening scene of *Yvain* before embarking on its companion narrative. For David Shirt, who refines upon Fourrier's hypothesis, the *Charrette* was composed in (at least?) three steps, with Chrétien inserting the tournament of Noauz episode between the scene of Lancelot's imprisonment by Meleagant's seneschal and the conclusion he had entrusted to Godefroi de Leigni *after* the commissioned conclusion had been completed.[8] Meanwhile, by inference, he states that *Yvain*, ll. 4738-39, because of its seeming unawareness of the Noauz episode, had been completed, as Fourrier suggested, either before or while Godefroi wrote his conclusion.

Interesting as they may be, these hypotheses are historically only more or less plausible. What, conversely, appears most striking, and true, in this linking of *Le Chevalier au Lion* and *Le Chevalier de la Charrette*—and note the ironic contrast in these two titles as well as their positioning in the respective texts!—is how sharply the linking focuses on Gauvain. To put it in another way, the stories of Yvain and Lancelot impinge directly on one another basically through the presence/absence of Gauvain; he is the go-between—the emissary from Arthurian centrality to the individualized worlds of two knights who, each in his own fashion, is a kind of outcast, or exile, from the Arthurian world (epitomized by Gauvain) and whose individuality criticizes that world. Yvain will learn to reject the Arthurian value system by essentially learning no longer to emulate Gauvain; he will go his own respectable (and perhaps somewhat dull) way. Meanwhile—and the irony is extraordinary—Lancelot, who is hardly "respectable" (but who is fascinating), will restore order (albeit a tenuous one) to the Arthurian world by rescuing the Queen, whom he loves passionately, by in fact betraying the King, his lord! But, we remember, this order had been initially destroyed, precisely, by the foolish rash boon accorded by Arthur at the start of the text. Gauvain's ineffectiveness during the quest for Guenevere's deliverance is, inevitably, total.

We shall have ample opportunity to study the implications for *Yvain* of Gauvain's function in both texts. At present, however, it would not be inopportune to suggest that, although *Le Chevalier au Lion* and *Le Chevalier de la Charrette* do stand on their own as "independent" texts, they, like so many other medieval literary works, clamor to be read intertextually, that is, in conjunction with other narratives and, in particular, conjointly, as in all likelihood—or so the Fourrier-Ménard "probabilities" suggest—they were experienced at the time—1177?—they were composed. Gauvain, as "shared attribute" of the two romances, serves to indicate a certain hollowness, a certain fundamental impotence (however glorious), that seems to lie close to the heart of Chrétien's depiction of "official," or "codified," "Arthurianism," when this latter is viewed from the diametrically opposed stories of both Yvain and Lancelot. And consequently, though "independent," the two narratives also may—even must—be understood as fusing together in a kind of "super romance," in which each is incomparably enriched by the other. The investigations of Fourrier, Ménard, Shirt, and others, show the great likelihood of a simultaneous composition. The contrasts, or oppositions, in the two texts, as well as the reciprocal allusions (Chrétien wished to make sure we got the point!) and certain "shared attributes," all point to and reinforce the conclusion presented here that *Yvain* and *Lancelot*, as fulfilled texts, depend on our recognizing the structural and poetic ties that bind them. The implications of such a recognition are at once important and numerous. Thus, for example, in order to grasp the sense of how the *Charrette* fits into Chrétien's on-going meditation on the *amour passion* question exemplified in the texts concerning Tristan and Iseut, it is essential—or so I believe—to understand the system of *Tristan* references in *Le Chevalier au Lion* as well as Gauvain's advice, after Yvain's marriage, to the effect that, in order truly to merit the love of his bride (and lady), Yvain ought to leave her. Not only is intertextual reading of this sort demanded by the two romances in question, but it also protects us from the abuses of such scholar-critics as have elaborated theories concerning Chrétien's "doctrine" (or "anti-doctrine") of "courtly love."

One final remark. Although my term "super romance" may be deemed by some to be an anachronistic neologism, it does correspond, on several pertinent levels, to medieval textual reality. As is well known, especially in respect to texts pre-dating, say, Machaut and, above all, post-printing press norms concerning the "integrity" of a given (vernacular) narrative, such supposed "integrity" did not—perhaps could not—prevail. Preservation of a canonical text as such was less a goal of scribes and their patrons than what, in their view, was considered proper transformation: amplification, abbreviation, recasting, continuation—these were the stuff of literary transmission during the Middle Ages. Textual transmogrification characterizes the medieval poetic process. Jean de Meung "continued" *The Romance of the Rose*, which had been "started," but left "unfinished," by Guillaume de Lorris; yet, as has often been pointed out, his "Continuation" constitutes in many important respects a refutation of his predecessor. Nevertheless, at approximately the midpoint of their two conjoined texts, Jean expresses great pride in the *fact* of his taking up where Guillaume left off. Refutation, along with other forms of recasting or perpetuation, belonged to the storehouse of poetic creativity—techniques, possibilities—which enabled medieval writers to function as they did. Not only "authors," but also scribes took part in this creative process. A case in point is the thirteenth-century scribe of a codex containing all five romances of Chrétien de Troyes. The codex (Paris, Bibliothèque Nationale, fonds français 1450) contains a transcription of Wace's *Brut* up to the point at which Wace describes the marvels of Arthur's kingship; then (folio 139v) the scribe intervenes to call upon Chrétien's "testimony" ("ce que Crestïens tesmogne") concerning Arthur, and, after transcribing Chrétien's romances, he returns to complete *Brut* (and other related narratives). B.N. f. fr. 1450, as codex and with this specific scribal-poetic intervention, both illustrates and justifies, I believe, the concept of "super romance." To be sure, this intervention focuses on thematic issues (are the Arthurian stories true?), but such matters in the twelfth and thirteenth centuries were not divorced from questions of form. It is by no means irrelevant that *Lancelot* was left "unfinished" by Chrétien—or rather, that he turned its completion over to Godefroi—whereas, as it is stated, Chrétien most decidedly *did* finish his *Chevalier au Lion* (ll. 6804-05). The scribe of B.N. f. fr. 1450, conjoining Wace and Chrétien, understood the value of Chrétien's "testimony" with regard to Arthurian "truth." Is it too much to expect that, in conjoining *Lancelot* and *Yvain* (and thereby poetically exploiting a medieval literary mode), Chrétien himself understood—perhaps helped invent—the potentialities of a "super (i.e., conjoined) romance"?[9]

Traditions of Scholarship

Although concerns of chronology have, as we have observed, played an important part in studies dedicated to *Yvain*, editorial questions have attracted much scholarly attention, too. These matters are treated in other sections of the present volume and so need not concern us here. Suffice it to say that, as early as 1581, the humanist-historian Claude Fauchet expressed interest in the work of Chrétien and especially in the text of *Yvain*, from which he printed extracts in *Recueil de l'origine de la langue et poësie françoyse, ryme et romans.*[10] Other matters have also fascinated scholars and antiquarians from the seventeenth century down to our own day.[11] For example, Chrétien's works have served to document numerous linguistic studies, e.g., the history of French, the structure of Old French, etymology, historical dictionaries. Wendelin Foerster's *Kristian von Troyes: Wörterbuch zu seinen sämtlichen Werken*,[12] though not so much a "dictionary" as a vast glossary, has become an indispensable tool for linguists interested in "classic" Old French. All in all, however, until fairly recently questions of literary history have claimed the lion's share of learned scrutiny given over to the whole of Chrétien's work as well as to *Yvain*. In addition to problems of dating, the attribution of given works, Chrétien's biography, and the like, scholars have concentrated on (1) relationships between the romances and possible "Arthurian," or Celtic, contexts (sources, influences); (2) Chrétien's *œuvre* and Classical tradition (e.g., Ovid, Virgil, the twelfth-century literary curriculum in the schools); (3) the French literary context of the twelfth century (e.g., Chrétien and Wace, *Tristan*, the *romans antiques*); (4) Chrétien's "influence" both in France and abroad (e.g., the *Perceval* "Continuations," *Yvain* and the Middle High German *Iwein* by Hartmann von Aue); (5) certain "doctrinal," or civilizational, values, like "courtly love," chivalry and religious ritual. Under one or more of these rubrics one finds also that considerable attention has been paid to such matters as "myth" (the Waste Land, the Grail, magic) and, especially since World War II, what, for lack of a more specific term, might be called Chrétien's literary art. Scholar-critics like Gustave Cohen, Stefan Hofer and, above all, Jean Frappier have provided acute analyses of Chrétien's deft handling of themes, of his ability to combine "realistic" observations and legendary—very romance-like and imaginative—storytelling, his gentle humor, his refined psychological perceptiveness. Little by little Chrétien has come to be recognized, perhaps even first and foremost, as a superbly sophisticated craftsman (as the "master" referred to by one of his German imitators); and, consequently, interest has increasingly been focused on his artistry: his versification; what he meant by, and how he achieved, *san* and *conjointure*; the nature of *clergie*, "clerkliness, learnedness" (see the Prologue to *Cligés*), an ideal, apparently, that he sought to exemplify; his all-important contributions to the forging of the Old French narrative instrument and its concomitant courtly diction.[13] Chrétien's quintessential "literariness" has helped prompt a number of present-day critics to attempt to work out, in terms of his *œuvre*, our own contemporary fascination for signs—their structures and their interrelationships (e.g., the interlocking and the coherence of different sign levels)—and to relate the documentation furnished by Chrétien to the wider documentation provided by equally "literary" Old French generic sets and subsets. Chrétien has thus served in the formulation by scholars of a kind of new, descriptively conceived literary history concerned primarily with poetic constructs (viewed as sign, or semiotic, functions) and intertextual relationships. In short, over the past forty years or so, textual relationships of a generic sort (sources, "influences") have tended to give way more and more to the description of textual analogues and even, though so far without signal success, to the analysis of what might be labeled "generative relationships." The relative accessibility as well as, of course, the intrinsic charm of Chrétien's romances have made of this corpus a virtual laboratory for philological (and other) experimentation over the past century or so.

Yvain has received its full measure of all these brands of critical attention and emphasis. For example, the nature of Chrétien's debt to Celtic materials has consistently preoccupied scholars for well over a century. Various schools of thought have taken shape. Certain impassioned *celtisants*, like Roger Sherman Loomis and Jean Marx, have in effect come close to affirming that texts like *Yvain* are in reality but recastings of a, or several, Celtic model(s);[14] other scholars, like Edmond Faral, in reaction against this view, have preferred to accentuate Chrétien's originality and/or his debt to Classical Antiquity. On occasion these debates have degenerated into acrimony. By and large, the *celtisants* have tended to consider *Yvain* (and the other romances) as a sort of patchwork, as a more or less adroit combination of Celtic stories, legends, moods, motifs, and the like; their opponents have stressed rather more positively the poetic organicity of the romances and their twelfth-century, peculiarly French literariness. The *celtisants*—like, on another level, their semiotician descendants of today—were less averse to conjecture (proofs of their assertions are frequently hard to come by) than their more textually-minded adversaries. Yet in the case of *Yvain*, Celtic elements, or components, are undeniably present. Understanding these elements is, to an important degree, what one wishes to make of them. An overriding interest in sources tends to foment in the scholar a main concern either for the reconstruction of lost, or only partially documented, mythic archetypes, or for processes of transmission; all too often a somewhat simplistic *post hoc ergo propter hoc* attitude has prevailed, namely, that if, say, a motif occurs in a text after it has appeared in an accessible previous text, then it must follow that the later work has borrowed from, and therefore is genetically related to, the earlier one.[15]

Yvain, to be sure, has been often utilized in the service of anthropologically oriented cultural history. Nevertheless, as Frappier and others have shown, any general interpretation of *Yvain* that does not cogently take into account the important Celtic elements present in Chrétien's text is the poorer for this failure. Without the magic, without faerie, without the marvelous fountain—not to mention the Arthurian backdrop itself—*Yvain* would hardly be the poem we now know. Yet what counts, of course, is what Chrétien did with these "components," and how, largely through his work, they entered the mainstream of European literature, even inspiring in some cases later works in a Celtic language like Welsh, notably the *Owein*.

By setting *Yvain* in the legendary world of King Arthur and the Round Table, Chrétien (like Marie de France in giving French versions of Breton lays) could distance himself and his work from the four narrative genres then prevailing in the French vernacular: the saint's life, the *chanson de geste* (e.g., *The Song of Roland*), the more or less fictionalized romance chronicle (e.g., Wace's *Brut* and *Rou*), the translation/adaptation of a Latin text (e.g., *Alexandre, Eneas, Thèbes, Troie*—all known as *romans*). As we shall see, Chrétien's romances share important characteristics with each of the above genres (and, naturally, the texts epitomizing them), but they also differ from these in highly significant ways. For Chrétien the Arthurian world is essentially fictional; as such, it enables the romancer to perform in ways that otherwise would have been impossible. (The same applies to the even more purely Celtic *Tristan* tradition, though the implications of Chrétien's stance with regard to the *Tristan* story are somewhat different.)[16] To put the matter succinctly, Chrétien's utilization of Arthurian legend and its concomitants—that is, how he used these materials and the purposes to which he put them—allowed him legitimately to request of his readers, or public, a voluntary suspension of disbelief (we are, after all, on romance—or story—territory, and belief in what is being told is secondary to other values) as well as an allegiance to the fact of their being told a story.

Let us look at a few cases in point.

When Lunete gives Yvain the magic ring rendering him invisible to Esclados' vengeful subjects, this Celtic motif is essentially a device of plot, enabling the story to progress in an interesting way. And the ring also contributes to the important dimension of faerie in the romance—it is part of a series of magical objects strung out along the length of the text. Moreover, it helps confirm in our minds Yvain's worthiness: Lunete is returning the favor of courtesy previously bestowed upon her by Yvain. A second magic ring, given to Yvain by Laudine, emblematic, as it is made out to be, of faithful love, adds to what might be called the moral dimension of authentic *courtoisie*; in a sense, Yvain's failure to return to Laudine means that he has, in effect, spurned this gift from his beloved and proved himself to be incapable of marriage service. Chrétien makes constant use of these magic artifacts up to, and including, Yvain's being cured of his madness-despair thanks to the good offices of the Lady of Norison and Morgue's miraculous balm. Subsequently, though we remain most assuredly in a *pays de roman*, such devices, to all intents and purposes, disappear: Yvain's redemption is owed to his own quite human efforts.

Analogues to these rings and other objects have, of course, been sought out and located in Celtic folklore. The same is true of many characters in *Yvain*: the frightful cowherd, for example, resembles the Irish Curoi (who might also have been a "source" for Esclados himself); the character Kynon in the Welsh *mabinogi* entitled *Owein and Lunet* (a text posterior in date to *Yvain*, but reflecting, many scholars agree, an earlier version with which Chrétien might have been familiar) shares many traits with Calogrenant; Laudine herself, a fairy figure, is clearly related to the tradition of the Celtic Lady of the Fountain (served by a giant knight known as Mabonagrain—an avatar of Esclados—who earns her love by defending the fountain); the Castle of Pesme Aventure as well as the hospitable vavasor and his daughter possess Celtic analogues, not to mention the devilish *netuns* destroyed by Yvain at Pesme Aventure. Indeed, certain bizarre features of the geography of *Yvain* have been accounted for with reference to supposed Celtic sources: "Carduel-en-Gales" (l. 7) has been identified as Carlisle; the fact that Chrétien neglects to note any crossing of the Channel has been attributed to his conflating his Celtic, British "source" with another Celtic legend, the Continental, or Breton, Brocéliande and its Fountain of Barenton.

Frappier (*Etude*, pp. 71-118) not only provides an excellent and judicious summary of these matters, but he also furnishes helpful clues for adequately understanding them. Carefully comparing each Celtic "source" so far identified with its counterpart in *Yvain*, he concludes that in every case the differences between the Celtic "original" and Chrétien's "adaptation" are easily as striking as their similarities. Not only does Chrétien transmit this material, but he thoroughly transforms it. Thus, though Laudine's fairy-like nature remains present and active in *Yvain*, it has receded into the background; she is much more—and other—than a Celtic water nymph. Also, in pointing out the extraordinarily "fluid" character of Celtic mythology (*Etude*, p. 83), compared to which, Frappier says, "the gods and heroes of Greece look like models of stability," he is very close to indicating what, to my mind, must surely have constituted much of the appeal for Chrétien of that mythology: it lends itself perfectly to the kind of fictional elaboration Chrétien was prepared to undertake. Chrétien could use these legends as he saw fit, taking what he wanted and transforming it to suit his own narrative purposes. As we noted, the first half of *Yvain* is far more ostensibly Celtic than what follows. Finally, Chrétien's consistent use of Arthurian legends and their trappings stands as a sign for his late twelfth-century "modernity"; like Marie de France, he distinguishes himself from the translator-romancers of *Eneas* and *Troie*, although, technically speaking, his romances owe a large debt to the *translatio studii* procedures employed by the practitioners of the *roman antique*. In the Prologue to *Cligés*, we recall, he is explicitly conscious of this "modernity."

The complexity of Chrétien's reliance on Celtic folklore is nowhere more evident in *Yvain* than in his use of the legend of the Magic Fountain. On the one hand, his antecedents here are strictly literary: the above-cited Celtic story contained in the Lady of the Fountain tale as represented by *Owein and Lunet*, which, however, makes no mention of Brocéliande or Barenton, and, among other twelfth-century texts, Wace's *Rou*, which does. Wace tells of his visiting "la fontaine de Berenton" in Brittany and trying to provoke rain by pouring water from it on the stone; unfortunately, nothing happens, and Wace concludes: "Fol i alai, fol m'en revinc" (Fool I went there, fool I returned).[17] Chrétien, it must be assumed, knew Wace's poem; the fact that the fountain never fails to perform properly in *Yvain* serves to distinguish Chrétien's *pays de roman* from the sort of chronicle-like text exemplified by *Rou*. Meanwhile, these literary antecedents—especially Wace—indicate the existence of a well-known and truly popular legend with which Chrétien might well have been familiar in his own right. The Fountain of Barenton still exists today much as Chrétien described it (except, of course, that the *perron* is not emerald and no basin of precious metal hangs from the tree beside it) in the Forest of Paimpont (Ille-et-Vilaine) about a mile's stroll up a hill from the tiny hamlet of Fol Penser (near the military school of Coëtquidan and approximately forty kilometers west of Rennes). Believers still have recourse to the fountain's marvelous properties in periods of drought. In Wace and in popular legend the fountain is beneficent, whereas, in Chrétien and British legends, the storm it provokes is terrible, as, of course, it must be in order to serve the purposes Chrétien assigns it in his story. Yet without the fountain Yvain and Laudine would never have met! In *Yvain*, clearly, the fountain is an essential device of plot. However, it is also magic, and, in so being, it participates in the wider gamut of mystery and magic we find in *Yvain*, in what Frappier has called the "other-worldliness" that pervades this romance—the mysterious, peculiarly romance, space/time in which, to a very considerable degree, the hero's adventures take place. Chrétien, so to speak, has his cake and eats it too: the Magic Fountain of Barenton, a conflation of "sources," does in fact refer to something anteceding his romance and existing "outside" of it, but the very mystery of the referent underscores its complete assimilation into the tissue of Chrétien's work, a work to which it is systematically subordinated.

What has just been noted applies with equal force to the "Iwenus," son of Urian (brother to the King of Scotland) mentioned by Geoffrey of Monmouth in his *Historia regum Brittaniæ*, and to "Ewein, le fiz Urien" described by Geoffrey's translator, Wace,[18] obvious sources (among others) for Chrétien. Chrétien's Yvain is no more and no less than the protagonist of his romance and, by extension, a participant in the Arthurian romance world his *œuvre* did so much to create. The same holds true for the many Classical "sources" of *Yvain*, which range from the model of Androcles and his lion to the many, often fleeting and epigrammatic allusions to Ovid, Virgil and perhaps Statius. The painstaking work of numerous scholars has made us conscious of these debts and textual analogues. Like other romances, *Yvain* reverberates with allusions and borrowings of all sorts. Yvain's madness and his commerce with the hermit reminds us, as Frappier has suggested, of Béroul's treatment of Tristan's exile in the Forest of Morois and his encounter there with Ogrin, but this, I believe, is less a matter of "influence," or "source,"[19] than, on Chrétien's part, a deliberate effort to situate his text purposefully within a recognizable literary system, a poetic economy, through a set of meaningful references.

The identification of sources has been closely related to the kinds of study devoted to what I have called the "doctrinal content" of Chrétien's work. For some scholars the fact of Chrétien's having been "influenced" by Celtic folklore and mythology suggests that he conceived of himself as a mouthpiece for Celtic "values" and "beliefs." And from this standpoint there is but a short step to take for scholars who have viewed his *pays de roman* as the more or less veiled expression of other value systems. Thus, in a famous article[20] Gaston Paris portrayed the Chrétien of *Lancelot* as the "epic poet" of *amour courtois,* courtly love—a doctrine, then, which Paris proceeded to define in great detail. About two decades ago, Mario Roques and especially the late Urban T. Holmes, Jr., and Sister M. Amelia Klenke sought to explain *Perceval* as a Judeo-Christian allegory celebrating the triumph of Ecclesia over Synagoga.[21] What, in the Prologue to *Lancelot*, Chrétien referred to as *san* has been interpreted by some as doctrinal meaning, and such scholars as have attempted to determine this kind of meaning have shown an energetic willingness to read between the lines—to interpret the romances—in such a way as to articulate it. Thus, for example, for Maxwell S. Luria[22] *Yvain* recounts the story of its protagonist's "symbolic baptism" (= the Fountain) and eventual understanding of Divine Love through a process of regeneration: it is a kind of allegorized "Knight's Progress."[23]

Allegorical readings of this sort have been searchingly criticized, in particular with respect to *Perceval*, by Frappier in a number of lengthy articles and reviews,[24] and, by and large, have made little headway among specialists in Old French literature. These views have enjoyed greater success among Anglicists, especially in the United States; Anglicists, we recall, once stood in the forefront of those concerned with Celtic matters. Meanwhile, Chrétien's "position" in *Yvain* with reference to "courtly love" has frequently been analyzed and discussed. Often described (like *Erec et Enide*, but in obverse fashion) as a paean to marriage, *Yvain* is seen as one of Chrétien's responses to the "fatal love" motif of *Tristan*, even as a rejection of the courtly "theory" that love can exist only outside the conjugal relationship. Moreover, love, chivalry and marriage, say these reader-critics, can—indeed, ought to—coexist harmoniously. Chrétien, consequently, is portrayed as a more or less rigorous moralist, with stern views not always shared by his supposed patrons. Such matters, I repeat, have absorbed a great deal of critical attention. But because the scholars involved in expressing views on them tend to attribute specific doctrines to Chrétien—he is seen as a kind of mouthpiece for such doctrine—and because the doctrines vary from scholar to scholar, undisputed, even cogent, conclusions have been hard to come by.

The particular influence of *Yvain* upon subsequent works like Hartmann's *Iwein* has also prompted considerable scrutiny, though perhaps not so much as one might expect. Once again, *Yvain* is seen as a "source." How Hartmann "translated" or "adapted" his French "model" is the chief issue.[25] Recent German theorists of *Rezeptionsästhetik* like Peter Kern[26] have contributed significantly to a renewal of these kinds of investigation. It has become more and more apparent that a better and more general understanding of the procedures of medieval romance narrative—its workings, its diffusion, its dynamics—must precede, that is, must provide a context for, the study of any given poem's fortune. We have become more conscious nowadays, I think, that a medieval text exists in a continuum of constantly varying contexts (manuscript tradition, adaptations, codicological compilations, etc.) and that knowledge of these necessarily forms an integral part of what in reality the "text" is and of how it functions. Conversely, study of the fortune of a given text (*Yvain*'s "destiny" differs markedly from that, say, of *Lancelot* and *Perceval*) helps us to articulate more sharply the nature of that text.

For these reasons and because so many scholars have come to mistrust the premises underlying traditional source study and doctrinal explications (also, for reasons of inevitable changes in fashion), recent Chrétien scholarship, including studies devoted in whole or in part to *Yvain*, has tended increasingly to focus on matters of form and structure, on the poetic nature and status of the romances. For even so ideologically a middle-of-the-road philologist as Jean Frappier, source study is valuable primarily for the light it sheds on how the romances—or romance in general—are put together. Thus, in discussing the "parallelism" between Celtic tales and "our Breton romances," he remarks, and I summarize, that only the Celtic notion of the Other World adequately accounts for the disconcerting strangeness one detects in *Lancelot, Perceval* or the Joie de la Cort episode of *Erec et Enide*;[27] furthermore, he adds, "the influence of Celtic stories explains why the typical adventure of the knight in Breton romances becomes the individual, solitary quest, substituted, as though through a process of brusque mutation, for the collective action of the heroes we find in the *chansons de geste*" (translation mine). Studies of what might be labeled Chrétien's poetic and/or literary consciousness as well as of the sign systems either contained in or augmented by his fictions have begun to appear in increasing numbers. Thus, Eugène Vinaver's pioneering studies of "interlacing" have helped center critical interest on medieval narrative composition, while, for his part, in a number of books and articles, Douglas Kelly has subjected Chrétien's literary terminology (and that of medieval Europe) to close scrutiny. Peter Haidu has examined in exhaustive detail Chrétien's use of rhetorical and poetic procedures in *Cligés* and *Perceval*; more recently, in connection with *Yvain* he has sought to describe and explicate the crucial semiotic systems at work in that poem and exemplified by it.[28] Pierre Gallais has combined concern for expressive devices, shapes and formulas with a desire to explore mythic structures and the subconscious as these lie latent in, and inform, Chrétien's romances.[29] Even trend-setting anthropologists like Claude Lévi-Strauss apparently have displayed renewed curiosity in how the romances document, or illustrate, matters of interest to their discipline.[30] Paul Zumthor's widely-read *Essai de poétique médiévale*[31] endeavors, in fact, to describe the conditions underlying—both supporting and modulating—all medieval "literariness": textual responses, or intertextuality; generic dynamics; "author-reader" relationships. Here, however, as the relatively few pages devoted to Chrétien indicate (esp. pp. 475-83), the emphasis is placed rather more heavily on "literature" than on given texts or *œuvres*. Indeed, the latter exemplify (by participating in) the former, which, consequently, bears the brunt of Zumthor's investigative activity.

Utilizing, at least to some degree, all these diverse (and sometimes magnificent) scholarly traditions, and with a view towards building on the foundations they provide, let us now return to the text—and what I have called the "textuality"—of *Le Chevalier au Lion*. Let us endeavor to see how that poem works and how it signifies. This will, I trust, help us understand *what* it signifies.

Opening Signals

The absence of any formal Prologue is, perhaps, what first strikes the reader of *Yvain*—the reader, particularly, who possesses some familiarity with Chrétien's other romances (all of which contain formal prologues) or who is conversant with twelfth-century romance. Prologues to Old French romance frequently take the form of the *exordium*, often beginning with a maxim (*sententia*) or a proverb; indicating a (real or supposed) "source" for the subsequent text; appealing to the reader's good graces (*captatio benevolentiæ*); conditioning, in one manner or another, the audience's response to what the author is trying to do. Thus, in the forematter to the *Roman de Troie*, Benoît de Sainte-Maure declares his work to be based not on remote Homer, but rather on the reports of Dares and Dictys, two self-described eye-witnesses to the Trojan War; his poem, consequently, will be "true." In the Prologue to *Lancelot* (a text, we recall, probably composed at the same time as *Yvain*), Chrétien's hyperbolic clerkly service, placed at the disposal of his patroness, the Countess Marie de Champagne, prefigures the equally hyperbolic love service Lancelot renders to Queen Guenevere. *Exordia* provide useful, sometimes essential, clues to how romances should be read, particularly in the case of literarily so self-conscious a body of texts as the romances of Chrétien de Troyes.

Yet like *Yvain*, so influential a mid-twelfth-century text as the *Roman d'Eneas* (a poem ostensibly "translating" Virgil's *Aeneid* and certainly known to Chrétien) has dispensed with a formal prologue; it begins in the mode known to the rhetorical and compositional theory of the time as *in medias res*, a perfectly legitimate procedure inherited from Antiquity. Furthermore, many early non-romance French narratives contain no elaborate *exordia* (for example, numerous *chansons de geste*). In the Oxford *Roland*, we remember, the narrator starts things off by situating his story (and his audience) in time and place: the time is that of "our great emperor" ("nostre emperere magnes"), namely, of "Charles the King"; the place is "Cordres," in Spain, where Charles and his army have spent seven full years in combat against the pagans. Only the stronghold of Saragossa and its ruler, King Marsile, remain to be reduced. Thus, these opening lines supply a present time (the time of the poem's actual performance) to which the events of a distant past (the late eighth century) are to be pertinently related. The place—far-off Spain—is implicitly contrasted with *dulce France*, the homeland not only of Charles and his Christian host, but also, presumably, of those to whom the narrator is addressing himself and to whose community he, too, belongs. The narrator is authoritative; his omniscience derives from his familiarity with a *geste*, "written text, story," which he claims is his source,[32] as well as from, one assumes, his own truthful character and his audience's memory. The poem's accuracy is no more to be doubted than that of Benoît's *Roman de Troie*. What Benoît's Prologue accomplishes for *Troie* is handled by other means—by a different system of "opening signals"—in the first *laisse*, or stanza, of the *Roland*. As we shall shortly see, the *Roland* system is not irrelevant to *Yvain*.

Yvain, however, is a romance, not a *chanson de geste*. Its subject matter is Arthurian, not the epic history of Christian France; it is composed in octosyllabic rhyming couplets, not in decasyllabic assonanced *laisses*. Its narrational procedures are, to all intents and purposes, the same as those we find in the rest of Chrétien's *œuvre* and in *romans antiques* like *Troie, Eneas* and *Thèbes*, or the Breton *Lais* of Marie de France. Though there exist striking similarities between the opening lines of *Yvain* and those of the *Roland*, these similarities, at least in terms of what they refer to, are superficial: different purposes are served, and these purposes are conditioned by the generic characteristics of romance and *chanson de geste*, respectively. It is, nevertheless, true that the opening lines of *Yvain*, like the first *laisse* of *Roland*, do function in a manner that orients the reader/ listener.

Before we examine in some detail the "opening signals" of *Yvain*, preliminary attention ought to be paid to a third important Old French narrative genre, the saint's life. Saints' lives, like most romances, frequently display formal *exordia*, though, as a rule, these, when compared to romances, are fairly rudimentary. The venerable eleventh-century *Life of Saint Alexis*, for example, begins with a *sententia*-like affirmation: "Bons fut li siecles al tems ancïenour" (The world was good in olden times).[33] Former times were replete with faith, justice and love; nowadays "all has changed, has lost its color." The narrator proceeds to supply a capsulized version of human history, a context for his tale of early Christian times, when "our ancestors" received *crestïantet* and there lived a "lord of Rome" whose about-to-be-born son Alexis will be the protagonist of his song. No explicit source for his poem is indicated by the narrator; a kind of "original source" is designated, however, later on in the text when the dead saint's holographic autobiography is read aloud to the Pope, the emperors, Alexis' family and the assembled Roman populace. At the same time as the poem bears witness to the saint's own testimony, it utilizes this witness in order to authorize its relating the events that take place subsequent to Alexis' death—miracles, salvation—and that fit the norms of hagiographic tradition. The *Alexis* narrator assumes the persona of the clerk rather more ostentatiously than is the case with the *Roland* narrator, yet, as does his *chanson de geste* counterpart, he, too, belongs to the community he addresses.

(Like that of Roland, Alexis' story is part of "our" history.) The *Alexis* clerk appears to resemble the clerkly narrator one finds in romance texts starting with Wace—as of the middle of the twelfth century, roughly—in his self-conscious awareness of his distinct role as transmitter of the material he is relating. However, he is not the *named* person we find in numerous romances (Wace, Benoît, Marie, Chrétien, Béroul, Thomas, et al.). He is, as it were, *professionally personalized*, though otherwise "anonymous." It is he who, at the poem's close, summons his audience to join him in keeping the saintly man's memory so that he might protect "us" from evil (ll. 621-22).

Neither the forematter to the *Alexis* nor that of the *Roland* provides any *open* hint as to how one ought to read, or respond to, the following narrative. It is sufficient that this forematter announce to us our presence, so to speak, on hagiographic or *chanson de geste* territory. This, I believe, is due in large part to the fact that epic and saint's life do not address themselves to a socially differentiated audience. The *Thèbes* narrator specifically shoos away any low-born listeners, since, as he puts it, a *vilain* hearing his story would be as inappropriate as a jackass at a harp recital. Also, we noted, hagiography and *chanson de geste* recount—that is, give formal, even ritualistic expression to—their public's *history*, its sense of itself in a transcendentally historical time/space. Conversely, what eventually came to characterize romance was its *peculiarity*, both social and literary. Derived from books and legends of one sort or another, romance stories had to be made meaningful in ways that would have been unnecessary in non-romance narrative. Alexis' sainthood, like Roland's heroism, is *naturally* relevant (or was perceived as such); all that is required, in fact, is that Alexis' Romanness be pertinently related to a Northern French community. The relevance, meanwhile, of, say, a Gauvain (King Arthur's nephew) or of the morally ambiguous Iseut is less readily accessible. Quite frequently romances play with the multifaceted character of appearances and realities. Subtlety and sophistication are romance hallmarks. Whereas saints' lives and *chansons de geste*, at their purest, furnish the place in which the celebration of religious and "national" values occurs, romances, though often textually open-ended within certain generic constraints and purviews, tend to be far more circumscribed; they establish value systems and meaning referents that remain, on several important levels, confined to the text itself or additionally, at most, to the textual subtradition to which the text pertains. To a significant degree, then, each romance constitutes an "art of romance composition," a self-conscious commentary on such composition; therefore, in romance, "reading" and "writing" are, in a sense, virtually coterminous. "Author" and "public" are consequently less concerned with *what* a romance says than with *how* it says. We, the public, are identified as those able to grasp and appreciate the "saying." This explains the prevalence of carefully constructed, sometimes elaborate *exordia* in romance narrative; it also justifies—indeed demands—our close scrutiny of "opening signals" in such romances—*Eneas, Yvain*—as do not ostensibly contain a formal, "detachable" prologue. And although, in some cases, the orientation procedures used in given romances might appear to resemble those we observe in texts like the *Roland* and the *Alexis*, they must be construed, then, as supplying, explicitly or implicitly, *open* hints designed to facilitate our grasp of the romance *as romance*, as examples of self-referential narrative textuality.

The forematter to *Yvain* consists of 41 lines; these lines provide neither a written (or personal) source for *Yvain* nor the name of the author, unlike numerous romances (including Chrétien's other works) whose forematter supplies this information. On the other hand, as in the *Alexis* and the *Roland*, the ostensibly implicit narrator figure acts as a knowing witness to the events and the meaning of the events he has undertaken to recount. What he reports is what he thinks and what he has seen (or sees). The *nos* (l. 2) *apparently* indicates a timeless *Roland*-like community made up of narrator and public: a "good king of Britain," Arthur, is he "who teaches *us* prowess and courtesy." He, like Charles at Cordres, holds court, or rather *held* court (the historical narrative tense), one Whitsunday at Carduel in Wales. Also, we note, the good-old-days topic similar to the one we observed in the *exordium* to *Alexis* contrasts, in *Yvain*, the knights and ladies of yore who were true disciples of the covenant of Love (l. 16) with those of nowadays (l. 18). Again, as in the *Alexis* and the *Roland*, in *Yvain* past and present tenses are deftly and quite unambiguously distinguished; Arthur's prowess *does* indeed teach us (by its example, presumably, and/or its reputation) to be "preu et cortois." And the narrator's job is to reveal (by narrating) that example to us, who, as he has explained, stand in sore need of learning (ll. 18-28). However, nothing as specific as this didactic commentary occurs either in *Roland* or, except at the end, in *Alexis*. In assuming this voice—a true "shape"—Chrétien's narrator undermines the genuinely implicit narrator figure of the *Alexis* and the *Roland*. He makes sure we get the point; he drives it into the ground, protesting, we start to suspect, a bit too much, all the while relying on a kind of editorial/communitarian "we": "Mes or parl*ons* de cez qui furent, / si leiss*ons* cez qui ancor durent" (ll. 29-30, my emphasis) (But now let *us* speak of those who were, and let *us* set aside those who are still alive). He then shifts into a first-person singular, "Por ce *me* plest a reconter" (l. 33) (For this reason it pleases *me* to tell), and he begins his narrative proper: an astounding *story*, told mainly in the narrative past and "historical" present, of Arthur's incivility and of his Round Table entourage's discourtesy (this latter epitomized by Keu's venomous tongue).

Beyond a shadow of a doubt, then, we are on romance terrain—a terrain of narrative problematics and of sophisticated textual inwardness (not only of Arthurian subject matter). The double complicity—a very straightforward complicity—of author/subject matter and narrator/public so characteristic of the non-romance *Alexis-Roland* construct is here totally undermined. Whom and what can we—ought we—believe? The narrator's (apparently wrong) judgments concerning Arthur's *courtoisie*, as expressed in the opening 41 lines of *Yvain*, or what he, as eye-witness, actually reports, starting with l. 42: "Mes cel jor molt se merveillierent" (But that day they were quite shocked)? Narrative, or the telling of an "historical" story, and commentary, or the relating of the past events to a present-day, desired value scheme by the "performing" narrator, are opposed within the poem on at least two levels. The "truth" of the text—there seems, really, to be no sure "Arthurian truth"—lies more deeply embedded in the verbal artifact than in that to which this artifact supposedly refers. It is the whole text itself, *not* the narrator, who is but a device *inside* the text, that teaches us what we learn here, namely, that, in and of themselves, verbal manipulation and narrative play constitute the *locus* of meaning.

What, then, the forematter to *Yvain* tells us is that this text is *not* an *Alexis* or a *Roland*, that, let me repeat, *Yvain* (perhaps like all Arthurian stories) is a romance—but, of course, a romance significantly different from other romances. The reader must infer from what he experiences as reader —as reader/writer, so to speak—the orientation which the text, in its organization, provides for him. Our confidence in the narrator—a narrator who rashly assumed the role we associate with hagiographic and epic narrative— is shaken, at least when he departs from recounting merely what, as it were, he sees and hears. It is ourselves, not he, whom we must trust when judgment is called for. His attempt at ritually structured storytelling is foiled by the behavior of Arthur and his court; no book, we recall, backs him up (indeed, in *Yvain* no source is *ever* alluded to); no "author"—no *maistre* Wace, no Benoît or, for that matter, no Chrétien—is depicted as being in charge. On the other hand, the narrator's witness to events—his "reporting"—is indispensable to the proper operation of the text; it is from the narrator that we receive the facts of the story. He is honest (no cover-up of Arthur's discourtesy); we respect this honesty.

The result of all this is that *Yvain*'s "opening signals" create in us a kind of poetic suspense. How will everything be worked out? Not, incidentally, how will every *thing* work out? We are concerned with the creation of meaning *by* the text, not with a pre-established meaning *in* the text. In a very real sense, the "opening signals" of *Yvain* instruct us to focus our attention on how the text will write itself out, as though it were doing this on its own. Provided, in other words, we grasp the intentional nature of Chrétien's experiment with romance form—his particular meditation on romance form in *Yvain* as distinct from the experiments he and his predecessors engaged in elsewhere—we stand a good chance of experiencing an extraordinary enlargement of the possibilities open to twelfth-century narrative fiction.

Narrator and Protagonist

There is something touchingly earnest about our narrator; in his own way he is striving to serve the memory of those fine knights of old whose deeds of bravery and whose fidelity to Love immediately come to mind whenever we think of Arthur (ll. 37-41). Remembrance of a worthy past is perhaps the most common justification for writing proffered in Old French romance prologues; only the ignorant, like animals, are unaware of the past. The narrator of *Yvain* means well; that, along with his honesty, gains him a measure of our sympathy, even if it does not, for the reasons summarized above, invariably earn him our trust. In his capacity as one of the textual devices present in *Yvain*, the narrator naturally incarnates the clerk figure one finds in virtually all twelfth-century narrative. Willy-nilly he stands for *clergie*, the set of qualities and the status which, in the Prologue to *Cligés*, Chrétien had at once associated with and distinguished from the values and status of knightly *chevalerie*. *Clergie* and *chevalerie*, within romance, are of equal rank; at times opposed, at times reconciled, they complement one another. To be sure, Arthur would not have existed as Arthur without his and the Round Table's feats of arms and of love; yet, as numerous texts take pains to make explicit, without clerkly accomplishment Arthur would have ceased to exist in our memory.

To what extent, we might well now ask, does Yvain—still within the text of Chrétien's romance—complement, as *chevalier*, the narrator's *clergie*? Are they at all similar to one another in any significant way? Together do they constitute, in *chevalerie* and in *clergie* respectively, a single, symmetrical construct? In my view, they do indeed form two aspects of a unit, and, when seen as such, the character Yvain and the narrator figure provide what the text has to "say" about the complex relationship of knightliness and literary learning.

I have already described the narrator's inadequacies at the beginning of *Yvain*. We know nothing about Yvain before the end of Calogrenant's story, except that he is in the party of knights who, along with the Queen, wish to hear that story. (He is, of course, a knight of the Round Table, and that provides him with a potential identity.) He takes no part in the quarrel between Keu and the others; to a sharp-eared listener the fact that Yvain, like Gauvain, is referred to as *mes sire* (l. 56) serves to single him out. It pairs him with Gauvain, who is consistently called *mes sire* and known traditionally as the paragon of knights in terms of whom the knight-protagonist of Chrétien's romances usually is measured. Yvain, who has not previously spoken, is the first to comment on Calogrenant's story; his words are kindly: he will avenge Calogrenant's humiliation (Yvain, we learn, is his first cousin). Once again Keu intervenes, sarcastically accusing Yvain of being a drunken braggart; the Queen answers Keu angrily, resuming the previous quarrelsome exchange. Yvain, addressing Guenevere, tries to calm matters (ll. 630-48): sagely he refuses to take Keu's accusation seriously, to let his taunts deter him. At this point Arthur joins the company and, after Guenevere has told him Calogrenant's tale, swears to visit the fountain. Yvain is unhappy at this turn of events, for ". . . il cuidoit aler toz seus" (l. 679) (he planned on going all alone). On the spot he decides to depart immediately for Brocéliande in secret.

Yvain, then, is singled out; he is presented as a loyal and kindly kinsman; he is capable of turning the other cheek when he is unjustly accused; he obviously loves adventure; he is impetuous (perhaps rash?), though hardly the braggart Keu makes him out to be. These facts, along with his noble—even royal—ancestry, are all we know about him, in contrast to Arthur's great reputation, about which the narrator has made such ado. In short, what we know of Yvain is, no more, no less, what the narrator records from his—the narrator's—direct observation. Yvain is not (yet) "famous," he has no previous reputation, nothing to "remember" him by. Up to this point—and, importantly, in terms of the text—he is unformed, incomplete. His "incompleteness" parallels, then, the narrator's own unfinished status as completely reliable clerk.

The double incompleteness of knight-protagonist and clerkly narrator (of *chevalerie* and *clergie*) provides the context for Calogrenant's remarkable story. This first-person narrative, we recall, recounts the tale of its protagonist's shame, not of his honor (ll. 59-60): the term *honte* occurs repeatedly, as a kind of leitmotif, throughout the story. Calogrenant tells what happened to him some seven years earlier when, having set out in search of adventure, he traveled to the Forest of Brocéliande, met a hospitable vavasor and his charming daughter, who received him graciously, and encountered a hideous looking keeper of wild bulls and other savage beasts. This *vilain* tells him about the Magic Fountain, which Calogrenant visits only to be ignominiously defeated in combat by the lord of the country. The story is detailed and, of course, marvelous. Even more interesting, to our purposes, is that the narrative is couched entirely in pure romance form and courtly diction. Calogrenant the *chevalier* narrates his own story in precisely the terms a romancer-*clerc* would have employed. Indeed, Chrétien provides us here with an astonishing preview of the technique "invented" by Guillaume de Lorris in the *Romance of the Rose*, where, we remember, a narrator, aged 25, tells of his own experience—an experience that took place at least five years before the time of the narrative proper. Like Calogrenant, the *Rose* protagonist/narrator is one and the same "person," acting at two moments of his life and functioning, so to speak, as an avatar of the knightly protagonist *and* subsequently as clerkly recorder: both Calogrenant and his *Rose* counterpart conjoin *chevalerie* and *clergie* in this manner, while at the same time the categories are kept separate.

Calogrenant's adventure leads to chivalric failure, however, at least as far as he is concerned. (Yvain will succeed where his cousin met defeat.) Conversely, his narrative *qua* clerkly achievement is classically perfect. Responding to Guenevere's plea that he tell his story, Calogrenant acts as Eneas had done when, at Carthage, he courteously recounts the story of Troy's destruction in answer to Dido's entreaty that he do so, despite the pain reliving these events would cause him.[34] Both Calogrenant and Eneas are eye-witnesses to their misfortune. The Epilogue to Calogrenant's tale is a direct borrowing from Wace's *Rou*. Wace, we recall, a *clerc* who claimed to have visited the supposedly magical "fontaine de Berenton," where no miracle happened during his stay there, summed up his experience by declaring: "Fol i alai, fol m'en revinc" (Fool I went there, fool I returned). Here is Calogrenant's fascinating—and very clerkly—borrowing from Wace:

> Ensi alai, ensi reving;
> au revenir por fol me ting.
> Si vos ai conté come fos
> ce c'onques mes conter ne vos.
> (ll. 577-80)

(Thus I went there, thus I returned; upon my return I held myself to be a fool. And so, like a fool, I have told you what I never wished to tell you.)

Wace, a *clerc* prototype, had behaved like a *chevalier* in seeking the "adventure" of the Fountain; his disappointment parallels that of the "real" *chevalier*, Calogrenant, who, in the context of *Yvain*, is, of course, behaving as though he were a *clerc*; the conflation of knight and clerk is remarkable in both instances. And, in Chrétien's reversal of Wace, Calogrenant stresses *conter*, "to tell a story," rather than the action, or "knightly adventure," as such.

The clerkly self-consciousness of Calogrenant's narrative is not limited to these romance-type allusions. The point of his (ironically) perfect *clergie* is driven home as carefully as is that of his knightly inadequacy. The *récit* proper is preceded by a Prologue of 23 verses; it starts out, naturally, with a *sententia*: "Cuers et oroilles m'aportez, / car parole est tote perdue / s'ele n'est de cuer entandue" (ll. 150-52) (Bring me your hearts and ears, for words are totally lost if they are not heard by the heart). The rest of the Prologue is given over to an amplified explanation of this statement; it concludes with a couplet (also foreshadowing Guillaume de Lorris)[35] designed, in classic romance fashion, to assert the story's truth: "car ne vuel pas parler de songe, / ne de fable, ne de mançonge" (ll. 171-72) (For I do not wish to speak of dreams or of fable or of lies). Wace's self-characterization as "fool," though blaming his own gullibility, also focuses on the falsehood of the Fountain's reputation; Calogrenant means no such thing: the Fountain's adventure is all too real! Calogrenant cites no written source for his story; his "source" is his own experience, which, however, confirms what the ugly animal-keeper had told him. He recounts what has befallen him, as befits a knight. His manner, though, is that of a romancer; what happens takes place in the world of romance, but it is reported as something "real." This is the curious result of the blend of *chevalier* and *clerc* epitomized by Calogrenant. Romance form is thus made to *contain* a certain authenticity, a new kind of meaning or relevance.

Romance procedures—for example, descriptions, wondrous events, narrator interventions, dialogue—pervade Calogrenant's report. Nowhere is this more evident than in what might be called the architecture of Calogrenant's narrative. I have mentioned the Prologue and the closure. What of the midpoint? Midpoints of entire romances or of important segments of romances, we recall, are often of considerable strategic importance, like prologues. They frequently bear upon the identity or name of the protagonist; they have to do with the text's *san*. For example, it is at the midpoint of *Yvain* that our protagonist meets the animal from whom he takes his name: Le Chevalier au Lion—also, eventually, the title of the poem. Lines 358-63 may be construed as the *exact* midpoint of Calogrenant's uninterrupted text, which, in Roques's edition, goes from l. 142 to l. 580. The animal-keeper has asked Calogrenant who he is and what he is looking for; the knight replies:

> —Je sui, fet il, uns chevaliers
> qui quier ce que trover ne puis;
> assez ai quis, et rien ne truis.
> —Et que voldroies tu trover?
> —Avanture, por esprover
> ma proesce et mon hardemant.
> (ll. 358-63)

("I am," says he, "a knight and seek what I cannot find; I have sought far and wide and found nothing." "And what would you wish to find?" "Adventure, in order to test my prowess and my courage.")

A more searching characterization of Calogrenant's state and being would be hard to imagine! His is gratuitous knight-errantry, open to whatever he might undergo just so long as he properly tests himself and his valor. This, of course, is an important theme throughout *Yvain* which, like other romances by Chrétien, is in great part a meditation on chivalry and its ideals. But these words have an even more far-reaching import. *Trover*, "to find," also means "to write, to compose, poetry," more precisely, in fact, "to invent, to discover the matter and the means of composing a poetic work." The midpoint of Calogrenant's text describes the knight in search of adventure as well as the clerk in the initial stages of invention seeking his proper subject matter, his *matière* and his *san*. This passage, located at what might be tagged the apex of Calogrenant's discourse, enunciates in authentic, credible romance style what the imperfect narrator at the beginning of *Yvain* was incapable of stating, namely, the problematic nature of *both* chivalry and clerkliness, particularly in their relationship to one another as this relationship forms the core of romance narrative. And, to an important degree, this problematic relationship is precisely what *Le Chevalier au Lion* is all about and will seek to resolve. Chrétien's meditation on knightliness is inextricably linked here to his meditation on *clergie*. Calogrenant's miniature *roman*, founded as it is on the double *experience* of knightliness/clerkliness, is meant to constitute the reference system underlying what will be the conjoined experiences and growth of both Yvain and the narrator who relates his story. The transformation of failure into success—into the "success" of marriage (not the gratuitous success Calogrenant presumably would have enjoyed had he managed to defeat Esclados)—will supply the dynamics of Chrétien's accomplishment. Finally, let me repeat, this accomplishment will be achieved through the purely romance means exemplified so startlingly by the function and form of Calogrenant's tale.

Both Yvain and the narrator "imitate" Calogrenant throughout the 300 or so lines following his Epilogue. Narrationally as well as experientially Calogrenant's *récit* mediates what occurs subsequently in the text. Yvain decides to undertake the same adventure as his cousin; the narrator relates the rationale of this decision (ll. 691-93), as well as what later happens, *in the third person*. And we believe him, despite the fantastic events, because Calogrenant's story authenticates what he says. Technically speaking, the narrator *abbreviates* Calogrenant's narrative in recounting Yvain's search for and exact replication of his cousin's adventure; even the vavasor's maiden daughter has apparently aged not a single day over the previous seven years! Like Calogrenant, and also in keeping with his own knightly character, Yvain seeks adventure, but, we remember, his motivation is not quite so gratuitous as was that of his predecessor. He hopes to avenge his kinsman's shame and to do so alone, with glory. In this sense, he *appropriates* Calogrenant's experience, making it his own. Similarly—and here Chrétien's artistry is most impressive—the narrator transforms Calogrenant's *récit* not only by abbreviating it (*amplificatio* and *abbreviatio* constituted two legitimate ways by which a clerk would rework, and make his own, material he "found"—*inventio*—in his source), but also by intervening into the substance of the story with personal commentary of a typically clerkly, though, in fact, at least partly unjustified, sort. Thus, in mentioning Yvain's arrival at the vavasor's domicile, the narrator states: "car plus de bien et plus d'enor / trueve il assez el vavasor / *que ne vos ai conté et dit*" (II. 779-81, my emphasis) (for greater good and honor does he plentifully find at the vavasor's *than I have told and said to you*). As though conscious, perhaps, of having stepped a bit out of line, he then refers directly to his source, though only to affirm his own (and maybe Yvain's) judgment: "et an la pucele revit / de san et de biauté cent tanz / *que n'ot conté Calogrenanz*" (II. 782-84, my emphasis) (and he saw in the maiden a hundred times more sense and beauty *than Calogrenant had told of*). Calogrenant's text/experience serves to mediate the subsequent conduct of both Yvain and the narrator; it also acts as a point of departure for the ensuing double, or parallel, adventure of narrator and protagonist, reinforcing at the same time the parallel nature of this adventure.

Yvain, I have said, assimilates Calogrenant's experience. Up to his defeat of Esclados, he does not, however, stray from the bounds of that experience. Thus, though impressed by her beauty, he does not dally with the vavasor's daughter any more than Calogrenant had done; that is, he does not play the Erec to this obvious avatar of Enide. Yvain's destiny truly becomes his own only after he mortally wounds Esclados and after his daring pursuit of his dying adversary into the castle. At this point Calogrenant's specific mediation—he is now avenged—becomes, as it were, sublimated into Yvain's own experience as reported by the narrator. The stress is on reporting, though some commentary, naturally, is included. Yet neither narrator nor protagonist can as yet fly with his own wings; both require further support, which is supplied by the character Lunete. It is she who makes things work at this juncture: she causes Yvain to be protected from the angry subjects of Esclados; she arranges the meeting between Laudine and Yvain as well as their marriage. It is thanks to her that Yvain's "story" progresses and, no less significantly, that the narrator has something to report. We shall analyze this personage in greater detail below, but for the time being, let it be said that her chief strength lies in her verbal power; this power is essentially *rhetorical*, not narrative. It consists in her ability to persuade those to whom she speaks of the virtue of her arguments. This, far more than her manipulation of magic artifacts, constitutes the authority through which she achieves her ends and inspires confidence in what is told about her. Her *verbal action* replaces, or is grafted upon, what I have called Calogrenant's mediation, and this both changes the course of Yvain's life (initiating at last his own *history*) and the narrator's attitude in regard to his subject, *his* "history," or *matière*. What Lunete promotes does in fact take place, and this conditions everything that happens in the rest of the story; she provides the logic of events: Yvain's despicable thoughtlessness with respect to his bride, his remorse and madness, his charitable knightly behavior, his eventual reconciliation with Laudine, as well as, of course, the narrator's faithful and ever more masterly depiction of all these events. Lunete supplies what will come to motivate, more and more profoundly, Yvain's chivalry and what will come to characterize the narrator's particular brand of *clergie*. Just as Yvain learns to put chivalry to good use, so—and analogously—the narrator will learn to derive purpose and truth from his literary training, his ability and his native honesty. Although *Yvain* in fact takes place in the Arthurian past, it appears—through romance sleight-of-hand—to unfold itself in the present. What is "worthy of memory" is being created by knight and clerk together before our very eyes.

Courtly Ambiguity

Yvain, we noted, has no "fame" apart from his royal descent and from his connection with Arthur's court—indeed, apart from the network of "courtly" situations and people with whom, in some ways, he is affiliated and from whom in other ways he is rendered distinct. In analogous fashion the narrator's status derives entirely from his position as narrator; unlike the narrator of *Lancelot,* he is not identified as, or with, an author, a "Crestïens." He is entirely he-who-narrates-the-story; his authority is shored up by none of the usual romance supports. And, as we saw, he is hardly the reliable clerkly figure his pronouncements and assumptions would seem to make him out to be. Yvain, then, belongs to the Arthurian world and to the romance narrative structure, but his manner of belonging to these differs radically from the manner, say, of a Gauvain, a Keu or a Guenevere. He is to *chevalerie* (ostensibly epitomized by Gauvain) what the narrator is to *clergie*. Yvain is integrated into the Arthurian court in nowhere near so complete a fashion as Gauvain, a knight whose identity is to be, *par excellence,* the Arthurian *mes sire*. But, we observed, the realities of Arthur's court—the king's lack of courtesy towards his guests, Keu's sarcasm, Guenevere's unladylike language—do not jibe with that court's reputation for graciousness and nobility. What actually takes place there contrasts with the court's fame. Furthermore, Calogrenant's search for adventure, a gratuitous, "purely Arthurian," quest, leads to his disgrace and shame. A certain emptiness threatens to characterize the courtly routines and the pretensions of those who participate in these routines. The Arthurian courtly reputation, we saw, is belied by facts both present and past. Thus, Yvain's lack of "history" not only parallels the narrator's inexperience; it also, in a kind of reversal, complements Arthurian inadequacies. Yvain's growth will take place both in respect and in contradistinction to a remarkably static Arthurian world; Yvain will learn to live outside this *pays d'Arthur* that, in effect, must also constitute the *locus* for the rite of passage he undergoes. Concomitantly, as we shall see, Chrétien's romance, *as text*, will also experience a definite transformation. The exploration and development of Yvain's *otherness*—of his uniqueness as protagonist—furnishes Chrétien with the means by which, within the economy of his poem, he will explore the nature of institutionalized courtliness: the courtly *reputation* of the Arthurian *matière* and, so to speak, ethos. Or, to put the matter in another way, the structure of *Yvain* will engender a commentary within the romance upon established fame and upon *a priori* "courtliness" in this text. Finally, and in conjunction with what has just been said, *Yvain* will put the romance genre itself to hitherto unexplored narrative uses.

It will consequently not suffice merely to extrapolate from *Yvain* a blanket condemnation by Chrétien of Arthurian ideals and chivalric claims. To be sure, *Yvain* does poke fun at those innocents who might wish to attribute to these ideals the same values one associates with the worlds of *Alexis* and *Roland*. Moreover, Chrétien exposes, with humor and with charm, the insufficiency of monolithic and one-dimensional social ideals when these are construed as model codes of behavior and applied rigidly in a world that never lives up to them. Elements of satire permeate *Yvain*. However, Chrétien refrains from offering any equally systematic alternative to inadequate Arthurian courtliness. No moralizing of the sort one detects, say, in Jean Bodel's polemical characterization of the matter of Britain as "vain and pleasant" (*Song of the Saxons*) can be pinpointed anywhere in Chrétien's text.[36] On the contrary, as we have noted, his narrator is deliberately rendered unable convincingly to voice moralizing of this sort. Chrétien no more condemns Arthur and his Round Table than Proust condemns Charlus, or Dickens Mr. Pickwick. *Yvain* employs the procedures of comedy in presenting Arthurian courtliness. Or rather, what modern scholarship has frequently construed to be "Arthurian courtliness" (since Gaston Paris and his predecessors), that is, a "doctrine," say, of "courtly love" or an aristocratic ideology of any more or less systematic type, is not only undermined as of the start of *Yvain*; the text's comic frame deliberately, and in interesting ways, places the Arthurian world at the service of other considerations. Whereas Yvain, the narrator and, by extension, the romance itself exist in a dimension of becoming, of self-completion, the Arthurian world—contained in such characters as Arthur himself, Calogrenant, Keu, Gauvain and, curiously, Laudine, too—remains entirely unchanging, totally unaffected by what happens. (The case of Lunete, as we shall see later in greater detail, differs from that of the others.) Yvain, I repeat, is at once *of* this comic structuring and opposed to it. Arthur and his companions constitute a pure datum—albeit an essential one—of the romance, as does the seldom-named Laudine.[37] What those like Calogrenant and especially Gauvain represent is not what Yvain must learn to emulate. To an important degree, rather, he must *un*learn to aspire to make of Arthur's court his *locus*, his home.

This conception of the Arthurian world, as befits its comic nature, is profoundly intellectual. Indeed, one might say, Yvain is called upon eventually to regard his relationship to Arthur's court, notably through his friendship for and emulation of Gauvain, in terms of intellectual and ironic detachment. Yvain's passionate nature is something other than Gauvain's splendid gratuitousness; he is also a "better knight" than his cousin Calogrenant. Moreover, Chrétien takes pains to include no direct hint of the tragically flawed character of the Arthurian world, no suggestion of the betrayals and of the coming demise of that world as had been "reported" by Geoffrey of Monmouth or Wace. These questions are opened and their implications faced squarely in the *Charrette* and above all in the *Conte du Graal*, the two romances which, we recall, led to numerous explicit continuations and recastings. Like Yvain, we, as readers-spectators-participants, are also invited to consider with intellectual (and smiling) detachment the Arthurian world depicted here. Again like that of Yvain, our detachment grows out of the comic frame which, as the romance progresses, we come increasingly to understand and appreciate; we, too, in a sense, lose our innocence. In its structurings and duration, the romance contains a double notion—or the two related notions—of courtly ambiguity. The ambiguous character of courtliness derives, then, from our *reading*, from, so to speak, our being created as readers; it is integrated into the poetic warp and woof of Chrétien's text. It is not something either underpinning the romance or to be concluded from it. As an idea, "courtly ambiguity" remains a function of the narrative poetics of *Yvain*; the intellectual nature of this idea is as entirely a part of the text as the "idea" of misanthropy in Molière's great play. Though, in point of fact, Arthur "the good King of Britain" does teach us "prowess and courtesy," as the initial couplet of the poem informs us, he does so in a fashion we, no more than Yvain or the narrator, would hardly have expected; his "teaching"—the place of the court, of his fame—is situated lock, stock and barrel in how the romance as a whole is worked out and grows: in how it becomes and in how it is completed.

Yvain, I suggested, takes the data of fame, rules of conduct and the "historical" trappings of the Round Table, turning these into components of highly self-conscious romance narrative composition. In a sense, they are trivialized, humorously and gently. One is reminded of what Chrétien had accomplished in *Cligés* and, when one considers Yvain's relative innocence, of what will become Perceval's eventual growth to knighthood. The Arthurian world is different in kind from the worlds of *Alexis* and *Roland*, just as Chrétien's text differs in kind from their brands of textuality. The process of gentle trivialization continues throughout the poem. For example, Gauvain's absence from the court at the time his niece and surviving nephews need defending (ll. 3910-14) against the horrible giant Harpin is due to his having departed on a quest to deliver Guenevere. This, we recall, is the plot of the *Charrette*, a *romance*. Gauvain is playing a role *in a story* when he ought to be protecting his sister's family. And, as if that were not enough, Gauvain's brother-in-law bitterly denounces Keu's having so badly advised, or deceived (*anbricona*, l. 3917), Arthur that he allowed the Queen to be carried off in the first place. Yvain will have to take on Gauvain's responsibility. It was also Gauvain, we remember, who taunted Yvain shortly after his marriage to Laudine, convincing his gullible friend to abandon Laudine and her castle, where he is truly needed, in order once again to display his valor in jousts and tournaments, namely, in the game-like routines of the Arthurian world. In his lengthy speech Gauvain mouths to a man who is genuinely loved and happily married the clichés of "courtliness" (ll. 2486-2540): marriage and chivalry must be complementary (and, therefore, incompatible?); honor (*pris*) must be maintained lest love come to nought and Yvain turn into a *jalos*, the unworthy jealous husband evoked in much courtly lyric and narrative and whose designation frequently rhymes with *cous*, "cuckold." Gauvain's rhetoric, couched in unregenerate courtly diction, assumes the existence of a value system directly opposed to the kind of situation Yvain has just chosen, a value system linked to reputation and *storybooks* and quite literally divorced from reality. He and Arthur wish to take Yvain away (l. 2484) from his newly found, real place in order to restore him to the romance-place of *la Bretaigne* (l. 2548). And Yvain obtains his release from Laudine through the typically romance—and *Charrette*—device of the rash boon, a ruse: he asks her to grant him a favor "for your honor and mine" (l. 2555) without, however, telling her what the favor is until she has trustingly agreed to accede to his request. Only then does he state his incomprehensible desire to "accompany the king and to participate in tournaments so that people will not call him *recreant*, 'coward, traitor'" (l. 2563). The request is granted on condition that he return within a year; his failure to do so—a genuine act of *recreantise*—leads to his despair and madness. All this occurs *after* the opening scene of the romance, in which the realities of Arthurian court life had been contrasted with the narrator's naïvely ideological presentation of what Arthur and the Round Table are supposed to stand for, their undying fame.

Whereas, in *Cligés*, all that happens, except for the very fashioning of the romance, takes place within a purely comic framework, in *Yvain* the experiences of both protagonist and narrator reverberate against a stiffly comic Arthurian order, which is identified both as place and as assembly of stock characters. The comicalicity of the Arthurian world is, therefore, a device. As such, it permits both the dynamics of the romance's composition—its completion—and a certain irony that pervades the story of Yvain's education and that of the narrator figure. Neither of these is to be taken with ponderous seriousness, despite the apparently cataclysmic disasters that befall our hero: his disgrace, the break-up of his marriage and his madness. Nor ought one ascribe a heavily moralizing tone to the story of Yvain's regeneration in the second part of the romance, after his cure by the Lady of Norison. Though quite authentic, on all counts, Yvain's achievement of genuine *pris* and *los*, as well as his reconquest of Laudine (brought off once again through a ruse by Lunete), cause the reader to smile contentedly, with amused understanding. Yvain does not move from the purely romance terrain of *Cligés* to the lands of *Alexis* or *Roland*; he merely learns to realize that Arthur's court is not for him, that it is not a real place. Gauvain's words of admonishment to him, he understands, present a false problem; courtliness as ideology is meaningless except as a game.

In this context, Chrétien's depiction of Yvain's love for Laudine (and her reciprocating this affection) shows masterful subtlety. As a character, Laudine is hardly more real than, say, Gauvain or Keu. She is at once the object of Yvain's love and the symbol of his duty. Her existence has no other dimension, no independence from his story, unlike the existence of Fenice, who at least is portrayed ostensibly as a strong-willed girl who refuses to give herself either to her husband, whom she does not love, or to Cligés, to whom she is not married. Moreover, Laudine resembles a patchwork of characteristically twelfth-century literary allusions: like Virgil's (and the *Eneas*') Dido, she is the passionate widow-ruler of a community of cowards, and she is, as well, perhaps too easily influenced by a Lunete-Anna; her behavior at Esclados' funeral has reminded scholars of Ovid's advice to would-be remarried widows that they take care to mourn unrestrainedly and to appear properly disheveled at their husband's funeral in order to attract a suitable new spouse (*Ars amatoria*, III, 431-32); in her association with the Magic Fountain as well as in her rapid according of her love, and withdrawal when betrayed, she follows the practice of numerous Celtic fairies in romance; her beauty and worth are the stock-in-trade of courtly lyric and narrative. She gives her love to Yvain and for "good reason" takes him as her husband. Her fountain, after all, must be defended —the mythic fountain denounced as such by Wace! Her subsequent anger towards Yvain, though quite plausible, is more necessarily a device of plot without which Yvain's story could not have been completed.

Had Laudine been depicted, as it were, more fully and less "literarily," the ambiguous character of courtliness in *Yvain* would necessarily have been sacrificed, as would have also the indispensable comic frame within which Arthurian conventions are exposed. The reader would have been too completely drawn into the "drama" of Yvain's marriage. For despite what numerous scholars have averred, *Yvain* does not methodically oppose one system of "authentic" courtliness—courtliness in marriage—to an inauthentic system of courtliness—the fame and behavior of those making up the Arthurian world. Elements of such an opposition, to be sure, are present in *Yvain*, but they are not pervasive. In her way Laudine is every bit as shadowy a figure as Gauvain. She and Yvain do not constitute the central couple in the romance; the essential twosome is formed, rather, by Yvain and the narrator. They are the only personages that may be described as growing; Laudine is simply there, an unchanging constant. And so it is, the romance tells us, with any reduction of human experience and values to a rule system, which, by its very nature, can neither contain the complexities —the dynamics—of such experience nor adequately serve to express them. Things properly work themselves out the other way around. What might be apprehended as an ideal set of rules in reality merely contributes a greater or smaller share to the thickness of realities that make up a human being and, for that matter, a text. In a certain sense, then, Yvain learns to be "courtly" while, and even more importantly, he disabuses himself of externally imposed rules of courtliness. One notes a similar, and analogously comic, development of this idea in the *Conte du Graal* as the young Perceval painfully learns to adjust the rules of conduct he learned from his mother and his tutor, Gornemant de Goorz, to the delicate and complex realities he faces throughout his chivalric adventures. In *Yvain* the ambiguity of courtliness—a remarkably fertile "idea"—derives, then, entirely from the seamless, yet highly self-conscious *conjointure* of Chrétien's text.

Lunete

She is the great artificer or, as I noted above, the prompter of the romance: she saves Yvain's life in gratitude for the kindness he had at one time displayed on her behalf; she brings Yvain and Laudine together, a *conjointure* entirely due to her persuasiveness; she provides Yvain with an opportunity to prove his true chivalry by defending her cause; she succeeds in reconciling him with his wife. Like Thessala in *Cligés*, she is a kind of mistress of the household in the service of her lady, but she is also something more: a craftswoman whose powers extend even to magic artifacts. The qualifier *mestre* is applied to Lunete at l. 1597; though usually glossed as "confidante" or as "governess," this term frequently carries the meaning of "crafts-man/woman" in romance texts, often designating the author (for example, the above-quoted *maistre* Wace). She partakes, as do Laudine and the Lady of Norison, of the romance's faerie. Finally, despite her status as serving-maid, she, unlike Thessala this time, also belongs to what might be called the courtly stratum of the romance. Indeed, her name is revealed during a charming dalliance she conducts with Gauvain after Arthur's arrival at Laudine's castle: she, a "little moon," is the counterpart of Gauvain, who is identified as the "sun of chivalry" (ll. 2400-16). Quite simply, without her the romance could not have happened as it did; in a sense, Lunete "takes over" from Calogrenant.

Lunete's strengths are chiefly verbal—verbal in an essentially rhetorical frame. She succeeds at almost every occasion in influencing the course of events according to her wishes. Her only mistake is to rely on Gauvain as her champion; he is off on the *Charrette* adventure-story when she needs him to defend her against the charges of three of Laudine's jealous retainers and possible immolation by fire. At the same time Lunete seems both to incarnate destiny in the romance, as its prime mover, and to be remarkably practical, even pragmatic. Her reaction to specific situations, like Yvain's entrance into the castle in pursuit of Esclados and his consequent mortal danger, are immediate and, to a great degree, improvised. Her advice and talent for persuasion consistently take the side of practical solutions against the tyranny of convention and rule systems. Thus, she convinces her mistress to marry the man who, if he is not her husband's willful murderer, is at least responsible for her widowhood. This, to some perhaps, shocking alternative is justified because Yvain, of whom she is fond, gives every sign of loving Laudine passionately and because Laudine requires a brave and capable knight to defend her fountain. Also, in reconciling the estranged spouses, Lunete does not shrink from utilizing a ruse, the typical romance "rash boon"; her ends, which are usually quite acceptable to the reader of the romance, plausibly justify her means.

It is surely no accident, then, that Lunete's name—her identity—is disclosed in the above-mentioned episode; it is entirely thanks to her efforts that the joy and happiness of visitors and hosts alike at Laudine's castle can occur. And, let us recall, Gauvain offers Lunete his love and knightly service precisely because she has saved the life of his dear friend. The juxtaposition of Lunete and Gauvain is not gratuitous; this juxtaposition is, as well, an opposition, a contrast central to the whole narrative. For immediately after describing the festivities and courtly *deduit*, the narrator records Gauvain's ill-fated admonishment to Yvain: "Honiz soit de sainte Marie / qui por anpirier se marie!" (ll. 2489-90) (Shamed be by Holy Mary he who marries only to be degraded thereby). His advice undoes the *conjointure* achieved by Lunete. Ever the "perfect knight," Gauvain serves merely to embody, because of his fame and reputation (not because of what he has actually done in *Yvain*), the rule system one is required to associate with Arthur's court. Gauvain leads to the disgrace and madness of his friend, the anger and dismay of Laudine and, almost, the death of the woman he has sworn to serve! He does all this in the name of Love (ll. 2495-97). By representing what might be tagged a courtly ideology, Gauvain is shown to be, quite simply, wrong. He epitomizes the inflexibility of rule systems, their inadequacy in real-life situations. Meanwhile, of course, Lunete stands for the freedom and the suppleness inherent in her practicality and living wisdom. Her free spirit and ability, as I noted, to move around within various categories—an ability analogous to that of the experienced rhetor and poet to move about in topics—are opposed, on all counts, to Gauvain's extreme one-dimensionality. His words, at best, are empty; hers are effective.

Interestingly enough, it is right after Yvain meets with and saves the lion from whom he will get his own identity and the romance, eventually, a title —the midpoint of the narrative—that he comes upon Lunete imprisoned in a chapel and sorely needful of a champion. She overhears Yvain outside lamenting his lost happiness and fainting from despair. She inquires as to who it is that carries on so pitifully, to which Yvain (whom she does not recognize) responds by asking in turn who *she* is. Lunete repiles, "The saddest being alive" (l. 3568). Lunete then argues that, whereas he "can go wherever he wishes" (ll. 3584-86), she is "ci anprisonee" (imprisoned here) and must face on the morrow a "mortel juïse," a judgment upon which her very life depends. She explains that three of her lady's retainers have accused her of treason because she had arranged the marriage between Laudine and Yvain. It is not her fault that Yvain reneged on his promise to return to Laudine after his year of absence. Of all the knights in the world, only two—*mes sire* Gauvain and *mes sire* Yvain—might successfully champion her cause against the three accusers and restore her freedom.

Gauvain, we noted, has departed to search for the abducted Guenevere. To anyone familiar with the *Charrette*, Lunete's assertion that he would not return to Arthur's court until he had found her surely must sound ironic. It was the "presently" imprisoned Lancelot, we remember, not Gauvain, who delivered the Queen.

Yvain accepts the challenge, but does so—a sign that he has at last perfected a sense of true chivalry?—on condition that Lunete not reveal his identity. He wishes to remain anonymous, or rather, perhaps merely to be known by his new name, as the Chevalier au Lion (ll. 4283-86, 4607-09). He courageously dismisses Lunete's concerns for his life ("It is better that you stay alive than both of us dying," ll. 3742-43), and promises her to do his duty at the appointed hour. Thus, once again Lunete is caused to have special access to information not generally shared by other characters in the romance.

This touching scene, involving as it does matters of identity and knightly responsibility at that crucial point in the narrative where past and present meet, underscores, I believe, what Lunete is meant to represent in the romance. Furthermore, it accomplishes this by showing up Gauvain's built-in limitations. Without Yvain's aid, Lunete's free spirit, her kindness and what she is capable of doing with words would be implacably destroyed by a cruel rule system, here symbolized by the rules of feudal justice, the ordeal. At times arms must courteously help *clergie*, the text seems to be telling us, and this service must be both genuine and responsible.

Yvain arrives at the place of Lunete's execution only in the nick of time; Lunete has been tied to the stake and has already received the rite of confession. Her impending death seems certain; a pathetic lament by court ladies who love her and praise her charity has been heard (ll. 4355-73). But on this occasion, Yvain's tardiness is not due to forgetfulness; he has just saved Gauvain's relations from the evil Harpin de la Montagne and has barely had the time to rush to Lunete's side. With the lion's help, we recall, he succeeds in defeating his three adversaries and in restoring Lunete to the good graces of her mistress. However, unlike the triumphs he enjoyed during his year and a half of tournaments, this victory was not meant to cover "Yvain"—his former name—with glory; he is introduced to Laudine as the Chevalier au Lion. Lunete repeats her promise not to divulge his real identity, and, after curing his own and his lion's wounds, he departs for further charitable adventures. Lunete alone is aware of this identity—of the Yvain of the first half of the romance and the new Chevalier au Lion/ Yvain of the second half.

Thus, the character of Lunete—a character entirely within the romance—constitutes, so to speak, the *locus* wherein and by means of which *Yvain* as romance comments upon the application of romance-type rule systems, or "ideologies," to real life. Her role is strikingly like that of a *servante* in a Molière play; in other ways she resembles an Anna, but one whose advice to her Dido-like Laudine turns out well in the end. The protean nature of her character makes of her a device *of* the romance—a metaphor of romance power, one might say—rather than solely a device *in* the romance. She very handily stands in for the absent author and for the equally absent authoritative "source," being both a part of what is going on in the romance and a conscious, motivating force. Through her Chrétien is able to depict directly the efficacy of words and of certain gestures as well as, under given circumstances, the limitations of these. Surely she is one of his most complex and sophisticated creations. Not the least interesting of her attributes is her ambiguously subservient social status; she is not permitted to run away with the text. She, like "Crestïens" himself perhaps, is beautifully controlled.

Yvain's Madness

Through the first half of the romance Yvain's character is presented as being composed, so to speak, of equal parts of impetuosity and genuine worth. He is fundamentally likeable (Lunete remembers his generosity to her, for example) even as he is rash and impulsive. This dialectic in his character is charmingly and amusingly brought out in the scene during which he witnesses, himself unobserved, Laudine's grief at her husband's funeral. Yvain falls in love on the spot, his passion rising to meet, and match, her sadness. A kind of counterpoint of strong feelings pervades this episode both within Yvain and in his juxtaposition to the beautiful woman who (and in very short order!) will become his wife. Chrétien pulls out all the Ovidian stops in the description of Yvain's lovesickness. *Charrette*-like hyperboles abound; God himself, not Nature, fashioned Laudine's beauty. Love is simultaneously an illness and its own cure; by inspiring him to love her, Laudine avenges Esclados. The very text seems to duplicate what is going on in Yvain's soul, so perfectly that the reader feels obliged to smile. Just as he will smile when, later, Lunete introduces the terrified and speechless (though freshly bathed and newly clothed) Yvain into Laudine's chamber so that he may formally meet and propose marriage to her. Nowhere does the narrator tell us directly that Yvain is impetuous or that he is worthy of our esteem. These character traits become apparent only in our observation, thanks to the narrator's reporting, of what Yvain does and thinks, as when Lunete can barely restrain him from rushing out of his hiding place to stop Laudine from tearing at herself in grief (ll. 1302-04).[38]

Similar techniques and analogous structures may be found in the scene of Yvain's madness, which in many respects constitutes the outgrowth of, and response to, the lovesickness episode. Yvain reacts to the denunciation of him by Laudine's messenger at Arthur's court immediately and decisively: hating himself for having betrayed his wife, he *chooses* to go mad. He *wants* to flee the court "all alone... to a land where no man or woman would know anything about him" (ll. 2786-88). Having, through his own fault, been stripped of his love, he repents by stripping himself of everything else: the esteem of the court, his fame and identity, even his clothes. He rushes wilfully into madness as, before, he had rushed into love. His commitment is total; his passionate impetuosity turns into an authentic literary sickness, and he becomes, for us, though still hyperbolically (that is, comically), an object of pity: "So great a turbulence affects his mind that he takes leave of his senses" (ll. 2806-07). As Laudine had done while mourning Esclados, so here Yvain tears at his clothes until, however, he is quite naked. But, as I remarked earlier, Chrétien also works into this scene a web of reminiscences of the *Tristan* story. His amazed narrator recounts how Yvain simply takes a bow and five barbed arrows away from a boy, hurries into the forest, slays several *bestes* and gorges himself on their raw flesh. The wood is a variation on Tristan's Forest of Morois—a place of involuntary exile, where Tristan also hunted with a bow and arrow—but, of course, Yvain has no Iseut to accompany him. In this episode *Yvain* systematically reverses the story we find in Béroul. And to make sure we get the point, Chrétien has Yvain meet a hermit. However, this hermit, who goes unnamed, is hardly the "wise" and very talkative Ogrin who advises Béroul's lovers to repent and make their peace with Mark. Unlike virtually all the hermits one finds in Old French romance, Yvain's hermit never says anything. Instead of boldly stepping in and taking charge of the madman, which is what a "normal" romance hermit would do, our hermit is so frightened that he stops his hoeing and withdraws inside his little house! He is reported to pray God on Yvain's behalf, but also that He prevent Yvain from returning! One suspects that, unlike Ogrin, Yvain's hermit behaves in a fashion befitting the behavior of real-life twelfth-century hermits. These upside-down *Tristan* references, like the Ovidian play in the lovesickness scene, underscore and maintain the essentially comic nature of Chrétien's text; they help keep the romance from getting out of hand.

Much is accomplished, then, by the scene of Yvain's madness. Not the least of these accomplishments is the commentary Chrétien effects here, once again, on the romance nature of the *Tristan* story, a matter, it may fairly be said, with which he was obsessed. This commentary, however, is woven integrally into his text. Thus, whereas the forest exile of Tristan and Iseut is depicted as a time of want for Béroul's protagonists,[39] *Yvain* does them one better. Though Yvain benefits from no spiritual sustenance offered by the hermit, he profits from the latter's material charity: bread and vegetables (l. 2840). Meanwhile, he shows the good side of his own character by giving meat to the hermit as well as the skins of the animals he has hunted, thereby allowing the hermit, who sells these skins, to improve the quality of the flour he buys for his bread. Unlike their counterparts in the Forest of Morois, they enjoy well-balanced meals! This material exchange, or collaboration, between hero and hermit, minutely detailed and reported by the narrator over some forty lines of text, constitutes both a comic reversal of *Tristan* and the exemplification of what will become the means through which Yvain will redeem himself: non-gratuitous good works. At the same time, Yvain's essential generosity—his worth, as contrasted with his dangerously impulsive impetuosity and passion—is also called into play. Although, we learn, Yvain cannot remember anything that he had done before his madness (ll. 2824-25), his character remains, nevertheless, entirely constant.

Yvain's madness takes place within a doubly-focused romance context: the world of the text that concerns him properly as well as the textuality of the *Tristan* world. This superimposition of two texts, a kind of blending, gently utilizes the resources of comedy—Yvain's exile into forest madness parallels the forest exile and the *folie* of Béroul's star-crossed lovers—in order to construct what, in the last analysis, is the genuinely narrative metaphor constituting the *san* of *Le Chevalier au Lion*. The depiction of Yvain's distress, relying as it does on the reader's intellectual grasp of this system of textual correspondences, is comic, as is the tale of his eventual cure. Two damsels and a lady encounter our naked hero lying fast asleep in the wood. We immediately remember Mark's visitation of the sleeping —and dressed!—lovers in the Forest of Morois. After lengthy and careful observation, one of the damsels finally looks at Yvain's face and recognizes him as "mes sire Yvains" because of a scar on his cheek—a typical romance device if ever there was one! But this comic depiction, undercutting the all-too-serious account of Tristan and Iseut's return to Mark's favor and court, a return achieved through false pretenses, serves, though still within the romance frame, as a powerful *understatement*, as an extended litotes, expressing both the grounds and the means of Yvain's return to his lady's good graces. Through comedy a lesson of *authentic* seriousness is provided here.

That, however, is not all. The episode is extraordinarily rich. It is here that the narrator truly begins to come into his own. He finds the style at which he excels: reporting exactly what he "sees." I have mentioned the minute description of the exchanges between Yvain and his hermit friend. We learn that the hermit's house was low-roofed and small, that he was hoeing when Yvain arrived on the scene, that the bread given Yvain by the hermit was rough-tasting because his flour cost but twenty *sous* the measure,[40] that Yvain ate the bread and drank the cold water offered him because he was ravenously hungry, that the food was served on a windowsill, that Yvain was sure to hunt at least one animal per week, etc. Details of this "realistic" kind also proliferate in the account of Yvain's discovery by the lady and her two damsels. One is under the illusion that absolutely everything that actually happened is being carefully and entirely reproduced, with nothing either added or subtracted. Furthermore, these depictions artfully avoid giving the impression that they pertain to set-piece categories like *descriptio* and *narratio*, or conventional amplifications of topics, of which so many twelfth-century romancers were fond and in which Chrétien ironically indulged himself to such good effect in *Cligés*.[41] A climate of verisimilitude is created; the narrator speaks with the sobriety and the authority of a truthful witness (a posture adopted also, but with different means, by Béroul's narrator, whose stance is modeled largely on that of the hagiographer). One finds oneself perfectly willing to believe even in the Lady of Norison's magic ointment, and this, I think, at least in part because she so carefully instructs the damsel to anoint only Yvain's temples and his forehead; his sickness, she states, is confined to his brain (ll. 2968-69), but, the narrator tells us, the damsel gets carried away and uses up all the ointment, rubbing not only "les temples et le front," but Yvain's entire body down to and including his big toe.

Virtually the entire second half of the romance is reported in this vein —factually, concretely. It is *as though* we have left the vague romance territory of legend, mystery and "literature." Even Arthur, for once, behaves with practical intelligence when he tricks the elder daughter of the Seigneur de la Noire Espine into restoring to her sister her share of their late father's inheritance. Interestingly, it is only when he recounts the duel between Gauvain, that storybook person *par excellence* who champions the unjust sister, and Yvain, who defends the younger sister's cause, that the narrator reverts momentarily to the style of rhetorical, romance-type set-pieces (ll. 5995-6074). Yet at the conclusion of these lines, after having just stated his belief that neither of these knights wished the other any harm, he is forced by what he "sees" to recant: "Or ai manti molt leidemant, / *que l'en voit bien apertemant* / que li uns vialt envaïr l'autre" (ll. 6075-77, my emphasis) (But I have just lied most nastily, *for anyone can clearly see* that they intend truly to attack one another). Accurate witness compels this contradiction of what the narrator "knows" to be true, or of what he thinks *ought* to be true. Yvain's madness has purged him of his impetuosity; his cure now can put him on the path to redemption. Meanwhile, the telling of this scene, with its reverberations of the earlier lovesickness episode and its reversal of *Tristan* all couched in a diction of highly contrived verisimilitude, purges the text of the inflexibly "ideological" and courtly bookishness, or "literariness," that had so interfered not only with Yvain's "life," but also with the narrator's ability to function properly and credibly.

The madness episode and its sequels (Yvain's cure, his defense of the Lady of Norison—an act reminding us of what he should have been doing for Laudine and her fountain instead of gallivanting about with Gauvain at tourneys—and his refusal of his benefactress' hand in marriage) prepare Yvain for meeting the lion from whom he acquires a new identity as the Chevalier au Lion. This meeting, we recall, takes place at the precise midpoint of the romance, a strategic *locus* in Chrétien's narratives and one that usually bears on the protagonist's identity (*Lancelot*) or on the nature of the text (Thessala's potion in *Cligés*).

Much has been written concerning Yvain's lion; he is a symbol of fidelity, of gratitude; he is a true companion, a throw-back to the Androcles story; he is Christ-like; etc. What, to my knowledge, has not been studied, let alone understood, is the fact that Yvain's lion behaves remarkably like a dog. Not only does he accompany his master everywhere, not only does he wish "to serve and keep him" (l. 3411), but he also smells out game. However, instead of leaping to the chase as, one supposes, a "natural" lion (l. 3419) would do, especially a very hungry lion (l. 3416), this literary lion awaits his master's order. Yvain responds by urging him on, crying out to him as one would to a *brachet*, a hunting dog (l. 3435). Only then does the lion leap forward, kill a roe-deer, drink its blood and retrieve the carcass, bringing it to his master's feet. The narrator, we note, explicitly assimilates the lion to a hunting dog.[42]

All this is very interesting, above all when we remember that Yvain meets his lion when he answers the terrified animal's cry for help ("un cri molt dolereus et haut," l. 3340); he delivers the animal from almost certain death, for a fearsome serpent has attacked him. (The serpent, amusingly, is described in exactly the same terms as Keu, by Guenevere, at the beginning of the romance: his "mouth" is full of *felenie*, he is "venomous," he is dangerous because of his mouth [ll. 3353-57].)

Now, then, without any doubt the most famous dog in twelfth-century romance is Husdent, Tristan's *brachet* (Béroul, l. 1541), who barks out loudly in the midst of the Forest of Morois; he has followed Tristan, Iseut and Governal in their escape from the court. His "story" parallels that of the lion. Tristan resolves to kill Husdent, despite his affection for him, because he fears that the dog's bark will lead Mark and other pursuers to the lovers' refuge in the forest. Yvain thinks of dispatching the lion, but instead rightly decides to do away with the Keu-like (that is, gossipy, evil-tongued) serpent, surely a transposition of the wicked *losengiers* who have caused the ruin of Tristan and his beloved. The prospect of eliminating Husdent pains Tristan, however:

> Et peise m'en, por sa franchise,
> Que il la mort a ici quise[,]
> *Grant* [= *Quant?*] *nature li faisoit fere;*
> Mais conment m'en pus je retraire?
> (II. 1565-68, my emphasis and emendations)

(It pains me that because of his frank nobility he has sought his death here[,] [*since*] *he was but obeying the rules of nature*; but how can I refrain from killing him?)

Yvain's lion is referred to as "la beste gentil et franche" (l. 3371) (the gentle, noble beast); his "nature" is to hunt with abandon, but he "trains himself," almost instinctively, to await his master's command, as we noted. At Iseut's urging, Tristan spares Husdent and accepts to train the animal both in order to hunt game with him and so that he will keep silent. A fairly detailed description of the training process ensues, with Tristan taking a good deal of trouble (Béroul, II. 1594, 1597, 1604) because the dog, unlike the instinctively trained lion, learns slowly (II. 1606-26). All is well that ends well, however; Husdent learns to control his impetuous barking (his nature) as well as to aid Tristan effectively in the chase. Tristan wounds game with his arrows, Husdent follows the fleeing animal, marks the spot where it eventually falls, and returns to lead his "lord" to their prey. Like Yvain's lion, Husdent is "de grant servise" (Béroul, l. 1636).

These parallels are no more fortuitous than the analogous, though different, kinds of parallels between *Tristan* and Chrétien's *Cligés*. The midpoint of *Yvain* constitutes a response to the Forest of Morois episode as we know it from the Béroul fragment, just as the madness episode had been. We note here the same procedure of parallelism-in-reversal that characterized Yvain's madness. Yvain is everything—or becomes everything—Tristan was not; it is he, I venture to say, who is Chrétien's most authentic "anti-Tristan," not Cligés or Erec.[43] In addition, it is, I think, a matter of more than passing interest that the *name* Yvain occurs in two passages of Béroul. The leper upon whom an enraged Mark bestows his wife Iseut and whose life Tristan has Governal spare when he rescues her because killing such a low-life individual is beneath the "preux et cortois" knight (II. 1269-70), is named Yvain; this Yvain is, then, already in Béroul the "anti-Tristan" *par excellence*. Furthermore, Yvain the leper is no ordinary leper: he is the chief of all the lepers, a true "realist," all too willing to take immediate advantage of his temporary good fortune. The second Yvain, "Evains" or "Ivain" (ll. 3483, 4057), "li filz Uriën," is none other than our Yvain, the Chevalier au Lion, who, however, belongs part and parcel to the entourage Arthur brings with him to Mark's court towards the close of Béroul's fragment.[44] The fact that, as a result of his betrayal of Laudine as well as his madness and adventure with the lion, Yvain chooses to be known as the Chevalier au Lion might well have something to do with these namings in Béroul, especially in defining Yvain/*Yvain* in their relationship to Tristan/*Tristan*— the hero and the work he appears in.

Surely, though, the most important features and results of Chrétien's transposition and integration of the Forest of Morois episode into the midpoint section of his romance have to do with the text's *san*, that is, with how its construction reveals meaning. The reversals take on considerable relevance. First, although it is the lion who parallels and, therefore, refers to the Morois story, it is not he, but Yvain, who, like Husdent, requires "training" in order to dominate his rash, "natural" impulses. "Real-life" contingencies furnish the material of his education, not storybooks or doctrinal systems. Again like Husdent, it is Yvain who is redeemed by this training. The lion is "naturally" able to overcome his "nature" by a free exercise of choice. The intertextual system adumbrated and fully controlled by Chrétien allows this to be "said," implicitly. Second, Chrétien reverses the sequence of events one finds in Béroul where, we recall, the lovers meet Ogrin the hermit after Husdent has been properly trained. As Ogrin provided the means for their return to court, so the lion will signify, in terms of Yvain's individuality, the state of mind that must be his if one day he is to be reunited with *his* beloved and recover his legitimate place. Finally, unlike that of Tristan and Iseut, Yvain's return will be definitive, not the pretext for a new disturbance of order.

Chrétien's rearrangement of the Morois episodes does not limit itself, however, to this simple reversal. Three scenes follow upon one another in Béroul: Husdent (the lovers' assuring themselves a good food supply), Mark's visit to the sleeping pair (i.e., a return to their present by, or of, their past; they, I repeat, are asleep, passive, until eventually Iseut awakens after a nightmare in which she is about to be devoured by two ferocious lions!), the discussions with Ogrin (who, incidentally, when they find him, is reading a book, not, like Yvain's hermit, tending his garden!). The "slot" created by Mark's visit in Béroul—the second scene in the sequence—is filled, in *Yvain*, by the scene involving his cure and the defense of his benefactress, the Lady of Norison. Unlike Tristan and Iseut, Yvain is *active*, he is *cured*. To be sure, in Béroul the love potion that has "maddened" Tristan and Iseut ceases to be effective; nevertheless, the lovers remain the prisoners of the history it has brought upon them. The Lady of Norison's equally potent magic balm succeeds in putting an end to Yvain's madness. Potion and balm are counterparts of each other, even to the point that, though for different reasons, they are both entirely consumed! And, as we noted above, the Lady of Norison is a Laudine figure; she serves, essentially, to provide Yvain with the possibility of a "grant servise" as well as to remind him of what he ought to have done for his own lady. Consequently, she is pertinent in regard to his past, as Mark was to the lovers, but she is also something new, part of his self-renewal, of his "training." It is, therefore, a "new" Yvain, the Chevalier au Lion, who, after saving his lion, can return to a past (Lunete, like Lancelot in the *Charrette*, imprisoned) that has become a present of changed circumstances.

Chrétien de Troyes, as some scholars have shown, employs from time to time the narrative procedure known technically as "interlacing" (*entrelacement*). That is, narratives are embedded in narratives: Adventure A, say, is interrupted by Adventure B, and is gone back to only after Adventure B is completed. Being thus conjoined, the two Adventures comment upon one another. Analogously, his narrators, in describing scenes of action, employ frequently what was known as the *ordo artificialis* rather than the *ordo naturalis*: they reject the chronological, or purely consecutive, order of events in favor of seizing first upon a salient feature of these and then, only subsequently, describing the rest. Thus, in *Yvain* the narrator first describes Esclados' funeral procession by concentrating upon the grief, and the beauty, of Laudine; only later does he return to describe the procession as it actually moved through the hall. But, as we have just seen, the poetics of interlacing also extends to systems of (inter)textual reference. The paradigmatic, or vertical, *Yvain-Tristan* relationship is as precious to the meaning of *Yvain* at its strategic midpoint as the chronologies linking *Lancelot* and *Yvain*, and as the horizontal, or syntagmatic (sequential), ordering of episodes proper to that specific text. Art, we must conclude, has at least as much to say as Nature. Or, perhaps to put the matter in more satisfactory terms, what "Yvain's Madness" illustrates—and tells us—is how the art of *Yvain* transforms the ostensibly—but in reality artificial—"natural" world of Arthurian and *Tristan* romance, a world characterized by stasis, by conflating it with the world of things observed, the dynamic and very present world of contingencies, of "real" Nature. Herein lies the source of *Yvain*'s comedy: the Arthurian and *Tristan* worlds are shown, within the context of *Yvain*, to be mechanical and unchanging, claims to the contrary (like those especially of Béroul) notwithstanding, and, therefore, incompatible with the "real life" Yvain is called upon to live. Chrétien turns the *Tristan* and Arthurian stories, including his own *Charrette*, into pure grist for the textual mill of his *Chevalier au Lion*. By systematically depicting Yvain, his fictional character, as an anti-Tristan, Chrétien reveals (as he had done, with different means, in *Cligés*) that Tristan, too, is a fictional character and ought to be regarded as such. Concomitantly, he invents, in Yvain, the concept of an authentically developing, growing romance hero, a concept he will, of course, further explore in the Perceval of *Le Conte du Graal*. Not only does *Le Chevalier au Lion* celebrate, as *Cligés* so sophisticatedly had done, the wonderful possibilities open to romance composition, this text adds an almost novelistic—a *Bildungsroman*-type—dimension to romance-style narrative.

Conclusion: Narrator and Author(ity)

As Yvain grows in chivalry, acquiring as he proceeds a new name, so the narrator grows in *clergie*; he acquires a form of mastery of his craft. He ends up where, given the structures present at the beginning of the text and given the expectations of readers of romance, he "ought to have started." Once he has completed his story, his former innocence and wrong-headedness are transformed into a consciously celebrative and charmingly phrased irony. In irony, Chrétien shows us, narrative and commentary—the worlds of story and discourse—can once again fuse, as in these pleasantly loaded lines:

> Or a mes sire Yvains sa pes;
> et poez croire c'onques mes
> ne fu de nule rien si liez,
> comant qu'il ait esté iriez.
> Molt an est a boen chief venuz
> qu'il est amez et chier tenuz
> de sa dame, et ele de lui.
> (ll. 6789-95)

(Now my Lord Yvain has his peace; and you may believe that never was he so happy about anything else, no matter how vexed he had been before. He has come to a very good end, since he is loved and held dear by his Lady, and she by him.)

Yvain and Laudine, we see, are finally reconciled, thanks to Lunete's intercession, the last of the romance's long series of *dons contraignants*, "rash boons." Let us examine in some detail how, precisely, this reconciliation is achieved and, subsequently, its implications for our grasp of the *san* of *Le Chevalier au Lion*.

After Yvain's duel with Gauvain—a draw, we recall—our protagonist has but one thought: to regain Laudine's good graces. Like the lion, Gauvain is at last "eliminated" from his life as well as from the text; Yvain had stood in for him, successfully, during his transfer to the *Charrette* story, when both his family and Lunete required defending, and proved (as Cligés had done!) to be Gauvain's match, even without the lion's help, during the duel. What Gauvain represents is no longer an obstacle to Yvain. On the contrary, Gauvain most courteously apologizes to Yvain for having unwittingly fought the knight who slew, on behalf of his own nephews and niece, the evil giant (ll. 6469-75). Consequently, since the Arthurian world has ceased to be in any sense Yvain's "place," only two alternatives are open to him if he is to fulfill his life and to complete his story: death or Laudine's love. He decides, then, to return to the fountain, his *real*, and fixed, place, and to provoke once again the storm; perhaps Laudine will make peace (*pes*) with him (l. 6513). More terrible than ever, the tempest—the fourth and last time it occurs in the text—causes the inhabitants of the castle to revile their ancestors who built their dwelling in so cursed a land (ll. 6537-43), but no one attempts to defend the fountain. Despite their supernatural overtones, the problems with which the place that is Laudine's castle must cope are genuine; they have to be dealt with, as it were, on a day-to-day basis, unlike the artificial, gratuitous concerns faced by the habitués of Arthur's court.

Laudine is distraught. In a delightfully ironic reprise of the arguments she used to persuade her mistress to marry Yvain in the first place, Lunete speaks to her of the noble and generous *chevalier* who slew the giant and vanquished the three knights (Yvain's post-madness exploits). Provided that Laudine agrees to do all in her power to reconcile this knight with his lady (the above-mentioned *don contraignant*), Lunete promises, he will in return endeavor to defend her fountain in service to her as he has been of chivalric service to others. Laudine swears to help the Chevalier au Lion, and the die is cast. Lunete brings the estranged spouses together; Yvain falls on his knees (once again!), but, as he is dressed in full armor, Laudine does not recognize him. Nevertheless, she promises to do "his will" (ll. 6729-30). Thereupon Lunete reveals Yvain's identity. Laudine is shocked; however, since she has given her word, she will not perjure herself. Yvain, realizing that "he will have his peace" (l. 6769), begs her to forgive him. The romance devices of the ruse and *don contraignant—Tristan* and *Charrette* devices *par excellence*—are here put to good use in "real life," in Yvain's case, presumably, for the last time. As the "myth" of Arthurian storybook prowess had interfered previously with Yvain's "life," so now, thanks to Lunete, romance procedures are pressed into service in order to put matters right. Eye-witness at once to *clergie* (i.e., romance) and to the events of Yvain's existence, our narrator conflates these in his text (his ("report"), and therein lies the justification for the delicate irony of ll. 6789-95—an irony, incidentally, that contributes in no small measure to maintain the text's comic tone right up to the end. This authentic and non-ostentatious eye-witnessing is, moreover, to be contrasted with the kind of self-conscious and typically romance (*pseudo*)-eye-witnessing one finds in other narratives, like Benoît de Sainte-Maure's reliance on Dares and Dictys in the *Roman de Troie*. In regard to the telling of the story of *Yvain*, the narrator has achieved a status remarkably analogous to the delicately ironic and pragmatic Lunete, who, of course, operates on the level of the events of the protagonist's life, the *matter* of the story. Both narrator and Lunete bring their respective tasks to a successful, and comparable, conclusion.

The last time Lunete is mentioned in the text follows immediately upon the description of Yvain's reconciliation with Laudine; Lunete is content at having again made "la pes sanz fin / de mon seignor Yvain le fin" (ll. 6801-02) (the endless peace of my Lord Yvain the refined). One assumes that our narrator is as content as she at completing *his* tale. All is well that *ends* well. Joy, completion, and *fin-esse* are at issue here.

A marvelous passage closes the text:

> Del *Chevalier au lyeon* fine
> Crestïens son romans ensi;
> n'onques plus conter n'en oï
> ne ja plus n'en orroiz conter
> s'an n'i vialt mançonge ajoster.
> (ll. 6804-08)

(Concerning the *Lion Knight* Crestïens finishes thus his romance; never did I hear anything more told about it, nor will you hear anything more told about it, unless lies are added to the story.)

Fine, the adjective describing Laudine in l. 6803 is figurally linked by paranomasia to the verb *fine* of l. 6804, the line that states at long last (!) the romance's title—a title reproducing, of course, Yvain's new name, the name he acquired, we remember, at the romance's midpoint. Like its protagonist, the romance *acquires* an identity, thanks, we might say, to its own hard work. Lunete's achievement—her closure of the events as reported by the narrator—is directly connected to the *san* and to what might be called the *authority* of the romance. The text generates this authority at its own end, upon its own completion. After having, as I remarked, "written itself out," it engenders an "author," the "Crestïens" of l. 6805. This Epilogue thus serves the most important functions performed by romance prologues: the identification of the romance as well as that of its "source" of authority.

The present and present perfect tenses (Lunete's *a fet* [l. 6801] and Crestïens' *fine* [l. 6804])—the tenses of "commentary" (Harald Weinrich's *besprochene Welt* and the late Emile Benveniste's *discours*)[45]—underscore the fact that the "story" (Weinrich's *erzählte Welt*, Benveniste's *histoire*) finally has a *san*, entire and complete unto itself. Truth is very much to the point here. Nothing must be added or, one assumes, subtracted from what has been said; addition or subtraction would involve *mançonge* (l. 6808). (We recall the honest Calogrenant, who told no *fable* or *mançonge* [l. 172] in *his* model report of his own shame and failure.) Interestingly, in distinguishing himself from the author "Crestïens," the narrator bears witness *to himself*: "n'onques plus conter n'en *oï*" (l. 6806), a statement of factual witness, related by a clear historical preterite.[46] We believe him. And we also believe him when he tells us that if *we* hear more about Yvain than what he has told, it will be a lie.

Now, then, as we noted in our discussion of the opening scene of *Le Chevalier au Lion*, Chrétien informs us that the truth of romance is in no way to be understood as the kind of truth we associate with the "worlds" of hagiography and of *chansons de geste*. There simply is no "truth" of that sort in the Arthurian "world." The narrator is wrong when he suggests in ll. 1-32 that somehow the Arthurian world exists, and exists nobly, *outside* the books that speak of that world, just as, he hints, the worlds of Alexis and Charlemagne do. Romance truth resides in the service provided by *clergie*, in how the romance text is put together, "conjoined," and in how that text is made to participate in the general processes of romance.

Each of Chrétien's five surviving romances constitutes, in its own unique way, a meditation on *clergie*—on clerkly service within the romance context and, by extension, within the world of the community to which it and other romances are directed (e.g., Wace's *riche gent*). It seems to me, then, that the meditation contained in and expressed by *Yvain* constitutes both the demonstration and the celebration of a certain kind of truthful witness. This is not the *Alexis* or *Roland* witness to a form of absolute truth, though, to a degree, it is related to their brand of witness. *Yvain* celebrates the witness—the carefully honest and unadulterated reporting—of fact, of what happens. Or, to put the matter in other terms, *Yvain* shows that reporting what one "sees" is a legitimate type of witness, of understanding; it, too, can grow into *clergie*, become the opponent of *mançonge*, a truth perfect, though not necessarily absolute. Some truths taken as absolute—e.g., *Tristan*, Arthurian courtly "ideology"—are, meanwhile, at once false and, when extrapolated out of the romance context, downright dangerous. *Yvain*'s truth strikes me as being a peculiarly novelistic truth; the text shows itself as being capable of generating its own authority within its own system of intertextuality—an authority quite as authentic as, say, that of the *translatio studii* process explored by and utilized in *Cligés*, but resolutely independent of such "exterior" concepts. Thus, in a very real sense, grasping the *san* of *Le Chevalier au Lion* means understanding how, and for what reasons, a "Crestïens" is derived from that text.

Finally, though couched in a gently ironic and amusingly comic frame, the moral implications of *Yvain* are considerable. There is, of course, no explicit moral of the kind we find at the end of *Cligés*, where we learn that Greek emperors now keep close watch on their wives! *Yvain* seems to tell us that a life, *like a poem*, is, to an important extent, a matter of little details, of "works," at times great, at times small; and these details, or works, need not invariably be "conventional." Indeed, works provide a safeguard against one's being duped by rigid, and misunderstood, rule systems; works constitute one's freedom to "find" one's own life as well as "invent" one's own poem. They are the expression of one's choices and of one's responsibilities. However, *Yvain* furnishes no model to be slavishly emulated. Its comic nature as well as the magic and the faerie it contains see to that! Rather, it very graciously tells us that we might do worse than endeavor to remain in charge of our own stories. Such, I believe, is the sense of *Yvain* as "commentary" upon "narrative"—a commentary that resides in Chrétien's novelistic conflation of clerkly *sapientia* and humane wisdom.

Rupert T. Pickens

Le Conte du Graal (Perceval)

Introductory Remarks

The *Perceval*—or, as Chrétien de Troyes himself calls his last romance, the *Conte du Graal*[1]—was most probably written between 1180 and 1190. Henry I the Liberal, Count of Champagne and husband of Marie, "ma dame de Chanpaigne" of the *Lancelot* Prologue (l. 1), died in 1181; Chrétien might then have quit the court at Troyes in the employ of his new patron, Philippe de Flandre, whom he praises in the *Perceval* Prologue as the donor of his romance's Latin source. This argument, which scholars generally find convincing, assumes that Chrétien had not left Troyes before Henry's death; since Philippe de Flandre was on crusade in 1177-1178, precisely when *Lancelot* and *Yvain* were underway in the Champenois court, Chrétien could not possibly have begun the *Conte du Graal* under his influence earlier than shortly before Henry himself took the cross in 1179. It may also be significant, as Frappier stressed, that in 1182 Philippe de Flandre, who was by then regent to the young Philip Augustus, visited Troyes in a vain attempt to win the widowed Marie's hand in marriage; thus, Chrétien could have conversed with him and undertaken their joint project during that year without ever leaving Troyes for Bruges. In any case, Philippe de Flandre took the cross a second time in 1190 and died on crusade in 1191; it is unlikely that Chrétien would have spoken about his patron as he does in the Prologue in his absence or after his death.[2]

Chrétien's last romance was left uncompleted. Gerbert de Montreuil, a continuator who did find a means to end the poem around 1220, tells us that Chrétien had died in the midst of writing.[3] Gerbert made the statement some thirty to forty years after the fact. His words need not necessarily be taken literally, for indeed the *narrator* "died" the moment the author finally stopped writing, whatever the reason Chrétien failed to finish his work.

A great teacher who devoted much of his scholarly life to the study of the *Conte du Graal* once observed that Chrétien's last romance was the most significant achievement in a vernacular literature before Dante's *Commedia*. Some scholars might argue that the completed *Roman de la Rose* should also be taken into consideration, but U.T. Holmes' assertion seems basically sound. Judging by the wealth and variety of responses it generated during the first hundred years after Chrétien stopped writing and beyond, Chrétien's poem created a sensation that can be compared only with the cultural impact produced by the two later masterpieces; but the Grail, like Dante's Hell, has stamped the popular imagination, as well as stirred minds and souls more learned, in profound ways that Deduit's garden has not.

So powerful and so mysterious—so seminal—is Chrétien's unfinished text that by the year 1200 or shortly thereafter, that is, within a decade or two of its inception, composition and publication, the *Conte du Graal* had inspired two anonymous attempts to continue its incomplete narration (neither succeeded in finding a conclusion) and had shaped the literary production of the twelfth century's "other" Grail poet, Robert de Boron; it had itself served as *matière* for two interpretive "translations" into prose: the so-called Didot-*Perceval*, which also amalgamates matter from Robert de Boron and the anonymous Second Chrétien Continuator, and the *Perlesvaus*.[4] During the first half of the thirteenth century, moreover, Chrétien's text plus the two anonymous continuations were completed independently by Gerbert de Montreuil, already mentioned, and by Manessier; in mid-century the ultimate French transformation of Chrétien was well underway: the vast Vulgate Cycle, often called the *Lancelot-Graal*, of which the prose *Lancelot* is but a part.[5] Significantly, the *Conte du Graal* is found in eighteen manuscripts from the thirteenth and fourteenth centuries, while most verse narratives composed in France before the *Roman de la Rose* survive in a mere handful of medieval copies; to be sure, the survival of a medieval text into modern times is to some degree a matter of chance, but few narrative poems from the twelfth century, and no other romance by Chrétien de Troyes, can testify to such widespread interest and popularity.[6]

No scholar or critic could hope to explain even the most obvious features of a narrative so rich and mysterious, much less aspire to account for every subtlety. In the following pages I attempt to identify some of the major themes in the *Conte du Graal* and discuss how they relate to the various levels of narrative discourse which the poem makes explicit.

The Prologue

The Prologue[7] to the *Conte du Graal* concludes with statements that recall theoretical themes developed in Chrétien's earlier *exordia*:

> Donc avra bien sauve sa peinne
> Crestïens, qui antant et peinne
> a rimoier le meillor conte,
> par le comandement le conte,
> qui soit contez an cort real:
> ce est li contes del graal,
> don li cuens li baill[a] le livre,
> s'orroiz comant il s'an delivre.
> (ll. 61-68 [ibid.])

(Therefore, he will have safely invested his labor—Chrétien, who attends and works to put into rhyme the best story, at the Count's behest, that can be told in a royal court: it is the *Story of the Grail*, of which the Count gave him the book; and you will hear how he acquits himself of it.)

In naming his source (l. 67), the poet implicitly places his work in the tradition of *translatio* which shapes the production of *Cligés* and *Erec et Enide*; in specifying that he writes at the command of a noble person (l. 64) who has given him the source (in this case it is Philippe d'Alsace, Count of Flanders), Chrétien explicitly relates noble patronage and inspiration to *translatio*—a reconciliation only to be inferred from the *Lancelot* Prologue.[8] Source and inspiration, translation, production, and reward define a system of poetic endeavor. The concept of recompense appears to close the system and to limit it to the causes and effects of noble patronage (the Count gave Chrétien a book to translate, he has translated it, he will be rewarded by the Count); but in reality the process is extended infinitely to embrace all of "us" who "will hear" Chrétien's poem.

The particular context in which these conventional assertions appear is of still greater significance, for as a whole the Prologue to the *Conte du Graal* suggests a profound revaluation by Chrétien of his function as literary artist. Even as he reaffirms and clarifies certain aspects of his artistic mission in accord with earlier statements, he also redefines them in light of a concept that has been described, with reference to Chrétien's contemporary Marie de France, as Christian modernism.[9] The art of translation and the intellectual, imaginative and poetic enterprises which make it possible are completely assimilated to the world of spiritual reality. In Marie the exercise of *translatio* is possible in the first place because human knowledge and the ability to communicate it increase with the passage of time; assuming the mediatory role of translator, the poet, as modern interpreter, perceives meaning hidden in an old text and reveals it to his modern audience. With respect to his own art, Chrétien's new awareness is that, while the poet and his translation are beneficiaries of history, they are also trapped in history. Thus, he recognizes both his artistic limitations and the fact that his product lacks absolute perfection. Chrétien's consciousness of his work's merits and his pride in achievement are evident in the Prologue to the *Conte du Graal*, but they are also tempered by a new sense of mutability and personal insufficiency. The products of translation can be a hundred times greater than the translation itself (cf. l. 4).

This paradox is expressed in Chrétien's use of the conventional topic of the seminal word:

> Qui petit seme petit quialt,
> et qui auques recoillir vialt,
> an tel leu sa semance espande
> que fruit a cent dobles li rande;
> car an terre qui rien ne vaut
> bone semance i seche et faut.
> Crestïens seme et fet semance
> d'un romans que il ancomance,
> et si le seme an si bon leu
> qu'il ne puet estre sanz grant preu,
> qu'il le fet por le plus prodome
> qui soit an l'empire de Rome.
> (ll. 1-12 [ibid.])

(Who sows little reaps little, and who wishes to harvest anything casts his seed in such a place that it may return fruit to him a hundred times over; for in worthless ground good seed dries up and fails. Chrétien sows and makes seed of a romance which he is beginning, and he sows it so and in such a good place that it cannot but be very profitable, for he does it for the noblest man who is in the empire of Rome.)

In the opening lines biblical intertextuality functions at many levels. "He which soweth sparingly shall reap also sparingly" (l. 1) is a well-known passage from II Corinthians (9:6) which was proverbial in Old French. Of primary importance, however, are Chrétien's extended references to the Parable of the Sower (Matthew 13:3-23, Mark 4:3-20, Luke 8:5-15), which the proverb serves to introduce.

On one level the proverb evokes the theme of direct material reward for Chrétien's having "sown" his romance; and in this his playful humor sets a dominant tone, as Haidu has shown. The verse in II Corinthians continues by asserting that he who sows with blessings ("benedictionibus" in the Vulgate) shall reap from those blessings, and this is followed, in verse 7, by the familiar "God loveth a cheerful giver." Thus, the "blessings" with which Chrétien sows are the fulsome praise of Philippe de Flandre that comprises the middle section of the Prologue (ll. 13-60), and Chrétien expects to be rewarded according to the fullness of his blessings: "Donc avra bien sauve sa peinne / Crestïens..." (ll. 61-62a) recalls "il ne puet estre sanz grant preu" (l. 10). However, as throughout the *Conte du Graal*, surface meaning, once evoked, can be overshadowed as the surface is transpierced and the same signs are regarded from another perspective. Whatever the "blessings" with which Chrétien labors, it is his translation, his *romans*, not his praise of his patron, that is sown. In fact, the "cheerful giver" who will reward the poet for his effort has already made him donations without which the system of poetic endeavor cannot have been made to function: the source text of which Chrétien's romance is a translation and the command to write. Moreover, Chrétien's poem is not addressed solely to Count Philippe de Flandre, but to a far vaster audience that includes all of "us" (l. 68). Thus, Chrétien fully exploits all implications in the double ambiguity in l. 11 (ambiguity in the meaning of the preposition *por* and in the function of the direct complement *le*): Chrétien makes it (i.e., the romance) /does it (i.e., sows) for the noblest man/because of him/on his behalf. In this light, the "good place" where Chrétien sows the romance (ll. 7-8), in imitation of Christ who sows the word of God in the parable, is not merely the Count, but also anyone else who hears it and lets it grow; and the rewards to be reaped are not only material gains won in the Count's court, but other kinds of treasure lying elsewhere.

In appropriating to himself and to his artistic enterprise the language of the Parable of the Sower, Chrétien underscores the conventional analogy between the poet, as mediator and translator, and Christ. Chrétien calls himself, as Jesus does, a sower of words; moreover, Jesus' parable is, like the Count's book, a story that requires interpretation (Jesus' role as mediator in the parable is, therefore, far more complex than the simplistic one of a narrator who, as pretended witness to events, merely testifies to their truth). Most people in the audience to which the parable is told do not understand it, but within that group are a select few, the disciples, for whom the account can be made truly meaningful through an act of interpretation. Jesus tells them that they are destined to "know the mysteries of the kingdom of heaven" (Matthew 13:11) and that their eyes and ears are blessed because they see and hear and understand (vs. 16). In fact, they are the "good ground" where the seed of the word of God takes root and flourishes (vs. 23). Potentially, the Count and members of Chrétien's wider audience are, analogously, just such an élite, and it is Chrétien's mission, in part, to make perceptible to them meanings hidden in an old text.

Indeed, Chrétien continues the Prologue by offering a specific example of interpretive translation. Jesus' admonition not to let "thy left hand know what thy right hand doeth" (Matthew 6:3), which is itself a statement about secrets and rewards (cf. vv. 31-36), is given a multileveled exegetical interpretation by Chrétien:

> L'Evangile, por coi dit ele:
> "Tes biens a ta senestre cele["?]
> La senestre, selonc l'estoire,

> senefie la vainne gloire
> qui vient de fause ypocrisie.
> Et la destre, que senefie?
> Charité, qui de sa bone oevre
> pas ne se vante, ençois coevre,
> que nus ne le set se cil non
> qui Dex et Charité a non.
> Dex est charitez, et qui vit
> an charité, selonc l'escrit,
> sainz Pos lo dit et je le lui,
> il maint an Deu et Dex an lui.
> (II. 37-50 [ibid.])

(Why does the Gospel say "Hide your good deeds from your left hand"? The left hand, according to the Latin text, signifies vainglory, which comes from false hypocrisy. And the right hand, what does it signify? Charity, which of its good work does not boast, but rather covers it up, so that none knows it except Him Whose name is God and Charity. God is Charity, and who lives in charity, according to what is written—St. Paul says it and I have read it—he dwells in God and God in him.)

This passage extends and supports the theme of the cheerful giver. More significantly, however, it also demonstrates Chrétien's powers to comprehend and to make known meanings that lie hidden in a received text. Yet, simultaneously, this display also betrays the limits of Chrétien's ability and the inexactitude of the comparison between himself and his divine model. In the Parable of the Sower, as well as in its interpretation for the elect audience, it is understood that, in Christ, God mediates between Himself and mankind; but Chrétien, as a human translator, requires a source other than himself—the history in the Count's book which is analogous to the text alone of the parable and to nothing else. Moreover, Chrétien seeks satisfaction for his artistic undertaking partly in the form of material profit. Certainly, in addressing the wider audience incapable of rewarding him directly, Chrétien offers a gift in an act of genuine charity; but, since Count Philippe is necessarily included in that audience, Chrétien seems to be giving with both hands at once. Irony turns back against the poet, therefore, and it functions to show his need for material gain despite his loftier motivations and aims. Ultimately contrasted with the concept of divine perfection, the faulty nature of Chrétien and of his endeavor is openly demonstrated in the very passage where he vaunts his powers of interpretation. The climactic biblical quotation ("God is love; and he that dwelleth in love dwelleth in God, and God in him") is beautifully and accurately translated, in the modern sense of that word, but it is emphatically attributed to St. Paul (I. 49); in reality, it is found not in a Pauline epistle, but in I John 4:15.

The erroneous reference reflects on the translator to his disadvantage. Nevertheless, it serves a positive and supportive purpose as well because it focuses attention on Paul, whose writings are quoted twice before in the Prologue without mention of the source. His words open the poem and introduce the topic of the seminal word. Furthermore, Chrétien's first statement about charity (ll. 43-44) is a quotation from the familiar encomium of charity in I Corinthians 13: "charity vaunteth not itself, is not puffed up" ("Pas ne se vante" can be a translation of both "non agit perperam" and "non inflatur" in vs. 6 of the Vulgate). Of particular importance to the *Conte du Graal* is the context in which this statement appears. At the end of the chapter the writer establishes the temporal bases of mankind's acquisition of knowledge through the operation of charity. They recall to the reader of Chrétien's Prologue both the gift bestowed upon the elect recipients of the Parable of the Sower and the interpretive roles of Chrétien, as translator of a book, and his own audience, as hearers of the romance: "When I was a child, I spake as a child, I understood as a child, I thought as a child; but when I became a man, I put away childish things. For now we see through a glass darkly; but then face to face; now in part; but then shall I know even as also I am known" (vv. 11-12). Speaking, understanding and thinking in childhood and in adulthood are a double metaphor. The writer's childhood is compared with his present, when he comprehends as though seeing an imprecise reflection of reality, while adulthood lies in the afterlife, when he will have perfect knowledge of God. More literally, however, as elsewhere (cf. Ephesians, ch. 4), Paul equates childhood with ignorance and suggests that adulthood, which comes after a conversion promoted by charity (as in his own case), is a time of greater knowledge and understanding, even if these are imperfect by norms lying outside time. These concepts, applied to the entire scope of human history, are the theoretical justification for Christian exegetes' claims that the Old Testament can be understood completely only in consideration of its fulfillment in the New.

Similarly, the theory explains *translatio* when the latter is associated with Christian modernism in context with the seminal word. Chrétien's literary, historical example functions in part to substantiate, in this light, the value of his literary enterprise in translating the book given by the Count:

> ... le plus prodome
> qui soit an l'empire de Rome:
> c'est li cuens Phelipes de Flandres,
> qui mialz valt ne fist Alixandres,
> cil que l'an dit qui tant fu buens.
> Mes je proverai que li cuens
> valt mialz que cist ne fist asez,
> car il ot an lui amassez

> toz les vices et toz les max
> dont li cuens est mondes et sax.
> (ll. 11b-20 [ibid.])

(the noblest man who is in the empire of Rome: it is Count Philip of Flanders, who is worthier than Alexander was, the one who people say was so good. But I will prove that the Count is a great deal worthier than he, for he had in him, all together, all the vices and all the evils of which the Count is pure and against which he is safe.)

> Donc sachoiz bien de verité
> que li don sont de charité
> que li bons cuens Felipes done,
> c'onques nelui n'an areisonne
> fors son franc cuer le debonere,
> qui li loe le bien a fere.
> Ne valt mialz cil que ne valut
> Alixandres, cui ne chalut
> de charité ne de nul bien?
> Oïl, n'an dotez ja de rien.
> (ll. 51-60 [ibid.])

(Therefore, know well in truth that the gifts are from charity which the good Count gives, for never does he speak to anyone about them except to his noble, gentle heart, which urges him to do good. Is he not worthier than was Alexander, who did not care about charity or any good deed? Yes, have no doubts about it!)

Chrétien doubtless refers to Alexandre the Great's medieval reputation as a model of largess, the greatest courtly virtue: people say ("l'an dit") that he was so good (l. 15). Yet despite his legendary generosity, he was a worthless man possessed of all sorts of vices, by comparison with Count Philippe de Flandre, a modern nobleman who may not (yet) have Alexandre's reputation for generosity, but whose largess is, nevertheless, superior. The difference is that the emperor from pre-Christian times cannot have known charity, while the Christian ruler, born in the new era of the "empire of Rome," possesses true virtue and wisdom ennobled by charity. Because charity, which is God (ll. 46-47), operates in the life of Philippe, he is an *imitator Christi* who "loves right justice, loyalty and Holy Church" (ll. 25-26); he also possesses, therefore, the highest values of courtly society to a degree impossible in Alexander's age: "he hates all villainy, and he is more generous than can be known, for he gives in accord with the Gospel, without hypocrisy and without guile" (ll. 27-30). (We recall the encomium of largess by another Alixandre—in *Cligés*, ll. 118-213—where the virtue is extolled in purely social terms. It is as though Chrétien revalorizes the truth of the earlier statement in light of new perceptions.)

Chrétien's historical scheme, the contrast of the pre-Christian and the Christian nobleman, recalls in a literal way the *translatio imperii/translatio studii* topics that are explicit in the *Cligés* Prologue and, in the latter form, implicit in other romances where he mentions a source such as the Count's book. But in the *Conte du Graal* the poet regards the phenomenon from a perspective that is wholly spiritual and wholly Christian. Christian love and the Christian God are forces that operate in history to elevate a vassal of the king of France above the ruler of an ancient empire. Furthermore, the very realm in which Philippe de Flandre resides is one whose spiritual reality has superseded a defunct political ideal: the "empire of Rome" is not the long dead ancient state or even, most probably, its medieval revival.[10] Rather, the "empire of Rome" is Christendom, the "empire" of the universal Church of Rome. Thus, in the *Conte du Graal* Chrétien shows precisely why the modern learning and knighthood of the *Cligés* Prologue are superior to the ancient forms from which they descend. He also shows why, in the life of an individual artist, *Cligés* surpasses his earlier works listed in that Prologue and why, now, he can boast that the *Conte du Graal* is "le meillor conte . . . qui soit contez an cort real" (ll. 63b-65). The life of a single man, which is the history of the world in microcosm, is a continuous advancement towards that time in the future when he will have access to all worthwhile knowledge. The *Conte du Graal* is "the best narrative" because it is the most recent version in the history of literature, an earlier stage of which is represented by the book from which the translation is made, and because it has been achieved by a gifted literary artist in response to a productive command.

Inevitably, however, the superiority of Chrétien's own poem is threatened by a gradual exposure, with the passage of time, of the narrator's intellectual and artistic limitations. Because the new book exists in history, some who hear Chrétien's words are bound to supersede him as interpreters and, potentially, as translators—not of the Count's book, but of Chrétien's *Conte du Graal*, which will be a new source. This is what happens when the literary artist limited by imperfectability engages, in imitation of Christ, in the fruitful enterprise of sowing words for others to hear and understand. The system of poetic endeavor has been set into motion, in charity, by a Count, a model of charity, who has given Chrétien a book and commanded him to translate. The artist obeys by creating and recreating, also in charity, because he, too, is an *imitator Christi*. Reward will come in two forms. Since, as a man, he needs to live, he hopes for a material return from the Count; but, as a participant in the divine order, he will be rewarded if his words bear fruit in those who cannot advance him materially. For Chrétien the act of artistic production is regenerative. Nowhere else than in this Prologue does he seem to possess greater consciousness of the powers as well as the limitations suggested by his name—the artist who is a Christian man.[11]

The Prologue and Romance[12]

The Prologue informs the narrative which it serves to introduce: the voice of the poet-narrator who comments on the regeneration of an old book is also that of the narrator who pretends to have witnessed events of past history and who interprets them for a modern audience. In fact, the Prologue provides means for evaluating two major aspects of the narrative to follow (each one, ultimately, inextricable from the other). First, in that the Prologue is an exposition of poetic theory, it alerts the reader to the significance of narrative artistry and narrative structure. Second, it introduces themes, in conjunction with its theoretical developments, that are primary in the story itself—most prominently, the growth of the individual, the human condition, perception of meaning, knowledge and charity which operates to distinguish two kingdoms by elevating over the other the one that values a Christian sense of history. In fact, the *Conte du Graal* is a narrative that both exemplifies the conditions and circumstances in which narrative artistry operates and contains models against which Chrétien's artistry as poet-translator—as narrator—can be evaluated.

As narrator, Chrétien affirms that two layers coexist in the *Conte du Graal*: the history and his interpretation of it. The history is presumed to be contained in the Count's book. For the modern reader, it cannot be a question here of what that book may or may not in reality have conveyed to Chrétien de Troyes about the Grail legend, Arthurian heroes, etc., or even of whether or not the book actually ever existed—of what, therefore, Chrétien de Troyes actually may have discovered there and how the romance came to be through his own invention. Because we do not possess that book and cannot directly compare with it Chrétien's narrative which asserts to be a translation of it, attention can be drawn only to the book's fictive role and its implications within Chrétien's poem.

To a certain extent, the book may be compared to Calogrenant's tale in *Yvain*. This tale was written by Chrétien de Troyes. Yet Chrétien's narrator does not claim authorship of it; on the contrary, he ascribes it to a character in his own story, reports it verbatim, and, when it is recited at court, offers no commentary that may color our perception of it. It functions as the source of the narrator's own *Yvain*, but his personal inventiveness hardly comes into play *at the level of events* until his new hero defeats Esclados and circumstances not found in Calogrenant's original are made possible. It remains true that Chrétien fictively portrays in *Yvain* the generation of one narrative from another and that poetic endeavor as defined in terms of that regenerative process is a primary focus of attention, despite the fact that Chrétien de Troyes, both as the actual author of Calogrenant's tale and of the romance containing it and as the creator of the narrator who "writes" that romance, undoubtedly had at hand a greater variety of "more tangible," "more influential" sources (a fund of Celtic lore, a body of opinion about love, Wace's *Rou*, and so on) useful in composing Calogrenant's tale as well as the entire romance of which that tale fictively serves as source.

The comparison with *Yvain* is enlightening in three ways. First, the author-narrator dichotomy is brought into clear definition. Chrétien's narrator is a creature of the author of *Yvain* who actually wrote Calogrenant's words and makes his narrator ascribe them truthfully (i.e., according to fictive truth) to a character and then truthfully report them word for word. Likewise, the narrator of the *Conte du Graal* is a creature of the author who makes him claim expertise in explicating biblical passages and then unconsciously slip in attributing one of them, with exaggerated emphasis, to Paul rather than to John. Second, the author-narrator dichotomy relates to the distinction between source and translation. The *Conte du Graal* does not "contain" its source in exactly the same sense that *Yvain* does because nothing in the *Conte du Graal* purports explicitly to be a verbatim rendering of the Count's book; indeed, the *Conte du Graal* claims from the beginning to be a translation already regenerated, so that the romance as a whole is like the portion of *Yvain* recounting the adventures of the narrator's hero prior to his victory at the fountain and may be said to "contain" its source in just the same way as that segment alone.

Finally, these discriminations involve a third crucial distinction between history and the narration of history. Within the fiction, events, characters, settings, situations, etc., are the inevitable components of history which the narrator is powerless to alter; in fact, they are what is in the "source" that requires interpreting. Calogrenant, as narrator of his tale, does not betray the essential truths of his personal experience (his own "source"). Nor does Chrétien's narrator change the events, their order, the settings or the characters met by the hero, in his translation of the tale, until he invents the defeat of Esclados. Yet the two accounts are different in other respects—different as translations: in narrational perspective (the shift from first person to third), the identity of the hero (as a consequence of that shift, "je" becomes Yvain), the quality of commentary (Calogrenant has a formal *exordium*, Chrétien's narrator does not; the knight tells a story of defeat, the clerk one of victory), historical distance (ironically, Calogrenant, who uses historical tenses exclusively, creates a sense of greater distance and objectivity than does Chrétien's narrator, who liberally sprinkles his account with presents and perfects), and amplitude (Chrétien's narrator abbreviates Calogrenant). Since the entirety of the *Conte du Graal* resembles the much smaller "translated" segment of *Yvain,* we may appreciate to the fullest extent the implications in the assertion by Chrétien's narrator that his romance derives from a written source for which he does not—indeed, cannot—claim authorship: his stance as mediator of history implies the role of regenerator, not that of creator. Things that happen to the hero(es), places where events occur, words spoken by characters (acts of speech as events), people and adventures encountered, the basic order of events, are in principle essential and inviolate; they constitute the history as found in the Count's book, the *estoire* of ll. 3250 [3262], 6009 [6217], etc. Chrétien de Troyes, creator of his narrator, is likewise the creator of his narrator's source history. However, the manner in which the history is represented—in translation—depends upon the perspicacity of the narrator and his artistry, neither of which is necessarily to be equated with the author's achievements. Chrétien's contribution, as narrator, is precisely his perception of meaning in characters and events from the perspective of the mature Christian artist. His poem consists of both history, as contained in the received old text, and its interpretation: text and gloss, as it were, but intermeshed in a cohesive translation.

Frequently, interpretive segments of the poem occur as direct, first-person commentary. For example, when in the history Perceval remains silent at the Grail Castle, the narrator remarks:

> se [= si] criem que il n'i ait domage,
> que j'ai oï sovant retraire
> que ausi se puet an trop taire
> com trop parler, a la foiee.
> (ll. 3236-39 [3248-51])

(so I fear that there may be harm in this, for I have often heard it stated that someone can keep silent for too long, just as he can talk too much—it all depends.)

This kind of commentary is the most obvious—and the most elementary—form of interpretation in a "critical translation" such as the *Conte du Graal.* In using *je,* verbs in the present and perfect tenses (*criem, ai oï*), and an aphorism (ll. 3238-39) which expresses its general truth in verbs also in the present tense, Chrétien draws attention to his "presentness" as narrator and emphasizes his stance as the modern judge of events in past history. The lines above are, in this respect, exactly comparable to such statements in the Prologue as "Qui petit seme petit qualt" (l. 1) and "Crestïens seme et fet semance / d'un romans que il ancomance" (ll. 7-8), etc.

Related to this mode of interpretation are remarks that demonstrate, though in a far more complex way, the essential contributions of Chrétien's modern artistry. In translating, the narrator imposes a new episodic order on events—not changing their historical sequence, but redirecting his audience's perception of them by interlacing. For example, the extraordinary Hermitage episode, in the course of which, on Good Friday and Easter morning, Perceval retrieves, to the fullest extent possible, the values of his heritage, is set apart from the causally unrelated Gauvain adventures by a commentative frame:

> De mon seignor Gauvain se test
> li contes ici a estal,
> si parlerons de Perceval.
> Percevax, ce conte l'estoire,
> . . . .
> (ll. 6006-09 [6214-17])

(Concerning my lord Gauvain the story falls silent right here, so we shall speak of Perceval. Perceval, the history tells, ...)

And, in closing:

> De Perceval plus longuemant
> ne parole li contes ci,
> ençois avroiz asez oï
> de mon seignor Gauvain parler
> que plus m'oiez de lui conter.
> (ll. 6288-92 [6514-18])

(Of Perceval no longer does the story speak here; rather, you will have heard a great deal spoken about my lord Gauvain before you hear me tell any more about him.)

Since the Hermitage episode is a five-year projection into the future with respect to the Gauvain adventures which it interrupts, the frame confirms the narrator's apparent (and, therefore, in the fiction, his real) manipulation of the order of events in the history. Chrétien contrasts the *estoire* (l. 6009), which is Count Philippe's book (*estoire* as written source, probably in Latin, such as the one which provides the narrator with his exegesis of "Tes biens a ta senestre cele"—cf. ll. 38-39), and his own narrative composition, which is the *conte* (ll. 6007, 6289), the *Conte du Graal* (cf. l. 66). Verbs whose subjects are *estoire* or *conte* (ll. 6006, 6009, 6289), as well as those indicating how the narrator's words are transmitted and received (ll. 6008, 6290, 6292), refer temporally to the moment of Chrétien's act of narration, which is also the time of the Prologue, of his expression of fear about the hero's silence, of his aphorisms, etc., rather than to the distant past of the history being recounted. The narrator indicates thereby, in the specific case of the Hermitage episode as well as in general, his own episodic segmentation, which, as an important aspect of his narrative artistry, is significant as an interpretive device. As it happens, the Hermitage episode is, in fact, crucial in our perception of the history's meaning.

Of another order are interpretive remarks blended into the temporal level of the history itself. For example, the narrator's critical judgment of his hero is implicit in statements like "Cler et riant furent li oel / an la teste au vaslet salvage" (ll. 972-73 [974-75]) (Bright and smiling were the eyes in the head of the wild boy). *Salvage* contrasts the crude behavior of the youth raised in a forest isolated from society with the civilized courtliness ideally associated with the Arthurian circle; *vaslet*, "boy," which also means, in the *Conte du Graal*, any aspirant for knighthood who is not yet dubbed (cf. ll. 7313-21 [7563-73]), remains the term used by the narrator in reference to his hero long after he receives arms and is inducted into the sacred order of chivalry (cf. ll. 1633-36 [1635-38]) and long after other characters acknowledge his prowess and call him *chevalier*. (For example, in Perceval's battle with Clamadeus, third-person pronouns referring to the hero are governed by "li vaslez" in l. 2613 [2615], cf. l. 2572 [2574]; but Clamadeus perceives him as "chevalier vermoil," as the narrator reports in indirect discourse, l. 2594 [2596], which refers only to his arms, and, in his "translation" of his defeat made before Arthur, as "li plus vaillanz chevaliers / a cui je onques m'acointasse," ll. 2854-55 [2856-57] [the most valiant knight I have ever known].) Similarly, Chrétien's narrator corrects in advance an erroneous assessment of Perceval, made by his mentor Gornemant de Goorz, when he observes:

> ... il [Perceval] comança a porter
> si a droit la lance et l'escu
> com s'il eüst toz jorz vescu
> an tornoiemenz et an guerres
> et alé par totes les terres
> querant bataille et avanture,
> car il li venoit de nature.
> (ll. 1470-76 [1474-80])

(... he [Perceval] began to carry so aright the lance and the shield, as though he had always lived in tournaments and in wars and gone throughout all lands searching for battle and adventure, for it came to him by nature.)

The mentor's judgment will be just the opposite. Although he is pleased with his pupil's performance, he thinks "que, se il fust tot son aaige / d'armes penez et antremis, / s'an fust il asez bien apris" (ll. 1484-86 [1488-90]) (that if he had been all his life concerned and occupied with arms, he would be quite adept). For the moment, it appears to Gornemant that his charge is a very promising beginner (cf. ll. 1498-1500 [1502-04]). Gornemant has never seen Perceval before, nor, to our knowledge, will he ever observe him again. But the narrator judges the same actions as the mentor from another point of view—that of the modern artist who already comprehends the entirety of Perceval's biography, his future as well as his past.

Such interpretive devices are wholly conventional demonstrations of a narrator's grasp of his materials, and they inspire confidence in his evaluations. Yet in the Prologue Chrétien's narrator reveals himself, both overtly and implicitly, to be capable of error; the adumbration is amply justified throughout his narrative. There are moments when his comprehension of events is superficial and his judgments irrelevant. His assessment of Perceval's martial talents is inappropriate at the point when he makes it, as is immediately borne out by subsequent events (cf. the hero's initial efforts at Biaurepaire, as when he does not know how to attack on horseback an enemy who has fallen to the ground, ll. 2220-23 [2224-27]), although it would be accurate as a reflection of later developments (e.g., when Perceval defeats the Orgueilleus de la Lande). More serious is his justification of Perceval's reticence at the Grail Castle, a judgment which flies in the face of informed opinions expressed elsewhere by characters who have knowledge of both Perceval's biography and the Grail mysteries. According to Chrétien's narrator, the hero remains silent because he remembers Gornemant's advice against garrulousness, while the Weeping Maiden and the Hermit both attribute his inability to speak to a primary cause, his abandonment of his mother who died of grief for him—of which his repudiation of her words in favor of Gornemant's, along with his rejection of Welsh clothing made by her for a civilized outfit, is a distant secondary effect. The narrator, who knows the primary cause because he has read the history, chooses to base his perception of reality on the young hero's thoughts (cf. ll. 3194-3200 [3206-12]) at the critical moment, not on more penetrating analysis expressed elsewhere in the history.

Just as disconcerting are the narrator's own long periods of "silence"— that is, when he sustains an air of mystery by refraining from interpreting events that seem to demand mediation. In the midst of the Gauvain adventures, where it appears that every minute of one day in the life of the second hero is accounted for, the narrator inexplicably jumps into the future to relate the Hermitage episode, ignoring five years of matchless knighthood in the primary hero. Moreover, it is incongruous that the narrator, who compares himself and his audience with those who "know the mysteries of the kingdom of heaven," avowedly does not know whether good or ill will befall Perceval after failure at the Grail Castle, but *fears* that something may be amiss (ll. 3236-41 [3248-53]). In fact, he never claims to possess knowledge of the mysteries of the Grail kingdom which surround the most important events in his poem and which, as the title indicates, are to be the major object of narration.

Far more laconic in the *Conte du Graal* than in his other romances, Chrétien's narrator frequently appears content to let his characters speak for themselves without his mediation, his "translation."[13] As the Perceval adventures progress, the narrator withdraws more and more and eschews direct confrontation with the other-worldly aspects of the hero's experience. An acute observer of ordinary reality, he penetrates the consciousness of some characters and explores their psychological complexities— especially the Tent Maiden, the Orgueilleus de la Lande, Gornemant de Goorz, Blancheflor, knights who attack her castle, knights at the Arthurian court. However, those who inhabit the Grail kingdom or who comprehend it have very little existence beyond the words they speak—the Fisher King, the Weeping Maiden, Perceval's Hermit Uncle, even the loathsome damsel who berates Perceval and whose physical presence is so memorably evoked. Perceval's mother is a case in point. The narrator vividly and touchingly portrays her as a distraught widow about to lose her last surviving son, but he apparently ignores those qualities in her character that might indicate her ties with the Grail kingdom and fails to analyze her motivations for isolating her son from the world outside the Waste Forest, other than to repeat her words suggesting that she has acted to protect him for her sake as well as for his own. Her niece (?), Perceval's cousin who was raised in the Waste Forest, her brothers (the Hermit and the so-called Grail King) and her nephew (the Fisher King) are of the "Grail nobility" (rulers in the Grail kingdom and/or people who comprehend the Grail mysteries), yet she does not single them out or allude to the kingdom's existence when she informs her son of his noble heritage (except to claim that her forebears were the greatest of knights, II. 418-24 [420-26]). Moreover, although she has knowledge of matters some understanding of which is essential in the Grail mysteries (world history in the Christian perspective, the history of Britain, the Eucharist), she has, nevertheless, raised her son largely in ignorance of the Church; and, until just before his departure from home, she has not imparted to him any but the most elementary religious concepts or taught him even the basic facts regarding his personal history, much less the history of the outside world. The "psychologically realistic" depiction of Perceval's mother as grieving widow, like the narrator's explanation of the hero's behavior at the Grail Castle, is convincing only until character is analyzed in the light of values maintained in the Grail kingdom—values which Chrétien's narrator rarely, if ever, professes overtly, except in the Prologue, to uphold in his perception of meaning in character and event, yet ones that are morally central in the history which he recounts. By the time he tells the last extant Perceval episode (the Hermitage), he has largely disappeared as a commentator (well over two-thirds of the episode are in direct discourse). In fact, it is precisely in this episode, as the framing devices suggest in part, that the sheer artistry of episodic structuring supersedes direct commentary as a means of interpretation.

Our sense of Chrétien's unreliability as narrator increases with his gradual effacement and the consequent loss of narrative distance: because of the relative paucity of mediatory narration, the *Conte du Graal* is more "dramatic" than any other romance by Chrétien de Troyes. This means that the narrator becomes just as much an object of speculation and judgment for the audience as his characters and the events he recounts are for him.

Fundamentally, the problem for Chrétien, as narrator, involves the effective use of language—a problem in communication which he shares with many of his characters; indeed, the *Conte du Graal* is, at the level of history, largely about the perception of meaning in linguistic forms and characters' ability to engage in verbal communication. Success in the history's central adventure, restoration of the Grail kingdom, can be achieved only through acts of language, and Perceval's failure is, precisely, his reluctance to enter into meaningful communication with the Fisher King—to ask questions and to hear answers about objects in the Grail procession.

The Prologue generally supports in analogous terms Chrétien's artistic enterprise of translation. However, the history also extends perception and expression of meaning in verbal signs to include problems in the interpretation of paralinguistic and non-linguistic signs as well: material and quasi-material signifiers that convey meaning in ways similar to those in which ordinary language operates. Perceval does not comprehend the truth in words addressed to him in charity, the Orgueilleus de la Lande refuses to believe his mistress, Arthur does not respond to Perceval's first salutation, the court does not understand the real implications of the Smiling Maiden's and the Fool's predictions; but these misapprehensions are, ultimately, of the same order as Perceval's misperception of the aural and visual signs of the intruding knights' real nature, these knights' interpretation of Perceval's attitudes of prayer and homage as signs of fear, the Orgueilleus's failure to understand the meaning of hoofprints at his tent, the initial belief at Biaurepaire that Perceval's silence is a sign that he is dumb, the Arthurian court's general confusion about the significance of Perceval's love-trance, the inability of the ladies at Tintaguel to perceive Gauvain's nobility. Comprehension of reality is impossible because perspective is limited either by cultural conditioning or by psychological disturbance. Perceval is innocent (in both senses: inexperienced and self-centered), the five knights share with the court prejudices against the Welsh, the Orgueilleus de la Lande is blinded by jealousy, the court is depressed at first and shows itself later to have few interests beyond its own immediate concerns. Perceptive failure is frequently due to lack of sufficient information on which to base judgments. Initially, Perceval has no knowledge of the world outside the Waste Forest, so he believes that knights are not ordinary human beings; the court hears only stories of the hero's successes, so it welcomes him back in joyful triumph despite his failure at the Grail Castle; Gornemant knows neither Perceval's background nor his future, so he misjudges his pupil's abilities. Finally, the Gauvain adventures are characterized by instances when perception of the second hero's qualities changes with the revelation of his identity.

The Prologue also acknowledges and warns against the destructive powers of language—"vilain gap" (lowbrow jesting), "parole estote" (stupid, or vainglorious, speech) and "mal dire" (slander), which grieve Philippe de Flandre (II. 21-24). In fact, by contrast, divine love, the very force that operates in translation and promotes the productive use of language, communicates most effectively in absolute silence: "Charité... de sa bone oevre / pas ne se vante, ençois la coevre, / que nus ne le set se cil non / qui Dex et Charité a non" (II. 43-46) (Charity, which of its good work does not boast, but rather covers it up, so that none knows it except Him Whose name is God and Charity). In the history, abusive language creates dangerous situations for the heroes and results in confusion. Subjected to vituperative abuse by others, Gauvain seeks to avenge his honor by adopting courses of action that threaten him with dishonor (e.g., at Tintaguel) or that lead to ever more humiliating defeats (e.g., at the hands of Greoreas, in the company of the Orgueilleuse de Logres). In an utter breakdown of communication, Perceval misinterprets Keu's mocking bestowal of arms in Arthur's name by understanding his words in their literal sense, rather than in their intended allegorical sense, which indicates that Perceval is incapable of becoming a knight at all, much less of facing and defeating a powerful opponent. Blancheflor misuses the language of *fin' amors* (signs both verbal and material) with a beguiling innocence in order to secure Perceval as her defender, and Gauvain engages in a silly (and dangerous) courtly charade in order to champion the spoiled Pucele as Manches Petites. The abuse of language results from the same causes as limit characters' perception of and expression of meaning. Keu is depressed, angry and prejudiced; the Orgueilleuse de Logres is beset by a pathological contempt for men; Blancheflor is desperate to save herself and her city; the innocence of the Pucele as Manches Petites recalls that of the boy Perceval.

Abusive language and the failure to communicate involve characters in acts of mistranslation. The adolescent Perceval, heroes and ladies associated with the Arthurian court or assimilated to it, Blancheflor and her subjects, even Gornemant de Goorz, are limited intellectually and spiritually in ways that are analogous to (though hardly the same as) the conditions which deprived Alexander the Great of the knowledge of true reality. Chrétien's narrator claims, with justification, to be superior to all of them because he is of the "empire de Rome" (I. 12) or because he succeeds them in history. Yet he also resembles them because he is trapped in time and because he speaks, in a "royal court" (l. 66), a human language whose absurdities of structure and vocabulary are ridiculed in the history, where it obfuscates reality as often as it clarifies it. And, like the characters who fail to communicate effectively, he also misinterprets and mistranslates. Unlike the characters who misuse and who abuse language, however, Chrétien is conscious of the limitations imposed on him by his medium of communication both in the perception and in the expression of meaning. The same narrator who comprehends the revelations of the New Testament, which make the perception of reality possible, who can quote it and translate it verbatim, and who can develop and sustain a multileveled interpretation of its meaning, can also attribute a key passage rendered literally to the wrong author; and, by justifying his art of translation in terms of the seminal word, he acknowledges the limitations and the imperfections—the transitoriness—of his own endeavor.

As the Prologue suggests, translation is, from Chrétien's point of view as narrator, a process involving two phases of activity: the rendering of a text from one language into another and the elucidation of its meaning. The Prologue contains models of both phases. Extreme examples are provided, on the one hand, by exact renderings of "qui parce seminat, parce et metet" (II Cor. 9:6, cf. l. 1) and "Deus caritas est; et qui manet in caritate, in Deo manet, et Deus in eo" (I John 4:16, cf. ll. 47-50), and, on the other hand, by Chrétien's commentary on "nesciat sinistra tua, quid faciat dextra tua" (Matt. 6:3) and his extended use of the Parable of the Sower. Intermediary between the two, but closer to the first than to the second, are interpretive renderings less exact than verbatim: "... ne saiche ta senestre / le bien, quant le fera la destre" (ll. 31-32) and "Tes biens a ta senestre cele" (l. 37).

Presumably, the Count's book which contains the history is, as the New Testament is for Chrétien, a text written in Latin to be translated into French. Fictively, direct discourse functions, in his narrative, like the exact renderings (words from the past are brought intact into the present), as do factual details, while indirect discourse (for example) is like the closely related intermediary mode. By contrast, Chrétien's interpretive matter interposed between his audience and the events being recounted is, fictively, extraneous to the history *per se*, although, to be sure, commentary derives from his comprehension of the source. Chrétien's frequent withdrawal as narrator consists, therefore, of his refusal to complete the act of translation, which requires interpretive mediation, direct and indirect verbal commentary, and explanation, while the initial phase (exact and interpreted renderings) continues to remain in play in the form of superabundant direct and indirect discourse, factual detail and description.

Perhaps accidentally, this feature of Chrétien's narration foreshadows his failure literally to finish his poem.

Ironically, it is in precisely those episodes where the poem's most significant events take place that the narrator's inadequacies as interpreter and the incompleteness of his translation are the most evident and the most troublesome—that is, in a narrative called the *Conte du Graal*, during those moments when the Grail appears and/or when its mysteries are the primary concern. The most obvious episodes in this category are the Grail Castle, the Weeping Maiden, the Hideous Damsel and the Hermitage; but, for reasons yet to be elucidated, parallels linking the Waste Forest episode with those in which avowed members of Perceval's family appear later suggest that the opening moments of the poem should be included as well. (In the Gauvain section, the character of these expisodes is reflected in Escavalon, when reference is made to the Bleeding Lance, and especially in the Roche del Canpguin.)

A focal point in each episode, except the Grail Castle, is that a character who has knowledge of the Grail mysteries (the Weeping Maiden, the Hideous Damsel, the Hermit), who is a member of the "Grail nobility" (Perceval's mother), or who has knowledge of local history (in the Gauvain adventures, Grinomalanz and the Ferryman) fulfills the role assumed by Chrétien with respect to his audience. They are secondary narrators; more importantly, they are translators of history. To be sure, any act of communication is, in the terms established by Chrétien in the Prologue, an act of translation; but, as the examples cited above indicate, communication in episodes other than those associated with the Grail is impossible partly because of the translators' intellectual, psychological and cultural limitations. (In the Gauvain section, the same may be true of Grinomalanz, although he recounts the history of the Roche del Canpguin before unleashing his irrational hatred on Gauvain; but it is not true of the impartial Ferryman.) Moreover, because of such deficiencies, these translators' consciousness of reality, as suggested by what they are and what they say, hardly extends beyond their own immediate concerns. In the Perceval section, until the arrival of the Hideous Damsel and Guiganbresil, who open new possibilities of adventure near the midpoint of the extant narrative, history, for the Arthurian court, begins with the assaults of the Vermilion Knight shortly before Perceval's first arrival—that is to say, the court is preoccupied only with events subsequent to a certain enemy's intrusion. Moreover, reality always centers spatially in the court and does not encompass places even a few days' ride away: the court does not know about or is utterly indifferent to the existence of the Waste Forest, Biaurepaire (where a siege has been going on for over a year), the Grail Castle and localities visited by

Gauvain. Finally, the Hideous Damsel's and Guiganbresil's news of adventures lying outside the Arthurian realm does not excite the court as a community (the messengers are received with silent disinterest by the court as a whole), but inspires only certain heroes as individuals. (The last, fragmentary scene ever written by Chrétien de Troyes suggests that even Perceval, the court's sole interest a short time before, has apparently been forgotten; only the absent Gauvain is longed for.) For the Orgueilleus de la Lande and his mistress, time begins when Perceval touches their lives, while for Blancheflor, her subjects and their attackers, it begins with the siege of Biaurepaire; for Clamadeus, his seneschal, the Orgueilleus de la Lande and the Tent Maiden, existence in history ends with their assimilation into the court of Arthur.

By contrast, Perceval's mother, the Weeping Maiden, the Hermit and the Hideous Damsel comprehend dimensions of reality far beyond the immediate and the material. Collectively, they know the biography of the primary hero, the history of Britain, the history of the Grail kingdom, the history of mankind, the ethics of chivalry, the mysteries of the Grail, mysteries of the Christian religion; furthermore, they possess moral and ethical values commensurate with their superior knowledge. Intellectually and spiritually, they resemble the Philippe de Flandre of Chrétien's Prologue, while Alexander the Great is the prototype of characters bound to the Arthurian kingdom, blindly preoccupied with the immediate and the material. As translators, moreover, the "Grail nobility" are superior even to Chrétien's narrator, who is also like the Count, but dependent upon him, because when they fail in acts of translation it is not necessarily owing to perceptive and perspectival limitations in themselves; rather, when their words do not bear fruit, it is because of intellectual, spiritual and cultural debilities in their audience.

Their audience is Perceval. Indeed, since a major problem in the *Conte du Graal* is communication, one measure of the hero's maturation is precisely the degree to which he successfully receives their words and the quality of his comprehension—that is, his perception of meaning and his interpretive perspective. In the beginning, Perceval is innocent (self-centered, ignorant of the world outside the Waste Forest). He fails to understand his mother's accounts of British and familial history (ll. 487-88 [489-90]), and he interprets her religious, moral and ethical instructions in accord with his selfish, materialistic nature. Hence, he degrades the Tent Maiden, blunders and blusters at court, behaves ridiculously in the company of his noble mentor. In the end, that is, in the last Perceval episode written by Chrétien de Troyes, words similar to his mother's uttered by penitents and by the Hermit, who also recalls aspects of the Weeping Maiden's forgotten narrations, result in the hero's acceptance of values honored in the Grail kingdom—specifically, the concepts of sin, redemption, charity and the sacraments. Interpreted correctly, his mother's words, which speak of the fall of Utherpendragon's kingdom, of religion and chivalric ideals associated with the past, might have prepared Perceval for success at the Grail Castle, but hearing them he lacks the awareness to adopt the requisite critical perspective. At the Hermitage, however, experience as an Arthurian knight and a renewed consciousness of his failure when confronted by the Grail mysteries provide a basis for comprehending what he hears on Good Friday. If it cannot be proved (because Chrétien's text is unfinished) that the later accounts accomplish what his mother's might have done earlier, at least Perceval finds means for release from the fault to which members of the Grail community attribute his inability to communicate with the Fisher King.

Before the crucial events at the Hermitage, the hero had grown from innocence to maturity by cultivating, consciously and unconsciously, an interpretive perspective in harmony with that of the Arthurian kingdom; he had become more like the Alexander of Chrétien's Prologue than like Philippe de Flandre. Thus, in hearing the Weeping Maiden's words, he is attracted to the immediate implications of what she recounts (his mother's death, which puts an abrupt end to his quest for her; the murder of the headless knight, which inspires an act of vengeance) and ignores (we know this because he forgets) the wondrous otherworldly aspects of her narratives (the history of the Grail Castle, the extraordinary life of the Fisher King, allusions to the Grail mysteries, her explanations of his failure, etc.). In fact, his pursuit of the immediate adventure leads to the Orgueilleus de la Lande and, ultimately, to his reunion with Arthur.

The culmination of the discrete Perceval section, the hero's joyful return to court, ends with the Hideous Damsel's public excoriation of him. This is the only occasion in Chrétien's extant poem when Perceval hears an account of Grail history in the company of others and from a secondary narrator other than an avowed member of his family whom he encounters by apparent chance. This translator seeks her audience out in the midst of Arthurian celebration. Her language is, therefore, properly suited to the court and to the Arthurian knight *par excellence,* which is Perceval; indeed, her mode of narration differs radically from that of the Weeping Maiden and the Hermit, who also "translate" Perceval's experiences for him, and from that of his mother, who speaks with simple eloquence. To be sure, the Hideous Damsel's account of Perceval's adventure at the Grail Castle and the consequences of his failure resonates factually with the Weeping Maiden's and the Hermit's; it is her interpretive commentary that, in general, does not correspond. Her extended metaphor evoking a pagan goddess and her social stigmatization of the hero are not consonant with the unadorned rebukes of the Weeping Maiden or the Hermit's charitable explanations:

> Ha! Percevax, Fortune est chauve
> derriers et devant chevelue,
> et dahez ait qui te salue
> et qui nul bien t'ore et te prie,
> que tu ne la retenis mie,
> Fortune, quant tu la trovas!
> (ll. 4622-27 [4646-51])

(Ah! Perceval, Fortune is bald behind and hairy in front—and curses on anyone who greets you, who wishes or prays that any good befall you; for you didn't hold fast to Fortune when you found her!)

Accordingly, she also refrains from introducing the concept of sin—the fault committed by Perceval in abandoning his stricken mother which the members of his family proffer as the reason for his failure. Indeed, her point of view supports the superficial interpretation already stated by Chrétien's narrator:

> Mout est maleüreus qui voit
> si bel tans que plus ne covaigne,
> si atant tant que plus biax vaigne.
> Ce es tu, li maleüreus,
> qui veïs qu'il fu tans et leus
> de parler, et si te taïs!
> (ll. 4638-43 [4662-67])

(He is most unfortunate who experiences as fine weather as could be wished for, and yet waits for it to be better. This is like you, the wretch who saw that it was time and place to speak, and yet said nothing.)

Neither the Weeping Maiden nor the Hermit expresses interest in Perceval's apparent desire to put off asking questions already formulated in his mind, whether out of indolence or in memory of Gornemant's warnings against unmanly garrulousness (cf. the narrator's comments, ll. 3234-41 [3246-53], 3282-86 [3294-98], 3291-98 [3303-10]); rather, both concentrate on what they consider to be the primary cause of his behavior. Finally, the Hideous Damsel places her account in context with other adventures proposed to the court at large (ll. 4660-90 [4684-4714]), so that Perceval's acceptance of her challenge to him, his vow to undertake a quest for the Grail Castle (ll. 4703-16 [4727-40]), is but one of fifty individual commitments made by Arthur's knights (ll. 4694-4702 [4718-26], 4717-22 [4741-46]). In her translation—in her audience's response to it—the supreme adventure in the *Conte du Graal* becomes an ordinary chivalric enterprise.

Although she has (imperfect?) knowledge of the future, her narration does not suggest that she possesses the global consciousness of the other

"Grail nobility" (whether she actually does or not is a moot point; she is to us only as she presents herself as translator). It is a mark of Perceval's Arthurian maturation that he perceives the truth in her narrative in exactly the same terms as she presents it. Clearly Perceval has forgotten his encounter with the Weeping Maiden—or, at least, her words bearing on the Grail kingdom. Otherwise, he might not have required the Hideous Damsel's prodding. Moreover, in the Hermitage episode all of his knowledge of the Grail Castle and of his failure (ll. 6160-64 [6372-80]) derives from the Hideous Damsel's excoriation only, and the Hermit reintroduces information from the Weeping Maiden's account as though Perceval were entirely ignorant of it: "et dit: 'Frere, mout t'a neü / uns pechiez don tu ne sez mot'" (ll. 6176-77 [6392-93]) (and he said: "'Brother, a sin you know nothing about has done you much harm"). In responding to the Hideous Damsel's words, therefore, Perceval is incapable of regarding her narrative from any other perspective than the courtly, Arthurian mode which she adopts as her own. Her words take root, in that they inspire Perceval to undertake a quest for the Grail, but they do not bear fruit. Imprisoned in his Arthurian orientation, Perceval is like rocky soil, where words grow at first, then wither and die, because he lacks the superior understanding of the "Grail nobility" who do not speak in Arthurian language. Thus, he continues to excel in knighthood, sending fifty prisoners to Arthur in imitation of his old habit, but he loses an essential faculty of the soul—memory of God (ll. 6009-29 [6217-37])—and he does not fulfill his mission.

The same limitations as influence the perception of meaning also determine the expression of thought. Perceval, like all beings human and divine who desire to communicate, is a translator; and, like everyone else in the poem, including Chrétien's narrator, he is to be judged according to the quality of his translations. In the Waste Forest, comic irony directed derisively against the hero emerges in the history in function of his misapprehensions of reality expressed verbally. He speculates that approaching knights are devils, then angels; he says that Arthur "makes" knights; having defeated the Vermilion Knight at Carduel, and remembering Keu's sarcastic bestowal of arms in Arthur's name, he expresses belief that Arthur has indeed "made" him a knight; etc., etc. As the hero matures in his ability to comprehend the meaning of signs, however, his powers to translate and to communicate increase necessarily; and, from the Biaurepaire episode onwards, overt derisive irony determined by a courtly perspective similar to that of the Arthurian circle decreases accordingly.

In fact, the kind of response elicited in him by the Hideous Damsel's excoriation is already signaled in the episode called Blood Drops on the Snow. Perceval is entranced by three drops of blood from a wounded goose that have fallen on fresh snow. Red on white reminds him of his lady

Blancheflor's beautiful face (ll. 4177-84 [4197-4206]). Certain knights in Arthur's nearby encampment, especially Keu, are irritated by Perceval's apparently arrogant demeanor and challenge him, but Gauvain, with a degree of insight, understands that "Li chevaliers d'aucune perte / estoit pansis qu'il avoit fete, / ou s'amie li ert fortrete, / si l'an enuiot et pesoit" (ll. 4336-39 [4360-63]) (The knight was absorbed in thought on some loss he had had, or his beloved had been taken away from him and he was vexed and grieved by it), and he advises that it is discourteous to have disturbed him (ll. 4326-35 [4350-59]). Later Perceval explains the reasons for the trance and Gauvain concludes that "cil pansers n'estoit pas vilains, / ençois estoit cortois et dolz" (ll. 4434-35 [4458-59]) (that trance was not rude; rather, it was courtly and gentle).

The ignorant Welshman incapable at first of interpreting correctly strange signs encountered in the Waste Forest now comprehends unusual, but natural signs in an extremely sophisticated way—as though the blood drops on the snow constituted an allegorical image, which is exactly what Chrétien's narrator calls it: "cele sanblance" (l. 4177A [4198]). And Gauvain, the epitome of Arthurian courtesy, applauds the hero's sentiments and calls his love-thoughts courtly and gentle. Recognition of Perceval's Arthurian prowess in the ensuing joyful celebration of his return to court is complemented, therefore, by indications of his newly refined sensibilities. Just as the savior of Biaurepaire and the manly conqueror of the Orgueilleus de la Lande develop from the country boy who savagely slays the Vermilion Knight with an unknightly javelin, so the sophisticated lover grows from the coarse adolescent who nearly ravishes the decorous Tent Maiden. All is in accord with the highest courtly ideals which, normally, the Arthurian kingdom is presumed to reflect; indeed, the episode in question signals Perceval's complete assimilation to that kingdom.

Yet the lover lost in courtly contemplation of an image of his now distant lady fails to perceive through that same kind of *sanblance* a reality that is, according to the extant fragment, of all-encompassing significance in Perceval's history: the Grail procession itself and, specifically, the Bleeding Lance. In fact, recollection of this mysterious phenomenon would have required somewhat less abstract thought processes than memory of Blancheflor. Perceval is well aware that the red spots in the snow are drops of blood (l. 4427 [4451]). In the Grail procession, a drop of blood falls from the tip of the lance against the white background of the weapon's head and shaft and runs onto the hand of the bearer who holds the lance upright (ll. 3179-89 [3191-3201]). Ironically, Perceval leans on his own lance to look down into the snow (l. 4177 [4197]).

This is not to suggest that Perceval should perceive through these signs an object in the Grail procession instead of his beloved, but that he ought to comprehend both. At the very least Biaurepaire and the Grail Castle have it in common that his promise to return to Blancheflor and his failure to save the Grail kingdom are the two potentials for further action that are not resolved in the discrete Perceval section. The narrator's awareness of the symbolic resonances suggesting an association between the blood drops on the snow and both Blancheflor's face and the Bleeding Lance is indicated by striking linguistic similarities linking his descriptions of Blancheflor and the Grail procession to the two translations (the narrator's own and Perceval's) of the hero's love-trance experience. Perceval speaks in the only words that can be ascribed with certainty to the history:

> ... devant moi an ice leu
> avoit .III. gotes de frés sanc
> qui anluminoient le blanc.
> An l'esgarder m'estoit avis
> que la fresche color del vis
> m'amie la bele i veïsse,
> ja mes ialz partir n'an queïsse.
> (ll. 4426-32 [4450-56])

(...there in front of me were three drops of fresh blood which illuminated the white. While looking at them I seemed to see the fresh color in the face of my beloved—I would not have sought to turn my eyes away from it.)

The narrator's account is more detailed:

> Si s'apoia desor sa lance
> por esgarder cele sanblance,
> que li sans et la nois ansanble
> la fresche color li resanble
> qui est an la face s'amie,
> et panse tant que il s'oblie.
> Ausins estoit, an son avis,
> li vermauz sor le blanc asis
> come les gotes de sanc furent
> qui desor le blanc aparurent.
> An l'esgarder que il fesoit
> li ert avis, tant li pleisoit,
> qu'il veïst la color novele
> de la face s'amie bele.
> (ll. 4177-88 [4197-4210])

(He leaned on his lance in order to gaze at that image, for the blood and snow together resemble the fresh complexion in the face of his beloved, and he thinks so long that he loses himself in contemplation. It seemed to him that the red was set on the white [in her face] as the drops of blood which appeared on white. In his gaze which pleased him so much, he seemed to see the fresh color in the face of his beautiful beloved.)

Ironically, it is Perceval's recollection that reverberates with Chrétien's description of the Bleeding Lance, particularly in the rhyme *sanc : blanc* (cf. ll. 4427-28 [4451-52]):

> et tuit cil de leanz veoient
> la lance blanche et le fer blanc,
> s'issoit une gote de sanc
> del fer de la lance an somet
> et jusqu'a la main [au] vaslet [i.e., the bearer]
> coloit cete gote vermoille.
> Li vaslez [i.e., Perceval] vit cele mervoille
> . . . .
> (ll. 3184-90 [3196-3202])

(and all those inside saw the white lance and the white iron; and there issued from the point of the lance's iron a drop of blood, and that red drop trickled down to the youth's [i.e., the bearer's] hand. The youth [i.e., Perceval] saw that marvel . . . .)

Chrétien's account of the love-trance recalls more immediately his earlier description of Blancheflor's face, even in the repetition of a whole line (l. 1822 [1824] = l. 4182 [4204]): "et mialz li avenoit el vis / li vermauz sor le blanc asis / que li sinoples sor l'argent" (ll. 1821-23 [1823-25]) (and the red set on the white in her face became her more than sinople set in argent), while both his and Perceval's summaries of the *panser* are linked to the description of Blancheflor in the intertwining rhymes *avis : asis* (ll. 4181-82 [4203-04]), *avis : vis* (ll. 4429-30 [4453-54]), and *vis : asis* (ll. 1821-22 [1823-24]). Curiously, Chrétien's account of the Bleeding Lance recalls an added commentary on Blancheflor's beauty that may explain why the hero is enthralled with his lady and neglects the Grail procession when he contemplates the *sanblance*. The lance is a "mervoille" (l. 3190 [3202]), while, in the case of the lady, "Por anbler san et cuer de gent / fist Dex de li *passemervoille*" (ll. 1824-25 [1826-27], my emphasis) (That she might steal people's minds and hearts, God made of her *more than a marvel*).

The subtle echoes reverberating among the four passages suggest the narrator's consciousness that two of Perceval's previous experiences, rather than just one, are related to the phenomenon that causes him to be lost in thought. In this light, his insistence that Perceval's interpretation is solely his own ("an son avis," l. 4181 [4203]; "li ert avis, *tant li pleisoit*," l. 4186 [4208], my emphasis; but Perceval uses the same expression in l. 4429 [4453]) indicates Perceval's limitations even more strongly. Perceval has forgotten the more important experience and can perceive reality through the signs only in terms of the self-centering Arthurian optic.

However, the narrator's message is, for its part, far from straightforward, and its subtle indirection requires a complex act of translation for comprehension of it. As narrator, Chrétien's evaluative perspective is, obviously, superior to that of the fictionalized Arthurian court—otherwise, he would be incapable of ironizing the Arthurian kingdom by emphasizing its moral, ethical and intellectual shallowness by drawing attention to the deficiencies of the heroes (Gauvain as well as Perceval) whom it embraces as embodiments of its ideals, even by delighting in the misapprehensions of reality that are the marks of its Alexandrine imprisonment. But it is equally obvious that the narrator's perceptive powers do not match those of characters who have knowledge of the other kingdom whose values incorporate the ethical center of the history, nor are his interpretations always expressed with the same directness and precision as theirs. This is because his own courtly language—in which the word *lance* absurdly refers to a weapon that is held fast rather than thrown (*lancier*) (cf. the ignorant Perceval's deflation of the noble term, ll. 196-97 [198-99]), which abounds in ambiguous rhetorical adornment (allegory: irony as well as personification) and proverbs, which, therefore, can obfuscate reality as well as illuminate it— resembles that of the Hideous Damsel more closely than it does the simple eloquence of Perceval's mother, cousin and uncle. He does not analyze the character, motivation or intellect of the "Grail nobility," including the Fisher King, nor does he confront their judgments, having once proffered an inadequate "psychologically realistic" explanation of Perceval's behavior at the Grail Castle which transforms a debilitating sin into a breech of etiquette. Concerning them and their words, he does not complete the process of translation because his language is ineffective. Self-effacement, limited self-ironization and the ultimate subversion of a perspective not completely dissimilar to his own or to that of his presumed immediate audience are means whereby Chrétien's narrator manifests consciousness of his own imperfection and draws attention to the perspective clarity produced by the light of the Grail. His incomplete translation, which, according to the poetics of the seminal word, is all that any literary activity can produce, continues to bear fruit to this day, having inspired early on endeavors to continue, to finish and to transform his story and, later, scholarly efforts to resolve the mysteries which he purposefully left "untranslated." Certainly, perception of the narrator's limitations and of the nature of the history which he recounts is possible only because of the creative genius and the authority of the Chrétien de Troyes in whom the words originate.

The Conte du Graal *and Romance*

The conceptual opposition of kingdoms introduced in the Prologue, where the "empire de Rome" supersedes the empire of Alexander the Great, finds material expression in the Perceval history of the *Conte du*

Graal, where the Arthurian kingdom and that of the "Grail nobility" are spatially and intellectually removed one from the other, and in the Gaúvain history, where the epitome of Arthurian courtliness and valor becomes the imprisoned savior of a mysterious, unknown fiefdom founded contemporaneously with the Waste Forest community, when Utherpendragon died (ll. 440 ff. [442 ff.], 8476 ff. [8740 ff.]), and a few years before the Grail Castle (compare l. 6213 [6429] and l. 8492 [8756]), a fiefdom totally isolated from the Arthurian world (at least for the present). Similar, though less absolute oppositions characterize Chrétien's work as a whole. In *Erec et Enide* the heroes' adventure is not complete until their kingdom of Estre-Galles is first set apart from, in imitation of the configuration in the first *vers,* then assimilated with Arthur's super-empire in the joyful celebration of their coronation at Nantes; in *Cligés,* by contrast, the failure of the primary hero is understood, in part, to lie in his inability to reconcile the ideals of Arthurian Britain with his achievements in Constantinople; in *Lancelot* experience in the otherworldly Gorre must be reduplicated in and/or justified in terms of Arthur's court, where the narrative begins and ends. In these poems the Arthurian kingdom functions as the locality with respect to which heroes must order their lives and, despite its imperfections, it furnishes the measure of human values. In *Yvain* Chrétien continues to oppose the Arthurian kingdom with a world beyond it; however, this time the court's inadequacies are stressed and its influence is viewed ultimately as potentially inimical and degrading. The hero is oriented away from court in his quest for identity as Fountain Defender, husband of Laudine and Lion Knight.

Quite conventionally, Chrétien's earlier romances are concerned with heroic progress—that is, problems inherent in heroes' character and circumstances are resolved, through the operation of adventure, in ways leading to unanticipated success. (*Cligés,* where the ideal is upheld, proves the convention in that its primary hero is unable to realize transcendent success and is, therefore, the object of particular ironic contemplation.) In the four earlier romances, heroes establish communication between the Arthurian kingdom and other worlds; throughout, contact is maintained either by acts of the will or by apparent chance, whether or not success depends ultimately upon a return to Arthur (*Lancelot*), assimilation with his kingdom (*Erec et Enide* and, potentially, *Cligés*) or rejection of it (*Yvain*). In fact, as Wilhelm Kellermann first demonstrated,[14] one significant aspect of episodic structuring in Chrétien is the pivotal nature of the Arthurian court perceived in periodic returns to and reunions with it. Furthermore, the quality of heroic progress is judged in terms of the quality of heroes' Arthurian or anti-Arthurian orientation (that is, with Arthur's court or another locality as the center of worlds in which they operate). In *Erec et Enide*, although there are hints that the court is in decline (Arthur has some difficulty in reestablishing a custom fallen into disuse since Utherpendragon's reign, II. 27-66, 1760 ff.), the positive moral standards of the Arthurian kingdom are never questioned; and, even when Erec refuses Arthur's hospitality after a chance encounter, in favor of pursuing his private adventure (II. 3907-4252), its beneficence is symbolized, in anticipation of the climactic joyous reunion, both by the miraculous medication given to Erec there and by the fact that, after the encounter, he begins directing his and Enide's experience outward in the service of others. In general, Chrétien maintains structures suggesting that heroic progress is possible only in Arthurian orientation—until *Yvain*.

With respect to this, the revolutionary feature of *Yvain* is not that the hero must venture outside the court in order to realize success (this is true of all the earlier romances), but that experience in the Arthurian kingdom can actually impede heroic progress. Having won a wife and a new identity, Yvain returns to court in pursuit of Arthurian honor, only to forget his new responsibilities in her domain and, once reminded of his neglect, to go insane. Redemption and reconciliation with Laudine are achieved independently of Arthur's influence. In thus isolating the hero from the Arthurian sphere, Chrétien places a new emphasis on the individual's involvement with adventure; he also begins to explore heroic progress more overtly in the light of values that are specifically religious in nature. Yvain's recovery from a state of bestial savagery is promoted by the cares of a charitable hermit (even though the first phase of his restoration is not complete until he is cured, like Erec, with an ointment from a fairy kingdom); he wins both a lion as a companion and another non-Arthurian identity after perceiving in the lion's life-and-death struggle with a dragon-like serpent a battle between good and evil with Christological overtones (even though Chrétien undercuts the lofty sentiments by making the lion pathetic as well as noble in his imitation of humanity).

In the *Conte du Graal* Chrétien broadens and deepens the implications of *Yvain*, indicating uncompromisingly that heroic success lies in consciousness of religious values and in individual achievement in a kingdom which the Arthurian court can hardly comprehend and to which it is oblivious—while yet the Arthurian kingdom, depite its decline and its limitations, has the same ethical functions as in *Erec et Enide*, to which, in this respect, *Yvain* is opposed absolutely. Perceval is called to attain a degree of heroic achievement that resembles and, potentially, surpasses Yvain's success in non-Arthurian orientation: restoration of the Grail kingdom. At the same time, unlike the Lion Knight, in whose case Arthurian values (for example, devotion to tournaments) militate against heroic progress, Perceval is also destined to realize Arthurian greatness before he can be ready for triumph in the anti-Arthurian kingdom. Gauvain is the counterpoise who demonstrates, by contrast, the weaknesses in the old pattern exemplified in the earlier romances—weaknesses revealed as such by the new pattern. Whether or not Chrétien's history intended Perceval ultimately to realize his potential to the fullest is, of course, impossible to determine; all that Chrétien's fragment permits is perception of what the way to heroic success is.

The insistence on experience in the Arthurian kingdom as prerequisite to achievement in another world resembles the function of Britain in *Cligés*, a narrative which the *Conte du Graal* recalls in many respects, in part because both are about adolescents growing to manhood. Heroes in both poems are boys or young men who venture into the Arthurian kingdom in order to attain a level of chivalric accomplishment, material and ethical, that is impossible to reach in their homelands. All succeed, in varying degrees, and the quality of their heroism lies in their ability to bring Arthurian education to bear in experiences awaiting them elsewhere. Alixandre and his son return to Constantinople, where they are heirs to the throne; Perceval enjoys two potentially transcendent adventures—at Biaurepaire, where he excels in knighthood, saves a besieged castle, wins a lady and is proclaimed lord, and at the Grail Castle, which houses members of his family who are the ruling nobility in a previously unknown kingdom.

But there is a major difference between *Cligés* and the *Conte du Graal* in the fact that in the former experience in Arthurian Britain is regarded as complementary to the heroes' initial condition and circumstances, while in the latter it supplants them absolutely. Perceval's upbringing in the Waste Forest inhibits knightly achievement, towards which he is impelled by birth and compelled emotionally, and Arthurian experience necessarily constitutes the abandonment of old values and attitudes, which keep him in ignorance, and the acquisition of something new. Biaurepaire offers the hero a supreme triumph as a new man in Arthurian orientation; and, when news of his victories reaches the court, it awakens anticipation for a joyful reunion eventually realized at Carlion. *Cligés* affirms the values of reconciliation of the old with the new; but in the *Conte du Graal* the discrete Perceval section, which sustains the hero's orientation in Arthur's kingdom, celebrates his triumphant rejection of his past associated with the Waste Forest and his progress in courtly acculturation (success in love and warfare, the adoption of attitudes that affect his language, perception of reality, and self-knowledge). Despite the differences in the pervasiveness of courtly education, however, both romances uphold the conventional worth of the Arthurian kingdom as reflected in *Erec et Enide*. Even the Hideous

Damsel's excoriation of Perceval, which disturbs the climactic celebration, does not undermine what is affirmed in the discrete Perceval section precisely because it translates the hero's failure at the Grail Castle into Arthurian language and implicitly proposes a Grail quest as a conventional Arthurian adventure.

Although severe limitations in the Arthurian court (e.g., preoccupation with the immediate and the material, failure to recognize transcendent values) come to light when events in the history are judged from the point of view of the Grail kingdom, the positive significance of Perceval's orientation in and around the court cannot be underestimated. This is because of another important difference between the *Conte du Graal* and Chrétien's earlier narratives. While other heroes may have other choices (e.g., Erec decides not to accept Arthur's hospitality, Yvain could prefer to remain with his wife), the Arthurian world provides Perceval with the only means possible for realization of his potential as a man. His mother and her vassals have contrived to maintain him in a state of childhood—a kind of ignorant purity that assures his blissful harmony with nature (cf. ll. 85 ff. [ibid.]), but that also imprisons him in unawareness of the world at large and unconsciousness of the worth of others. It is only his fatal awakening to the new reality of Arthur's existence as the "king who makes knights" that offers him freedom from isolation and egocentrism. It is clear, of course, almost from the beginning of Perceval's history, that, by comparison with a past age (the reign of Utherpendragon), Arthur's kingdom is in a state of disarray—an implication in the account of British history by Perceval's mother (ll. 440 ff. [442 ff.]) that is amply demonstrated at Carduel in the court's impotence before the Vermilion Knight and its cruel rudeness towards Perceval, which seems to be a fulfillment of the inchoate decline suggested in the opening of *Erec et Enide*. "Arthurian knighthood" is conferred on Perceval not as a generous grant of arms from the king, who sees only the absurd surface of the boy's request, but by the bitterly sarcastic voice of the angry seneschal Keu (ll. 999-1005 [1001-07]).

Yet those who have knowledge of superior chivalry are limited in their powers to enhance practically Perceval's mental and moral growth or to promote the full exercise of his physical skills in service to others. Indeed, his mother is a cause of his debilities. And Gornemant de Goorz, whose concept of "God's highest order" (ll. 1633-36 [1635-38]) harmonizes with the ideals expressed by Perceval's mother, is himself isolated from society: he implies a distance between himself and Arthur's court (cf. ll. 1367-71 [1371-75]), although physically Carduel is a short ride from his castle, while he seems never to have aided his niece Blancheflor in her year-long struggle at Biaurepaire, a day's ride away. With an afternoon's instruction, Gornemant remains unconvinced of his pupil's merits (ll. 1482-86

[1486-90]), but he is content to give Perceval his spurs and—his most significant bestowal—words of advice (ll. 1620-96 [1624-98]). Of necessity, therefore, in possession primarily of his mentor's words, Perceval is left to his own devices in defending Biaurepaire and, ultimately, in gaining a degree of achievement that recalls, in some ways, conventional heroic transcendence. He gradually excels in knightly prowess thanks as much to innate ability and instinct as to Gornemant's instructions, but, in the end, circumstances force Perceval to interpret his mentor's words in terms that are wholly Arthurian. In granting mercy to Clamadeus and his seneschal, in memory of these words, he becomes convinced (with justification) that his adversaries would be endangered if sent to Blancheflor or to her uncle for imprisonment; therefore, he dispatches them to the only other suitable prison he knows—Arthur's court (ll. 2239-2321 [2243-67], 2680-97 [2684-99]). In fact, the center of the Arthurian kingdom is the single place where Gornemant's words can have true meaning for the hero who persists in claiming that Arthur, rather than Gornemant, has "made" him a knight (cf. ll. 3941-45 [3959-63]). Furthermore, the imprisonment of Clamadeus and his seneschal materially advances the establishment of the Arthurian context of Perceval's knighthood. The prisoners' accounts of Perceval's victories excite the king's interest in the savage boy who has so quickly become an extraordinary knight (ll. 2765-2907 [2785-2909]). Later, a similar story told by the Orgueilleus de la Lande moves the court to search for the missing hero, whom it eventually succeeds in recognizing as one of its own (ll. 4025-4120 [4045-4140]).

Thus, the convention of Arthurian centrality in *Erec et Enide* prevails both in the history, where circumstances as well as his own beliefs force Perceval to define his mother's and Gornemant's chivalry in Arthurian terms, and in the narrator's account of it, which structures events so that the hero's experiences have meaning only in light of the reunion at Carlion. In fact, it is the very conventionality of the discrete Perceval section, with its midpoint episode at Biaurepaire, that affirms the worth of Arthurian values. Certainly, this is true to the extent that it reflects generally the pattern of *Erec et Enide*, but structural details as well support the assertion. An important feature of the Perceval history is that, like all successful heroic ventures in Chrétien, Perceval's pursuit of knighthood constitutes an "ironic quest." Erec follows Yder in order to avenge his dwarf's insult, Alixandre goes to Britain in order to win glory in Arthur's court, Yvain reenacts Calogrenant's adventure in order to measure his prowess and avenge his cousin's dishonor, but all unexpectedly find wives; Lancelot intends to rescue the Queen, but in so doing he discovers the pains and rewards of love. By contrast, Cligés gains little more in Britain than he anticipates—hence, his failure as a hero.

Similarly, in leaving the Waste Forest, Perceval has no goals beyond the acquisition of arms at Carduel in adherence to his mother's counsel about chivalry as he understands her words (ll. 525-96 [527-94]). By the time he departs from Gornemant's castle, not only does he possess "Arthurian" arms, but, in memory of his mother's advice, he also thinks that he has visited a church (the Tent Maiden's *tref*), successfully wooed a lady (the Tent Maiden), and been in the company of a noble man (Gornemant); therefore, in reflection of the intentional aspect of the quest, it is natural that, having realized his expectations, he should now respond for the first time to the implications of his mother's faint and seek to return home (ll. 1575-88 [1580-92]). At this point in the history, the primary ironic element in Perceval's quest is its comic subversion and the humor directed against the hero with delusions of grandeur and not the slightest degree of sophistication. However, the way back home to the Waste Forest leads Perceval to Biaurepaire, and it is in defending Blancheflor and her castle that, in imitation of Chrétien's earlier heroes, Perceval acquires what he has not, and cannot have, anticipated before. Like all of them, he wins a lady and potentially, like Yvain, a new identity and new responsibilities as the future lord of her domain; moreover, his victory over her enemies and liberation of her castle are in harmony with a divine plan of restoration (ll. 2521-58 [2523-60]). The degree of chivalric perfection achieved by the hero is justly admired at Arthur's court when the defeated knights tell their stories and when all finally see the hero for themselves. In large measure, Perceval's successes cause a reversal in the trend of comic subversion established early on in the history and in its narration.

It is noteworthy that the kind of irony operating against the hero until he begins to excel in knighthood depends entirely upon a concept of positive Arthurian values that is quite conventional according to norms affirmed by Chrétien in other romances, but that, prior to the Biaurepaire episode and the arrival of prisoners at Arthur's court, does not otherwise find material support in the history. Indeed, in paradoxical fulfillment of predictions made at Carduel, it turns out to be Perceval himself (at Biaurepaire and in others' narrative accounts of his victories) in whom the convention of excellence in Arthurian knighthood is reflected the most effectively. Yet, as Chrétien presents Biaurepaire—that is, as it appears in the history and in the narrator's interpretation of it—the quality of the hero's success is compromised. The narrator describes Blancheflor's town with a realism that exposes its materialistic concerns. Under siege, Biaurepaire is starving, and Blancheflor and her subjects are desperate in their preoccupation with survival. When, according to Chrétien's narrator (l. 2526 [2528]), God intervenes on their behalf, the miracle takes the form of a commercial enterprise: a merchant barge is blown off course, and commodities are bought and sold. No lofty ideals exist in Biaurepaire to counteract the effects of its materialistic needs and interests, and Perceval himself suggests that a major concern of the town's two religious houses is money (ll. 2962-65 [2968-71]). The degree to which Biaurepaire as a community compromises Perceval's heroism is, ironically, the degree to which conventional Arthurian values are upheld in the text—values that are noble, courtly, anti-urban, anti-bourgeois. These same values operate, in fact, in two different kinds of Arthurian translation which change the focus on Perceval's experience at Biaurepaire by filtering out the baser, materialistic elements: the defeated knights' accounts of Perceval's victories and his own explanation of the love-trance in the snow affirm, for the court, the worth of the hero's chivalry and assure his acceptance as the embodiment of its ideals. But Chrétien's depiction of Biaurepaire justifies by itself, from a viewpoint complimentary to Arthurian values, the history's requirement of a greater test of the hero's character and abilities—the adventure at the Grail Castle.

Like Yvain in Laudine's domain, Perceval at Biaurepaire is compelled by a memory of his old world to return there and attempt to resolve a problem impeding his acceptance of a new status as lord of a castle. In fact, Perceval proposes, much more explicitly than Yvain, a reconciliation of the old with the new. He must find his mother in the Waste Forest. If she is alive, he will bring her back to Biaurepaire; if she is dead, he will return and pay to have masses said for her repose (ll. 2948-65 [2952-71]). But instead of the Waste Forest, Perceval finds the Grail Castle.

The hero's failure when confronted with the Grail mysteries indicates severe deficiencies in the values which he has adopted outside the Waste Forest. The deficiencies are indicated directly by the facts that a new sword is destined for the hero to replace his "Arthurian sword" won from the Vermilion Knight, with which Gornemant conferred "God's highest order of chivalry" (ll. 1630-36 [1634-36]),[15] and that a newly acquired concern for appearing courtly and not boorish motivates Perceval to refrain from asking questions at the right time (cf. ll. 3198-3200 [3210-12]). Yet the history and the narrator do not subvert those values as a consequence of Perceval's failure. As grave as his errors are in the eyes of the "Grail nobility" (sinful abandonment of his mother, refusal to communicate with the Fisher King, etc.), his faults do not inhibit his conventional heroic progress either materially or ethically. On the contrary, as a result of his failure —that is, when he meets his cousin the Weeping Maiden while looking for the Fisher King's men who have disappeared—he becomes conscious for the first time of his identity as Perceval the Welshman (l. 3561 [3575]), and, having learned that his mother is dead and that, therefore, there is no need to return to the Waste Forest (ll. 3607-11 [3621-25]), he begins a series of adventures that increasingly demonstrate the ethical worth of his orientation in the Arthurian world. Vowing to avenge the murder of his cousin's lover, Perceval defeats the Orgueilleus de la Lande. In so doing, he expiates a wrong committed earlier, in his blind innocence, against the Tent Maiden, purges the Orgueilleus of his pathological jealousy, reconciles the lovers, and unites them with the court. Their account of his heroism further enhances his reputation and, in fact, eventually brings about his reunion with Arthur. The hero's love-trance convinces Gauvain that he has nobility and courtesy in love as well as prowess at arms. And, by defeating Keu, he fulfills the Smiling Maiden's and the Fool's mysterious predictions and, in the judgment of the court, has proved himself to be, as they foretold, "the one who will have complete dominion in chivalry" (ll. 1059-60 [1061-62]).

The discrete Perceval section, an effect of *conjointure* as episodic structuring, culminates in the celebration at Carlion in fulfillment of the potential in Perceval's visit at Carduel. This turn of events is implicitly endorsed by the narrator who arranges his account so that periodic returns to Arthur and reviews of the events at Carduel in light of more recent achievements forecast, in harmony with the king's anticipations, the kind of reunion typical in Chrétien's romances. However, because of the hero's failure, its causes and effects, the discrete Perceval section in actuality resembles not a completed romance, but the first *vers* of *Erec et Enide*: in what might otherwise have suggested a complete action, the Grail mishap generates another action (or another phase of the same action) that is the object of narration in a "second *vers*." The primary difference between *Erec et Enide* and the *Conte du Graal*, in this respect, is that the existence and the nature of Perceval's faults are made explicit throughout much of the first section, while in Chrétien's earliest extant romance the narrator does not even hint that the hero who returns to court with his betrothed will neglect chivalric and princely duty in favor of nuptial pleasure or that his lady will utter, in her first words recorded by the narrator, a fateful lament. Despite this, the joy at Carlion recalls that of Caradigan, even when the Hideous Damsel disrupts it to make Perceval's private sins public. Just so, it is public knowledge of Erec's negligence that precipitates the second action in the earlier poem; and, as a reflection of this, there are many reasons for the expectation that Perceval's problems, as understood from the Hideous Damsel's excoriation, can be resolved in a way permitting a conclusion that resembles the coronation at Nantes and, in the *Charrette*, the celebration of Lancelot's final victory. Perceval "belongs" in the Arthurian kingdom because experience there is ultimately positive and ameliorative for him, in that he excels in knighthood and acquires courtliness, by contrast with the debilitating effects of his Waste Forest heritage. In Chrétien's world in general and specifically in the *Conte du Graal*, the hero cannot have progressed physically, intellectually or socially under any other conditions. Regardless of what arises elsewhere in the poem to contradict this sense in the conclusion of the discrete Perceval section or to alter the significance of Perceval's orientation in the Arthurian kingdom, the typical implication in the narrator's episodic segmentation remains intact because supported by the material isolation of the Perceval section from subsequent events in the history to which it relates directly. Interlacing operates to remove the Hermitage episode from it by some 1300 lines of Gauvain adventures that are causally independent of any Perceval episode.

Nevertheless, the Hermitage episode profoundly affects our perception of meaning in the Perceval history because it forces a revaluation of past events in a new light and a reinterpretation of meaning in the discrete "first *vers*" which affirms typical Arthurian values. As noted before, in the Hermitage episode Chrétien both achieves maximum withdrawal as narrator, in that he translates "less completely" than anywhere else in the Perceval adventures, and establishes, explicitly and implicitly, artificial episodic segmentation as a primary interpretive device. In so doing, he recreates for and in his audience, more fully than heretofore, conditions that resemble those operating in translation, the very activity in which the narrator is himself engaged—the perception, in retrospection, of the truth in past events and of realities which language is incapable of expressing directly. All in recognition of the powers of the seminal word.

Perceval's orientation in the Arthurian kingdom is recalled in the opening lines of the Hermitage episode. For five years the hero has wandered in quest of chivalric adventure and, in imitation of his practice established at Biaurepaire, has sent some fifty knights to be imprisoned in Arthur's court (II. 6016-27 [6224-35]). During this time, however, he has forgotten God and has, therefore, utterly neglected his religious obligations (II. 6010-15 [6218-23], 6028-29 [6236-37]). This loss of memory is usually regarded as the equivalent of insanity.

Otherwise, the episode constitutes primarily a review of events the essence of which is apparently irrelevant in the Arthurian kingdom: the hero's experience in a world—the Grail kingdom and places inhabited by "Grail nobility"—whose existence the court can comprehend only dimly, thanks to the Hideous Damsel's diatribe, and a world in which the court has manifested no interest whatsoever. At the Hermitage, attention focuses on the Grail Castle and on the mysterious procession, some aspects of which Perceval's uncle interprets for the hero; and, although the Weeping Maiden is never referred to directly in any way, the Hermit replays her role as mediator and translator and repeats her words, which Perceval has forgotten, about his debilitating sin.

Equally striking are the resonances that relate the Hermitage and the Waste Forest. Physical resemblance is limited to the fact that the Hermitage is in a springtime forest (l. 6094 [6304]) or a wood (l. 6125 [6337]) isolated in a wasteland ("un desert," l. 6031 [6239]). More significant are the conceptual and verbal links. Just as, in the Waste Forest, the boy unexpectedly meets strangers and asks them comically absurd questions about their knighthood, so, in approaching the Hermitage, Perceval the man encounters knights in unexpected garb (on Good Friday they are without arms) and asks simplistic questions about them as penitent Christians. But the history reverses the situations of man and boy and, consequently, the bases on which they ground their questions. In the Waste Forest Perceval is innocent and the knights are incongruous intruders; on Good Friday it is the experienced Perceval who is the incongruously intrusive knight because he wears arms, while the penitents are "innocent" because they have made confession and received absolution. The boy is awakened to knighthood, but the man is awakened from the "sleep" of knighthood and is made aware yet again of a new dimension of reality; as before in the Waste Forest, he later learns from a member of his family (this time his mother's brother) facts in the history of his family that relate to what he has just begun to comprehend. The Hermitage suggests a new beginning for the hero, but it is a reawakening that accounts for the entirety of his experience. At the close of the episode, Perceval, having confessed and taken communion on Easter, is an "innocent" penitent knight like those encountered on the way into the forest where he finds refuge—that is, he is cleansed of his sin and ready to do penance and atone for his wrong.

In addition to projecting matter from the Waste Forest episode onto a different—and higher—plane in providing for that new beginning, the Hermitage is also a fulfillment of the potential in the hero's first awakening. In this, Chrétien imitates the pattern according to which Perceval's reunion at Carlion harks back to Carduel and fulfills it, but the structure reflected in the Waste Forest-Hermitage relationship functions in unprecedented ways partially to subvert what the discrete Perceval section affirms. On the one hand, Perceval's mother regards the Arthurian kingdom and, therefore, its knighthood as inferior ethically to what was known under Utherpendragon and even as inimical to the welfare of her family (ll. 405-86 [407-88], esp. 425-32 [427-34]). The Waste Forest shelters a society in refuge from Arthur's fallen kingdom; Perceval's elder brothers were sent to serve not Utherpendragon's son, but foreign kings; Perceval has been raised in ignorance of knighthood (and, therefore, of courtly society) lest he suffer the same fate as his brothers, who were killed in combat (one's body was gruesomely ravaged by birds of prey), and implicitly lest his mother, like her husband, die of grief (ll. 479-86 [481-88]; cf. her extreme reactions to Perceval's brief absence from home, ll. 372-76 [374-78]). The death of the hero's mother as a result of his departure is doubtless the realization of one of her fears; Perceval's insanity in Arthurian service is the unanticipated form in which her concerns about the destructive nature of his vocation are fulfilled—indeed, the Hermit tells his nephew that only the power of his mother's dying words has stayed his imprisonment and death (ll. 6190-92 [6406-08]).

On the other hand, the Hermitage completes a pattern of actualization, throughout the Perceval history, of the predictive and imperative forecasts made by the hero's mother as he prepares to leave her—another manifestation of the power of her words. (In this, her words resemble Calogrenant's tale, except that their generative power operates at the level of history alone.) The comically successful and disastrous Carduel episode demonstrates both the obvious and the mysterious aspects of her predictions concerning Perceval's projected request for arms at Arthur's court (ll. 508-24 [510-26]). Since her son is totally inexperienced, she says, he cannot know what to do with arms when he receives them. What is initially incredible in her words is the illogical outcome they predict. They accurately forecast events at Carduel: in accord with Perceval's plans, "Vos irez a la cort le roi, / si li direz qu'armes vos doint" (ll. 510-11 [512-13]) (You will go to the king's court and you will tell him to give you arms); but in response to the inept boy's groundless demand, "De contredit n'i avra point, / qu'il les vos donra, bien le sai" (ll. 512-13 [514-15]) (There will be no argument about it, for he will give them to you, I know it well). Irony in these words resonates, precisely, with Keu's sarcasm, which, because Perceval misunderstands it, reinforces, in its turn, the process whereby the hero's destiny is accomplished. (The widow's insistence that the king will grant her son arms doubtless also reinforces Perceval's naïve conviction that he received the Vermilion Knight's arms from Arthur, when, in reality, Keu only pretends to speak for the king.)

The widow's imperative statements, which constitute her advice to Perceval (ll. 525-92 [527-94]) (what she calls "un san," l. 525 [527: "un sens"]), are fruitful in another way because they bear upon the ethical dimensions of chivalry—specifically, courtesy with respect to ladies (including the rudiments of *fin' amors*), association with noble men, and religious obligations. Both Perceval's consciousness of his mother's commands and the manner in which he comprehends them propel the action even after he decides to return to the Waste Forest (a compulsion also determined, although indirectly, by his mother) and Gornemant de Goorz substitutes his own *parole* for the widow's. The pattern of fulfillment of the widow's words, despite the overlay of Gornemant's advice, which, in all events, is not incompatible with hers, takes form first in the comic inversion of the intention of each piece of advice, then in the manifestation of each in harmony with her serious intent. Perceval is drawn to a magnificent tent because he thinks it is a church (ll. 653-64 [655-66], cf. ll. 565-70 [567-72]); he mistreats the lady inside in a bungling attempt at playing the courteous suitor (ll. 680-84 [682-86], 710-13 [712-15], cf. ll. 531-54 [533-56]); he addresses a charcoal burner as a nobleman (l. 837 in Roach's edition only) and finds ignoble men at Arthur's court (cf. ll. 555-64 [557-66]). Increasingly serious realization of the serious import of the widow's words, not without comic overtones at first, begins to occur in reverse order as Perceval passes beyond the Arthurian court and finds the truly noble Gornemant de Goorz (ll. 1398-1402 [1402-06]) and then Blancheflor at Biaurepaire. Reduplications occur subsequently in encounters with noble men (the Grail Castle and Carlion, where the court is enhanced by the presence of Gauvain) and ladies (the Weeping Maiden and again the Tent Maiden, then Blancheflor once more, symbolically present in Perceval's perception of her through the blood drops on the snow).

Obscured in the neat rounding out of episodes in the discrete Perceval section is the fact that only the question of religious obligation, materially the most important part of the widow's history-shaping discourse, never recurs, after its comic manifestation in Perceval's first perceptive mistake in the world outside the Waste Forest, as a factor in the hero's physical and moral development, much less as the major theme of an entire scene or episode. In this light, it is undoubtedly significant that, in the succession of episodes, the Grail Castle follows Gornemant de Goorz, where the hero encounters a truly noble man, and Biaurepaire, where he comes to love a lady in distress—that is to say, the Grail Castle occurs in the place of an episode where, in the reverse order of Perceval's comic misapprehensions of his mother's words, a serious transformation of her religious themes is anticipated. But a vacuum exists in the Perceval section precisely because nothing happens at the Grail Castle either to advance or to impede Perceval's heroic progress as defined in terms of success in Arthurian knighthood. To be sure, the Grail Castle is not a church (to recall Perceval's early misunderstanding about the tent), but if the hero had inquired about the Grail procession, he might, as the Hermit's explanation suggests later, have heard answers relating the Grail and/or its contents to the Eucharist. However, since Perceval remains silent, and the narrator characteristically does not comment on the nature of the procession, religion fails to be reintroduced into the texture of the discrete "first *vers*" and themes in the history revert to the first two points in the widow's discourse: the ethical aspects of inter-human relationships according to her chivalric code as reinterpreted by Perceval with reference to Gornemant's advice. The Hermitage episode completes the pattern. Perceval responds to the penitents' account of divine history relative to the sacraments with a kind of desperate fervor unlike the boyish curiosity in his reactions to his mother's almost identical explanations (compare ll. 6047-6104 [6255-6314] and ll. 565-92 [567-94]). Guided by his uncle, he comes to terms with the implications of those words in light of his own experience, which knows both joy and madness, success in the Arthurian kingdom and failure in the Grail kingdom. Finally, as if in response to his mother's wishes, he is introduced to participation in the sacraments for the first time in the narrator's account of his history.

Retrospectively, thematic and structural components of the Hermitage suggest a configuration of events in the discrete Perceval section that is simultaneously at odds with the sense of Arthurian context inherent in the pattern of the "first *vers*" and complementary to it. This configuration indicates both that achievement in Arthur's kingdom is insufficient preparation for triumph at the Grail Castle, even that restoration of the Grail kingdom is impossible because of heroic progress in Arthurian knighthood, and that excellence in ordinary chivalry is a necessary prerequisite to victory in the romance's ultimate test. The new episodic pattern recalls the construction of both sections of *Cligés*, where both heroes visit Britain as a foreign kingdom and return home, and especially that of the second part of *Yvain*, where adventures group around Laudine's castle, a center where Arthur does not hold court. The difference in the *Conte du Graal* is that identification of the localities suggesting orientation in a world outside Arthur's kingdom depends upon similarities relating episodes in the history conceptually, rather than upon periodic returns to the same place (Laudine's domain, Constantinople): the Hermitage is linked to the Waste Forest, the Grail Castle and the Weeping Maiden .

In the Hermitage episode the history explicitly summarizes, in the form of direct discourse, events occurring in the Waste Forest (e.g., Perceval's mother's faint) and at the Grail Castle (e.g., the procession), and, by reintroducing the problem of the hero's fault, it relates the earlier episodes causally. The Hermit's words deepen the association between the Waste Forest and the Grail Castle, and between these and the Hermitage, by elucidating the familial ties linking Perceval to the principal interlocutors—his mother in the Waste Forest, her brother at the Hermitage, their nephew at the Grail Castle, where their brother is hidden in an inner chamber. Implicitly, the Hermitage also recalls the Weeping Maiden episode because the Hermit reduplicates the role of Perceval's cousin as interpreter of his Grail experience, often to the point of repeating her words verbatim. Other similarities, such as the parallels between the Hermitage and the Waste Forest already noted, the fact that the Weeping Maiden's history of the Grail Castle and the widow's account of British history are mutually illuminative, and the knowledge displayed by Perceval's cousin both of the Waste Forest and the Grail, strengthen the associations still further. The Hermitage affords a perspective for regarding the construction of Perceval's adventures in terms of a departure from, then periodic visits to, a world inhabited by members of the hero's family who are of the "Grail nobility" and who have knowledge of realms of experience, history as well as the Grail mysteries, which the Arthurian court does not appear to comprehend. Without canceling it out, this view of events in Perceval's history drastically alters the sense of heroic achievement in orientation around Arthur's court as indicated in the joyful celebration at Carlion and, once the Hideous Damsel makes Perceval's failure known publicly, by the hero's conception of the Grail adventure as an "ordinary" Arthurian quest like the collective and the private journeys to see the wonders of Laudine's fountain.

From the point of view of the "Grail nobility," Perceval's advancement in the Arthurian kingdom constitutes a gradual falling away from a superior form of life—just as, according to Perceval's mother, the glorious age of Utherpendragon vanished, with disastrous results for society in general and for her family in particular, when his kingdom fell and Arthur inherited it in a time of devastating warfare. The sin that impedes Perceval's success at the Grail Castle is his abandonment of the superior values associated with his mother. The fault, as explained by his cousin and uncle, lies in his failure to return to his stricken mother after he saw her fall, at a time when he was subject to the overwhelming compulsion to leave the Waste Forest and to embrace the very knighthood from which she and her servants had tried to protect him (and themselves). Thus, the compulsion to abandon the Waste Forest is bound up in a problematic lack of charity. A kind of "original sin." But the effects of the sin are extended throughout the entirety of the discrete Perceval section and are manifest in the hero's gradual abandonment, both conscious and unwitting, of all things connected with the world of the Waste Forest as he acquires the characteristics of an accomplished courtly knight.

Perceval leaves home equipped in a manner hardly becoming a knight, with clothing (pants, a coarsely woven shirt, a leather jerkin), arms (a javelin), a horse, a mode of speaking and a way of behaving that invariably brand him as a Welsh innocent abroad in the world of courtly sophistication. The derogatory attitude of the Tent Maiden, Arthur and his courtiers, perhaps of Gornemant de Goorz, towards the interloper from Wales is defined by the knights who awaken Perceval to the existence of the new, Arthurian world:

> ... Galois sont tuit par nature
> plus fol que bestes an pasture.
> Cist [Perceval] est ausi come une beste.
> Fos est qui delez lui s'areste,
> s'a la muse ne vialt muser
> et le tans an folie user.
> (ll. 241-46 [243-48])

(... Welshmen are all by nature more foolish than beasts at pasture. This one [Perceval] is also like a brute. Anyone who tarries beside him is a fool, unless he wants to dawdle with trifles and waste time in foolishness.)

Commensurately with his acquisition of knightly prowess and Arthurian values, the hero loses first his javelin (in killing the Vermilion Knight to take his arms) and his horse (given to Yonez in exchange for the dead man's charger), then his rough clothing (for finery offered by Gornemant), his manner of speaking (when he agrees to substitute Gornemant's words for his mother's) and finally his mode of behavior (when, at Biaurepaire, he practices restraint instead of garrulousness, gradually displays manly skill instead of clumsiness, and begins to acquire the refined sentiments of the *fin amant*). From the point of view of the court at Carlion, the transformation signifies an achievement to be acknowledged in celebration.

In large measure, the knights' judgment is supported by the history, in that irony turns against Perceval because of his social and military ineptitude during the early and middle stages of his career and because of the destructive nature of Welsh innocence; this perspective is also maintained in the narrator's interpretation, which is partially consonant with Arthurian opinion. Yet the history also indicates that something essential for success at the Grail Castle—something ineffably quintessential, perhaps—is lost in the process. It is precisely this point that the narrator explicitly ignores in his direct commentary on the history, a point that emerges on the level of history alone (an achievement of the author despite the reticence of his narrator) and one perceived only dimly thanks to the new episodic configuration suggested by the Hermitage episode, which is the only major sign of the narrator's consciousness of this aspect of his matter.

The Weeping Maiden berates Perceval when, having failed at the Grail Castle, he articulates, for the first time in his life, his name, which he has never known before: Perceval the Welshman ("Percevax li Galois," l. 3561 [3575]). Because he has failed to restore the Grail kingdom, however, she changes, for her own purposes, his name to "Percevax li chetis" (l. 3568 [3582]). The *Conte du Graal* makes explicit the special significance of characters' names that is implicit elsewhere in Chrétien, for, in her seminal advice, Perceval's mother remarks that what a man is is indicated by his name (ll. 556-60 [558-62]). In castigating her cousin, the Weeping Maiden places particular emphasis on the hero's surname (the version of the widow's advice in Roach's text likewise underscores the significance of surnames, l. 562). The Weeping Maiden suggests that if Perceval had succeeded at the Grail Castle, he might be worthy of bearing his true name, of being known as the Welshman, but since he has condemned inhabitants of the Grail kingdom to renewed suffering, he must be called instead the Wretched or the Captive. In her view, to be Welsh is not to be wretched and not to be imprisoned.

As a "Welshman" in the Waste Forest, Perceval would have asked the Grail questions without hesitation. How can the lance bleed (cf. ll. 3192-93 [3204-05])? Why does the lance bleed (cf. ll. 3538-39 [3552-53], 4633-34 [4657-58], 6194-96 [6410-12])? Where does the Grail procession go (cf. ll. 3554-55 [3568-69])? Whom does the Grail serve (cf. ll. 4635-37 [4659-61], 6197-98 [6413-14])? Confronted by five shining knights in the Waste Forest (no less a dumbfounding marvel to an untutored country boy than the mysterious, magnificent procession ought to be for the victor at Biaurepaire), the young Perceval unleashes a barrage of similar questions. What are you (l. 173 [175])? What are you carrying (l. 189 [191])? What is this and *how does it serve you* (l. 212 [214])? But the same Gornemant de Goorz who advises him that it is unmanly to quote his mother (ll. 1673-82 [1675-84]) and substitutes his own for her words (ll. 1684-86 [1686-88]) also urges him not to be "trop parlanz ne trop noveliers" (l. 1648 [cf. 1650]) (too talkative or too gossipy). Garrulousness is uncourtly, and, according to a proverb that is ironic in light of Perceval's "pechié ... de ta mere" (ll. 3579-80 [3591-92]) (fault concerning your mother), "Qui trop parole pechié fet" (l. 1652 [cf. 1654]) (Who talks too much does wrong). Consequently, during the Grail procession the narrator notes that Perceval would have asked the right questions at the right time had he not been afraid, because of his mentor's advice, to appear discourteous (cf. ll. 3190-3200 [3202-12]), and the narrator *fears* that something may be wrong because he has heard it said that keeping quiet for too long a time can be just as bad as talking too much (ll. 3236-39 [3248-53]). (It is Perceval's decision apparently not to embarrass the Fisher King by waiting to ask a servant unobtrusively the next day, cf. ll. 3291-97 [3303-09], that is referred to in the Hideous Damsel's diatribe, ll. 4638-44 [4662-68]).

The problem for the hero is not just the paradoxical confrontation of two opposite truths supported by biblical authority, the one fresh in his mind, thanks to Gornemant, while he observes the Grail procession ("silentium est signum sapientiæ et loquacitas est signum stultitiæ"),[16] and the other, which the narrator and the Hideous Damsel say he ought to have followed, not introduced into the history (and into Perceval's consciousness) until much later at Carlion ("omnia tempus habent ... tempus tacendi et tempus loquendi").[17] If this were the case, the primary concern of Chrétien's history would be merely the difficulties in educating and in socializing a backwoodsman who lacks the grace to act appropriately in unfamiliar surroundings. This accords with judgments made by the Hideous Damsel, who translates the Grail adventure for a particular courtly audience at Carlion (a group that derides Welsh innocence), and expressed by the narrator, who translates for sophisticated audiences in general. But such an explanation clouds the truth as perceived by the "Grail nobility," for in the eyes of the Weeping Maiden and the Hermit, not the uncritical application of a particular rule of conduct, but Perceval's fault in abandoning his mother is the real cause of his silence—the ultimate cause of which acquisition of knowledge from Gornemant is but one of many effects, the cause to which the hero's every act of abandoning something Welsh (javelin, horse, clothing, words) points as a sign, as a consequence and as a fulfillment.

The *Conte du Graal* history is determined more pervasively by a pattern of fall and redemption than that of any other romance by Chrétien. Unlike *Erec et Enide, Lancelot* and *Yvain,* it is the biography of a boy who rises to manhood and, unlike *Cligés,* it overtly casts human growth against a background resonant with religious and quasi-religious, as well as historical, prototypes. This is true not only because of the unusually explicit religious language of the Prologue, where translation and modern narrative are viewed as possible after Christ's redemptive act and in terms of the history of mankind (where, therefore, Chrétien affects a convergence of poetics and theme), but also because of the exceptionally complex nature of Chrétien's own history. Both Perceval's mother and the penitent knights whom the hero meets on Good Friday evoke Christ's sacrifice in terms of man's fallen condition and subsequent liberation from imprisonment in hell:

> . . . si sofri angoisse de mort
> por les homes et por les fames,
> qu'an anfer aloient les ames
> quant eles partoient des cors,
> et il les an gita puis fors.
> (ll. 582-86 [584-88])

(. . . so he suffered agony of death for men and women whose souls had gone to hell when they left their bodies, and he then cast them out of there.)

> Hui [i.e., on Good Friday] fu cil an croiz estanduz
> qui trante deniers fu vanduz,
> cil qui de toz pechiez est monde.
> Por les pechiez de tot le monde,
> don toz li monz ert antechiez,
> devint il hom, bien le sachiez.
> . . . .
> que a tel jor por verité

> com hui est fu an la croiz mis
> et trest d'anfer toz ses amis.
> (ll. 6061-80 [6269-88])

(Today [on Good Friday] was he stretched out on a cross who was sold for thirty deniers, he who is pure from all sin. For the sins of the whole world, with which everyone was stained, he became man, know it well.... For on such a day, in truth, as it is today he was put on the cross and brought all his friends out of hell.)

Both the hero's mother and the penitents stress the continued commemoration and/or reenactment of the central historical events—the latter by the repeated *hui*, "today" (ll. 6061 [6269], 6079 [6287], cf. ll. 6056-58 [6265-66]), the former by her explicit references to the Eucharist (ll. 578-79 [580-81], 590-92 [592-94]). The pattern is reduplicated in the more recent history of Britain, in the fall of Utherpendragon's throne (ll. 437-47 [438-49]) and the apparently simultaneous disasters in the Grail kingdom (ll. 3498-3513 [3512-27], cf. ll. 6208 [6424], 6213 [6429]). Britain continues to suffer the consequences of the catastrophic fall of Utherpendragon, according to the widow, and her Waste Forest community is a refuge against a fallen world; warfare, sickness and exile continue in the Grail kingdom (ll. 3572-76 [3586-90], 4646-59 [4670-83]). Meanwhile, in the Grail kingdom, the Fisher King awaits a restorer, which might have been Perceval himself, had he only asked the questions in accord with his suppressed Welsh nature (ll. 3569-76 [3583-90], 4646-50 [4670-74]), just as other people in other places actually find redeemers in Perceval and Gauvain (Biaurepaire, the Tent Maiden and her lover, Tintaguel, the Roche del Canpguin). Within Chrétien's history, consciousness of profound meaning in the pattern is reserved for members of the "Grail nobility" and those under their influence (e.g., the penitents, but not Perceval, of course, until the Hermitage); the Arthurian kingdom conceives history (e.g., events since Carduel, the narratives of Clamadeus and the Orgueilleus de la Lande) in its own self-centered terms and ritually acknowledges "ordinary" achievements of the romance hero by offering him acceptance and celebration.

The pattern is, finally, implicated in the life of Chrétien's primary hero. Perceval's innocent state in the paradisiacal Waste Forest (a self-sufficient, isolated society associated with the fruitfulness of springtime; an orderly refuge against the outside world) recalls the innocence of human childhood in general and, in particular, of humanity's "childhood" in Eden. Perceval "falls" from that state of innocence into manhood by yielding to the compulsion to rebel against his mother and her values in response to a genetically determined call to knowledge about knighthood despite all efforts to keep him in ignorance. He abandons his mother and her values and enters the Arthurian world, the only world where he can experience growth and freedom, where he can realize fulfillment of his innate potential. Yet by leaving his mother and following his destiny, he also, paradoxically, commits a fault that prevents progress beyond a certain point and impedes reconciliation with a community, the Grail kingdom, from which he has sprung and whose spiritual ideals he is forced to confront from time to time.

Reconciliation with this community and restoration of it to a former position of peaceful preeminence constitute the hero's highest calling. Only members of the "Grail nobility" have knowledge of Perceval's experience in the Waste Forest and understand the nature of his fault in leaving it, for his "sin committed with respect to his mother" prevents him from entering into fruitful communication with the Fisher King as he fails in the first confrontation with the Grail community. Yet the results of that fault are also prerequisite to success because if the maturing man fails to speak, the untutored boy who would have asked questions instinctively would not have comprehended the significance of the act of communication. Moreover, the Fisher King's gift of a wonderful sword predestined for the hero (ll. 3155-57 [3167-69]) is a sign of the Grail community's approval of his introduction to knighthood: the new sword replaces, supersedes, the "Arthurian sword," but Perceval can never have won even it without first taking and using the Vermilion Knight's sword (see my n. 15). Following his initial failure, Perceval is led, despite it and in consequence of it, to increased self-knowledge (e.g., in learning his name) and further accomplishment in chivalry that is justly celebrated in the Arthurian world. At the same time, however, he forgets his experience at the Grail Castle, as first suggested by the Hideous Damsel, and he later forgets God.

The links between the pattern of fall and redemption and the Christian view of world history are explicitly put into context with religious doctrine in the Hermitage episode, which simultaneously brings into focus the configuration of episodes that opposes those associated with the "Grail nobility" to those centering on the Arthurian court. The view of human history as a story of fall and redemption is reimposed as the penitents recount and interpret the significant events on the very day when they are especially commemorated. Furthermore, the Hermit reveals that the Grail procession is associated, at least in an ancillary way, with the Eucharist, in that the Grail contains the Host, and that, therefore, to some extent events in the Grail Castle itself recall daily the central act of divine charity. Finally, Perceval finds means of freeing himself from the effects of his particular "original fault" in confession and Easter communion. Reconciliation with God, long forgotten by the hero, is simultaneous with reconciliation, in a sense, with his family, against one of whose members he committed the fault with far-reaching consequences and with another of whom he failed, as a result, to communicate. With his mother dead, the Hermitage, which resembles the Waste Forest, constitutes a form of "return" to his point of departure, but on a plane that, as reflected in Chrétien's history, may well be judged superior: not only has the man profited from the experience of Arthurian knighthood, but he also benefits from contact with the world of spiritual reality in ways denied him in the Waste Forest. In this respect, Perceval's history seems determined by the dynamics of the *felix culpa,* the "happy fault":[18] reconciliation of the old with the new in a sense that neither minimizes the seriousness of the act of rebellion nor negates amelioration in freedom.

Just as the narrator's Prologue is a revaluation of romance poetics with Christian justification of the dual structure of history and narration, so do the double configuration of the Perceval adventures and the emergence in Chrétien's history of explicitly religious values indicate a revaluation by the author of the significance of Arthurian matter. No longer does the narrator regard either the episodic pattern of *Erec et Enide,* which, with its variations in *Cligés* and *Lancelot,* suggests the ethical superiority of the Arthurian kingdom to kingdoms outside it, or that of *Yvain,* which opposes Laudine's domain to Arthur's realm, as structures that by themselves are sufficient for the portrayal of human experience. The limits of the old patterns are exposed in the history by ironization that, because of the earlier literary compositions recalled in the forms, borders on the parodic: the Gauvain adventures deprecate the noble hero imprisoned in Arthurian chivalry, while the early movements of the Perceval adventures testify to dangers in the rejection of the Arthurian kingdom. Rather, the new structure of the *Conte du Graal* simultaneously affirms the worth of both patterns in mutual tension. But, as the historical model in the Prologue demonstrates, one kingdom, whose values are, nevertheless, worthwhile and even essential, is ultimately superseded by and subsumed in the other, which possesses more complete knowledge of spiritual reality. Similarly, Chrétien's history ascribes to the "Grail nobility" a degree of religious consciousness, in language and perception, that is unprecedented in his career as a writer of romance. Perceval's heroic destiny is, in the end, that which Chrétien's earlier heroes signify only imperfectly—whether the history intends that he return to the Grail Castle in triumph or be denied the opportunity. But Chrétien's narrator is limited, by the nature of his courtly language, in his ability to translate that history. To a certain extent he is trapped into following his earlier romance structures, but he finally begins to withdraw as a voice commenting directly and to point indirectly to meanings in the history which he is scarcely able to articulate.

The Grail Procession and the Conte du Graal

In a narrative characterized by ambiguity and mystery, the most important events, which are in the Grail Castle episode, are the ones that remain the most mysterious. The Grail procession itself—the central event in the episode where the dish[19] named in the title as the major object of narration appears in context with a bleeding lance and dazzling light—seems fraught with significances which Chrétien's fragment barely hints at. In the history and in its reading, the pageant and the objects carried in it constitute a mystery in every sense of the word: a wondrous means of heroic transcendent redemption (of others and of oneself), but a puzzle for the hero whose function and meaning still lie hidden for the reader. The obvious attraction of the multiple mystery has caused some scholars to focus with such intensity on the Grail procession and the Grail Castle that the larger context of the fragment itself, in which the event is never reenacted, although occasionally referred to, is frequently distorted out of all proportion.[20] It is always tempting to say much more about the mystery than can be justified by Chrétien's words in the history or in its narration.

This is due, of course, in large measure to the strategy that Chrétien adopts for his narrator: his only interpretive judgments in the Grail Castle episode are directed at the young man watching the procession rather than at the procession itself or the other important witness, the Fisher King. The apparent inadequacies of this limited interpretation have already been suggested. In fact, Chrétien's narrator never claims to possess knowledge of any aspect of the Grail procession or of the castle where it takes place, let alone the mysteries, except as "pure" history partially translated without commentary. Richly detailed description does abound; for example, in recounting the procession the narrator emphasizes the beauty of the human figures, their concerted movements and the extraordinary material properties of the objects they carry: a drop of blood falling from the tip of a white lance onto the hand of the young man holding the weapon upright, ten-branched candelabra, light surrounding (or emanating from) a golden, jewel-encrusted grail and growing more intense as the grail passes, a silver carving platter from which sumptuous meats are served (ll. 3178-3230 [3191-3240], 3272-77 [3284-89]), the grail returning time after time "tot descovert" (l. 3289 [3301]) ("uncovered" or "in plain view") (ll. 3278-82 [3289-92], 3287-89 [3299-3301]). But such description, no matter how exquisite, is not, strictly speaking, interpretive; although it must necessarily be selective, the poem offers no basis for judging the quality of the narrator's choices. However, implications in the narrator's reticence about the Grail procession, even his denial of knowledge about the moral consequences of the hero's failure to ask questions, are borne out in the remainder of the fragment. Subsequent interpretive references to events at the Grail Castle are never made by the narrator, but in the history by characters in unmediated direct discourse.

In the narration the Grail Castle resembles episodes preceding it in that it is a seminal source of translation within the history itself. Perceval's visit at Carduel is rehearsed by members of the court immediately after his departure (II. 1204-96 [1208-1300]), retold by Arthur to Gauvain at Carlion (II. 4059-4120 [4077-4140]), and evoked again in detail at the encampment where the hero rejoins the court (e.g., II. 4522-54 [4546-78]). Meanwhile, Perceval recalls specific events when he tells Gornemant de Goorz that Arthur has "made" him a knight (II. 1365-66 [1369-70]) and when he entrusts first Anguinguerron (II. 2309-21 [2313-23]), then Clamadeus (II. 2690-97 [2692-99]) with messages for the king. Clamadeus, in his turn, repeats the events of Carduel (known to him at second hand) to the court at Disnadaron as he begins a new translation, his account of his defeat at Biaurepaire (II. 2835-47 [2837-49], 2852-61 [2854-63]); his story inspires additional references to Carduel in light of the hero's proven successes (II. 2862-74 [2864-76]). Later the Orgueilleus de la Lande conveys to Arthur Perceval's account of the Smiling Maiden's humiliation (II. 3932-62 [3950-80]) in conjunction with his own story (II. 4028-53 [4046-71]), and precipitates the reunion of Perceval with the court. The words of Perceval's mother, the Tent Maiden episode and Biaurepaire are likewise translated and retranslated with Carduel or independently of it —even by the author himself, it might well be argued, in inverted, ironic transformation in the Gauvain section.

Similarly, the central events at the Grail Castle are subsequently translated in three versions manifesting differing degrees of insight: (1) by the Weeping Maiden in conversation with Perceval (II. 3469-3676 [3483-3686]) —her questions prompt him to recall the procession in detail as event, then she supplies limited interpretive matter relating to the Fisher King's affliction, his very identity and the consequences of Perceval's failure to speak; (2) by the Hideous Damsel (II. 4621-59 [4646-83]), who offers a translation suitable for her Arthurian audience; (3) in the Hermitage episode, by Perceval, who remembers not his experience as illuminated by the Weeping Maiden, but only the words of the Hideous Damsel, and by the Hermit, who reintroduces the Weeping Maiden's commentary, then adds explanatory details of his own.

Functional differences distinguishing the Grail Castle from preceding episodes, however, highlight its uniqueness. In large measure, the Grail

Castle episode is "pure" history. By contrast, the others are themselves richly detailed translations. For example, Chrétien's narrator recounts the Tent Maiden's plight in a perspective sympathetic with her courtliness (Perceval is brutish, she is a lady who remains faithful to her lover), and he proffers plausible explanations in direct commentary for the participants' behavior, including that of the pathologically jealous Orgueilleus de la Lande (l. 813 [815]). At Carduel the narrator deftly shifts point of view from that of the courtiers, with whom he shares condemnation of the hero's uncouth Welsh manners, to that of Perceval and to that of objective observer, with emerging irony that allows for judgment against the court for ignoble behavior. In limiting his evaluations in the Grail Castle episode to Perceval, however, not only does the narrator shrink from an ethical stance with respect to values associated with the Grail kingdom, but he also, as already suggested, leaves himself subject to tests of his own abilities as translator.

It is also significant that the episodes prior to the Grail Castle have a dual function in the romance. Subsequent accounts, within the history, of the Tent Maiden, Carduel and Biaurepaire episodes work in concert to bring about the court's climactic reunion with Perceval and his affirmation as an example of Arthurian chivalry. But each episode is also pivotal in and of itself because it represents an aspect of Perceval's heroic development. When the hero sees a marvelous tent, he puts his mother's words into practice for the first time, and he simultaneously sets into motion the processes whereby he will eventually achieve expiation, vengeance and recognition; at Carduel he wins arms, at Biaurepaire he saves a castle with God's help and finds a lady. By contrast, nothing of the sort happens at the Grail Castle. Indeed, the hero's failure is *lack* of action—which, in any case, should not have been physical at all, but intellectual (to ask questions and to comprehend answers). As a result of his failure to act, nothing changes whatsoever. The hero continues to advance conventionally towards Arthurian celebration; meanwhile, the Grail kingdom remains unrestored and subject to continued suffering.

The unique features suggest, in fact, that the *sole* function of the Grail Castle episode (at least as it figures in Chrétien's fragment) is virtually to serve as pure history to be translated within the history. Ironically, this new assertion also demonstrates the limitations of Chrétien's narrator because he fails to accomplish what his characters achieve in producing more informative translations than his and because his own reticence about the Grail mysteries resembles in some ways that of the hero whom he observes and judges.

As the narrator presents it, the Grail procession is a two-part pageant (ll. 3178 ff. [3190 ff.]). The "act" in which the Grail appears is a procession for the service of food at a rich banquet. The Grail, as material object in the procession, does not have special meaning because of what it is—something quite ordinary at a banquet, a serving dish, even if, in this instance, it is spectacular in its own right. In his first reference to it outside the Prologue, where it is singled out specially as the object of narration (l. 66 [ibid.]), the narrator introduces it as "un graal" (l. 3208 [3220]). Even Perceval knows what *a* grail is. When the Weeping Maiden asks him if he saw *the* grail—that is, the grail belonging at a certain castle—he immediately replies in the affirmative (ll. 3542-43 [3556-57]). In the history this grail becomes *the* Grail, in fact, only because it figures prominently in a *particular* banquet procession, where candelabra and a silver platter are also perfectly fitting. Moreover, its distinctive attributes, aside from the accidental features of its manufacture (gold, jewels), result from what it contains: instead of ordinary food, a Host. For this reason, it is holy (l. 6209 [6425]). However, although, as suggested already, the episodic structure as determined by the words of Perceval's mother indicates that the hero ought to encounter the world of religion here, it does not appear that the *immediate* function of the Grail is to inspire justification of it as a serving piece in Eucharistic celebrations. Rather, the Grail is a conveyer of meaning: it exists to direct attention to realities beyond itself. To what it conveys literally (the Host), to be sure, but more immediately to the place where it is taken. Rather than serving the Fisher King and his guest, as one might expect in an ordinary banquet procession, the maiden passes them by and carries the Grail elsewhere.

Accordingly, in light of the Weeping Maiden's remarks, the first Grail question is not "What is it?" or even "Whom does it serve?" but "Where are the Grail bearer and her companions going?": "Demandastes vos a la gent / quel part il aloient ensi?" (ll. 3554-55 [3568-69]). It is clear from the text that Perceval knows the answer. His cousin exposes his momentary total recall of the procession as pageant; he tells her that the Grail maiden went from one chamber into another and passed in front of him (ll. 3545-46 [3560; l. 3546 not in Roach]), which corresponds factually with the narrator's account (cf. ll. 3228-30 [3240-42]). It is equally clear, however, that mere knowledge of the existence of the "other chamber," which the hero comprehends only from the point of view of one sitting in the great hall outside it, is insufficient. The answer to the Weeping Maiden's version begs for more penetrating inquiry; hence the Hideous Damsel's translation: "What rich man is served with the Grail?" (l. 4637 [4661, which reads "nobleman," not "rich man"]), which Perceval transforms and retains in his confession to his uncle as "Who is served with the Grail?" ("cui l'an an sert," l. 4712 [4736], cf. ll. 6163-64 [6379-80]). (The latter is also the narrator's version, l. 3233 [3245].) Just as Perceval already knows what his cousin's question asks for, so the Hermit answers the Hideous Damsel's question, identifying the man as his and Perceval's mother's brother (scholars often refer to him as the Grail King) and revealing the extraordinary meal served by the Grail. Significantly, however, the Hermit abruptly changes the subject when he brings up the "other chamber" where the man has lived for fifteen years sustained by the Host alone:

> ... que hors de la chanbre n'issi
> ou le graal veïs antrer.
> Or te voel anjoindre et doner
> penitance de ce pechié [the cause of Perceval's silence].
> (II. 6214-17 [6430-33])

(... for he did not leave the chamber where you saw the Grail enter. Now I want to impose on you penance for this sin.)

The author maintains the mystery in his history: Perceval still knows nothing about the "other chamber" itself.

In appearance the Grail procession proper (candelabra, platter, Grail) is distinguished from an ordinary banquet procession only by the intense light that is, doubtless, a sign of the Grail's miraculous contents. However, the procession is preceded by an astonishing "first act": the passage of a bleeding lance. In a romance by Chrétien de Troyes a lance is certainly an even more banal object than a grail. Yet, unlike the Grail, this lance is made extraordinary by a special property as well as by its presence in the great hall. In this instance, the narrator's very vagueness with respect to the question-provoking events illuminates the general effects of the Bleeding Lance's passage: "si s'est [Percevax] de demander tenus / *comant cele chose avenoit*" (II. 3192-93 [3204-05], my emphasis) (so he [Perceval] refrained from asking *how that thing was happening*). "How can it happen that a lance bleeds?" It is the Weeping Maiden who first specifies the Lance question as "Why does it [i.e., a particular lance] bleed?" (II. 3538-39 [3552-53], cf. II. 4633-34 [4657-58], 4715 [4739]). Like the various Grail questions, what is crucial in the Lance questions is that they direct inquiry beyond the extraordinary object itself to its incongruous attributes and ultimately to the event that has caused it to bleed.

The Gauvain history later reveals that the Bleeding Lance will destroy Arthur's kingdom of Logres (II. 5959-65 [6162-71]) and hints that it may belong to the king of Escavalon: Gauvain is charged to seek the lance and *return* it to him. It is perhaps pertinent that Perceval's eldest brother was sent to serve not Arthur, but the king of Escavalon—the present king's father?—and was killed returning to the Waste Forest (II. 461-78 [463-80]). The history of the Lance given by the wise vavasor in Escavalon contains the only direct evidence of actual enmity between the Grail kingdom and Arthur's kingdom; the implicit links between Escavalon and the Grail kingdom are all the more significant in light of the fact that Gauvain is accused of murdering the father of the present king of Escavalon (cf. l. 5797 [5863]).

Perceval ought to have asked questions in order both to heal his interlocutor, the Fisher King, who suffers from a wound that is suggestive of sexual mutilation (ll. 3495-3501 [3509-15]), and to restore him to a peaceful kingdom, thereby accomplishing the highest achievement possible in this history. But Chrétien's *Conte du Graal* is not a question-unspelling fairytale. If it were, then the ignorant boy in the Waste Forest, not a knight for whom a marvelous sword is predestined, would suffice for the triumph. The point of the Grail and Lance questions in their various versions is that questions lead to questions and, ultimately, to fruitful, revelatory discourse with another human being—communication with the Fisher King. More importantly, the desired act of communication with reference to the phenomena at the Grail Castle would have involved both men in significant acts of translation in relating a grail to the Grail, a lance to the Bleeding Lance, an ordinary banquet in a great hall to the Eucharistic feast in an inner chamber, a two-act pageant to the threatened destruction of Arthur's kingdom, Perceval's family to the "Grail nobility." History and the narration of history.

If these and other possible associations remain unilluminated in Chrétien's poem, it is because, at a certain moment in the history, the hero fails to set into operation the processes of translation and communication. It is also because Chrétien's narrator, conscious of the limitations of his language and of convention, fails to complete his own translation despite his poetic mission and, more significantly, in realization of the restrictions which it imposes with respect to his artistic endeavor and perfectability. Subsequent translations of the Grail Castle episode within the history reveal, in fact, its true centrality in the poem: poetics, theme and structure converge to suggest the extent to which Chrétien's narrator is prefigured by his own hero. Both are silent when confronted by the Grail mysteries, both lack experience in Christian adulthood (in differing degrees, to be sure) sufficient to the task of communicating about them. But this also indicates something about the audience for which the narrative is immediately destined. Thus, the translating voice within the history that resembles most closely the narrator's is that of the Hideous Damsel, rather than of members of the "Grail nobility," for she limits her view to a certain courtly perspective, and her language is incapable of illuminating the essence of the Grail mysteries. Finally, the Grail mysteries remain unelucidated because of circumstances that forced Chrétien de Troyes to interrupt the composition of his history and his narrator to end his act of translation. Perhaps the interruption is not unintentional (and, in this case, the example of *Lancelot* may be illustrative). The *Conte du Graal* is the (incomplete) translation of a history that embodies (incomplete) translation and is about (incomplete) translation. What remains of it is the most beguiling literary mystery of the French Middle Ages.

Alfred Foulet

Appendix I

On Editing Chrétien's *Lancelot*

Appendix I comprises four sections:
1. A presentation of the projected Foulet-Freeman edition of Chrétien's *Lancelot*
2. A list of its rejected readings
3. The text of about 250 corrected lines
4. A list of transcriptional errors in the Roques C.F.M.A. text

1. The Foulet-Freeman edition

Michelle A. Freeman and I are at work on a new edition of Chrétien's *Lancelot*. Our goal is a text that will come significantly closer to what the poet actually wrote than the flawed version of the *Chevalier de la Charrette* encountered in Mario Roques's edition, the one most scholars quote from nowadays.

So far *Lancelot* has been edited by P. Tarbé (Paris, 1849) (base: B.N. fr. 12560), W.J. Jonckbloet (The Hague, 1850) (base: B.N. fr. 794), Wendelin Foerster (Halle, 1889) (base: B.N. fr. 794—to the extent one can speak of a basic manuscript for Foerster's eclectic text), and Mario Roques (Paris, 1958) (base: B.N. fr. 794).

Like his predecessor Jonckbloet, Roques hewed as close as possible to his chosen base, B.N. fr. 794, unquestionably the best manuscript among those still extant. Roques has introduced no more than some sixty corrections in the manuscript's 7112 lines, roughly one per every 120 lines. A conservatism so extreme reduces his text almost to the level of a diplomatic edition, thereby, I claim, doing Chrétien a grievous disservice.

The Foulet-Freeman edition now in preparation, like those procured by Jonckbloet and Roques, is based on the Guiot manuscript (B.N. fr. 794);

but after incorporating the textual corrections introduced by Roques or proposed by Jean Frappier, we have been led to add about 260 more, which we have borrowed in nearly every case from Foerster.

To achieve the establishment of an acceptable Chrétien text, one worthy of his reputation as an outstanding versifier and narrator, we committed ourselves to the following principles:

(a). Ascribe to Chrétien an earnest desire to make sense. When the late Jean Frappier decided to translate the Guiot-Roques text into modern French, he found himself compelled, in the interest of a coherent and logical narrative, to depart over sixty times from his exemplar by resorting to readings taken from Foerster's edition; see Frappier's *Le Chevalier de la Charrette,* 2nd. ed. (Paris, 1967), pp. 19-25.

(b). Ascribe to Chrétien a distaste for imperfect rhymes (such as assonances or violations of the two-case declension).

(c). Ascribe to Chrétien a strong reluctance to have the same word appear twice as rhyme-word in the same distich.

(d). Ascribe to Chrétien a predilection for rich rhymes.

(e). Ascribe to Chrétien a sporadic indulgence in *annominatio*-linked rhyme-words spread over two or more distichs.

(f). Ascribe to Chrétien (and his continuator Godefroi de Leigni) the authorship of all 7134 lines of the Foerster edition, versus Roques's 7112.

Our text, then, greatly resembles Foerster's so far as number of lines, attention paid to narrative coherence, observation of the rules of Old French grammar and prosody, and cultivation of the rich rhyme. On the other hand, we have retained Guiot's graphies, making no attempt à la Foerster to reach back to Chrétien's presumed spelling (after all, Guiot was also a Champenois and followed Chrétien by only forty to fifty years). Also, we did not select tenses and moods of verbs to accommodate our personal notion of the correct syntax of a given sentence or passage, or prefer one synonym to another because it pleased us more. In other words, we aim at a critical edition, not like Foerster at a critical text. With Foerster, the reader is ever uncertain whether a given spelling has the backing of any manuscript. Whereas the Foerster text has very little documentary value, our own faithfully reflects Guiot for some 6724 lines out of 7112.

Examples of our editing, collated in each case with the Roques text and followed by a few comments of mine, will help assess the judiciousness of our departures from the basic manuscript:

End of Prologue and beginning of narrative (ll. 27-35, Roques 27-33)

... et il s'antremet	... et il s'antremet
De panser, si que rien n'i met	de panser, que gueres n'i met
Fors sa painne et s'antancion.	fors sa painne et s'antancïon.
Des or comance sa raison.	
A un jor d'une Acenssion	Et dit qu'a une Acenssïon
Fu venuz de vers Carlion	
Li rois Artus et tenu ot	li rois Artus cort tenue ot,
Cort molt riche a Camaalot,	riche et bele tant con lui plot,
Si riche com au jor estut.	si riche com a roi estut.

The Guiot version lacks two lines given by the other manuscripts (*A*: Chantilly 472; *E*: Escorial M iii 21; *G*: Princeton, Garrett 125; *T*: B.N. fr. 12560—except that *A* does not include ll. 1-30). It is open to criticism on two counts: it fails to mark a clear separation between prologue and narrative, and it does not tell us where Arthur is holding court. Let us turn to Chrétien's other romances. In *Erec, Cligés* and *Perceval* prologue and narrative remain distinct (*Yvain* has no prologue); when Arthur first appears, he is to be found at Caradigan (*Erec*, l. 28), at Winchester (*Cligés*, l. 287) and at Carduel (*Yvain*, l. 7; *Perceval*, ll. 336, 387). These two facts seemingly prove *AEGT*'s superiority over *C* in this passage. If it be objected that a group of four successive lines rhyme in -*on*, one may answer that even if such "quatrains" are most unusual in Chrétien's romances, they nevertheless do occur, e.g., *Lancelot*, ll. 3721-24 (Roques 3703-06), which rhyme in -*et*.

Lancelot faces two murderous opponents (ll. 1138-46, Roques 1126-34)

Maintenant jusqu'a l'uis s'aproche	Maintenant jusqu'a l'uis s'aproche,
Et bote anz le col et la teste	et bote anz le col et la teste
Et esgarde amont vers le feste:	et garde a mont par la fenestre:
Si voit deus espees venir;	si voit les espees venir,
Arriers se tret et retenir	adonc se prist a retenir.
Li chevalier lor cos ne porent.	Li chevalier lor cos ne porent
De tal aïr meüz les orent	detenir, qu'esmeüz les orent:
Qu'an terre les espees fierent	an terre les espees fierent
Si qu'anbedeus les peçoierent.	si qu'anbedeus les peçoierent.

The assonance *teste:fenestre* is quite clearly due to Guiot. When Chrétien uses *fenestre* at the end of a line, he rhymes it with *estre* or *senestre* (Roques 3141-42, 559-60). The Guiot version of the above-quoted passage, quite apart from a faulty distich, limps along most awkwardly. What is this *fenestre* which allows Lancelot to peer inside a bedroom, when its door has already been mentioned as open (Roques 1062-67)? When Guiot states that Lancelot *se prist a retenir*, he seems to mean something like "he begins to stop dead in his tracks," which hardly qualifies as the equivalent of *arriers se tret*. The verb *detenir* comes too soon after *retenir*: read aloud, *Li chevalier lor cos ne porent / detenir* becomes an unexpected alexandrine coupled in lopsided fashion with octosyllabic *adonc se prist a retenir*, a prosodic blunder few of us should want to ascribe to Chrétien. Finally, *de tel aïr*, "with such fury," words which accentuate the dynamism of the two descending swords, are nowhere present in MS C. In fairness to scribe Guiot let us listen to Roques (p. 222, note to his l. 1128): "Comment Lancelot serait-il amené à tourner ses regards vers le faîte de la salle pour voir venir les épées qui doivent être à hauteur d'homme? Etant donné que Lancelot s'est rapproché de la porte et qu'il y a passé seulement sa tête et son cou, il semble naturel de comprendre *fenestre* comme désignant non pas une ouverture dans la muraille, mais une partie mobile et non fermée de la porte, telle qu'un judas, ou la partie haute d'une porte coupée en hauteur par le milieu." The Roques interpretation of the danger faced by Lancelot arises from a misunderstanding of what his two opponents have in mind. Looking upwards (*amont* or *a mont*), Lancelot sees two swords raised high, ready to cleave him asunder in their mighty downward impact; they are not to be thrust at him in a piercing assault. It is *taille* and not *estoc*! Note also *EGTV*'s *deus espees*, which is preferable to *CA*'s indefinite *les espees* (*V*: Vatican, Regina 1725).

The Sword Bridge (ll. 3058-61, Roques 3044-47)

Malveisemant est fez et joinz	Malveisemant est fez et joinz
Cist ponz, et mal fu charpantez.	cist ponz, et mal fu charpantez.
Se a tans ne vos repantez,	S'a tant ne vos an retornez,
Au repantir vanroiz a tart.	au repantir vanroiz a tart.

Lancelot is being warned by his two companions not to cross a most perilous bridge. Guiot has botched the passage in several ways. He has replaced *repantez* with *retornez*, thereby eliminating a word which provided a rich rhyme for *charpantez* and a striking contrast between borrowings from two opposite vocabularies (*repantez*, a spiritual-emotional term, versus *charpantez*, a technical-material term), and he has likewise destroyed the chiasmic structure *a tans—repantez—repantir—a tart*.

Meleagant's angry outburst (ll. 3238-48, Roques 3224-32)

Et dit: "Joinz piez et jointes mains,	Et dit: "Joinz piez et jointes mains,
Volez espoir que je devaigne	volez espoir que je devaigne
Ses hom et de lui terre taigne?	ses hom et de lui terre taigne?
Si m'aïst Dex, ainz devandroie	Si m'aïst Dex, ainz devandroie
Ses hom que je ne li randroie	ses hom que je ne li randroie.
La reïne! Dex m'an desfande	
Qu'en tel guise je la li rande!	
Ja certes n'iert par moi randue	Ja certes n'iert par moi randue,
Mes contredite et desfandue	mes contredite et desfandue
Vers toz ces qui si fol seront	vers toz ces qui si fol seront
Que venir querre l'oseront."	que venir querre l'oseront."

Lines 3243-44, missing from Guiot and the Vatican manuscript, have two things to be said in their favor. They extend the *annominatio*-interlocking of distichs from two (*randroie—randue*) to three (*randroie—rande —randue*), and they add fire to Meleagant's rage. It is worth noting that at no point in this passage does Roques resort to an exclamation mark.

Lancelot's attempted suicide (ll. 4313-20, Roques 4295-4302)

Quant a terre cheü le voient	Quant a terre cheü le voient
Cil qui avoec lui chevalchoient,	cil qui avoec lui chevalchoient,
Si cuident que pasmez se soit,	si cuident que pasmez se soit,
Que nus del laz ne s'aparçoit	que nus del laz ne s'aparçoit
Qu'antor son col avoit lacié.	qu'antor son col avoit lacié.
Tot maintenant l'ont anbracié,	Tot maintenant l'ont redrecié,
Sel relievent antre lor braz,	sel relievent antre lor braz,
Et si ont lors trové le laz.	et si ont lors trové le laz.

By replacing *anbracié* with *redrecié*, Guiot has obliterated the chiasmus *lacié-anbracié-braz-laz*, and reduced the richness of the rhyme in 4317-18.

Meleagant's seneschal scolds his wife (ll. 6082-92, Roques 6062-72)

Et la dame qui li avoit	Et la dame qui li avoit
Ses armes vermoilles bailliees,	ses armes vermoilles bailliees,

Beles et bien apareilliees,	bien et beles apareilliees,
Et son hernois et son cheval,	et son hernois et son cheval,
Le voir an dist au seneschal,	le voir an dist au seneschal,
Comant ele l'ot anvoié	comant ele l'ot anvoié
La ou en avoit tornoié,	la ou en avoit tornoié,
A l'ahatine de Noauz.	a l'ahatine de Noauz.
"Ne poïssiez faire noauz,	"Dame, voir, fet li seneschauz,
Dame, voir, fet li seneschaus;	ne poïssiez faire noaus;
Molt m'an vanra, ce cuit, granz maus.	molt m'an vanra, ce cuit, granz maus.

By displacing l. 6090 (Roques 6071) and altering the spelling of *seneschaus* and *noauz*, Guiot derhymed two distichs, the first (*Noauz:noauz*) rhyming in *-auz* and the second (*seneschaus:maus*) in *-aus*: rhyme has yielded to assonance.

I have limited to six the examples of Guiot's indifference to the finer points of Chrétien's versification, but many more could have been adduced. The need for new critical editions of Chrétien's romances, editions which would attempt to approximate what he must have written, has been forcefully advocated in recent years. Among the most persuasive of these advocates one should list Jean Frappier ("Remarques sur le texte du *Chevalier de la Charrette,*" in *Mélanges offerts à Charles Rostaing* [Liège, 1974], I, 317-31), T.B.W. Reid ("Chrétien de Troyes and the Scribe Guiot," *Medium Aevum*, 45 [1976], 1-19) and Tony Hunt ("Chrestien de Troyes: The Textual Problems," *French Studies*, 33 [1979], 257-71).[1]

2. *The Rejected Readings*

In addition to the rejected readings of the basic manuscript (B.N. fr. 794), I have listed all lines it has omitted, repeated or transposed; (*sic*) indicates that Guiot has twice used the same rhyme-word within the same couplet.

Concordance with the Roques Edition

1-29 = 1-29, 31 = 30	2437-3242: deduct 14
33-362: deduct 2	3245-3716: deduct 16
365-756: deduct 4	3719-4780: deduct 18
763-1082: deduct 10	4783-6690: deduct 20
1085-2434: deduct 12	6693-7134: deduct 22

17 pailes — 28 De p. q. gueres — 30 *omitted* — 31 Et dit qu'a u. A. — 32 *omitted* — 33 cort tenue ot — 34 R. et bele tant con lui plot — 35 c. a roi e. — 40 aus — 60 avoir — 71 des — 79 Q. s. an prison — 89 boenemant — 111 demorance — 112 porloignance — 113 f. il — 114 setier — 119 f. il — 136 dire *repeated* — 178 La reïne q. je voi ci — 211 Ha rois — 212 ne l'otroiesiez — 213 Que Kex me menast un seul pas — 218 q. l'oïrent — 235 isnelemant — 275 Apantoisant — 289 baillessiez — 292 b. nest — 295 monta tantost — 302 v. armez — 330 A ces q. m. et larron sont (*sic*) — 338 S'a. t. enors p. — 344 l'ancontreras — 363-64 *omitted* — 372 n' *omitted* — 386 P. li d. nains — 398 voldras (*sic*) — 408 nel c. — 426 q. ert — 427 Qui delez — 429 Et d'autre part — 463 mangié — 465 En une s. — 477 M. en cest lit q. e. deça — 479 a voz cors — 480 r. lors — 496 Ne ge ne l'ai pas f. p. — 510 Se c. sor — 569 Et q. il ne — 581 la m. — 582 Qu'il a en la c. e. — 615 *repeated* — 638 toz — 647 servitune — 690 deus *omitted* — 757-62 *omitted* — 802 me feristes — 803 Se ge au f. u. d. m. — 837 Se — 841 verras — 869 s'antrevient — 883 T. set — 970 tristesce — 971 orguel et p. — 976 voloir — 980 hauz murs — 982 que e. atandoit

1038 Car lavez s'alez asseoir — 1039 M. v. et cil s'asiet — 1040 Et c. lez l. cui molt siet — 1083-84 *omitted* — 1097 mie talentos — 1098 Ne tant ne quant n'an ert jalos — 1140 Et garde a. par la fenestre — 1141 Si v. les e. v. — 1142 Adonc se prist a r. — 1144 Detenir qu'esmeüz l. o. — 1145 An t. — 1147 Q.e. furent peçoiees — 1150 Puis saut entra'x — 1166 porra la p. — 1198 tuit cil de laienz — 1205 Et — 1230 convert — 1237 Qu'aillors a mis del tot s'antante — 1238 M. ne p. mie n'a. — 1295 si r. — 1310 Et conduire me devïez — 1358 Que il voient u. f. — 1371 Se — 1376 de *omitted* (*-1*) — 1426 les chevox — 1479 liez — 1480 soing — 1498 Si — 1507 Et que feroie ge — 1526 vos (*sic*) — 1547 *repeated* — 1556 Les granz galoz — 1558 Qu'il ne c. mie g. — 1559 boens eürez — 1574 tres bien — 1575 Cele ore a — 1601 an eise (*-1*) — 1673 .xxiij. — 1742 r. itant — 1750 Je t'acreant — 1755 Honte feroie — 1762 angingnier — 1766 meüst — 1805 conuis — 1810 Ce qu'il — 1824 Et — 1833 s. siudra — 1851 murs — 1863 Que par dedanz ces murs avoit (*sic*) — 1867 l'en mainne — 1868 El cemetire a. le mainne (*sic*) — 1869 A. l. tres p. b. t. — 1876 lors les nons — 1884 et s. e. de l'uevre — 1885 S. t. les a. plus b. — 1891 Dou — 1900 B. e. dedanz et defors p. — 1916 ne clers ne g. h. — 1917 Des l'ore qu'il i est antrez — 1940 Dom — 1946 delivrera — 1984 secorre — 1985 secorra

2052 lëaumant — 2086 dongier — 2198 Qui m. amoit la c. — 2224 C. q. l'esgarde — 2238 p. desoz — 2282 a e. tel c. — 2339 T. que il v. a l'i. — 2341 qu'il furent f. — 2342 Lor l. a. les c. — 2373 defors — 2405 granz — 2412 Qu'il r. et f. et si d. — 2413 E. et lances et h. — 2423 au fil — 2435-36 *omitted* — 2454 pristrent — 2551 & 2564 deus — 2567 oste — 2569 li miaudres — 2572 C. l. ch. alumer — 2611 montez — 2633 chevalier — 2649

Ou ce non — 2656 Cui soit la honte ne li diax — 2692, 2693 *transposed* — 2696 a bandon (*sic*) — 2709 jusque — 2731 a la — 2743 et *is lacking* — 2788 je cuit m. — 2789 cest — 2812 besoig — 2827 E. feras a. et bien — 2828 rien — 2867 Merci donc ne l'avra il donques — 2874 baast — 2877 le vialt (*sic*) — 2924 Et cil se haste ne puet plus — 2945 haoie — 2963 asseoir — 2975 Et au moins autrui p. s. — 2978 Dex vos en oie! — 2980 et l'ot abessiee — 2985 Boen m. avrïez — 2987 v. le demandesiez — 2993 bien v. e. m.

3030 betee — 3044 Si ne sanble il pas qui la voit — 3045 puisse — 3054 Que il t. tuit de p. — 3060 S'a tant ne v. an retornez — 3073 voidier — 3111 desire et s. m. — 3122 el p. — 3124 A la g. d. c'on li fist — 3142 Si cuida estre d. — 3143 Mes — 3188 A c. dedanz soi r. — 3190 suens (*sic*) — 3234 D. le c. — 3243-44 *omitted* — 3253 Ce sez tu bien que hontes iert — 3254 Au chevalier s'il ne conquiert — 3264 (*repeats 3252*) Je te lo et pri qu'an pes soies — 3265 Et — 3289, 3290 *transposed* — 3293 Si prodon — 3301 nel vos consantiromes — 3310 prodon — 3332 garnir — 3335 plaiez — 3372 f. sener — 3406 M. je g. trop le t. ici — 3448 E. est venuz p. p. — 3497 u. hom ancïens — 3524 Se — 3558 De braz de janbes et de piez — 3616 varengle — 3691 s'a. — 3708 Lancelot — 3717-18 *omitted* — 3726 Se — 3736 chanceler — 3801 la nostre — 3810 Se — 3854 *first* tu *repeated* — 3899 que semont l'avra — 3905 Artus — 3931 g. feste — 3948 Quex — 3979 m. belemant

4000 Lancelot — 4044 Rien — 4059, 4060 *transposed* — 4076 *repeated* — 4133 Et de ce ne s. pas irié — 4135 Se — 4175 vait — 4176 A la r. fu retrait — 4205 Qui — 4210 L'a — 4225 Se — 4250 Don ne me doit ma vie n. — 4293 m'ocirrai — 4294 (*repeats 4288*) Comant n'autremant n'en porrai — 4318 redrecié — 4323 *repeated* — 4336 Se — 4342 P. f. le lessas — 4358 acheson — 4375 Riens — 4389 Nes sor la charrete — 4393 conuist — 4401 m'anertume — 4430 Se — 4461 pristrent — 4483 a lor plaisir (*sic*) — 4536 Et — 4588 Que conpaignie n'i trova — 4604 l'a salüee — 4637 Que an . . . couchiee — 4659 La p. ongle s'an crena — 4662 Et — 4668 Kex — 4717 de s. sanc — 4732 qu'an an — 4733 Nus — 4770 Kex — 4781-82 *omitted* — 4845 & 4853 Kex — 4874 Artus — 4897 Li d. li v. m. — 4905 Que — 4911 m'amez — 4928 Nus chevaliers — 4941 l'osent — 4975 Quex — 4977 M. l. armes d. — 4978 L. chevax amener c. — 4979 L'an l. amainne armé se sont (*sic*) — 4987 et li s.

5029 lor *repeated* — 5052 hontes — 5092 Lancelot — 5114 Ne quele part — 5124 Si bien que de rien ne se tordent — 5150 Rot son c. d. et sa d. — 5163 Et il repondirent — 5164 Lanceloz del Lac font se il — 5167 Et avoec nos autres trestoz — 5172 qu'il a mesfet — 5198 Des ore se — 5200 *transposed after 5202* — 5201 s'aprocherent — 5202 erent — 5223, 5224 *transposed* — 5240 Q. j'en preiez g. p. a. (*-1*) — 5271 Queus — 5324 Artus

— 5361 les *repeated* — 5369 si p. — 5382 Li dameisel l. d. — 5393 v. amer — 5394 S. feront s. et c. — 5414 Venir v. — 5503 V. d. je voir au r. — 5531 ou *repeated* — 5595 La — 5671 Qu'il — 5711 Se — 5719 si mespoise — 5720 A la r. pas n'an poise — 5721 Einz an e. l. — 5724 E. t. nuit — 5749, 5750 *transposed* — 5757 Et li neanz — 5759 Ou est alez — 5791 Et c. lor — 5807 mitiez — 5823 E. d. des les l. — 5830 cuens d'E. — 5850 qu'e. l'a. — 5881 vermoilles (*sic*) — 5883 q. fet il — 5896 pucel (*-1*) — 5944 esbaudi — 5967 Li uns p. l'autre d. — 5968 Et li autres p. l'e. — 5969 seignors — 5993 Que il n'e. hom q. a. p.

6004 Et c. chevalier le suioient — 6022 se — 6029 meïsmes — 6064 G. d. en a — 6084 Bien et beles a. — 6090 noaus — 6091 seneschauz — 6139 Ençois qu'e. f. tote f. — 6140 et la p. t. — 6149 Forz et e. et longue et lee — 6150 fu ensi fondee — 6152 Et en la t. ensi le m. — 6153 barrer — 6162 dongier — 6199 Kex — 6263, 6264 *transposed* — 6263 Cele e. s. M. — 6297 Lancelot — 6301 Artus — 6340 A l'uevre — 6355 *repeated* — 6363 resbez — 6376 conuis — 6378 Et d. q. ja c. — 6392 E. si a p. t. p. — 6402 quant le c. — 6415 trueve (*sic*) — 6458 menee (*sic*) — 6466 Si v. la t. et longue et l. — 6467 Mes m. a ce q. p. e. — 6476 L. le vet — 6481 merveilleuse — 6494 p. le feisoies — 6500 A n. e. — 6503, 6504 *transposed* — 6504 & 6528 Gauvain — 6529 Certes — 6530 quant v. n. s. — 6542 je *omitted* (*-1*) — 6545 le destine — 6546 Q. a t. h. me define — 6557 Lancelot — 6580 Belemant — 6586 mes il la v. — 6609 jorz *omitted* (*-1*) — 6622 a grant s. — 6625 *repeated* — 6630 Com puisse — 6634 p. de c. (*+1*) — 6643 et boté — 6668 A. que ele coneüst — 6690 mie *omitted* (*-2*) — 6691-92 *omitted* — 6701 *repeated* — 6702 fet *repeated* — 6711 Artus — 6718 Lancelot — 6726 Ne — 6756 requiert — 6764 q. je vos t. — 6768 randrai — 6779 l. un tapiz d. s. — 6780 Isnelemant font sanz esfroi — 6781 Tot s. c. li e. — 6786 Cil saut sus einz n'i aresta — 6816 decevant — 6829 Va s'an li r. — 6841 rapele — 6847 bienvenue — 6911 trop e. p. — 6912 Et je meïsmes resui prez (*sic*) — 6913 s'an *omitted* (*-1*) — 6934 Il ne cuide ja veoir l'ore — 6962 quanque li m. f. — 6963 F. ce cuit la m. trestote

7003 Chevalier d. et p. — 7004 Por Lancelot gentes et b. — 7038 s. taingnant — 7057 n'estriés — 7060 Et chieent a la terre v. — 7063 l'autre et m. — 7086 Et q. il — 7098 an s'antraille — 7118 an f. o.

3. Corrected Lines

Only those lines which cannot be visualized from an examination of section 2 (The Rejected Readings) are listed below. Among those that are excluded are the lines corrected by Mario Roques (see his C.F.M.A. edition,

p. 220), it being assumed that scholars using Appendix I will normally refer to the easily obtainable Roques text rather than to the much rarer Foerster edition.

17	Vaut de pelles et de sardines
28	De panser, si que rien n'i met
30	Des or comance sa reison
31	A un jor d'une Acenssion
32	Fu venuz de vers Carlion
33	Li rois Artus et tenu ot
34	Cort molt riche a Camaalot
35	Si riche com au jor estut
60	Par quoi tu les puisses ravoir
79	Qui sont an essil an ma terre
89	Rois, servi t'ai molt longuemant
178	Sire, ma dame que voici
211	"Ha! ha! se vos ce seüssiez,
212	Ja, ce croi, ne me leissessiez
213	Sanz chalonge mener un pas!"
218	Tuit cil et celes qui la virent
235	Qu'aprés n'alasse maintenant
275	Et pantoisant et tressüé
295	Einz sailli molt tost sor celui
302	S'an vet poignant par la forest
330	Qui traïson ou murtre font
338	S'avoit puis totes lois perdues
363	Qu'il ne l'atant ne pas ne ore.
364	Tant solemant deus pas demore
386	Puis dit au nain: "Car me consoille
398	Et g'irai la ou tu iras
408	Les genz, mes mie n'an consoillent
426	Vers une tor qui tot a plain
427	Par devers la vile seoit
429	Et par delez estoit assise
463	Qant il orent assez veillié
465	Anmi la sale haut et lonc
477	Mes an celui qui est dela
479	Ne fu pas fez cist a vostre ués.
480	Li chevaliers li respont lués
496	L'an ne l'a mie fet parer
510	Se couche soz un samit jaune

569	Et quant plus ne la pot veoir
581	Par tot de sa maleürté?
582	Des qu'il a en charrete esté
757	Mes li chevaliers ne l'ot mie,
758	Et cil tierce fois li escrie:
759	"Chevaliers! n'antrez mie el gué
760	Sor ma desfanse et sor mon gré;
761	Que par mon chief je vos ferrai
762	Si tost come el gué vos verrai."
802	Bien sachiez que mar le feïstes
803	Se au frain a une des mains
971	Molt i avra travail et painne
976	Son pleisir et sa volenté
982	Fors celui qu'ele i amenoit
1038	Cil leve, si se va seoir
1039	Molt volantiers, et si li siet;
1040	Et cele delez lui s'asiet
1083	Ne troverai qui le m'an ost;
1084	Et se tu ne me secors tost
1097	Si n'en ert il mie jalos
1098	Ne ja de lui ne sera cos
1140	Et esgarde amont vers le feste,
1141	Si voit deus espees venir.
1142	Arriers se tret et retenir
1144	De tel aïr meüz les orent
1145	Qu'an terre les espees fierent
1147	Quant cil voit qu'eles sont brisiees
1150	Entr'ax se lance et fiert del cote
1166	Randre li voldra sa promesse
1198	Lors s'an vont cil hors de laienz
1237	S'estoit ele molt bele et gente,
1238	Mes ne li pleist ne atalante
1310	Et se vos me conduisïez
1358	Qu'il vienent pres d'une fontainne
1376	Qu'ele fors de sa voie l'ost
1507	Mes por coi feroie lonc conte?
1556	Le grant cors vint ancontre aus deus
1558	Que ses pas ne cuide gaster
1574	Et s'il eüst tot fors josté
1575	A cele ore un tornoiemant
1601	Et quant je vos truis ci an eise
1742	Cil par orguel respont: "Comant!

1755	Et cil respont: "Honiz seroie
1755	Et cil respont: "Honiz seroie
1766	De mon voloir ne me neüst
1824	Con cil qui amander nel puet
1833	An mainne, sel suefre mes sire.
1863	Que ce estoit qu'il ne savoit
1867	—Volentiers, sire." Lors l'i moinne.
1868	Li chevaliers aprés le moinne
1869	Antre et voit les plus beles tonbes
1884	De marbre, si sanble estre nueve,
1885	Sor totes autres riche et bele.
1900	Biax est defors et dedanz plus
1916	Don n'ist ne sers ne gentix hon
1917	Qui ne soit de la antor nez
1940	Qui estes vos et de quel leu?
2052	Molt volantiers et lieemant
2198	Que molt aime lor conpaignie
2224	Cil qui le garde li reproche
2238	Trestot droit par desus la panne
2282	Puis qu'il a enprise grant chose.
2339	Vont tant qu'il vienent a l'issue
2341	Mes maintenant que cil fu fors
2342	Li lessierent aprés le cors
2412	Que il ront et fant et depiece
2413	Escuz et hiaumes et haubers.
2435	Quant ceste novele ont oïe,
2436	Molt an est lor genz esjoïe.
2569	Que toz li mandre s'aprestoit
2572	Et cil les chandoiles gaster
2611	De ce que tu i fus menez
2633	Qui cestui valoir resanblast
2656	Cui qu'an soit la honte et li diax
2788	Mialz voldroie estre cent fois morz
2827	Einçois sera aumosne et biens,
2828	Que c'est la plus deslëax riens
2867	Merci, ne l'avra il adonques?
2924	Et cil li crie, et plus et plus
2945	De la rien que je plus voloie.
2963	Qu'al mangier rasseoir voloient
2975	Et a maint autre preuz seroit
2978	Et cil respont: "Bien le savoie."
2980	Sa parole et sa voiz bessiee
2985	Se mestier aviez del prendre

2987	Tant que vos demandé l'aiez
2993	En manroiz, qu'il vos est mestiers
3030	Ausi com an la mer salee
3044	Que tant i avoit il d'esploit
3045	Qu'ele pooit grant fes porter.
3054	Qu'il tranblent andui de peor
3060	Se a tans ne vos repantez
3111	Que ses piez desarme et ses mains
3124	A grant dolor si con li sist
3142	Qu'anchantez fu et deceüz,
3143	Car il n'i avoit rien qui vive.
3188	An cui dormist et reposast
3190	Plus que pröesce enor as buens.
3243	La reïne! Deus m'an desfande
3244	Qu'en tel guise je la li rande!
3253	Ce sez tu bien que enors iert
3254	Au chevalier se il conquiert
3264	Molt me poise quant tu foloies,
3265	Mes se tu mon consoil despis
3293	Si piteus ne si charitables
3301	Por ce ne nos correceromes
3335	Et cil qui molt estoit bleciez
3372	Et voz plaies faire atorner
3406	Mes je gast le tans et pert ci
3448	Einz vient por enor porchacier
3497	Iluec fu uns cirurgïens
3558	Et li haubers menu mailliez
3616	Estriés ne resne ne sorcengle
3691	Ne puis l'ore qu'il l'aparçut
3717	Qu'arriere main gietes tes cos,
3718	Si te conbaz deriere ton dos.
3736	Que il le fet tot trestorner
3899	Des le jor qu'il le semondra
3979	Se li respont mout humblemant
4133	Et de ce sont molt correcié
4175	Ceste novele par tot va
4176	Tant que la reïne trova
4205	Qu'il suens avoit esté toz dis
4250	Por quoi? Doit don mon ami nuire
4293	Tant que mal gré suen m'ocirra
4294	Morz qui onques ne desirra
4318	Tot maintenant l'ont anbracié

4342	Par felenie m'espargnas
4389	Neïs sor charrete monter
4483	Puis parlerent a grant leisir
4588	Qu'onques nul home n'ancontra
4604	D'un dolz salu l'a enerree
4637	Qu'an mon lit soie recouchiee
4717	Mes de son cors tant i remaint
4781	Molt a or bele garde feite
4782	Mes pere qui por moi vos gueite!
4977	Maintenant lor chevaus demandent,
4978	Lor armes aporter comandent;
4979	L'an lor aporte tost a mont
5124	Si bien que de rien n'i descordent
5150	Et del cuer delivre ot la doiz
5163	Et il li respondent: "Oïl!
5164	Qui? —Lanceloz del Lac, font il
5167	Et avoec li nos autres toz
5172	Nos ne savons qu'il en a fet
5198	De seür s'i pueent atandre
5240	Que ja en sui prez grant piece a.
5369	La reïne et tuit li prison
5382	Les dames et les dameiseles
5393	Dïent que les voldront avoir
5394	Sel firent crïer et savoir
5503	Vos doing et jur le revenir.
5595	Ja sont assanblees les rotes
5671	Que ne l'ot veisins ne veisine
5719	Qu'el monde n'a rien si coarde."
5720	Et la reïne qui l'esgarde
5721	An est molt liee et molt li plest
5724	Ensi tote jor jusqu'au soir
5757	Et li noauz, et li despiz?
5759	Ou iert trovez? Ou le querrons?
5791	Et cil les armes lor devisent
5823	Ensi devisent cil des loges.
5830	Si l'en aporta Kex d'Estrax.
5850	Talanz li prist qu'ele i anvoit
5883	Est revenuz, mes que quiert il?
5967	Li un por celui desconbrer
5968	Et li autre por l'enconbrer.
5969	Li un lor seignor eidier cuident

5993	Qu'il n'est riens qui armes ne port
6139	An ce que ele fust tost feite.
6140	Sor la mer fu la pierre treite
6149	Haute et espesse et bien fondee.
6150	Quant ele fu a ce menee
6152	Par nuit et an la tor le mist
6153	Puis comanda les huis murer
6263	Qui suer estoit Meleagant
6378	Dahait et qui ja cuidera
6392	Estoit ja si par tans perie
6415	N'ele nel set n'ele nel rueve
6458	Fortune qui tant l'a penee.
6466	La tor voit fort et haute et lee
6467	Mervoille soi que ce puet estre
6476	Lors le viaut apeler par non
6494	Las, chaitis, por coi t'i fioies
6500	A neant t'est comant qu'il aut.
6530	Mes espoir que vos nel savez
6545	Soit maudiz, et Dex le destruie,
6546	Cil qui a tel honte m'estuie!
6580	Foiblemant, petit et petit
6586	Ne la conut quant il la voit
6622	Lors vos metrai a boen sejor
6630	Don puissiez croistre cest pertuis
6643	Et tant a feru et chevé
6668	Aucuns s'il les reconeüst
6691	Or est plus tornanz et plus vistes
6692	Qu'onques rien aussi ne veïstes.
6756	Puis li enquiert de Lancelot
6764	"Des qu'ainsi est que je nel truis
6768	Ce fet Gauvains: "Bien vos tandrai
6779	Iluec devant soi un tapi.
6780	Ne se sont mucié ne tapi
6781	A son comant li escüier
6786	Lors s'assiet cil qui le manda
6816	Mes nel va lors riens detenant
6841	Joie, qui formant les revele.
6847	Com ore a de sa revenue
6911	Por l'atandre, car toz est prez
6912	Li gaainz, la monte et li prez
6934	Car molt li delaie et demore

6962	Mes je cuit qu'ainz que li murs faille
6963	Faudra la mers et l'eve tote
7003	La reïne, dames, puceles
7004	Dom avoec li avoit de beles
7038	Es escuz qui bien sont tenant
7060	Que de seignor fu tote vuide
7086	Et quant cil se sant domagié
7098	Li a fait tele osche an sa taille
7118	Cil qui plus lié ne furent onques

4. Mistranscriptions in the Roques Text

The numbered lines are those of the Roques C.F.M.A. edition. In each case the Guiot reading comes first, being followed within round brackets by Roques's transcriptional error.[2]

201 enmi (anmi) — 206 sopiranz (sospiranz) — 219 trestot (tretost) — 234 ce (cel) — 259 Keu (Kex) — 401 troi (trois) — 472 cist (cil) — 473 lit (li) — 481 desfanse (deffanse) — 520 panon (pannon) — 668 autres (autre) — 712 desfanse (deffanse) — 726 ne (que) — 755 an (en) l'eve — 764 desfandu (deffandu) — 812 dit (dist) — 816 Nel (Non) — 845 porent (poeent) — 846 desfandre (deffandre) — 851 desoz (dessor) — 873 set (sen) — 892 lest (leist) — 995 trovee (trouvee)

1002 sa (la) — 1013 l'en (l'an) — 1076 volanté (volenté) — 1080 vileinnemant (vileinemant) — 1141 codes (cotes) — 1145 lo (le) — 1147 tote (toste) — 1161 jusqu'as (jusqu'es) — 1162 & 1170 desfandre (deffandre) — 1192 main (maint) — 1209 se (le) — 1232 an (en) — 1364 qu'ele (que ele) — 1544 granz (grans) — 1643 plusor (plusors) — 1646 queroles (quaroles) — 1669 & 1672 com (con) — 1697 que (qui) — 1700 queroles (quaroles) — 1757 por (par) — 1773 que (qui) — 1872 uevre (ueve) — 1884 uns (un) — 1906 ancor (ancors) — 1952 seüremant (seürement) — 1954 li (les)

2197 tant (tanz) — 2255 troi (trois) — 2296 conbatuz (conbatus) — 2425 le (la) — 2556 qu'a (que) — 2773 griés (grief) — 2802 afeire (a faire)

3099 venuz (venus) — 3119 deus (deux) — 3203 li (lui) — 3403 sosferroie (sosferoie) — 3519 feste (feite) — 3552 com (con) — 3737 menace (mennace) — 3857 & 3859 ocirroit (occirroit) — 3879 sanz (sans)

4570 n'i (ne) — 4655 braz (bras) — 4670 & 4672 qant (quant) — 4825 mosterrai (mosterrrai) — 4978 des (del)

5065 vos (voz) — 5185 traïson (traïsons) — 5187 qui (que) — 5684 as (a) — 5694 forsenez (forcenez) — 5754 s'a (l'a) — 5852 li (lit) — 5878 que ele (qu'ele) — 5961 resbaudist (resbaudit)

6090 an (en) — 6097 eüst (eüt) — 6224 li (le) — 6342 li (le) — 6688 fui (sui) — 6759 son (con)
7112 malmetre (mal metre)

Addendum

The Prologue to Chrétien's *Lancelot*

The text printed below conforms by and large to the one established by Wendelin Foerster, yet it includes one important change: ll. 12-13, instead of reading *Tant con li funs passe les vanz, / Qui vante en mai ou en avril*, have become *Tant con les funs passe li vanz / Qui vante en mai ou en avril*. Karl D. Uitti (*Romania*, forthcoming) demonstrates why such a departure from the Foerster text (which, with the exception of *Si* versus *Tant*, is also the text procured by Roques) is required by rhyme, rhetoric and syntax.

For ll. 1, 8, 17, 19, 28 and 30, Foerster rejected *C* (Guiot) in favor of *ET*; Roques, of course, did not. In each case the *ET* reading, now backed by *G*—a manuscript unknown to both Foerster and Roques—proves superior to that of *C*. But in 26 Guiot's *san* is preferable to *GTE*'s *sens* (*E*: senz).

   Des que ma dame de Chanpaigne
   Vialt que romans a faire anpraigne,
   Je l'anprendrai molt volentiers
4 Come cil qui est suens antiers
   De quanqu'il puet el monde feire,
   Sanz rien de losange avant treire.
   Mes tex s'an poïst antremetre
8 Qui i volsist losenge metre,
   Si deïst—et jel tesmoignasse—
   Que ce est la dame qui passe
   Totes celes qui sont vivanz,
12 Tant con les funs passe li vanz
   Qui vante en mai ou en avril.
   Par foi, je ne sui mie cil
   Qui vuelle losangier sa dame;
16 Dirai je: Tant com une jame

>   Vaut de pelles et de sardines,
>   Vaut la contesse de reïnes?
>   Naie, je n'en dirai ja rien,
> 20   S'est il voirs maleoit gré mien.
>   Mes tant dirai ge que mialz oevre
>   Ses comandemanz an ceste oevre
>   Que sans ne painne que g'i mete.
> 24   Del *Chevalier de la Charrete*
>   Comance Crestïens son livre;
>   Matiere et san li donne et livre
>   La contesse, et il s'antremet
> 28   De panser, si que rien n'i met
>   Fors sa painne et s'antancion.
>   Des or comance sa raison.

Manuscripts
C: B.N. fr. 794 (basic text: Guiot); *E*: Escorial M iii 21; *G*: Princeton, Garrett 125; *T*: B.N. fr. 12560

Rejected readings
1 Puis — 8 Qu'il i — 12 Si c. li f. p. les v. — 17 pailes — 19 N. voir je n'en d. r. — 28 De p. q. gueres n'i m. — 30 *C omits line*

Variants
1 la d. *E* — 3 l'emprenderai v. *G* — 4 e. bien *E*, s.e. *G* — 6 riens *ET* — 8 Que il *E* — 9 je t. *ET* — 12 li feuz *E*, le fu *G*, li f. *T*, les v. *E* — 13 Q. en m. v. *G*, et an a. *T* — 16 Mais je d. *E*, Diré et *T* — 17 pierres *E* — 18 des r. *E* — 19 Et ja n'en die nule r. *E*, Nenil *T* — 20 Si e. il m. g. m. *EG* — 24 a la Ch. *G* — 26 sens *GTE*, l'an *T*, li baille *G*, *GT omit second* et (*sic*)

Note
Since *EGT* all give *ja* in l. 19—an excellent illustration of textual *collegiality*—I have rejected the otherwise acceptable reading provided by *C*.

December 1983

Alfred Foulet

Appendix II

Chrétien's Indebtedness to the *Alexandre décasyllabique*

The *Alexandre décasyllabique* (ADéca), a Southwestern French (Poitevin) narrative poem, recounts the birth, childhood and early exploits of Alexander the Great. Written in the style of a *chanson de geste*, it is relatively short: 785 verses divided into 76 *laisses*.[1] Though no exact date can be assigned to it, the probability is strong that the ADéca was composed in the mid or late 1160s.[2]

Chrétien's indebtedness to the *Eneas* is sufficiently documented, but little has been said, so far as I know, about his utilization of the ADéca, likewise a representative of the *matière de Rome*.[3] It is this gap which the present Appendix seeks to fill.[4]

The ADéca contains five passages which apparently influenced Chrétien. I shall transcribe them—except in one case, where, because of the passage's length, the transcription will be replaced by a summary—transcription or summary to be followed by various comments of mine.

1. The taming of Bucephalus
(ADéca, ll. 130-32, 137-38)

Li fers chivaus   vit son segnor venir,
Les pez devant   començar a flatir,
Baisa lo chef,   semblant fait de servir.
. . . .
Quant Bucifaus   vit venir sun segnor,
Baisa la testa,   signe li fait d'amor.

The ADéca author presents Bucephalus as a man-eating horse, duly locked up on account of his ferociousness, but, when with utter fearlessness Alexander enters his pen, Bucephalus immediately recognizes his future master, behaving with all the humility expected of a human vassal.

Bucephalus' suddenly submissive posture is duplicated in a grateful lion's kneeling before an Yvain who has just saved his life from the deadly fangs of a fire-spewing serpent:

> Oëz que fist li lions donques!
> Con fist que frans et de bon' eire,
> Que il li comança a feire
> Sanblant que a lui se randoit,
> Et ses piez joinz li estandoit
> Et vers terre ancline sa chiere,
> S'estut sor les deus piez deriere;
> Et puis si se ragenoilloit
> Et tote sa face moilloit
> De lermes par humilité.
> (*Yvain*, ed. Reid, ll. 3392-3401)

Though Chrétien's actual wording of the scene described by him is not specially close to the terms used by the ADéca author, it should be noted that both poets make it clear that the homage rendered is the action of a quadruped.[5]

2. Alexander demands to be knighted
(ADéca, ll. 139-73)

Alexander leaps onto Bucephalus' back and rides right into his father's banquet hall. King and courtiers are greatly affrighted. Alexander dismounts and tells Philip that the time has come to confer knighthood on his son.

A similar scene occurs in *Perceval* (ed. Roach, ll. 900-99). On his first appearance at Arthur's court, Perceval rides into the main hall, stopping within arm's length of the King, who is seated at table and has just finished his meal. His request is the same as Alexander's had been: he wishes to be knighted.

The striking link between *Perceval* and the ADéca is not an impetuous young man's desire to be dubbed, but that the would-be knight has entered the royal banquet hall on horseback. This, of course, is a most unusual procedure when one craves a boon.

While Chrétien has borrowed situation and scene from the ADéca, he has introduced a notable difference between Perceval's behavior and that of Alexander. The latter dismounts before he makes his request for knighthood; Perceval does not, even when invited to do so by Arthur. His reason?

At this early stage of a problematic career he firmly believes that to become a *chevalier* he must remain astride a *cheval*, an absurd notion fully on a par with Perceval's wish to be made a RED knight. He has been dazzled by *Li Vermauz Chevaliers'* shining red armor: no one, he is convinced, can be knighted unless he be encased within a suit of armor, preferably red.[6]

>   *3. Alexander's lustral bath in the sea*
>   (ADéca, ll. 203, 205-06, 211-211.1)
>
>   Quant la reïne oït le roi parler,
>   . . . .
>   Per la cité fait aus donceus mander
>   Que begner s'augent la jus au port de mer.
>   . . . . . .
>   Li doncel sallent qui anz anz en la mer,
>   N'i a celui qui atendist son per.

Philip having acceded to Alexander's request that he be made a knight, the ritual ceremony then follows. Among its features figures the lustral bath. Somewhat surprisingly, Alexander and his companions, who will also receive knighthood, bathe in the sea.

In *Cligés* the Mediterranean is replaced by the English Channel, but the lustral bath remains a communal one: the *Cligés* Alixandre is surrounded by young companions just as was the ADéca Alexander:

>   Droit sor la mer se desvestirent,
>   Si se laverent et baingnierent,
>   Car il ne vostrent ne daignierent
>   Qu'an lor chaufast eve an estuve:
>   De la mer firent baing et cuve.
>   (*Cligés*, ed. Micha, ll. 1134-38)

Chrétien improved on his ADéca model by having Cligés' father himself choose the sea-bath, whereas in the ADéca it was Olympias who ordered her son to bathe off the Greek shore. Chrétien's Alixandre conceives of his lustral bath as a test of his physical toughness. For the month is October ("Tot droit a l'entree d'oitovre," l. 1045): immersion in a warm bathtub would be so much more comfortable.

4. Alexander dons a precious shirt
(ADéca, II. 264-69)

> Danz Alixandres demanda sa chamise,
> Et la reïne la li a el dos mise.
> Unques ne fu cosue ne reprise,
> Ovree fu sur l'aiqua de Tamise,
> Per haute mer en fu portee en Frise
> Au rei Felipe, cui ele fu tramise.

The Adéca author recounts at length how Alexander, after his bath, gets dressed in brand-new clothes: shirt, *bliaut*, *peliçon* and mantle (II. 241-306). Of all this finery Chrétien has retained only the shirt:

> Trestoz ses escrins cerche et vuide,
> Tant c'une chemise en a traite;
> De soie fu, blanche et bien faite,
> Molt delïee et molt soutil.
> Es costures n'avoit un fil
> Ne fust d'or ou d'argent au mains.
> . . . .
> La reïne[7] prant la chemise,
> Si l'a Alixandre tramise.
> (*Cligés*, II. 1144-49, 1161-62)

It is Guenevere now who, wishing to honor the young foreign prince at her court, selects the finest shirt she can find, but it is Soredamor, Gauvain's lovely sister, who has greatly enhanced its (sentimental) value by weaving into it one of her long golden hairs. Had the *Cligés* Alixandre but known this, he would have been overjoyed. He will have to wait till a later time to be apprised of his great good luck.

Chrétien may have remembered the ADéca shirt, since, strange to say, it was woven in the land where flows the Thames and sent there to Phrygia. Be it as it may, the author of *Cligés* has known how to integrate it, or rather a similar English shirt, within his narrative, making of it an important element of the Alixandre-Soredamor love intrigue.

5. The word graal
(ADéca, II. 598-603, 609-12)

> Li seneschaus conut ben lo meschin
> Et dist au rei sempres en son latin:

"Per ma fei, sire, ça vei un pelerin,
Il but erser a ma copa d'or fin,
Se li donai e pain e char e vin;
De mon ostal se leva oi matin."
. . . .
Li proz Sanson conut lo seneschal.
"Sire, dist il, Deus te porgart de mal.
Ot tei manchai erser a ton graal
E oi matin esi de ton ostal."

In his *Perceval and the Holy Grail* William A. Nitze pointed out that the word *graal* appeared in the Adéca some ten years earlier than in Chrétien's *Perceval* and that in both texts it has the meaning of "dish" or "platter."[8]

Because the word was relatively rare—at least in literary texts—before Chrétien conferred on it an ever-increasing celebrity, one may well wonder whether he picked it up in the ADéca.[9] Several reasons favor such a view. The ADéca passage is attention-attracting: two consecutive stanzas, of similar structure, emphasize the difference which exists between a cup out of which one drinks and a *graal* off which one eats. Since the ADéca cup is of gold, the ADéca *graal*, by implication, is equally of precious make, which, quite apart of its magic effulgence, is most certainly the case of Chrétien's *graal* (see *Perceval*, ed. Roach, ll. 3232-39). Finally, if one concedes as proven that Chrétien borrowed from the ADéca the passages mustered above under 1, 2, 3 and 4, one might as well add the word *graal* to his borrowings.

Chrétien, of course, is no vulgar imitator. All his borrowings from the ADéca are widely dispersed through his *œuvre*. They are more like reminiscences than borrowings, and reminiscences which have acquired an entirely new life, be it in *Cligés*, *Yvain* or *Perceval*. Put to new purposes in each case, they have become thoroughly fused with their new contexts.

NOTES

Preface

1. Jean Frappier, *Chrétien de Troyes* (Paris: Hatier, 1968); L.T. Topsfield, *Chrétien de Troyes: A Study of the Arthurian Romances* (Cambridge: Cambridge Univ. Press, 1981).
2. Wolfgang Brandt, *Chrétien de Troyes: Zur Dichtungstechnik seiner Romane*, Freiburger Schriften zur romanischen Philologie, 19 (Munich: Fink, 1972); Norris J. Lacy, *The Craft of Chrétien de Troyes: An Essay on Narrative Art*, Davis Medieval Texts and Studies, 3 (Leiden: Brill, 1980).

"Chrétien de Troyes: The Narrator and His Voices," by Douglas Kelly

1. Unless otherwise indicated, references throughout this volume are to the following editions: *Erec et Enide*, ed. Mario Roques, Classiques Français du Moyen Age, 80 (Paris: Champion, 1966); *Cligés*, ed. Alexandre Micha, C.F.M.A., 84 (Paris: Champion, 1957); *Le Chevalier de la Charrette*, ed. Mario Roques, C.F.M.A., 86 (Paris: Champion, 1970); *Le Chevalier au Lion (Yvain)*, ed. Mario Roques, C.F.M.A., 89 (Paris: Champion, 1971); *Le Conte du Graal (Perceval)*, ed. Félix Lecoy, 2 vols. C.F.M.A., 100, 103 (Paris: Champion, 1973-1975), with line references in square brackets to *Le Roman de Perceval ou le Conte du Graal*, ed. William Roach, 2nd ed., Textes Littéraires Français, 71 (Geneva: Droz; Paris: Minard, 1959). Pertinent studies are indicated in the notes; for bibliography, see pp. 343-53. On the importance of Chrétien's Prologues for an understanding of his art, see Tony Hunt, "The Rhetorical Background to the Arthurian Prologue: Tradition and the Old French Vernacular Prologues," *Forum for Modern Language Studies*, 6 (1970), 1-23, and "Tradition and Originality in the Prologues of Chrestien de Troyes," *Forum for Modern Language Studies*, 8 (1972), 320-44; Marie-Louise Ollier, "The Author in the Text: The Prologues of Chrétien de Troyes," *Yale French Studies*, 51 (1974), 26-41; Pierre-Yves Badel, "Rhétorique et polémique dans les prologues de romans au moyen âge," *Littérature*, 20 (1975), 81-94; and Beate Schmolke-Hasselmann, "Untersuchungen zur Typik des arthurischen Romananfanges," *Germanisch-romanische Monatsschrift*, n. s., 31 (1981), 1-13.
2. Eugène Vinaver, *The Rise of Romance* (Oxford: Clarendon Press, 1971), p. 32.
3. Roger Sherman Loomis, *Arthurian Tradition and Chrétien de Troyes* (New York: Columbia Univ. Press, 1949), esp. pp. 38-58. See also Constance Bullock-Davies, *Professional Interpreters and the Matter of Britain* (Cardiff: Univ. of Wales Press, 1966); Ian Lovecy, "Exploding the Myth of Celtic Myth: A New Appraisal of the Celtic Background of Arthurian Romance," *Reading Medieval Studies*, 7 (1981), 3-18. But cf. as well Claude Luttrell, "The Arthurian Traditionalist's Approach to the

Composer of Romance: R.S. Loomis on Chrétien de Troyes," *Oeuvres et Critiques,* 5, No. 2 (1980-1981), 23-30.

4. Jean Fourquet, "Le Rapport entre l'œuvre et la source chez Chrétien de Troyes et le problème des sources bretonnes," *Romance Philology,* 9 (1955-1956), 298-312. Cf. Vinaver, *A la recherche d'une poétique médiévale* (Paris: Nizet, 1970), pp. 105-28; and Rainer Warning, "Formen narrativer Identitätskonstitution im höfischen Roman," in *Le Roman jusqu'à la fin du XIIIe siècle,* Vol. IV, Pt. 1 of *Grundriss der romanischen Literaturen des Mittelalters* (Heidelberg: Winter, 1978), pp. 25-59; Michel Zink, "Une Mutation de la conscience littéraire: Le langage romanesque à travers des exemples français du XIIe siècle," *Cahiers de Civilisation Médiévale,* 24 (1981), 3-27.

5. Besides the still useful Alwin Schultz, *Das höfische Leben zur Zeit der Minnesinger,* 2 vols. (Leipzig: Hinzel, 1878-1880), see Badel, *Introduction à la vie littéraire du moyen âge* (Paris: Bordas, 1969); Hunt, "The Emergence of the Knight in France and England 1000-1200," *Forum for Modern Language Studies,* 17 (1981), 93-114 (good overview with extensive bibliography); and, especially, the articles by Jean Flori, "Chevalerie et liturgie: Remise des armes et vocabulaire 'chevaleresque' dans les sources liturgiques du IXe au XIVe siècle," *Moyen Age,* 84 (1978), 247-78, 409-42; "Les Origines de l'adoubement chevaleresque: Etudes des remises d'armes et du vocabulaire qui les exprime dans les sources historiques latines jusqu'au début du XIIIe siècle," *Traditio,* 35 (1979), 209-72; and "Pour une histoire de la chevalerie: L'adoubement dans les romans de Chrétien de Troyes," *Romania,* 100 (1979), 21-53.

6. Georges Duby, *Medieval Marriage: Two Models from Twelfth-Century France,* Johns Hopkins Symposia in Comparative History, 11 (Baltimore: Johns Hopkins Univ. Press, 1978). See as well David J. Shirt, "*Cligés*: A Twelfth-Century Matrimonial Case-Book?" *Forum for Modern Language Studies,* 18 (1982), 75-89.

7. Reto R. Bezzola, *Les Origines et la formation de la littérature courtoise en Occident (500-1200),* 3 vols. (Paris: Champion, 1944-1963).

8. Erich Köhler, *Ideal und Wirklichkeit in der höfischen Epik: Studien zur Form der frühen Artus- and Graldichtung,* Beihefte zur Zeitschrift für romanische Philologie, 97, 2nd. ed. (Tübingen: Niemeyer, 1970); French trans. by Eliane Kaufholz, *L'Aventure chevaleresque: Idéal et réalité dans le roman courtois: Etudes sur la forme des plus anciens poèmes d'Arthur et du Graal* (Paris: Gallimard, 1974) (page references to the translation are given in square brackets). See as well Köhler's "Literatursoziologische Perspektiven," in *Le Roman jusqu'à la fin du XIIIe siècle,* pp. 82-103 (cf. above, n. 4).

9. See especially D.W. Robertson, Jr., "Some Medieval Literary Terminology, with Special Reference to Chrétien de Troyes," *Studies in Philology,* 48 (1951), 669-92, and *A Preface to Chaucer: Studies in Medieval Perspectives* (Princeton: Princeton Univ. Press, 1962); Friedrich Ohly, *Schriften zur mittelalterlichen Bedeutungsforschung* (Darmstadt: Wissenschaftliche Buchgesellschaft, 1977); Hennig Brinkmann, *Mittelalterliche Hermeneutik* (Darmstadt: Wissenschaftliche Buchgesellschaft, 1980); Jacques Ribard, *Chrétien de Troyes, Le Chevalier de la Charrette: Essai d'interprétation symbolique* (Paris: Nizet, 1972), "Les romans de Chrétien de Troyes sont-ils allégoriques?" *Cahiers de l'Association Internationale des Etudes Françaises,* 28 (1976), 7-20, and "Ecriture symbolique et visée allégorique dans *Le Conte du Graal*," *Oeuvres et Critiques,* 5, No. 2 (1980-1981), 103-09.

10. Köhler, *Ideal,* pp. 236-61 [*Aventure,* pp. 269-98].

11. In this respect, Vinaver's evaluation of criticism up to 1960 is still perti-

nent; see especially his "L'Exemple de Bédier," in *A la recherche*, pp. 15-47. See as well the important article by Alberto Vàrvaro, which, if it does not deal explicitly with Chrétien, is relevant to his romances: "La Teoria dell'archetipo tristaniano," *Romania*, 88 (1967), 13-58.

12. Hans-Robert Jauss, "The Alterity and Modernity of Medieval Literature," *New Literary History*, 10 (1978-1979), 182; see also his *Alterität und Modernität der mittelalterlichen Literatur: Gesammelte Aufsätze 1956-1976* (Munich: Fink, 1977). For recent studies, see the review article by Marie-Louise Ollier, "Modernité de Chrétien de Troyes," *Romanic Review*, 71 (1980), 413-44.

13. See Wesley Trimpi, "The Ancient Hypothesis of Fiction: An Essay on the Origins of Literary Theory," *Traditio*, 27 (1971), 3.

14. Warning, "Formen," pp. 45-47. Cf. Lacy, *Craft*, pp. 34-66.

15. See Roger D. Ray, "Medieval Historiography through the Twelfth Century: Problems and Progress of Research," *Viator*, 5 (1974), 33-59. As a good illustration, consult Erich Kleinschmidt, *Herrscherdarstellung: Zur Disposition mittelalterlichen Aussageverhaltens, untersucht an Texten über Rodolf I. von Habsburg*, Bibliotheca Germanica, 17 (Bern: Francke, 1974).

16. On the problem of dating Chrétien's romances, see especially Anthime Fourrier, "Encore la chronologie des œuvres de Chrétien de Troyes," *Bulletin Bibliographique de la Société Internationale Arthurienne*, 2 (1950), 69-88; Jean Misrahi, "More Light on the Chronology of Chrétien de Troyes?" *Bulletin Bibliographique de la Société Internationale Arthurienne*, 11 (1959), 89-120; Frappier, *Chrétien*, pp. 8-9. A recent, but controversial new chronology is proposed by Luttrell, *The Creation of the First Arthurian Romance: A Quest* (Evanston: Northwestern Univ. Press, 1974), pp. 26-46.

17. The attribution to Chrétien of the *Chevalier à l'épée* and the *Mule sans frein* has not gained general acceptance. Cf. D.D.R. Owen, "Two More Romances by Chrétien de Troyes?" *Romania*, 92 (1971), 246-60; and R.C. Johnston, "The Authorship of the 'Chevalier' and the 'Mule,'" *Modern Language Review*, 73 (1978), 496-98.

18. Frappier, "Le Concept de l'amour dans les romans arthuriens," *Bulletin Bibliographique de la Société Internationale Arthurienne*, 22 (1970), 119-36.

19. Matilda Tomaryn Bruckner, *Narrative Invention in Twelfth-Century French Romance: The Convention of Hospitality (1160-1200)*, French Forum Monographs, 17 (Lexington, Ky.: French Forum, Publishers, 1980).

20. See notably Rita Lejeune, "Rôle littéraire de la famille d'Aliénor d'Aquitaine," *Cahiers de Civilisation Médiévale*, 1 (1958), 319-37; Bezzola, *Origines*, vols. II-III; John F. Benton, "The Court of Champagne as a Literary Center," *Speculum*, 36 (1961), 551-91; June Hall Martin McCash, "Marie de Champagne and Eleanor of Aquitaine: A Relationship Reexamined," *Speculum*, 54 (1979), 698-711.

21. Lejeune, "Rôle littéraire d'Aliénor d'Aquitaine et de sa famille," *Cultura Neolatina*, 14 (1954), 1-57, and "Rôle littéraire de la famille d'Aliénor d'Aquitaine."

22. See Mary D. Stanger, "Literary Patronage at the Medieval Court of Flanders," *French Studies*, 11 (1957), 214-29. For further discussion of Philippe, as well as of his relations with Marie de Champagne, see Rupert T. Pickens, "*Le Conte du Graal*," below, esp. pp. 232 and 336, n. 2.

23. Karl D. Uitti, "The Courtly Narrator Figure in Old French Hagiography and Romance," *Medioevo Romanzo*, 2 (1975), 394-408.

24. Köhler, *Ideal*, pp. 67-88 [*Aventure*, pp. 77-102]; and his "Il Sistema sociologico del romanzo francese medievale," *Medioevo Romanzo*, 3 (1976), 321-44. But cf. Philippe Ménard, "Le Chevalier errant dans la littérature arthurienne: Recherches

sur les raisons du départ et de l'errance," in *Voyage, quête, pèlerinage dans la littérature et la civilisation médiévales*, Senefiance, 2 (Aix-en-Provence: CUER-MA, Paris: Champion, 1976), pp. 289-311. The divergent views, as Köhler suggests, and as I agree here, are not necessarily irreconcilable; see Flori, "Chevalerie" (above, n. 5).

25. Herbert Grundmann, "Litteratus-illitteratus: Der Wandel einer Bildungsnorm vom Altertum zum Mittelalter," *Archiv für Kulturgeschichte*, 40 (1958), esp. 9-10, and "Die Frauen im Mittelalter: Ein Beitrag zur Frage nach der Entstehung des Schrifttums in der Volkssprache," *Archiv für Kulturgeschichte*, 26 (1935), esp. 149-50, n. 66. See also Helene Jacobius, *Die Erziehung des Edelfräuleins im alten Frankreich nach Dichtungen des XII., XIII. und XIV. Jahrhunderts*, Beihefte zur Zeitschrift für romanische Philologie, 16 (Halle: Niemeyer, 1908), esp. pp. 55-69.

26. Cf. R. Howard Bloch, *Medieval French Literature and Law* (Berkeley, Los Angeles, London: Univ. of California Press, 1977).

27. Ernst Robert Curtius, *Europäische Literatur und lateinisches Mittelalter*, 2nd ed. (Bern: Francke, 1954), pp. 38-39.

28. Flori, "La Notion de chevalerie dans les chansons de geste du XIIe siècle: Etude historique de vocabulaire," *Moyen Age*, 81 (1975), 211-44, 407-45.

29. For what follows, see Frappier, "Le Prologue du *Chevalier de la Charrette* et son interprétation," *Romania*, 93 (1972), 337-77; and Douglas Kelly, "The Source and Meaning of *Conjointure* in Chrétien's *Erec* 14," *Viator*, 1 (1970), 179-200.

30. See Edmond Faral, *Les Arts poétiques du XIIe et du XIIIe siècle: Recherches et documents sur la technique littéraire du moyen âge*, Bibliothèque de l'Ecole des Hautes Etudes, 238 (Paris: Champion, 1924); Hennig Brinkmann, *Zu Wesen und Form mittelalterlicher Dichtung* (Halle: Niemeyer, 1928; rpt. Darmstadt: Wissenschaftliche Buchgesellschaft, 1979); Frappier, *Chrétien*, pp. 13-19; Vinaver, *Rise*, pp. 15-52.

31. Michelle A. Freeman, *The Poetics of* Translatio Studii *and* Conjointure: *Chrétien de Troyes's* Cligés, French Forum Monographs, 12 (Lexington, Ky.: French Forum, Publishers, 1979). See in general the special issue on "Intertextualités médiévales" edited by Daniel Poirion in *Littérature*, 41 (1981).

32. See the important study of the idea in Elisabeth Gössmann, *Antiqui und Moderni im Mittelalter: Eine geschichtliche Standortbestimmung*, Veröffentlichungen des Grabmann-Institutes zur Erforschung der mittelalterlichen Theologie und Philosophie, n. s. 23 (Munich, Paderborn, Vienna: Schöningh, 1974). On Marie de France in particular, see Alfred Foulet and Karl D. Uitti, "The Prologue to the *Lais* of Marie de France: A Reconsideration," *Romance Philology*, 35 (1981-1982), 242-49; Rupert T. Pickens, "La Poétique de Marie de France d'après les prologues des *Lais*," *Lettres Romanes*, 32 (1978), 367-84.

33. Curtius, *Europäische Literatur*, pp. 388-89; Uitti, "Clerkly Narrator," esp. pp. 397-99.

34. Köhler, "Zur Selbstauffassung des höfischen Dichters," in his *Trobadorlyrik und höfischer Roman: Aufsätze zur französischen und provenzalischen Literatur des Mittelalters*, Neue Beiträge zur Literaturwissenschaft, 15 (Berlin: Rütten & Loening, 1962), pp. 9-20.

35. J.D. Burnley, "*Fine Amor*: Its Meaning and Context," *Review of English Studies*, n. s. 31 (1980), 129-48; John M. Steadman, "'Courtly Love' as a Problem of Style," in *Chaucer und seine Zeit: Symposion für Walter F. Schirmer* (Tübingen: Niemeyer, 1968), pp. 1-33; Kelly, *Medieval Imagination: Rhetoric and the Poetry of Courtly Love* (Madison: Univ. of Wisconsin Press, 1978), pp. 14-22.

36. Köhler, *Ideal*, pp. 22-36 [*Aventure*, pp. 26-43].

37. Ed. Léopold Constans, S.A.T.F., 6 vols. (Paris: Firmin-Didot, 1904-1912); see Zink, "Mutation," pp. 14-17.

38. Ed. G. Perrie Williams, C.F.M.A., 38 (Paris: Champion, 1929).

39. Ed. Jean Rychner, C.F.M.A., 93 (Paris: Champion, 1968).

40. "De l' 'Enéide' à 'Eneas': Mythologie et moralisation," *Cahiers de Civilisation Médiévale*, 19 (1978), 213-29; cf. Fourquet, "Rapport," and Warning, "Formen."

41. *De vulgari eloquentia*, ed. Pier Vincenzo Mengaldo, Vulgares Eloquentes, 3 (Padua: Antenore, 1968). See Marcia L. Colish, *The Mirror of Language: A Study in the Medieval Theory of Knowledge*, Yale Historical Publications: Miscellany, 88 (New Haven, London: Yale Univ. Press, 1968), pp. 224-341.

42. On the Grail, its meanings, origins and etymology, see Frappier, "La Légende du graal: Origine et évolution," in *Grundriss*, Vol. IV, Part 1, pp. 292-331.

43. *Li Torneimenz Antecrit*, ed. Georg Wimmer, Ausgaben und Abhandlungen aus dem Gebiete der romanischen Philologie, 76 (Marburg: Elwert, 1888), II. 1336-37.

44. Cf. Frappier, "Sur la versification de Chrétien de Troyes: L'enjambement dans *Erec et Enide*," *Research Studies* (Washington State Univ.), 32 (1964), 41-49; "La Brisure du couplet dans *Erec et Enide*," *Romania*, 86 (1965), 1-21; *Etude sur Yvain ou le Chevalier au Lion de Chrétien de Troyes* (Paris: S.E.D.E.S., 1969), pp. 245-72; and *Chrétien de Troyes et le mythe du Graal: Etude sur Perceval ou le Conte du Graal* (Paris: S.E.D.E.S., 1972), pp. 257-72.

45. Cited from Ulrich Mölk, *Französische Literarästhetik des 12. und 13. Jahrhunderts: Prologue–Exkurse–Epilog*, Sammlung romanischer Übungstexte, 54 (Tübingen: Niemeyer, 1969), p. 95; see in general, pp. 92-97.

46. Köhler, "Sistema," pp. 341-44; Flori, "Origines," pp. 237-40, 247-48. Note that in Chrétien there is *no* example of ecclesiastical participation in dubbing a knight, although such participation is everywhere prominent in marriages and coronations.

47. See Richard Glasser, "Abstractum agens und Allegorie im älteren Französisch," *Zeitschrift für romanische Philologie*, 69 (1953), 43-122.

48. *Claris et Laris* and Girard d'Amiens's *Escanor* are the last known thirteenth-century verse romances; only Froissart's *Meliador*, written almost 100 years after them, survives in part as a testimony to Arthurian verse romance. See Beate Schmolke-Hasselmann, *Der arthurische Versroman von Chrestien bis Froissart: Zur Geschichte einer Gattung*, Beihefte zur Zeitschrift für romanische Philologie, 177 (Tübingen: Niemeyer, 1980); and Peter F. Dembowski, "Considérations sur *Meliador*," in *Etudes de philologie romane et d'histoire littéraire offertes à Jules Horrent* (Liège: n.p., 1980), pp. 123-31.

49. Cf. Freeman, "Problems in Romance Composition: Ovid, Chrétien de Troyes, and the *Romance of the Rose*," *Romance Philology*, 30 (1976-1977), 158-68.

50. The two most influential—and opposing—readings of the *Rose* are Daniel Poirion, *Le Roman de la Rose* (Paris: Hatier, 1973), and John V. Fleming, *The Roman de la Rose: A Study in Allegory and Iconography* (Princeton: Princeton Univ. Press, 1969).

51. Fanni Bogdanow, *The Romance of the Grail: A Study of the Structure and Genesis of a Thirteenth-Century Arthurian Prose Romance* (Manchester: Manchester Univ. Press, 1966), pp. 215-20; Vinaver, *Rise*, pp. 53-67.

52. *Rise*, pp. 30-32; Lacy, *Craft*, pp. 2-6.

53. First enunciated by Wendelin Foerster; see his *Kristian von Troyes: Wörterbuch zu seinen sämtlichen Werken*, Romanische Bibliothek, 21 (Halle: Niemeyer,

1914), pp. 43*-45*.

54. On the theoretical problems in editing Chrétien manuscripts and the editorial principles used in the available modern editions, see Alfred Foulet and Mary B. Speer, *On Editing Old French Texts*, Edward C. Armstrong Monographs on Medieval Literature, 1 (Lawrence: Regents Press of Kansas, 1979); and see below, Appendix I.

55. Paul Zumthor, *Essai de poétique médiévale* (Paris: Seuil, 1972), pp. 65-75. See as well Pierre Le Gentil, "Réflexions sur la création littéraire au moyen âge," in *Chanson de geste und höfischer Roman: Heidelberger Kolloquium 30. Januar 1961*, Studia Romanica, 4 (Heidelberg: Winter, 1963), pp. 9-20. There are useful observations in this context in Elspeth Kennedy, "The Scribe as Editor," in *Mélanges de langue et de littérature du moyen âge et de la Renaissance offerts à Jean Frappier*, 2 vols. (Geneva: Droz, 1970), I, 523-31.

56. Benoît Lacroix, *L'Historien au moyen âge*, Conférence Albert-le-Grand 1966 (Montreal: Institut d'Etudes Médiévales, Paris: Vrin, 1971), p. 75.

57. Daniel Koenig, *"Sen"/"sens" et "savoir" et leurs synonymes dans quelques romans courtois du 12e et du début du 13e siècle*, Publications Universitaires Européennes, series 13: Langue et Littérature Françaises, 22 (Bern: Herbert Lang, Frankfurt: Peter Lang, 1973).

58. See the examples of literary *accessus ad auctores* in R.B.C. Huygens, ed., *Accessus ad auctores*, Collection Latomus, 15 (Brussels: Latomus, 1954); and, by the same editor, Conrad of Hirsau, *Dialogus super auctores*, Collection Latomus, 17 (Brussels: Latomus, 1955). See in general, Edwin A. Quain, "The Medieval Accessus ad Auctores," *Traditio*, 3 (1945), 215-64; Paul Klopsch, *Einführung in die Dichtungslehren des lateinischen Mittelalters* (Darmstadt: Wissenschaftliche Buchgesellschaft, 1980), pp. 48-64; Leslie G. Whitbread, "Conrad of Hirsau as Literary Critic," *Speculum*, 47 (1972), 234-45.

59. Frappier, "Prologue," pp. 344-60.

60. Foulet and Uitti, "Prologue," p. 247; cf. Ollier, "Nom, désir, aventure: Les structures latentes d'un roman courtois," *Far-Western Forum*, 1 (1974), 226.

61. Albert Gier, "Das Verwandtschaftsverhältnis von afr. *sens* und *sen*," *Romanistisches Jahrbuch*, 28 (1977), 54-72; and Uitti, *Story, Myth and Celebration in Old French Narrative Poetry 1050-1200* (Princeton: Princeton Univ. Press, 1973), p. 135, n. 6 (to p. 137).

62. Kelly, "Rhetoric in French Literature: Topical Invention in Medieval French Literature," in *Medieval Eloquence: Studies in Theory and Practice of Medieval Rhetoric*, ed. James J. Murphy (Berkeley, Los Angeles, London: Univ. of California Press, 1978), pp. 231-51. For an excellent *mise au point* on the theory of topical invention, see Lothar Bornscheuer, *Topik: Zur Struktur der gesellschaftlichen Einbildungskraft* (Frankfurt: Suhrkamp, 1976).

63. Köhler, "Selbstauffassung."

64. Frappier, "Concept," and "'D'amors,' 'par amors,'" *Romania*, 88 (1967), 433-74; Kelly, *Medieval*, pp. 13-22; Joan M. Ferrante, "*Cortes' amor* in Medieval Texts," *Speculum*, 55 (1980), 686-95; Burnley, "*Fine amor.*"

65. Kelly, "Courtly Love in Perspective: The Hierarchy of Love in Andreas Capellanus," *Traditio*, 24 (1968), 119-47.

66. Trimpi, "The Quality of Fiction: The Rhetorical Transmission of Literary Theory," *Traditio*, 30 (1974), 81-89.

67. Marie-Claire Zai, ed., *Les Chansons courtoises de Chrétien de Troyes*, Publications Universitaires Européennes, series 13: Langue et Littérature Françaises, 27 (Bern: Herbert Lang, Frankfurt: Peter Lang, 1974), p. 78, ll. 28-36.

68. See Marc Bloch, *La Société médiévale* (Paris: Albin Michel, 1939, 1968), pp. 197-208, 416-33; Duby, *Medieval Marriage*.

69. *Le Roman de Thèbes*, ed. Guy Raynaud de Lage, 2 vols., C.F.M.A., 94, 96 (Paris: Champion, 1966-1971); cf. Köhler, "Literatursoziologische," pp. 86-88.

70. "Literatursoziologische," pp. 90-91.

71. *Ideal*, pp. 89-90 [*Aventure*, pp. 102-03].

72. Ollier, "Nom," pp. 221-32.

73. Kelly, "Source," pp. 179-88.

74. Bruckner, *Narrative*.

75. Edgar de Bruyne, *Etudes d'esthétique médiévale*, 3 vols. (Bruges: De Tempel, 1946), II, 31-34, 173-202; Alice M. Colby, *The Portrait in Twelfth-Century French Literature: An Example of the Stylistic Originality of Chrétien de Troyes* (Geneva: Droz, 1965).

76. Hugh of Saint Victor, *Didascalicon: De studio legendi*, ed. Charles Henry Buttimer (Washington: Catholic Univ. Press, 1939), p. 16; *The Didascalicon: A Medieval Guide to the Arts*, trans. Jerome Taylor (New York, London: Columbia Univ. Press, 1961), p. 55.

77. De Bruyne, *Etudes*, II, 255-301; Brian Stock, *Myth and Science in the Twelfth Century: A Study of Bernard Silvester* (Princeton: Princeton Univ. Press, 1972), esp. pp. 11-62; Peter Dronke, *Fabula: Explorations into the Uses of Myth in Medieval Platonism*, Mittellateinische Studien und Texte, 9 (Leiden, Cologne: Brill, 1974).

78. Kelly, "Theory of Composition in Medieval Narrative Poetry and Geoffrey of Vinsauf's *Poetria Nova*," *Mediaeval Studies*, 31 (1969), 117-30; Dronke, "Medieval Rhetoric," in *The Mediaeval World*, ed. D. Daiches and A. Thorlby, Literature and Western Civilisation, 2 (London: Aldus, 1972), pp. 315-46; Kelly, *Medieval*, pp. 26-45.

79. Winthrop Wetherbee, *Platonism and Poetry in the Twelfth Century: The Literary Influence of the School of Chartres* (Princeton: Princeton Univ. Press, 1972); Stock, *Myth*.

80. Wetherbee, *Platonism*, pp. 255-66; Poirion, *Roman*, pp. 174-86.

81. Uitti, "A propos de philologie," *Littérature*, 41 (1981), 30-46; Thomas Elwood Hart, "Chrestien, Macrobius and Chartrean Science: The Allegorical Robe as Symbol of Textual Design in the Old French *Erec*," *Mediaeval Studies*, 43 (1981), 250-96.

82. That stage in narrative composition intermediate between the *disiecta membra* of the source (cf. *depecier* and *corronpre*) and the *conjointure*; see *The Medieval French Roman d'Alexandre*, ed. E.C. Armstrong, et al., Elliott Monographs, 37 (Princeton: Princeton Univ. Press, 1937), pp. ix-xi. De Bruyne in fact translates *(con)-iunctura* in Alain de Lille's *De planctu Naturæ* by the same word: "pour peindre un tableau plus élégant, composé de thèmes variés, le poète *amalgame*, par sa jonglerie fabulatrice, des faits historiques d'origine diverse avec des fictions fabuleuses" (*Etudes*, II, 281).

83. Cf. the introduction to the description of Fenice, above, p. 35. Marie de France's conception of inventing the obscure meaning in her sources is the same, and relies on traditional methods of textual elucidation and composition; see Foulet and Uitti, "Prologue."

84. De Bruyne, *Etudes*, II, 14-49; R.R. Bolgar, *The Classical Heritage and Its Beneficiaries* (Cambridge: Cambridge Univ. Press, 1954), pp. 194-200. Cf. Stock, *Myth*, pp. 119-37.

85. These are the traditional fields of topical invention in medieval schooling;

see Bornscheuer, *Topik,* pp. 170-71.

86. Thomas, *Les Fragments du Roman de Tristan,* ed. Bartina H. Wind, T.L.F., 92 (Geneva: Droz, Paris: Minard, 1960).

87. See Burnley, *"Fine amor,"* pp. 142-44; see also Zink, "Mutation," pp. 21-23. For a different interpretation of these lines, see Tony Hunt, "The Significance of Thomas's *Tristan," Reading Medieval Studies,* 7 (1981), 41-61.

"Erec et Enide,"
by Edward J. Buckbee

1. For editions of Chrétien, see above, p. 311, n. 1 to p. 13.

2. Pierre-Yves Badel, *Introduction à la vie littéraire du moyen âge* (Paris: Bordas, 1969), p. 181.

3. E. Peter Nolan, "Mythopoetic Evolution: Chrétien de Troyes' *Erec et Enide, Cligés* and *Yvain," Symposium,* 25 (1971), 142.

4. Ibid., p. 145.

5. Roger Sherman Loomis, *Arthurian Tradition and Chrétien de Troyes* (New York: Columbia Univ. Press, 1949), pp. 22-36, 61-184. See also Jean Frappier, "Chrétien de Troyes," in *Arthurian Literature in the Middle Ages,* ed. Roger Sherman Loomis (Oxford: Clarendon Press, 1959), pp. 161-71.

6. Winthrop Wetherbee, *Platonism and Poetry in the Twelfth Century: The Literary Influence of the School of Chartres* (Princeton: Princeton Univ. Press, 1972), pp. 220-41.

7. Stefan Hofer, *Chrétien de Troyes: Leben und Werke des altfranzösischen Epikers* (Graz, Cologne: Böhlaus, 1954), pp. 9-86.

8. For a major general treatment of these themes in Chrétien and with particular remarks on *Erec,* see Erich Köhler, *Ideal und Wirklichkeit in der höfischen Epik,* 2nd ed. (Tübingen: Niemeyer, 1970), pp. 5-180 (*L'Aventure chevaleresque: Idéal et réalité dans le roman courtois,* trans. Eliane Kaufholz [Paris: Gallimard, 1974], pp. 7-207).

9. Jean Frappier, *Chrétien de Troyes* (Paris: Hatier, 1968), p. 95.

10. Norris Lacy, "Thematic Analogues in *Erec," L'Esprit Créateur,* 9 (1969), 274.

11. A.R. Press, "Le Comportement d'Erec envers Enide dans le roman de Chrétien de Troyes," *Romania,* 90 (1969), 533.

12. Kelly, *Sens and Conjointure in the* Chevalier de la Charrette, Studies in French Literature, 2 (The Hague, Paris: Mouton, 1966), pp. 36-39.

13. Reto R. Bezzola, *Le Sens de l'aventure et de l'amour (Chrétien de Troyes)* (Paris: La Jeune Parque, n.d. [1947]), p. 78.

14. Kelly, "La Forme et le sens de la quête dans l'*Erec et Enide* de Chrétien de Troyes," *Romania,* 92 (1971), 343-44.

15. Frappier, *Chrétien de Troyes,* p. 101.

16. Kelly, "The Source and Meaning of *Conjointure* in Chrétien's *Erec* 14," *Viator,* 1 (1970), 179-200.

17. "Escïence," in Tobler-Lommatzsch, *Altfranzösisches Wörterbuch* (Wiesbaden: Franz Steiner, 1954), III, cols. 904-05.

18. For an elucidation of key theoretical pronouncements on his literary craft made by Chrétien in the prologues to his romances, see Marie-Louise Ollier, "The

Author in the Text: The Prologues of Chrétien de Troyes," *Yale French Studies*, 51 (1974), 26-41.

19. Alfred Adler, "Sovereignty as the Principle of Unity in Chrétien's *Erec*," *PMLA*, 60 (1945), 936.

20. Compare the reading of Roques's l. 6677 with that of *Erec und Enide*, ed. Wendelin Foerster, 2nd ed. (Halle: Niemeyer, 1909), ll. 6738-39: "Si an trai a garant Macrobe, / Qui au descrivre mist s'antante" (And I take for authority Macrobius, who applied himself to the subject of description). Such a reading would underscore that Macrobius is a model of descriptive technique, as such, whatever the actual subjects of his descriptions.

21. Claude Luttrell, *The Creation of the First Arthurian Romance: A Quest* (Evanston, Ill.: Northwestern Univ. Press, 1974), p. 25.

22. A promising approach, one which suggests a response by Chrétien to the Old French *Eneas* and medieval Virgilian commentaries, is presented by Joseph S. Wittig, "The Aeneas-Dido Allusion in Chrétien's *Erec et Enide*," *Comparative Literature*, 22 (1970), 237-53.

23. J.-J. Salverda de Grave, ed., *Eneas, roman du XIIe siècle* (Paris: Champion, 1964), ll. 4047-68. See Erich Auerbach, "Camilla, or, the Rebirth of the Sublime," in his *Literary Language and Its Public in Late Latin Antiquity and in the Middle Ages*, trans. Ralph Manheim (New York: Pantheon, 1965), pp. 181-233.

24. Only manuscript *A* (Guiot's copy), the manuscript Roques favors, gives *haster* here; the others read *gaster*, which would yield this translation of l. 5527: "and I do not at all want to waste it." Roques explains his preference: "la leçon *haster*: *haster* permet un sens qui ne serait pas sans intérêt: '... ce serait sottement mal employer le temps que de détailler la broderie, et ce temps je ne veux pas non plus le presser (par une description trop rapide); c'est plutôt moi que je veux presser en allant droit mon chemin sans faire de détour ou m'égarer.' Conviendrait-il d'attribuer cette subtilité à Chrétien ou à Guiot? Elle ne serait étonnante ni chez l'un ni chez l'autre; et elle donnerait une justification de plus à ces rimes du même au même, dont le nombre ne permet guère de les expliquer par de simples distractions" (*Erec et Enide*, p. 229, note to ll. 5527-28).

25. Jean Frappier, "Pour le commentaire d'*Erec et Enide*: Notes de lecture, I. 'Bilis, li rois d'Antipodés' (éd. Foerster, v. 1994; éd. Roques, v. 1942)," *Marche Romane*, 20, No. 4 (1970), 15-17. In general, see Wilhelm Kellermann, *Aufbaustil und Weltbild Chrestiens von Troyes im Percevalroman*, Beihefte zur Zeitschrift für romanische Philologie, 88 (Halle: Niemeyer, 1936; rpt. Darmstadt: Wissenschaftliche Buchgesellschaft, 1967).

26. See the general study of this matter by Erich Köhler, "Le Rôle de la 'coutume' dans les romans de Chrétien de Troyes," *Romania*, 81 (1960), 386-97.

27. Pierre-Yves Badel, *Introduction*, p. 194.

28. Charles Foulon, "Le Rôle de Gauvain dans *Erec et Enide*," *Annales de Bretagne*, 65 (1958), 147-58.

29. Ibid., p. 156.

30. Ibid., 158.

31. Speaking generally of Chrétien's romances, Köhler observes: "L'aventure est ... le moyen qui permet au chevalier, en tant qu'individu, d'atteindre à une compréhension complète de soi-même et à l'harmonisation de la réalité de son existence avec l'image idéale qu'il s'en fait. Elle sert d'instrument pour rétablir à la fois l' 'ordo' et la perfection individuelle à laquelle, dès maintenant, semble lié l'ordre d'un état

féodal idéal" ("Rôle," p. 396).

32. T.A. Shippey, "The Uses of Chivalry: 'Erec' and 'Gawain,'" *Modern Language Review*, 66 (1971), 243.

33. Donald Maddox, *Structure and Sacring: The Systematic Kingdom in Chrétien's* Erec et Enide, French Forum Monographs, 8 (Lexington, Ky.: French Forum, Publishers, 1978), p. 24.

"Cligés," by Michelle A. Freeman

1. "The word *transfertur* [in Ecclesiasticus 10:8] ('is transferred') gives rise to the concept of *translatio* (transference) which is basic for medieval historical theory. The renewal of the Empire by Charlemagne could be regarded as the transferal of the Roman *imperium* to other people. This is implied in the formula *translatio imperii*, with which the *translatio studii* (transferal of learning from Athens or Rome to Paris) was later coordinated. The medieval Empire took over from Rome the idea of world empire; thus it had a universal, not a national, character." E.R. Curtius, *European Literature and the Latin Middle Ages*, trans. W.R. Trask (New York, Evanston, Ill.: Harper and Row, 1963), pp. 28-29.

2. This chapter reflects, in large part, revised work already completed on Chrétien's *Cligés* that I first published in an article, "Chrétien's *Cligés*: A Close Reading of the Prologue," *Romanic Review*, 67 (1976), 89-101; in my monograph, *The Poetics of* Translatio Studii *and* Conjointure: *Chrétien de Troyes's* Cligés, French Forum Monographs, 12 (Lexington, Ky.: French Forum, Publishers, 1979); and in "Transpositions structurelles et intertextualité: Le 'Cligés' de Chrétien," *Littérature*, 41 (1981), 50-61. For editions of Chrétien, see above, p. 311, n. 1 to p. 13.

3. *The Gothic Cathedral: Origins of Gothic Architecture and the Medieval Concept of Order,* Bollingen Series, 48 (Princeton: Princeton Univ. Press, 1962), p. 14.

4. For discussions of the Classical rhetorical tradition and its directives for *exordia*, see Edmond Faral, *Les Arts poétiques du XIIe et du XIIIe siècle*, Bibliothèque de l'Ecole des Hautes Etudes, 238 (1924; rpt. Paris: Champion, 1962); E.R. Curtius, *European Literature*; and Tony Hunt, "The Rhetorical Background to the Arthurian Prologue: Tradition and the Old French Vernacular Prologues," *Forum for Modern Language Studies*, 6 (1970), 1-23, and "Tradition and Originality in the Prologues of Chrestien de Troyes," *Forum for Modern Language Studies*, 8 (1972), 320-44.

5. Ovid, *Metamorphoses*, trans. Frank Justus Miller, The Loeb Classical Library (Cambridge, Mass.: Harvard Univ. Press, London: Heinemann, 1944).

6. Pseudo-Cicero, *Ad C. Herennium: De ratione dicendi (Rhetorica ad Herennium)*, trans. Harry Caplan, The Loeb Classical Library (Cambridge, Mass.: Harvard Univ. Press, London: Heinemann, 1954), I, v, 8.

7. See, for example, Joseph Anglade, *Grammaire élémentaire de l'ancien français*, Collection U (Paris: Armand Colin, 1965), p. 179.

8. See Anthime Fourrier, *Le Courant réaliste dans le roman courtois en France au moyen âge*, I: *Les Débuts (XIIe siècle)* (Paris: Nizet, 1960), pp. 392-94.

9. On the Chrétien-*Tristan* problem, see Douglas Kelly, *Chrétien de Troyes: An Analytic Bibliography*, Research Bibliographies and Checklists, 17 (London: Grant and Cutler, 1976), p. 129.

10. All references in this chapter to Thomas's *Tristan* are taken from *Les Fragments du roman de Tristan, poème du XIIe siècle*, ed. Bartina H. Wind (Leiden: E.J. Brill, 1950). References to Béroul's *Tristan* are taken from *Le Roman de Tristan, poème du XIIe siècle*, ed. Ernest Muret, 4th ed. revised by L.M. Defourques, C.F.M.A., 12 (Paris: Champion, 1967).

11. Concerning the two varieties of potions, see Jean Frappier, "Structure et sens du *Tristan*: Version commune, version courtoise," *Cahiers de Civilisation Médiévale*, 6 (1963), 255-80, 441-54, esp. pp. 266-79.

12. "'*Lameir* is what distresses me,' answered Love's falcon, Isolde, 'it is *lameir* that so oppresses me, *lameir* it is that pains me so.'

"Hearing her say *lameir* so often he weighed and examined the meaning of the word most narrowly. He then recalled that *l'ameir* meant 'Love,' *l'ameir* 'bitter,' *la meir* 'the sea': it seemed to have a host of meanings. He disregarded the one, and asked about the two. Not a word did he say of Love, who was mistress of them both, their common hope and desire. All that he discussed was 'sea' and 'bitter.'" Gottfried von Strassburg, *Tristan*, trans. A.T. Hatto (Baltimore: Penguin, 1967), p. 199.

13. This sort of avowal scene is not new. It was handled previously in the Old French *Eneas* in the scene between Lavine and her mother, a scene which itself is an adaptation of Ovidian examples. Beyond transforming the Thomas example, then, Chrétien manages to invent a parallel with an earlier romance that itself goes back at least as far as Ovid, one of our poet-narrator's avowed masters. This is complex intertextual strategy indeed, but one that is characteristic of the poetics of *Cligés*.

14. For an example of this kind of analysis, see Tristan's internal monologue-dialogue in which he debates whether or not he should try to forget Iseut by marrying Iseut aux Blanches Mains (Thomas, Sneyd Fragment, ll. 5-182), or the narrator's open-ended debate concerning which of the two couples, Mark and the Blond Iseut or Tristan and Iseut White-Hands, suffers more (Thomas, Turin Fragment, ll. 144-83).

15. For an example of the *cors/cuers* dichotomy in Thomas's *Tristan*, see the Turin Fragment, ll. 83-183.

16. Kelly, "Theory of Composition in Medieval Poetry and Geoffrey of Vinsauf's *Poetria Nova*," *Mediaeval Studies*, 31 (1969), 126; numerous examples are found in Henri de Lubac, *Exégèse médiévale*, 4 vols. (Paris: Aubier, 1959-1964), II, Part 2, pp. 41-60.

17. See Gertrude Schoepperle Loomis, *Tristan and Isolt: A Study of the Sources of the Romance*, 2nd ed., Vol. I (1913; rpt. New York: Burt Franklin, 1960): "The episode, as given in Eilhart, presents almost without modification, a folk tale which was common in the fiction of the Middle Ages, as it still is in popular tradition: A king sees a hair on the waters of a stream or in the beak of a bird. He decides that he must have to wife the woman to whom the hair belongs. A young hero undertakes the quest and succeeds in obtaining her for the king.

"As will be observed on examining versions of the folk tale of the Swallow's Hair, one of the essential elements of the story is that the princess and her whereabouts are unknown. This requirement seems incompatible with the story of the hero's healing at the hands of that same princess a few months before. The difficulty is met in Eilhart by the slightest possible change in the first narrative—we are told that Isolt does not tend the wounded Tristan in person: she sends a messenger to him with healing herbs and he departs from Ireland without seeing her.

"In Thomas the two incidents have undergone a thorough remodeling, and are fused to the advantage of the story. Tristan is healed by Isolt in person during the first visit. The second voyage is not introduced by a story of two swallows and a mysterious hair; the quest which Tristan undertakes is no longer for a princess whose identity is unknown. On the contrary, it is introduced by Tristan's praises, on his return from his visit to Ireland, of the princess who has healed him there. It is decided that this princess would be a suitable wife for Mark, and Tristan undertakes to set out and win her. When Isolt finds him, after the slaying of the dragon they of course recognize each other. It is clear, however, from the passages in Gottfried and *Sir Tristrem* which allude to the Swallow's Hair and reject it as improbable, that Thomas' model gave the Béroul-Eilhart version and that Thomas has given it, on his own responsibility, the modified form which we have just read" (pp. 86-87).

The story of the quest of a bride for Mark is told in the *estoire* as follows: "After a month of aimless sailing, Tristan commands the boatmen to avoid Ireland and declares that they must make a thorough search through all lands. The boat is, however, driven by a storm to the shore on which Tristan was healed. He knows that, in revenge for the death of the Morholt, every person who approaches this shore is put to death. With evil forebodings he plans a ruse. The Irish king, angered by the nearness of a boat, commands the marshal to go down and kill those on board. Tristan offers the marshal a golden cup, and asks him to tell the king that they are merchants come from England to sell food" (pp. 186-87).

"A favorite ruse of the wooer in the folk tales is to pretend that he and his men are merchants. In *Tristan* the account of the famine in Ireland in the Voyage for Healing serves to explain this motif. The hero pretends that he is bringing provisions to the distressed country. In the folk tales and popular epics the maiden is lured on board the ship in order to examine the merchant's goods. The strangers then lift anchor and sail away. This plan is followed at two other points in the Tristan story. In the version of Thomas, the Norwegian merchants thus kidnap the youthful hero. In the *estoire* the messenger sent by the dying Tristan to Cornwall employs the same ruse with the complicity of Isolt" (pp. 192-93).

In the *estoire*, the quest prompted by the swallow's hair, connected with Tristan passing himself off as a merchant and giving a golden cup to the King in order to allay his anger, puts all three motifs together. Only two of these features—Tristan the merchant and the golden cup (repeated in the Kaherdin-Iseut scene in Thomas)—are taken up by Chrétien to supply the missing detail of the strand of hair in the shirt.

18. See above, Buckbee, "*Erec et Enide*," pp. 74-75.

19. See Winthrop Wetherbee, *Platonism and Poetry in the Twelfth Century: The Literary Influence of the School of Chartres* (Princeton: Princeton Univ. Press, 1972), pp. 236-39, on Enide's saddle and the relevance of the comparison between the *Eneas* and Chrétien's romance. See also an earlier study on the same topic by Joseph S. Wittig, "The Aeneas-Dido Allusion in Chrétien's *Erec et Enide*," *Comparative Literature*, 22 (1970), 237-53.

20. Lewis and Short, *A Latin Dictionary* (Oxford: Clarendon Press, 1975), p. 555.

21. Cicero, cited as an example for this frequent usage of the meaning of *describo*, is all the more interesting for our text, since the second time in this episode that Chrétien mentions the term *descrivre*, he does so to invoke the authority of Macrobius: "Macrobe m'anseigne a descrivre" (l. 6679). Since we know that Macrobius wrote a commentary on Cicero's *Dream of Scipio*, we might be authorized to understand the reference to *descrivre* in this context, seeing the art of commentary as a kind of copy in the sense of a redoing of an original text. See Karl D. Uitti, "A propos de philologie," *Littérature*, 41 (1981), 30-46, for further discussion. Chrétien is

himself elaborating a kind of commentary in his *Erec et Enide* (albeit a poetic one) on such other original texts as the *Eneas*.

22. In his review, "A Man with an Eye" (*The New York Times Book Review*, February 24, 1980), James Breckenridge makes the following remark which is pertinent to my discussion of the thrones in *Erec et Enide*: "This is in the article 'The Joseph Scenes on the Maximianus Throne in Ravenna' [from Meyer Schapiro's book *Late Antique, Early Christian and Medieval Art* (New York: George Braziller, 1980)] in which Professor Shapiro seems to think that this assemblage of ivory panels served as the functional seat of the Archbishop. It is generally agreed that ivory seats of this sort were never intended for people; their purpose was to dignify books of the Gospel and the liturgy in the cathedral sanctuary" (p. 42).

23. The original use to which description is put near the very end of Chrétien's text might explain in part the abrupt ending of that romance. Chrétien has done what needs doing once he has described the thrones and Erec's regalia, including the robe embroidered with the figures of the quadrivium. Any attempt to describe the rest of the sumptuous feast and its decorative riches for their own sake would detract from this other function of description. Such a display would recall, or imitate, in all likelihood, the sorts of splendiferous and exotic descriptions carried on at length in, for example, the *Roman d'Eneas*. This latter romance also ends abruptly, in a manner which serves to undercut the matter so quickly glossed over after the references to the wedding and coronation. The matter at stake is Eneas' lineage. If historical matters are somewhat brushed aside in this text in order to emphasize instead matters of craft, then, by deploying an analogous treatment at the end of *Erec*, Chrétien could ask his audience to draw a conclusion with respect to description in the *Eneas* vis-à-vis description in the *Erec et Enide* similar to that desired by the *Eneas* poet in regard to his treatment of Virgil's epic, as this treatment differed from the concerns of his model. Each case serves to underscore the departures from, and innovative treatments given to, an original.

24. The distinction I refer to was drawn originally by Uitti, *Story, Myth, and Celebration in Old French Narrative Poetry 1050-1200* (Princeton: Princeton Univ. Press, 1973).

"*Le Chevalier de la Charrette (Lancelot),*" by Matilda Tomaryn Bruckner

1. For editions of Chrétien, see above, p. 311, n. 1 to p. 13. Roques's edition closes the quotation after l. 20. I have corrected this obvious mistake by moving the end marks to l. 18.

2. *Ille et Galeron*, ed. Frederick A.G. Cowper (Paris: Picard, 1956), p. 5 (ll. 79-102, in manuscript *P*). A number of Gautier's images recur in the *Charrette*: the lady compared to a gem (ll. 16-18), the brilliance of refined gold used to describe Guenevere's hair (ll. 1488-89). The second image is varied slightly, but its function is similar, since it indicates how one bright thing surpasses another. Gautier also uses a verb important in Chrétien's romance: "s'aüne" (l. 83).

3. Anthime Fourrier, *Le Courant réaliste dans le roman courtois en France au moyen âge*, I: *Les Débuts (XIIe siècle)* (Paris: Nizet, 1960), pp. 206-07; Jean Rychner, "Le Prologue du *Chevalier de la Charrette*," *Vox Romanica*, 26 (1967), 6-8.

4. Cf. Calogrenant's instructions to his audience on listening with both ears

and heart to the tale of his adventure (*Yvain*, ll. 150-74), and below, Uitti, *"Yvain,"* p. 207.

5. William A. Nitze, "Sans et matière dans les œuvres de Chrétien de Troyes," *Romania*, 44 (1915-1917), 19-21; Pierre-Yves Badel, "Rhétorique et polémique dans les prologues de romans au moyen âge," *Littérature*, 20 (1975), 83-84; and Erich Köhler, *Trobadorlyrik und höfischer Roman* (Berlin: Rütten & Loening, 1962), p. 10.

6. Cf. Emile Benveniste, *Problèmes de linguistique générale* (Paris: Gallimard, 1966), esp. pp. 225-32.

7. Marie-Louise Ollier, "The Author in the Text: The Prologues of Chrétien de Troyes," *Yale French Studies*, 51 (1974), 28.

8. For the Celtic thesis, see, for example, Roger Sherman Loomis, "The Modena Sculpture and Arthurian Romance," *Studi Medievali*, n. s. 9 (1936), 1-17; and T.P. Cross and W.A. Nitze, *Lancelot and Guenevere: A Study on the Origins of Courtly Love* (Chicago: Univ. of Chicago Press, 1930). Alexandre Micha, "Sur les sources de la *Charrette*," *Romania*, 71 (1950), 345-58, argues for a hagiographic source, while H.C.R. Laurie sees in the *Charrette* a combination of Ovid, Christian mystical fervor and the worshipping lover of the troubadours. See her *"Eneas* and the *Lancelot* of Chrétien de Troyes," *Medium Aevum*, 37 (1968), 142-56.

9. Karl D. Uitti, *Story, Myth and Celebration in Old French Narrative Poetry 1050-1200* (Princeton: Princeton Univ. Press, 1973), pp. 135-36, n. 6; see also Alfred Foulet and Karl D. Uitti, "The Prologue to the *Lais* of Marie de France," *Romance Philology*, 35 (1981), 247 and n. 9, for a brief discussion of Marie's use of san/sans.

10. See Albert Gier, "Das Verwandtschaftsverhältnis von afr. *sens* und *sen*," *Romanistisches Jahrbuch*, 28 (1977), 54-72. His argument would eliminate the necessity of any direct Germanic influence, since the complete range of meanings (from direction to "understanding") is fully represented in the Latin usage of *sensus*. Gier follows up the argument with a series of Old French examples to demonstrate that *sen* and *sens* both express the same complex of meanings.

11. Jean Rychner denies this distinction in "Prologue," pp. 1-23. He would interpret ll. 26-29 as part of Chrétien's conventional compliment to Marie: the patroness inspires her poet by nourishing his faculties (science, discernment, ideals, talent) more than his desire or will to write (p. 13). But see Jean Frappier's rebuttal in "Le Prologue du *Chevalier de la Charrette* et son interprétation," *Romania*, 93 (1972), 337-77.

12. "Prologue," p. 342.

13. Andreas Capellanus, *The Art of Courtly Love*, trans. John J. Parry (New York: Norton, 1969), pp. 106-07.

14. *Chrétien de Troyes* (Paris: Hatier, 1968), p. 122.

15. Frappier reaffirms the gap between Chrétien's ethic and Marie's instructions in "Prologue," pp. 337-77. See also Richard L. Michener, "Courtly Love in Chrétien: The 'Demande d'amour,'" *Studia Neophilologica*, 42 (1970), 353-60; David J. Shirt, "Chrétien de Troyes and the Cart," in *Studies in Medieval Literature in Memory of Frederic Whitehead* (Manchester: Manchester Univ. Press, 1973), pp. 279-301.

16. See, for example, John Benton, "The Court of Champagne as a Literary Center," *Speculum*, 36 (1961), 578-82; Michael D. Cherniss, "The Literary Comedy of Andreas Capellanus," *Modern Philology*, 72 (1975), 223-37; Wesley Trimpi, "The Quality of Fiction: The Rhetorical Transmission of Literary Theory," *Traditio*, 30 (1974), 75-118, esp. pp. 81-89.

17. Once Marie has thus been set up as an arbitrary *domna*, sympathy for or complicity with Chrétien leads some scholars to turn the tables on her. For example,

in "Proper Behavior in Chrétien's *Charrette*," *French Review*, 48 (1975), 683-89, Jerome Mandel speculates on how Marie's shortcomings may have permitted her agile poet-servant to outwit her.

18. Cf. Norris J. Lacy, *The Craft of Chrétien de Troyes: An Essay on Narrative Art*, Davis Medieval Texts and Studies, 3 (Leiden: Brill, 1980), pp. 54-60. His discussion on the Prologue (p. 57) points out Chrétien's distancing techniques, without equating such irony with criticism of Marie.

19. Cf. the Prologue's treatment of the truth motif, ll. 7-20.

20. This recalls Marie's exceptional status as described in the Prologue hyperboles.

21. The narrator comments favorably when the Proud Son decides to give up his pursuit of Lancelot; this time he has properly interpreted the situation: "Del retorner a fet grant *san*" (l. 1996, my emphasis) (He showed great *sense* in returning).

22. Ollier, p. 32.

23. Uitti, *Story*, p. 137, n. 6.

24. The *Prose Lancelot* will adapt this aspect to Lancelot's own biography. Since the Lady of the Lake conceals his name, Lancelot knows nothing about his identity until he achieves his first great adventure, the capture of the Dolorous Guard. In a scene which shows how the prose romancer reinvents his narrative at least partially from materials already used in the *Charrette*, Lancelot discovers his name written on a tombstone reserved for the liberator of the castle. Elsewhere we learn that Lancelot's original name was Galahad.

25. The word *panser* appears with another meaning in the Prologue, where it describes Chrétien's own arrangement of *san et matiere*.

26. The Queen's name appears for the first time in the *Charrette* during Lancelot's monologue, when he is debating whether or not to risk his quest by going to the Immodest Damsel's aid. The only other time Guenevere's name occurs in the romance is in Bademagu's conversation with his son immediately preceding this combat scene. There also the relationship between Lancelot and the Queen is emphasized, since Bademagu is describing the hero's mission: "Il quiert la reïne Ganievre" (l. 3207) (He is searching for Queen Guenevere).

27. Cf. the description of his *panser* cited at the beginning of this section.

28. The *pucele*'s repeatedly indirect manner of referring to the Queen suggests that where one can speak of Lancelot by name, "Guenevere" must be concealed: see the later discussion of public and private worlds, the Queen's court function distinguished from her role as woman and lover (below, p. 155).

29; This is a variation of the formula used in the Prologue (l. 20) to describe Chrétien's own predicament through hyperboles.

30. Jean Dornbush, " 'Conjointure' and Continuation in the Old French Prose 'Lancelot': Essays on Form and Craft in the Thirteenth-Century Romance," (diss. Princeton University, 1976), pp. 192-96.

31. Cf., for example, the episode with the Ford Knight: Lancelot's *panser* first makes him oblivious to the challenges shouted out; later, once he realizes how long the combat has gone on, shame makes him hasten towards victory.

32. Or at least almost equal: the narrator indicates how eagerly Lancelot rushes out to fight *au mialz*, eager to show off his prowess (ll. 5918-21).

33. Cf. Lancelot lost in thought as his thirsty horse heads straight for the ford, rider and horse equally unmindful of the knight's threats.

34. Unlike Chrétien's earlier romances, the *Charrette* contains no portraits of hero or heroine. The accent is placed not on physical beauty *per se* (that is taken for

granted in the idealized world of Arthurian society), but rather on the magnitude of its effect on others (see, for example, ll. 3540-49).

35. The same pattern appeared in the midpoint scene with the momentary gap between Lancelot's past reputation and his current action.

36. The herald's cry is repeated in ll. 5563-64, 5571, 5617-18, 5678-84, 5963. The notion of "better or worse" occurs in ll. 5370-74, 5589, 5622, 5632-33, 5645, 5654, 5661-62, 5685-88, 5704-05, 5708-18, 5736-43, 5772, 5842, 5853, 5864-65, 5879, 5889, 5912-15, 5958-60, 5988-92, 6019-27 (cf. also the repetition of the same idea during the first combat between Lancelot and Meleagant, ll. 3546-49, 3626-33, 3826-37).

37. Note that the public revelation of his name in the midpoint scene is not his doing. Later at the tournament, he leaves the red shield in the middle of the melee and disappears without collecting the victory prize.

38. Lancelot gives this information on his origin just as it becomes significant: the cemetery episode apparently occurs in a region just between Logres and Gorre, since Lancelot's next stop puts him in the company of prisoners. Lancelot serves Arthur's kingdom best as he moves away from and back to it.

39. When Lancelot arrives for the final combat with Meleagant, Gauvain sees immediately that it is Lancelot (the verb used is *veoir*, not *reconoistre*). Anonymity and identity are no longer in question in this final scene: since he has been absent for over a year, it is Lancelot's visibility that strikes Gauvain.

40. Lacy, "Thematic Structure in the *Charrette*," *L'Esprit Créateur*, 12 (Spring 1972), 16-17.

41. This is not to say that Lancelot is Chrétien's *porte-parole* or that the *Charrette* on the whole eliminates such conflicts: see my closing discussion of *san*.

42. Cf. Frappier, *Chrétien*, p. 139.

43. Douglas Kelly, *Sens and Conjointure in the* Chevalier de la Charrette, Studies in French Literature, 2 (The Hague, Paris: Mouton, 1966), p. 66.

44. Marie-Claire Zai, ed., *Les Chansons courtoises de Chrétien de Troyes* (Bern: Herbert Lang, 1974), p. 59.

45. Fanni Bogdanow, "The Love Theme in Chrétien de Troyes's 'Chevalier de la Charrette,'" *Modern Language Review*, 67 (1972), 52-61.

46. The adoration of Guenevere's golden hairs recalls a similar scene in *Cligés*, when Alixandre is stunned to discover one of Soredamor's hairs woven into his shirt. The motif of the golden hair, like Chrétien's use of the bloody sheets episode, suggests an implicit reference to *Tristan* material (see for example, in Béroul's version, ll. 731-79, and above, Freeman, "*Cligés*," pp. 119-23). But these echoes point out Chrétien's comic exploitation of the *matière* in contrast to the *Tristan's* tragic development. The same preference for humorous treatment of potentially tragic materials appears in the *suicides manqués* of Lancelot and Guenevere, drawn from the Pyramus and Thisbe story (Lancelot himself is explicitly described shortly before as loving more than Pyramus, l. 3803).

47. This father-son couple parallels and serves as a gloss on the Bademagu-Meleagant pair. See Mandel, "Elements in the *Charrette* World: The Father-Son Relationship," *Modern Philology*, 62 (1964), 97-104.

48. The double line indicates a couple already formed by defending knight and lady. The broken lines link challenger and lady. A solid line links the two rival knights. The direction of the arrows in the triangles indicates "who desires whom." For example, in the first, Meleagant desires the Queen, but she does not return his desire. Mutual desire exists only between Lancelot and Guenevere.

49. Strictly speaking, Keu does not desire the Queen so much as the opportunity to display his prowess in her defense. Nor is Meleagant's motivation clear in the opening scene. Only later, in the conversation with Bademagu, do we learn that he loves the Queen (l. 3279). It is tempting to speculate that this unexpected desire arises in Meleagant primarily from his position in the series of triangular relationships and from his frustration at being denied the fruits of his victory over Keu (cf. the intensity of his anger later when Meleagant thinks Keu has enjoyed the Queen's favors, ll. 4756-67, 4785-4818).

50. Cf. Kelly, *Sens*, pp. 214-15.

51. See ll. 4588-89, 4654-61, 4669-84, 5872-75.

52. Cf. Juri Lotman's discussion of the "personnage mobile" who is unbound by the text's binary oppositions and who thus possesses the solution for actions forbidden to other, immobile characters, in *La Structure du texte artistique*, trans. A. Fournier, et al. (Paris: Gallimard, 1973), pp. 332-39.

53. The twelfth century witnessed not only the rise of courtly romance, but also the rapid spread of Cistercian spirituality, St. Bernard's religion of love and the spiritual quest of the soul seeking union with Christ. For a discussion of resemblances and differences between secular and sacred love of the twelfth century, see Robert Javelet, "L'Amour spirituel face à l'amour courtois," in *Entretiens sur la Renaissance du XIIe siècle* (The Hague, Paris: Mouton, 1968), pp. 309-36; and Jean Leclercq, *Monks and Love in Twelfth-Century France: Psycho-Historical Essays* (Oxford: Clarendon Press, 1979).

54. While Frappier, *Chrétien*, p. 128, merely alludes to Lancelot's messianic role, these Christological attributes have led Jacques Ribard to interpret the entire romance as Christian allegory, in *Chrétien de Troyes, Le Chevalier de la Charrette: Essai d'interprétation symbolique* (Paris: Nizet, 1972).

55. Source studies identify Meleagant with a Celtic god of the Other World. In the Celtic myth, he kidnaps a married woman and carries her off to his kingdom, from which she is subsequently rescued by her husband. Such is the story of Melwas (king of the summer country) as reported by a Welsh clerk in his *Vita Sancti Gildæ*, an early version of the kidnapping of Arthur's Queen. See Kenneth G.T. Webster, *Guinevere: A Study of Her Abductions* (Milton, Mass.: The Turtle Press, 1951), pp. 2-4.

56. See my *Narrative Invention in Twelfth-Century French Romance: The Convention of Hospitality (1160-1200)*, French Forum Monographs, 17 (Lexington, Ky.: French Forum, Publishers, 1980).

57. 15, iv, 31-32, quoted by Bogdanow, "Love Theme," p. 51, from Bernard de Ventadour, *Chansons d'amour*, ed. Moshé Lazar (Paris: Klincksieck, 1966).

58. 13, iii, 20-21, quoted by Bogdanow, "Love Theme," p. 55.

59. Cf. Jean-Charles Payen, "Lancelot contre Tristan, ou la conjuration d'un mythe subversif," in *Mélanges Pierre Le Gentil* (Paris: S.E.D.E.S. and C.D.U., 1973), pp. 617-32.

60. In "Godefroi de Lagny et la composition de la *Charrete*," *Romania*, 96 (1975), 27-52, and "How Much of the Lion Can We Put before the Cart? Further Light on the Chronological Relationship of Chrétien de Troyes' *Lancelot* and *Yvain*," *French Studies*, 31 (1977), 1-17, David J. Shirt argues that Chrétien wrote the tournament episode after Godefroi wrote his part of the romance, in order to counterbalance a budding romance between Lancelot and Meleagant's sister. Whatever may be the merits of this argument, it is true that later medieval writers from the *Prose Lancelot* to Malory's *Morte d'Arthur* did spin a tale about Lancelot and maiden love. The

maidens in question are never, however, Meleagant's sister, and Lancelot never willingly betrays the Queen's love.

61. The word *aventure* itself is related both to *evenio-eventus* and *advenio-adventus*. While both verbs mean "to happen, occur," *eventus* signifies a result or a favorable issue (referring to the influence of some outside power), while *adventus* describes an arrival (with obvious Christian connotations). See Elena Eberwein, *Zur Deutung mittelalterlicher Existenz*, Kölner romanistische Arbeiten, 7 (Bonn, Cologne: Roehrscheid, 1933), pp. 26 ff., cited by Erich Köhler, *L'Aventure chevaleresque: Idéal et réalité dans le roman courtois*, trans. Eliane Kaufholz (Paris: Gallimard, 1974), p. 77, where Köhler discusses as well other relevant scholarship.

62. Cf. the herald's description of Lancelot as "cil qui l'aunera." The bed is a measure of Lancelot's worth, just as Lancelot himself will set the measure for excellence at the tournament.

63. The description of the bed, a set piece in courtly romance, is also an occasion for hyperbolic pyrotechnics.

64. Cf. Peter Haidu, *Lion-queue-coupée: L'écart symbolique chez Chrétien de Troyes* (Geneva: Droz, 1972).

65. Later information about the magic ring that reveals enchantments (ll. 2345-50), given to him by the Lady of the Lake, will hint about the marvelous in Lancelot's life prior to the events of the *Charrette*.

66. *Aventure*, pp. 118-19. The problem of credibility, the fundamental characteristic of legend, is absent from fairy tales.

67. Cf. Meleagant's amazement when Lancelot arrives in the closing scene: Lancelot's presence itself is a *mervoille* (ll. 6915-17).

68. Frappier's analysis in "Le Concept de l'amour dans les romans arthuriens," *Bulletin Bibliographique de la Société Internationale Arthurienne*, 22 (1970), distinguishes "merveilleux magique," the negative pole of adventure opposed to Love's triumph, and "merveilleux courtois," the positive pole of adventure representing the irresistible power of Love (pp. 132-33). See also Jean Fourquet, "Le Rapport entre l'œuvre et la source chez Chrétien de Troyes et le problème des sources bretonnes," *Romance Philology*, 9 (1955-1956), 298-312.

69. The following analysis is based on Köhler's chapter, "L'Aventure: Réintégration et quête de l'identité," in *Aventure*, pp. 77-102. His argument relates the character of adventure in Chrétien's romance to the situation of the *petite noblesse* in contemporary feudal society. The need to found the concept of nobility on courtly virtues, rather than on property, was accepted by the higher levels of the aristocracy as an answer to the uncertainty of their own self-definition as an exclusive class. For a critique of Köhler's argument, see Philippe Ménard, "Le Chevalier errant dans la littérature arthurienne: Recherches sur les raisons du départ et de l'errance," in *Voyage, quête, pèlerinage dans la littérature et la civilisation médiévales*, Senefiance, 2 (Aix-en-Provence: CUER-MA, Paris: Champion, 1976), pp. 294-96; and Köhler's response to criticism in "Literatursoziologische Perspektiven," in *Grundriss der romanischen Literaturen des Mittelalters* (Heidelberg: Winter, 1978), IV, Part 1, pp. 89-93.

70. Arthur's court does not always wait for outside intruders: in the opening scene of *Erec* and later in Erec's own conduct in the Joie de la Cort episode we see a policy of "deliberate recklessness" combined with a conservative maintenance of custom and tradition. See T.A. Shippey, "The Uses of Chivalry: *Erec* and *Gawain*," *Modern Language Review*, 66 (1971), 241-50.

71. Ménard, "Le Temps et la durée dans les romans de Chrétien de Troyes," *Moyen Age*, 73 (1967), 397.

72. See Kelly, *Sens*, pp. 156-63, on surprise and suspense.

73. Eugène Vinaver, "Les Deux Pas de Lancelot," in *Mélanges Jean Fourquet* (Paris: Klincksieck, 1969), pp. 355-61.

74. *Essai de poétique médiévale* (Paris: Seuil, 1972), p. 357.

75. Underscored by repetition (II. 7098-7100 and 7111-12).

76. Robert Guiette, "Questions de littérature," *Romanica Gandensia*, 8 (1960), 54.

77. Cf. Vinaver on *digressio* in medieval arts of rhetoric and in romance practice, in *Form and Meaning in Medieval Romance*, Modern Humanities Research Association Presidential Address (London, 1966), p. 12.

78. Jean Deroy, "Chrétien de Troyes et Godefroi de Leigni, conspirateurs contre la Fin'Amor adultère," *Cultura Neolatina*, 38 (1978), 67-78. While Deroy sees both authors as opposed to adultery (a subject imposed by Marie de Champagne, in Deroy's view), David J. Shirt argues for a possible disagreement between Chrétien and Godefroi in the treatment of Lancelot and Meleagant's sister ("Godefroi de Lagny," p. 49, and "How Much," pp. 1-17).

79. Rychner, "Le Sujet et la signification du *Chevalier de la Charrette*," *Vox Romanica*, 27 (1968), 72-73; Elaine Southward, "The Unity of Chrétien's *Lancelot*," in *Mélanges de linguistique et de littérature romanes offerts à Mario Roques*, Vol. II (Paris: Didier, 1953), pp. 281-90.

80. These criticisms generally focus on the closing scene's "inadequate" treatment of the love element. Lancelot's thoughts are concentrated on his desire to fight Meleagant. In the larger context of the romance, Lancelot's feelings for the Queen have certainly been sufficiently explored to certify his love for her. Moreover, the connection between that love and his hatred for Meleagant has also been clearly established. As far as the details of the closing scene itself are concerned, the love theme does appear in the Queen's private joy and desire to welcome Lancelot with kisses. The combat itself takes place in a typical setting for love: a *locus amœnus* complete with fresh grass, ancient sycamore and clear fountain (II. 6983-98).

81. *Structure in Medieval Narrative* (The Hague: Mouton, 1971), p. 40.

82. P. 168.

83. *Chrétien Studies: Problems of Form and Meaning in* Erec, Yvain, Cligés *and the* Charrette (Glasgow: Univ. of Glasgow Press, 1973), pp. 112-18. She specifically discusses bipartition and tripartition in her analysis of (and disagreement with) Kelly's divisions, pp. 154-56.

84. Kelly, *Sens*, pp. 193-94.

85. Pp. 173-80.

86. Kelly, *Sens*, p. 179:

    A Lancelot's arrival, II. 3136-41
    B Bademagu and Meleagant's first discussion, II. 3142-3302
    A Lancelot's reception by Bademagu, II. 3303-3422
    B Bademagu and Meleagant's second discussion, II. 3423-77
    A Lancelot cared for during the night at Bademagu's, II. 3478-88

87. Here there is a slight variation, since Lancelot's delay takes the form of an interior debate on whether or not he should become involved (II. 1097-1125).

88. Cf. Lacy, *Craft*, pp. 90-92, for a brief discussion of the hesitation and humiliation motifs as major themes of the *Charrette*.

89. A random selection gives us: "Li chevaliers sanz nul arest / S'an vet armez par la forest" (II. 299-300) (The knight with no stopping goes off armed through the forest); "Et cil qui rien ne se delaie / ne se plaint mie de sa plaie" (II. 1149-50) (And

the one who delays not at all does not complain about his wound); "Et Lanceloz pas ne sejorne, / mes tost an sa prison retorne" (ll. 6057-58) (Lancelot sojourns not, but quickly returns to his prison).

90. Cf. ll. 1010, 1046, 1111, 2268 (both meanings implied), 3182, 3412, 4284, 4487, 4536, 5214, 5326, 6488, 6911, 7020.

91. See Alfred Foulet, "Guenevere's Enigmatic Words: Chrétien's *Lancelot*, vv. 211-213," in *Jean Misrahi Memorial Volume: Studies in Medieval Literature* (Columbia, S.C.: French Literature Publications Co., 1977), I, 175-79; and Kelly, *Sens*, pp. 105-06, n. 7, and p. 106, n. 8.

92. See ll. 1900-09, 2092-2115, 3899-3901.

93. Cf. the ABABA pattern mentioned above, p. 169.

94. Cf. ll. 3506-07 (*respitiers—pes*) and 3875-98.

95. Cf. Arthur's and Guenevere's earlier deference to Keu in order to detain him at court.

96. Lazar, "Lancelot et la *mulier mediatrix*," *L'Esprit Créateur*, 9 (1969), 243-56.

97. Cf. the descending pattern in the number of verses devoted to the actual fighting between Lancelot and Meleagant in their three consecutive encounters (ll. 3584-3846, 4991-5028 and 7002-89).

98. Ll. 1345, 1359-60, 1363-83.

99. In addition to those just given, see ll. 613-15, 680-82, 726-27, 1507, 2142-58, 2467, 3003, 6109-10, 6148-49, 6246-51, 6437-38. Lancelot's mission is often expressed in terms of the "voie . . . enprise" (ll. 868-69, 2143-44, 2962-63, 4608-15).

100. Cf. ll. 2988-93, 3181-84, 7098-7100, 7111-12.

101. "Etudes sur les romans de la Table Ronde. Lancelot du Lac, II. Le Conte de la Charrette," *Romania*, 12 (1883), 459-534. The four points enumerated are: (1) courtly love is adulterous and secret, (2) because of that the lover is always in a position of timid inferiority before his lady, (3) in order to deserve her love he demonstrates great prowess, (4) love is an art with its own set of rules (pp. 518-19). Cf. Frappier, "Sur un procès fait à l'amour courtois," *Romania*, 93 (1972), 145-93.

102. See my extended analysis of the Immodest Damsel episode in "An Interpreter's Dilemma: Why Are There So Many Interpretations of Chrétien's *Chevalier de la Charrette?*" (forthcoming in *Romance Philology*).

103. Recent articles have concentrated on the *Charrette*'s treatment of social conduct. See Mandel, "Elements," pp. 97-104, and "Proper Behavior," pp. 683-89; Emanuel Mickel, Jr., "The Theme of Honor in Chrétien's *Lancelot*," *Zeitschrift für romanische Philologie*, 91 (1975), 243-72.

104. See Paule Le Rider, "*Or est venuz qui l'aunera* ou la fortune littéraire d'un proverbe," in *Mélanges Jeanne Lods* (Paris: Collection de l'Ecole Normale Supérieure de Jeunes Filles, 1978), I, 393-409, for a valuable discussion of the proverb's social context and associated metaphorical meaning.

105. Gerard J. Brault, "Chrétien de Troyes' *Lancelot*: The Eye and the Heart," *Bulletin Bibliographique de la Société Internationale Arthurienne*, 24 (1972), 147-50; Lacy, "Thematic Structure," pp. 17-18, and *Craft*, pp. 92-93.

106. Cf. ll. 666-67, 2072, 6414-15, 6769.

107. The narrator first tells us he does not know whose comb lies on the fountain (l. 1350), but shortly thereafter he reports the Immodest Damsel's identification of its owner to Lancelot.

108. The narrator refuses to describe Lancelot and Guenevere's joy, since it should not be spoken of in a story (ll. 4680-81).

109. For example, II. 6664-65: "... je n'an porroie / la mitié deviser ne dire" (I couldn't describe or tell half [the care lavished on Lancelot by Meleagant's sister]).

110. Cf. Köhler's argument in *Aventure*, esp. pp. 95-99.

111. The Classical method of arguing on both sides of a question (*in utramque partem*) was passed on to the Middle Ages through the graded exercises of the *præexercitamina*. See Wesley Trimpi, "The Quality of Fiction in the Rhetorical Transmission of Literary Theory," *Traditio*, 30 (1974), 1-118 (esp. pp. 75-81, where he discusses how the exercises of confirmation and refutation lead into narrative problems of truth and verisimilitude).

112. Cf. André Jolles's definition of the "Case," in *Formes simples,* trans. A.M. Buguet (Paris: Seuil, 1972), pp. 137-45. He specifically mentions the problems debated by medieval "love courts" (at least in their literary representations) as characteristic of courtly culture (p. 153).

113. The inadequacy of the secular ideal appears only gradually in Chrétien's work, which may explain his shift in the *Perceval* to an ideal explicitly connected with Christian values.

114. In this respect the *Charrette* reflects the exuberant optimism of the twelfth century, but already contains the seeds of conflict that will burst forth in the more pessimistic Vulgate Cycle.

115. Jean-Charles Payen, "Les Valeurs humaines chez Chrétien de Troyes," in *Mélanges Rita Lejeune*, 2 vols. (Gembloux: Duculot, 1969), II, 1087-1101.

"Le Chevalier au Lion (Yvain)," by Karl D. Uitti

1. For editions used throughout, see above, p. 311, n. 1 to p. 13; whenever appropriate I also cite the earlier edition by Wendelin Foerster, *Der Löwenritter (Yvain) von Christian von Troyes* (Halle: Max Niemeyer, 1887).

2. See Foerster's note to II. 3707-08 in his above-mentioned edition, p. 312.

3. "Encore la chronologie des œuvres de Chrétien de Troyes," *Bulletin Bibliographique de la Société Internationale Arthurienne*, 2 (1950), 69-88.

4. *Etude sur Yvain, ou le Chevalier au Lion, de Chrétien de Troyes* (Paris: S.E.D.E.S., 1969), p. 15.

5. "More Light on the Chronology of Chrétien de Troyes?" *Bulletin Bibliographique de la Société Internationale Arthurienne*, 11 (1959), 89-120.

6. See Frappier's above-mentioned *Etude*, p. 16; also Mario Roques's "Introduction" to his edition of *Lancelot*, p. vii.

7. "Note sur la date du *Chevalier de la Charrette*," *Romania*, 92 (1971), 118-26.

8. See "Godefroi de Lagny et la composition de la *Charrete*," *Romania*, 96 (1975), 27-52.

9. The *molt bele conjointure* (very beautiful conjoining) referred to by Chrétien in the forematter to *Erec et Enide* (l. 14) and reflecting, as it does, certain Chartrian concepts of mythopoesis—which, ultimately perhaps, derive from such late Latin authors as Macrobius and Martianus Capella (for recent discussions of these matters, see Karl D. Uitti, "A propos de philologie," *Littérature*, 41 [February 1981], 30-46, and Michelle A. Freeman, *The Poetics of* Translatio Studii: *Chrétien de Troyes's Cligés*, French Forum Monographs, 12 [Lexington, Ky.: French Forum, Publishers, 1979], pp. 11-13, 57-88)—appears to be a compositional constant in Chrétien's entire

œuvre. As was noted above, the pairing of *Yvain/Lancelot* seems itself to pair off against the earlier romance coupling of *Erec/Cligés*; and, filtered through this fundamental dichotomy, there may be ascertained links between, on the one hand, *Yvain* and *Erec et Enide* (e.g., the theme of regenerated marriage) and, on the other, between *Lancelot* and *Cligés* (e.g., ironic, and double, focus on the artifice of romance constructs). Meanwhile, *Le Conte du Graal* is at once the culmination of Chrétien's œuvre —the processes set in motion by the previous romances are fulfilled in it—and the text to be paired against all four earlier romances. Systematic pairing—doubleness or binarism—pervades Chrétien's work; after all, in *Erec et Enide*, *conjointure* has to do both with poetry and with the relationship (that is, something more than the simple addition) of the two protagonists. "Conjoining," as Freeman has remarked (*Poetics*, pp. 67-69), lies at the heart of metaphor, the process underlying all of Chrétien's artistry and which, furthermore, may be what he meant by *san* (cf. Douglas Kelly, *Sens and Conjointure in the* Chevalier de la Charrette, Studies in French Literature 2 [The Hague, Paris: Mouton, 1966]): each romance (a narrative) stands in relationship to another (or others) which comment(s) upon it, and *Perceval* constitutes Chrétien's ultimate narrative-commentary on the nature of romance—and of his œuvre as a whole. This narrative-commentary system explodes the boundaries of any single "text." The true "place" is, then, "textuality," which thereby constitutes a "critical mass," a most dynamic—and productive—place of meaning. A systematic study of at least one set of these "pairings," it seems to me, would be of great utility at this juncture.

    10. See Janet Girvan Espiner-Scott, *Claude Fauchet: Sa vie, son œuvre* (Paris: Droz, 1938), esp. pp. 176-79.

    11. For an obviously outdated, but as yet not fully replaced survey of early philological scholarship concerning Chrétien, see Wilhelm Ludwig Holland, *Crestien von Troyes: Eine literaturgeschichtliche Untersuchung* (Tübingen: L.F. Fues, 1854); also, Gustav Gröber, *Grundriss der romanischen Philologie* (Strasbourg: K.J. Trübner, 1888-1902), esp. Vol. II, Part 1, pp. 497-506. It should be recalled that Holland's edition of *Yvain, Li Romans dou Chevalier au Lion, von Crestïen von Troies* (Hanover: Carl Rümpler, 1862), the first complete and philologically defensible text of modern times of this romance, was, like that of Roques and unlike that of Foerster (Holland's successor), based on the Guiot manuscript (B.N. f. fr. 794). It is thus substantially the same text as—though more richly annotated than—that given by Roques, who, curiously, fails entirely to mention Holland in the forematter to his edition.

    12. (Halle, 1914); and, particularly, as revised by Hermann Breuer, 3rd edition (Tübingen: Max Niemeyer, 1964).

    13. Chrétien's fame as a stylist was recognized by his medieval successors—for example, Huon de Méry, who, in his *Torneimenz Anticrist* (ed. Margaret O. Bender, Romance Monographs, 17 [University, Miss.: Romance Monographs, 1976]), not only writes of "having found" (*trovai*) Yvain's fountain (ll. 101-05), but on several occasions praises Chrétien's poetic art (*pris de trover* [excellence in invention], descriptive talent and *bel françois* [beautiful French], ll. 22-26, 2600-05, 3534-39). Also, though to my knowledge this has not as yet been thoroughly studied, Guillaume de Lorris' *Romance of the Rose* owes a substantial debt to Chrétien. See Freeman, "Problems in Romance Composition: Ovid, Chrétien de Troyes, and the *Romance of the Rose*," *Romance Philology*, 30 (1976), 158-68. Guillaume's "unfinished" text also contains what appears to be numerous, and highly significant, allusions to *Yvain* (especially to Calogrenant's "story within a story" in respect of both the Prologue and the Narcissus episode, with its Perilous Fountain). Perhaps Guillaume's amorous semi-failure is not

unrelated to Calogrenant's chivalric "shame." The question deserves close examination; see below, p. 207 and n. 35. Might not Part I of the *Rose* be *Yvain*'s authentic "Continuation"?

14. For examples of studies dealing with matters of Celtic sources and influence, pro and con as well as moderate, see the list provided by Kelly, *Chrétien de Troyes: An Analytic Bibliography*, Research Bibliographies and Checklists, 17 (London: Grant and Cutler, 1976), pp. 91-100.

15. Loomis himself warned against this tendency among the more dogmatic *celtisants*; see his *Arthurian Tradition and Chrétien de Troyes* (New York: Columbia Univ. Press, 1949), pp. 41-42.

16. See Freeman, *Poetics*, esp. pp. 101-27; also, her chapter on *Cligés* in the present volume.

17. *Roman de Rou et des ducs de Normandie*, ed. Hugo Andresen, Vol. II (Heilbronn: Gebr. Henninger, 1879), l. 6419.

18. *Le Roman de Brut*, ed. Ivor Arnold, Vol. II (Paris: Société des Anciens Textes Français, 1940), l. 13189.

19. With his customary flair for significant detail, Frappier points out several of these tantalizing analogues, in *Etude*, p. 78.

20. "Etudes sur les romans de la Table Ronde. Lancelot du Lac, I. Le *Lanzelet* d'Ulrich de Zatzikhoven; Lancelot du Lac, II. Le *Conte de la Charrette*," *Romania*, 10 (1881), 465-96; 12 (1883), 459-534; 16 (1887), 100-01.

21. See their *Chrétien, Troyes, and the Grail* (Chapel Hill: Univ. of North Carolina Press, 1959).

22. "The Storm-Making Spring and the Meaning of Chrétien's *Yvain*," *Studies in Philology*, 64 (1967), 564-85.

23. Similar ideas may be found in Tom Artin, *The Allegory of Adventure: Reading Chrétien's Erec and Yvain* (Lewisburg, Pa., London: Bucknell Univ. Press, 1974).

24. "Le *Conte du Graal* est-il une allégorie judéo-chrétienne?" *Romance Philology*, 16 (1962-1963), 179-213; 20 (1966-1967), 1-31; "Le Graal et ses feux divergents," *Romance Philology*, 24 (1970-1971), 373-440.

25. See Frances L. Decker, "The Development of the Narrator Figure in Old French and Middle High German Courtly Epic" (diss. Princeton 1975), and Hans-Peter Kramer, *Erzählerbemerkungen und Erzählerkommentare in Chrestiens und Hartmanns Erec und Iwein*, Göppinger Arbeiten zur Germanistik, 35 (Göppingen: Kümmerle, 1971) (diss. Marburg 1971).

26. See his "Der Roman und seine Rezeption als Gegenstand des Romans: Beobachtungen zum Eingangsteil von Hartmanns *Iwein*," *Wirkendes Wort*, 23 (1973), 246-52.

27. See his review of Jean Marx, *La Légende arthurienne et le Graal*, in *Romania*, 73 (1952), 252. (Edmond Faral's vitriolic anti-*celtisant* critique of Marx follows immediately upon Frappier's more temperate remarks in this same issue of *Romania*.)

28. *Lion-queue-coupée: L'écart symbolique chez Chrétien de Troyes* (Geneva: Droz, 1972).

29. See "Hexagonal and Spiral Structure in Medieval Narrative," *Yale French Studies*, 51 (1974), 115-32; and *Perceval et l'initiation: Essais sur le dernier roman de Chrétien de Troyes, ses correspondances "orientales" et sa signification anthropologique* (Paris: Editions du Sirac, 1972).

30. Thus, as reported by Donald Maddox, in *Structure and Sacring: The Systematic Kingdom in Chrétien's* Erec et Enide, French Forum Monographs, 8 (Lex-

ington, Ky.: French Forum, Publishers, 1978), pp. 195-96, n. 27: "Lévi-Strauss has successfully revitalized the study of primitive myth as a useful approach to comparative ethnography. Moreover, in a recent seminar at the Collège de France, Lévi-Strauss examined mythic aspects of the Grail romances. An account of the seminar may be found in *L'Annuaire du Collège de France*, 74 (Paris, 1974), 303-09. See also *Anthropologie structurale deux* (Paris, 1973), pp. 31-35, where Lévi-Strauss analyzes comparatively the structures of the myth in the Grail cycle and the Oedipus myth."

31. (Paris: Seuil, 1972).

32. Ed. Joseph Bédier (Paris: H. Piazza, 1964), l. 2095: "Ço dit la Geste" (Thus says the written text).

33. Ed. Gaston Paris, C.F.M.A., 4 (Paris: Champion, 1903), l. 1.

34. Cf. *Yvain*, ll. 131-49; also, *Eneas, roman du XIIe siècle*, ed. J.-J. Salverda de Grave, Vol. I, C.F.M.A., 44 (Paris: Champion, 1964), ll. 839-58.

35. Cf. the initial couplet of the *Rose*: "Aucunes genz dïent qu'en songes / n'a se fables non et mençonges" (Some people say that in dreams there are but fables and lies). Ed. Félix Lecoy, Vol. I, C.F.M.A., 92 (Paris: Champion, 1970).

36. For two differing, but, I trust, complementary approaches to Jehan Bodel's characterization of the "matter of Britain," see Robert Guiette, "'Li conte de Bretaigne sont si vain et plaisant,'" *Romania*, 88 (1967), 1-12; and Uitti, *Story, Myth, and Celebration in Old French Narrative Poetry 1050-1200* (Princeton: Princeton Univ. Press, 1973), pp. 71, 144, 152, 233-35.

37. See Alfred Foulet and Karl D. Uitti, "Chrétien's 'Laudine': *Yvain*, vv. 2148-55," *Romance Philology*, 37 (1983-1984), 292-302.

38. See Uitti, *Story*, pp. 183-203, for a more detailed analysis of this scene of Yvain's lovesickness.

39. Béroul, *Le Roman de Tristan*, ed. Ernest Muret, 4th edition revised by L.M. Defourques [=Lucien Foulet and Mario Roques], C.F.M.A., 12 (Paris: Champion, 1967), ll. 1761-73.

40. See ed. Foerster, ll. 2845-55, for a more detailed and, to my mind, more authentic description of these matters than that furnished by Guiot-Roques, ll. 2847-49.

41. For a study of these conventional descriptions, see Alice M. Colby, *The Portrait in Twelfth-Century French Literature: An Example of the Stylistic Originality of Chrétien de Troyes* (Geneva: Droz, 1965).

42. Frappier was perhaps the first to notice the possible connection between Yvain's lion and Tristan's Husdent implied by this use of *brachet*; see his brief recapitulation of *Tristan* "reminiscences" in *Le Chevalier au Lion*, in *Etude*, p. 78. See also his highly suggestive remarks concerning the *Yvain/Lancelot* relationship, pp. 12-17.

43. Parallelism-in-reversal, we recall, also characterizes the relationship of Calogrenant's tale to Wace's *Rou* (see above, p. 206); Wace-becomes-Calogrenant prefigures, within the text, the "paradigmatic" *Tristan*-becomes-*Yvain* construct.

44. Béroul introduces the Arthurian—that is, a "storybook"—world into the frame of his *Tristan* narrative; this Yvain, as part of that world, is presented as a storybook figure, albeit a minor one, in the more "real" universe of Tristan and Iseut, an interesting ploy when one considers Gauvain's role in *Le Chevalier au Lion*.

45. Weinrich's *besprochene Welt* and Benveniste's *discours* are linked to the present, the present perfect and the future tenses; Weinrich's *erzählte Welt* and Benveniste's *histoire*, meanwhile, are associated with the past (e.g., imperfect, preterite and conditional) tenses. See Harald Weinrich, *Tempus: Besprochene und erzählte*

Welt (Stuttgart, Berlin, Cologne, Mainz: Kohlhammer, 1964, 1971); French translation of the first edition: *Le Temps: Le récit et le commentaire,* trans. Michèle Lacoste (Paris: Seuil, 1973). See also Emile Benveniste, "Les Relations de temps dans le verbe français" (1959), rpt. in *Problèmes de linguistique générale* (Paris: Gallimard, 1966). Cf. Uitti, "Narrative and Commentary: Chrétien's Devious Narrator in *Yvain,*" *Romance Philology,* 33 (1979-1980), 160-67.

46. Compare, and contrast, this ending with Godefroi de Leigni's Epilogue to the *Charrette* (ed. Roques, ll. 7098-7112), in which Godefroi both names himself and claims to derive his authority for finishing (*parfinee*) "La Charrete" directly from "Crestïen."

"*Le Conte du Graal (Perceval)*," by Rupert T. Pickens

1. For the editions used, see above, p. 311, n. 1 to p. 13. Unless noted otherwise, line references to Lecoy's edition of *Perceval* are given first, followed in square brackets by the corresponding lines in Roach's text. In Alexandre Micha's judgment, the Guiot copy (B.N. f. fr. 794 = manuscript *A*, mid-thirteenth century) is the "best" *Conte du Graal* text in a confused manuscript tradition for which a stemma cannot be established: *La Tradition manuscrite des romans de Chrétien de Troyes* (Paris: Droz, 1939; rpt. Geneva: Droz, 1966), pp. 167-90, 233-53, 393. However, Lecoy's recent edition of Guiot does not supersede Roach's edition of manuscript *T*, early thirteenth century, which is not directly related to *A*. Micha's conclusions about the preeminence of *A*, followed by three other manuscripts, none of which is *T* (p. 393), should not imply, as they do, that *T* is not worthy of study; on the contrary, Micha's own analysis (summarized, pp. 252-53) shows just how conservative the tradition of *T* is. Also important is Alfons Hilka's critical edition, *Der Percevalroman von Christian von Troyes* (Halle: Niemeyer, 1932), Vol. V of *Christian von Troyes sämtliche Werke,* completing the series begun by Wendelin Foerster and continued by him through Vol. IV. Occasionally in the present study, citations of Lecoy's edition contain emendations based on Hilka's text and notes; all changes in Lecoy's text, some of which merely correct printer's errors, are indicated by the use of square brackets. But Hilka's text, based primarily on Guiot's copy, *A*, should be consulted with great care, and attention must always be directed to the variants and rejected readings; the language of the text represents Hilka's attempt to reconstruct late twelfth-century Champenois. However, the copious variants, notes and appendices remain most useful. Roach has adjusted the line numbers of his text so that they invariably correspond to Hilka's. Most scholars agree that Chrétien de Troyes wrote the entire fragment of the *Conte du Graal* attributed to him in *A*, where the poem is called "Percevax le viel" to distinguish it from the Continuations, and in other manuscripts not directly related to *A* (see Micha, *Tradition,* pp. 28-64). The few scholars who dispute the integrity of "Percevax le viel" do so primarily because they cannot accept that Chrétien intended to join the Gauvain adventures to the discrete Perceval section and/or because the tenor of the Hermitage episode (a return to Perceval in the midst of Gauvain's adventures) seems to them not to accord with their perceptions of the other Perceval episodes (therefore, Chrétien did not write it); thus, they are unwilling to deal with the totality of the text as manifested by the manuscripts, our only reliable source of information, for reasons relating to their interpretations of a part of that text. The

most notable are Philip-August Becker, "Von den Erzählern neben und nach Chrétien de Troyes," *Zeitschrift für romanische Philologie,* 55 (1935), 400-16; Stefan Hofer, "La Structure du Conte del Graal examinée à la lumière de l'œuvre de Chrétien de Troyes," in *Les Romans du Graal dans la littérature des XIIe et XIIIe siècles* (Paris: C.N.R.S., 1956), pp. 15-30; Martín de Riquer, "Perceval y Gauvain en *Li Contes del Graal,*" *Filologia Romanza,* 4 (1957), 119-47; Leo Pollmann, *Chrétien de Troyes und der Conte del Graal* (Tübingen: Niemeyer, 1965), pp. 3-79; D.D.R. Owen, *The Evolution of the Grail Legend* (Edinburgh, London: Oliver and Boyd, 1968), pp. 165-75. For counterarguments supporting the integrity of "Percevax li viel," see Jean Frappier, "Sur la composition du 'Conte du Graal,'" *Moyen Age,* 64 (1958), 67-102, and *Chrétien de Troyes et le mythe du Graal* (Paris: S.E.D.E.S., 1972), pp. 60-62, 213-18.

2. The Historical facts—Henry's second crusade venture, his return to Troyes and subsequent death; Philippe de Flandre's first trip to Palestine, his return, his wooing of the widowed countess of Champagne, his second departure on crusade; etc.— are well known; the problem has been how to interpret them in light of the *Conte du Graal* and Chrétien's identification of a new patron. On the dating of *Lancelot* and *Yvain,* see Karl D. Uitti, *"Le Chevalier au Lion,"* above, pp. 183-85. See also Anthime Fourrier, "Encore la chronologie des œuvres de Chrétien de Troyes," *Bulletin Bibliographique de la Société Internationale Arthurienne,* 2 (1950), 69-88; Jean Misrahi, "More Light on the Chronology of Chrétien de Troyes?" *Bulletin Bibliographique de la Société Internationale Arthurienne,* 11 (1959), 89-120; Jean Frappier, "Chrétien de Troyes," in *Arthurian Literature in the Middle Ages,* ed. Roger Sherman Loomis (Oxford: Clarendon Press, 1959), esp. pp. 157-59.

3. "... Crestiens de Troies / ... de Percheval commencha, / Mais la mors qui l'adevancha / Ne li laissa pas traire affin" (Chrétien de Troyes ... began about Perceval, but death, which overtook him, did not allow him to draw it to an end). Gerbert de Montreuil, *La Continuation de Perceval,* ed. Mary Williams, 2 vols., C.F.M.A., 28, 50 (Paris: Champion, 1922-1925), II. 6984-87.

4. *The Continuations of the Old French Perceval,* ed. William Roach, Vols. I-IV (Philadelphia: Univ. of Pennsylvania Press/American Philosophical Society, 1949-1971); Robert de Boron, *Le Roman de l'Estoire dou Graal,* ed. W.A. Nitze, C.F.M.A., 57 (Paris: Champion, 1927)—cf. *Merlin, roman du XIIIe siècle,* ed. Alexandre Micha, T.L.F., 159 (Geneva: Droz, 1979), a prose rendering of a verse original by Robert de Boron of which only a fragment survives; *The Didot Perceval,* ed. William Roach (Philadelphia: Univ. of Pennsylvania Press, 1941); *Le Haut Livre du Graal: Perlesvaus,* ed. William A. Nitze, 2 vols. (Chicago: Univ. of Chicago Press, 1932-1937).

5. Manessier's termination is in *Perceval le Gallois ou le Conte du Graal,* ed. Charles Potvin, vol. VI (Mons: Société des Bibliophiles Belges, 1871); *The Vulgate Version of the Arthurian Romances,* ed. H. Oskar Sommer, 7 vols. (Washington: Carnegie Institute, 1909-1913). Other works from the period influenced by the *Conte du Graal* include Renaut de Beaujeu, *Le Bel Inconnu,* ed. G.P. Williams, C.F.M.A., 38 (Paris: Champion, 1929) (cf. D.D.R. Owen, *Evolution*); and Huon de Méry, *Li Torneimenz Antecrit,* ed. Georg Wimmer (Marburg: Elwert, 1888), more recently, ed. Margaret O. Bender, Romance Monographs, 17 (University: Miss.: Romance Monographs, 1976). Not to mention the *Conte du Graal*'s enormous influence abroad— cf. Wolfram von Eschenbach's *Parzival,* begun before 1200.

6. The *Conte du Graal* exists completely in fifteen manuscripts and more or less extensively in three more fragments, one of which (Annonay) was copied right around the year 1200. See Hilka's Introduction; Lecoy, II, 97-99; and Micha, *Tradi-*

tion, pp. 28-64. Also exceptionally well preserved are, for example, the *Roman d'Alexandre* in 28 manuscripts and Wace's *Brut* in eighteen. The early branches of the *Roman de Renart* survive in "numerous" copies, according to Studer and Waters, *Historical French Reader* (Oxford: Clarendon Press, 1924), p. 97; there are twelve. Of Chrétien's romances, *Lancelot* is found in eight manuscripts, whole or fragmentary; *Cligés* and *Yvain* in nine each; and *Erec et Enide* in seven. The best preserved *chansons de geste*, those of the William of Orange cycle, survive in eight cyclical codices, six of which are very closely related. Among other important twelfth-century narratives cited in this volume, the *Tristan* of Thomas d'Angleterre exists in five fragmentary manuscripts (the fragments range in length from 52 to 1815 verses), and Béroul's *Tristan* is in a single fragment of 4485 verses. The *Roman de Thèbes* is manifested by five copies, and the complete *Lais* of Marie de France by two, only one of which contains the General Prologue. By contrast, the *Roman de la Rose* is found in well over 260 medieval copies.

7. Of particular interest in the study of the Prologue are Tom Artin, *The Allegory of Adventure: Reading Chrétien's* Erec *and* Yvain (Lewisburg, Pa.: Bucknell Univ. Press; London: Associated University Presses, 1974), ch. 1, "Sowers of the Word," pp. 31-54; Peter Haidu, *Aesthetic Distance in Chrétien de Troyes: Irony and Comedy in* Cligès *and* Perceval (Geneva: Droz, 1968), pp. 115-17; Urban Tigner Holmes and Sr. M. Amelia Klenke, O.P., *Chrétien, Troyes, and the Grail* (Chapel Hill: Univ. of North Carolina Press, 1959), pp. 91-94; Tony Hunt, "The Rhetorical Background to the Arthurian Prologue: Tradition and the Old French Prologues," *Forum for Modern Language Studies*, 6 (1970), 1-28, and "Tradition and Originality in the Prologues of Chrestien de Troyes," *Forum for Modern Language Studies*, 8 (1972), 320-44; Marie-Louise Ollier, "The Author in the Text: The Prologues of Chrétien de Troyes," *Yale French Studies*, 51 (1974), 26-41; Beate Schmolke-Hasselmann, "Untersuchungen zur Typik des arthurischen Romananfangs," *Germanisch-romanische Monatsschrift*, n. s. 31 (1981), 1-13.

8. On *translatio*, translation and related concepts, see Ernst-Robert Curtius, *European Literature and the Latin Middle Ages*, trans. Willard Trask (New York: Harper and Row, 1963), pp. 28-30, 384 ff.; Michelle A. Freeman, *The Poetics of* Translatio Studii *and* Conjointure: *Chrétien de Troyes's* Cligés, French Forum Monographs, 12 (Lexington, Ky.: French Forum, Publishers, 1979); Douglas Kelly, "*Translatio Studii*: Translation, Adaptation, and Allegory in Medieval French Literature," *Philological Quarterly*, 57 (1978), 287-310; Karl D. Uitti, "Remarks on Old French Narrative: Courtly Love and Poetic Form," *Romance Philology*, 26 (1972-1973), 77-93, 28 (1974-1975), 190-99, and *Story, Myth, and Celebration in Old French Narrative 1050-1200* (Princeton: Princeton Univ. Press, 1973); Paul Zumthor, *Essai de poétique médiévale* (Paris: Seuil, 1972), pp. 54-106. In Marie de France: Leo Spitzer, "The Prologue of the *Lais* of Marie de France and Medieval Poetics," *Modern Philology*, 41 (1943), 96-102; Emanuel J. Mickel, "The Unity and Significance of Marie's Prologue," *Romania*, 95 (1974), 83-91; Rupert T. Pickens, "La Poétique de Marie de France d'après les prologues des *Lais*," *Lettres Romanes*, 32 (1978), 367-84, and "History and Meaning in the *Lais* of Marie de France," in *Studies in the Seven Sages of Rome and Other Essays in Medieval Literature*, eds. H. Niedzielski, H.R. Runte, W.L. Hendrickson (Honolulu: Educational Research Associates, 1978), pp. 201-11; Alfred Foulet and Karl D. Uitti, "The Prologue to the *Lais* of Marie de France: A Reconsideration," *Romance Philology*, 35 (1981-1982), 242-49. See also Jacques Monfrin, "Humanisme et traductions au moyen âge," *Journal des Savants* (1963),

161-90, and "Les Traducteurs et leur public en France au moyen âge," *Journal des Savants* (1964), 5-20. Below (pp. 241-43, 250-52) the processes of "fictive translation" are related to narratology as discussed in Gérard Genette, *Figures III* (Paris: Seuil, 1972).

9. Mortimer J. Donovan, "Priscian and the Obscurity of the Ancients," *Speculum*, 36 (1961), 75-80.

10. Although now called "of Alsace," Philippe held no lands from the German emperor in his father's native region, but he did possess domains across the Escaut constituting "Imperial Flanders." However, the County of Flanders (cf. the title and name given to Philippe by Chrétien, l. 13) was a fiefdom of the French king. Moreover, all of his important political activities involved Philippe intimately with Louis VII or Philip Augustus: support of Thomas Becket, serving as godfather and then regent to Philip Augustus, quarrels then reconciliation with the new king, accompanying him on crusade, etc.

11. Cf. Buckbee, *"Erec et Enide,"* above, pp. 51-52, and Donald Maddox, *Structure and Sacring: The Systematic Kingdom in Chrétien's* Erec et Enide, French Forum Monographs, 8 (Lexington, Ky.: French Forum, Publishers, 1978), pp. 20-24.

12. This and the following section constitute in part a revision and refinement of work I have previously published in *"Estoire, Lai* and Romance: Chrétien's *Erec et Enide* and *Cligés," Romanic Review*, 66 (1975), 248-62; in *The Welsh Knight: Paradoxicality in Chrétien's* Conte del Graal, French Forum Monographs, 6 (Lexington, Ky.: French Forum, Publishers, 1977); and in a paper on the function of secondary narration, entitled "Temporal Style in Chrétien's *Conte del Graal,"* presented at the City University of New York Conference on Language and Style, April 2, 1977. Of particular interest in reading the *Conte du Graal* are Frappier, *Chrétien de Troyes et le mythe du Graal*, and "Le Graal et ses feux divergeants," *Romance Philology*, 24 (1970-1971), 373-440; Pierre Gallais, *Perceval et l'initiation: Essais sur le dernier roman de Chrétien de Troyes, ses correspondances "orientales" et sa signification anthropologique* (Paris: Editions du Sirac, 1972); Haidu, *Aesthetic Distance*, pp. 115 ff.; Stanton de V. Hoffman, "The Structure of the *Conte del Graal,"* Romanic Review, 52 (1961), 81-98; Paul Imbs, "L'Elément religieux dans le conte del Graal," in *Les Romans du Graal*, pp. 31-53; Erich Köhler, *Ideal und Wirklichkeit in der höfischen Epik* (Tübingen: Niemeyer, 1956), French trans.: *L'Aventure chevaleresque*, trans. Eliane Kaufholz (Paris: Gallimard, 1974); Norris J. Lacy, *The Craft of Chrétien de Troyes: An Essay on Narrative Art*, Davis Medieval Texts and Studies, 3 (Leiden: Brill, 1980), esp. ch. 4, and "Gauvain and the Crisis of Chivalry in the *Conte del Graal,"* in *The Sower and His Seed: Essays on Chrétien de Troyes*, ed. Rupert T. Pickens, French Forum Monographs, 44 (forthcoming); Jean Marx, *La Légende arthurienne et le Graal* (Paris: Presses Universitaires de France, 1952), and "La Quête manquée de Gauvain," in *Mélanges offerts à Etienne Gilson* (Toronto: P.I.M.S., 1959), pp. 415-36; Per Nykrog, "Two Creators of Narrative Form in Twelfth Century France: Gautier d'Arras—Chrétien de Troyes," *Speculum*, 48 (1973), 257-76; Volker Roloff, *Reden und Schweigen* (Munich: Fink, 1973), esp. pp. 139-69; Sara Sturm-Maddox, "Lévi-Strauss in the Waste Forest," *L'Esprit Créateur*, 18, No. 3 (1978), 82-94.

13. My findings show that the *Conte du Graal* contains over 51% direct discourse and about 1.3% commentary (exclusive of the Prologue), figures typical of the *chanson de geste* rather than works associated with learning and writing (i.e., works that purport to be translations). In the Hermitage episode, the frequency of direct discourse rises to about 67%, while commentary is directed to the subject of poetics

(in the opening and closing frames) rather than to the history. See my "Historical Consciousness in Old French Narrative," *French Forum*, 4 (1979), 168-84.

14. *Aufbaustil und Weltbild Chrestiens von Troyes im Percevalroman* (Halle: Niemeyer, 1936).

15. Following l. 3908 (Roach 3926), two manuscripts not directly related continue with passages in which Perceval breaks the sword given him by the Fisher King, thus fulfilling the Weeping Maiden's prediction (ll. 3644 ff. [3658 ff.]) that it will fail him in battle (he is fighting the Orgueilleus de la Lande). Perceval replaces the broken sword with the one taken from the Vermilion Knight with which Gornemant de Goorz inducted him into the order of chivalry. One of the two manuscripts is *T* (cf. Roach, ll. 3926a-t). In *A* and the other manuscripts, the Grail Castle sword is not mentioned again after it is awarded to Perceval, but it is implicit that he continues to wear it and to use it.

16. "Silence is a sign of wisdom, loquacity is a sign of folly." Quoted by Hilka from the *Disciplina clericalis*, 8, 11 (p. 652, n. 1654), along with relevant Old French proverbs. Cf. "Judicium determinat causas, et qui imponit stulto silentium, iras mitigat" (Proverbs 26:10); "... sic indecens est in ore stultorum parabola" (Proverbs 26: 7); "qui odit loquacitatem, extinguit malitiam" (Ecclesiasticus 10:5).

17. "To everything there is a season, ... a time to keep silence and a time to speak" (Ecclesiastes 3:1, 7). Cited by Hilka (p. 684, n. 3250-51), along with related Old French proverbs recalling the narrator's. See Roloff, pp. 24-85.

18. See Herbert Weisinger, *Tragedy and the Paradox of the Fortunate Fall* (East Lansing: Michigan State Univ. Press, 1953); Joseph Campbell and Henry Morton Robinson, *A Skeleton Key to Finnegans Wake* (New York: Viking Press, 1961); and Pickens, *Welsh Knight*, pp. 158-59, n. 22.

19. See Frappier, *Chrétien de Troyes et le mythe du Graal*, pp. 1-2; William A. Nitze and Harry F. Williams, *Arthurian Names in the Perceval of Chrétien de Troyes* (Berkeley: Univ. of California Press, 1955), pp. 275-77; Mario Roques, "Le Nom du Graal," in *Les Romans du Graal*, pp. 5, 8-14; and Alfred Foulet, Appendix II, below, pp. 308-09.

20. Various interpretations, all of which involve the "origins" of the Grail and Chrétien's use of Grail sources, are summarized dispassionately by Urban Tigner Holmes in *Chrétien de Troyes* (New York: Twayne, 1970), pp. 137-50, and with more bias by Klenke in Holmes and Klenke, *Chrétien*, pp. 168-94. See especially Harry F. Williams, "Interpretations of the *Conte del Graal* and Their Critical Reactions," forthcoming in *The Sower and His Seed*. Noteworthy examples include Jessie L. Weston, *From Ritual to Romance* (Cambridge, 1920; rpt. Garden City, N.Y.: Doubleday, 1957) (reference to vegetative myths); Leonardo Olschki, *The Grail Castle and Its Mysteries*, trans. and ed. J.A. Scott (Berkeley, Los Angeles: Univ. of California Press, 1966) (heterodox Christian meaning); Roger Sherman Loomis, *Arthurian Tradition and Chrétien de Troyes* (New York: Columbia Univ. Press, 1949) (meanings in supposed Celtic sources as understood by Chrétien); Eugene J. Weinraub, *Chrétien's Jewish Grail*... (Chapel Hill: Univ. of North Carolina Department of Romance Languages, 1976) (the Grail procession refers to the Seder); Mario Roques, *Le Graal de Chrétien et la demoiselle au Graal* (Paris: S.P.R.F., 1955) (on the Grail procession as Christian allegory); and Holmes and Klenke, *Chrétien* (on the Grail procession as a multi-leveled allegory depicting the supplanting of Synagoga by Ecclesia).

Appendix I
"On Editing Chrétien's *Le Chevalier de la Charrette*,"
by Alfred Foulet

1. A seventh instance of Guiot's unfaithfulness to the Chrétien text should not be overlooked, especially as it is not included among Frappier's emendations of the Roques-Guiot text. When one compares Foerster, ll. 4133-34 ("Et de ce sont mout correcié / Que li mal pas sont depecié") with Roques, ll. 4115-16 ("Et de ce ne sont pas irié / que li mal pas sont depecié"), it becomes apparent that Guiot has both done away with Chrétien's rich rhyme (*-ecié: -ecié*) and completely altered the meaning of the first line of the distich. Whereas Chrétien speaks of the people of Gorre's anger at Meleagant's defeat, Guiot is telling us that the prisoners from Logres are happy at being freed.

2. On the first page of his edition, Roques lists six manuscripts of the *Lancelot*: B.N. f. fr. 794, B.N. f. fr. 1450, B.N. f. fr. 12560, Vatican 1724 (read: Reg. 1725), Chantilly 572 (read: 472), and Escorial M. iii. 21. The Princeton manuscript, Garrett 125, was unknown to him, but, surprisingly enough, Roques fails to mention a manuscript he himself had described in *Romania*, 68 (1944-1945), 213. Institut de France MS 4676 contains two *Lancelot* fragments: Foerster, ll. 3615-3774 (Roques, ll. 3599-3756) and Foerster, ll. 4741-4900 (Roques, ll. 4723-4880).

Appendix II
"Chrétien's Indebtedness to the *Alexandre décasyllabique*,"
by Alfred Foulet

1. A critical edition of the ADéca is part of Edward C. Armstrong's *The Medieval French Roman d'Alexandre*, III, 8-11, 61-100. Hereafter cited as *MFRA*.

2. See *MFRA*, III, 9.

3. In his "Alexanderroman—Erec und die späteren Werke Kristians" (*Zeitschrift für romanische Philologie*, 60 [1940], 245-61), Stefan Hofer pointed out close verbal links between *Erec*, ll. 6673-76, 6683-85 (Foerster edition) and several lines of the *Mort Alixandre* Prologue: MS *A*, ll. 4624, 4627, 4655; MS *B*, ll. 10730, 10733 (*MFRA*, Vols. I and VII).

4. That the ADéca may have influenced Chrétien meets with no chronological obstacle in regard to *Cligés*, *Yvain* and *Perceval*. "On peut tenir comme probable pour *Cligés* la date de 1176" (*Cligés*, ed. Alexandre Micha, p. viii). Scholars are agreed that both *Yvain* and *Perceval* postdate *Cligés*. See Uitti, "*Yvain*," above, pp. 183-85.

5. In her *Bisclavret* Marie de France presents a man who, changed into a werewolf, has not ceased to be human. Pursued by hunting dogs, he begs for mercy of the king (who sits astride his horse) by grasping and kissing one of his legs in a feudal gesture of surrender and humility (Jean Rychner's C.F.M.A. edition of the *Lais*, ll. 145-54). Whether Marie had in mind the ADéca's Bucephalus passage remains uncertain. Rychner, p. xii, ascribes the *Lais* to the 1160s.

6. Gaston Paris, the first editor of the *Lai de Tyolet* (*Romania*, 8 [1879], 40-50), commented on the close resemblance between the adventures of its protagonist with Perceval's, up to and including their respective arrivals at Arthur's court. Neither

he nor Mario Roques (in *Romania*, 81 [1960], 33-38) could decide which text inspired the other. In my view, it is the *Tyolet* author who has imitated Chrétien, and most clumsily at that. Note *Flamenca*, ed. Merton J. Hubert and Marion E. Porter (Princeton, 1962), ll. 672-73: "L'autre comtet de Persaval / Co venc a la cort a caval."

7. The Guiot reading ("Soredamors prant la chemise") is contextually inadmissible. All other *Cligés* manuscripts read: "La reïne . . . ."

8. *University of California Publications in Modern Philology*, 28, No. 5 (1949), 321.

9. The question has been raised by Carl Theodor Gossen, in *Vox Romanica*, 18, No. 2 (1959), 181-82, 215-19. I owe my knowledge of Gossen's "Zur etymologischen Deutung des Grals," to Jean Frappier's *Chrétien de Troyes et le mythe du Graal* (1972), p. 12.

Sandra Ihle

SELECTED BIBLIOGRAPHY

This Bibliography is not meant to be inclusive; full bibliographies exist elsewhere (two of these are listed below; let me also mention at this juncture the annual MLA *Bibliography,* which contains rubrics dedicated to works dealing with Chrétien de Troyes and related subjects). Rather, it is intended as a guide to the reader of this volume who wishes to explore further Chrétien's art of composition. Thus, in addition to the standard editions and a list of both English and modernized French versions of Chrétien's romances, the Bibliography contains studies providing background material—historical, sociological and esthetic—to an understanding of Chrétien's literary context, as well as studies illuminating the art of writing demonstrated in his romances. The emphasis of the Bibliography, however, is on such studies as throw further light on the special concerns of the authors of this volume. It therefore stresses critical analyses that broaden our understanding of Chrétien as *romancier* and narrator. The self-conscious manipulation of sources and sophisticated shifting of narrative perspectives reveal an intention for these romances as well as demonstrate Chrétien's mastery of the art of romance. The studies that follow elucidate Chrétien's romance art from diverse points of view, but with the common goal of furthering our appreciation of that art.

Editions

Les Romans de Chrétien de Troyes, édités d'après la copie de Guiot (Bibl. nat. fr. 794). Ed. Mario Roques [unless otherwise indicated]. Classiques Français du Moyen Age. Paris: Champion, 1952-1975.
  1. *Erec et Enide.* C.F.M.A., 80. Paris: Champion, 1952.
  2. *Cligés.* Ed. Alexandre Micha. C.F.M.A., 84. Paris: Champion, 1957.
  3. *Le Chevalier de la Charrete.* C.F.M.A., 86. Paris: Champion, 1958.
  4. *Le Chevalier au Lion (Yvain).* C.F.M.A., 89. Paris: Champion, 1960.

5. *Le Conte du Graal (Perceval)*. Ed. Félix Lecoy. 2 vols. C.F.M.A., 100, 103. Paris: Champion, 1973-1975.

Christian von Troyes. *Sämtliche erhaltene Werke*. Ed. Wendelin Foerster [unless otherwise indicated].
    1. Grosse Ausgabe. Halle, 1884-1899. 4 vols. I: *Cligés* (1884); II: *Der Löwenritter (Yvain)* (1887); III: *Erec und Enid* (1890); IV: *Der Karrenritter und das Wilhelmsleben* (1899).
    2. Kleine Ausgabe. Halle, 1886-1932. 5 vols. I: *Erec und Enid* (1896, 1909, 1934); II: *Cliges* (1888, 1901, 1921 (abridged, ed. Alfons Hilka], 1934 [ed. Hermann Breuer]; III: *Yvain* (1891, 1902, 1906, 1912, 1913, 1926 [ed. A. Hilka], 1942 [ed. T.B.W. Reid (Manchester: Manchester Univ. Press), rpt. 1948, 1952, 1961]; IV: *Wilhelm von England* (1911); V: *Der Percevalroman (Li Contes del Graal)*. Ed. A. Hilka (1932, 1966).

Le Roman de Perceval ou le Conte du Graal. Ed. William Roach. Textes Littéraires Français, 71. 2nd ed. Geneva: Droz, Paris: Minard, 1959.

Philomena: Conte raconté d'après Ovide. Ed. Cornelis De Boer. Paris: Geuthner, 1909.

Guillaume d'Angleterre. Ed. Maurice Wilmotte. C.F.M.A., 55. Paris: Champion, 1927 [sometimes attributed to Chrétien de Troyes].

Les Chansons courtoises de Chrétien de Troyes. Ed. Marie-Claire Zai. Bern: Herbert Lang, Frankfurt: Peter Lang, 1974.

English Translations and Modern French Versions

Arthurian Romances by Chrétien de Troyes (*Erec, Cligés, Yvain, Lancelot*). Trans. W. Wistar Comfort. Everyman's Library, 698. London, Toronto: J.M. Dent, New York: E.P. Dutton, 1914. Revised [frequent reprintings].

The Story of the Grail (Perceval). Trans. Robert White Linker. Chapel Hill: Univ. of North Carolina Press, 1952.

Erec et Enide. Trans. René Louis. Paris: Champion, 1954.

Cligès. Trans. A. Micha. Paris: Champion, 1969.

Le Chevalier de la Charrette (Lancelot). Trans. Jean Frappier. 2nd ed. Paris: Champion, 1971.

Le Chevalier au Lion (Yvain). Trans. Claude Buridant and Jean Trotin. Paris: Champion, 1972.

Perceval le Gallois ou le Conte du Graal. Trans. Lucien Foulet. Paris: Editions Stock, 1947; rpt. Paris: A.G. Nizet, 1970, 1975.

Bibliographies

Kelly, Douglas. *Chrétien de Troyes: An Analytic Bibliography.* Research Bibliographies and Checklists, 17. London: Grant and Cutler, 1976.
Bulletin Bibliographique de la Société Internationale Arthurienne—Bibliographical Bulletin of the International Arthurian Society. Published since 1949.

Critical Studies

Adler, Alfred. "Sovereignty as the Principle of Unity in Chrétien's *Erec.*" *PMLA*, 60 (1945), 917-36.
Artin, Tom. *The Allegory of Adventure: Reading Chrétien's* Erec *and* Yvain. Lewisburg, Pa., London: Bucknell Univ. Press, 1974.
Auerbach, Erich. "Camilla, or, the Rebirth of the Sublime." In his *Literary Language and Its Public in Late Latin Antiquity and in the Middle Ages.* Trans. Ralph Manheim. New York: Pantheon, 1965.
Badel, Pierre-Yves. *Introduction à la vie littéraire du moyen âge.* Paris: Bordas, 1965.
―――. "Rhétorique et polémique dans les prologues de romans au moyen âge." *Littérature*, 20 (1975), 81-94.
Benton, John. "The Court of Champagne as a Literary Center." *Speculum*, 36 (1961), 551-91.
Bezzola, Reto R. *Les Origines et la formation de la littérature courtoise en Occident (500-1200).* 3 vols. Paris: Champion, 1944-1963.
―――. *Le Sens de l'aventure et de l'amour (Chrétien de Troyes).* Paris: La Jeune Parque, 1947.
Bloch, Howard. *Medieval French Literature and Law.* Berkeley, Los Angeles, London: Univ. of California Press, 1977.
Bogdanow, Fanni. "The Love Theme in Chrétien de Troyes's *Chevalier de la Charrette.*" *Modern Language Review*, 67 (1972), 50-61.
Brault, Gerard J. "Chrétien de Troyes' *Lancelot*: The Eye and the Heart." *Bulletin Bibliographique de la Société Internationale Arthurienne*, 24 (1972), 142-53.
Brinkmann, Hennig. *Zu Wesen und Form mittelalterlicher Dichtung.* Halle: Niemeyer, 1928; rpt. Darmstadt: Wissenschaftliche Buchgesellschaft, 1979.
Bruckner, Matilda Tomaryn. *Narrative Invention in Twelfth-Century French Romance: The Convention of Hospitality (1160-1200).* French Forum Monographs, 17. Lexington, Ky.: French Forum, Publishers, 1980.

Burnley, J.D. "Fine Amor: Its Meaning and Context." *Review of English Studies*, n. s. 31 (1980), 129-48.

Cohen, Gustave. *Un Grand Romancier d'amour et d'aventure au XIIe siècle: Chrétien de Troyes et son œuvre.* Paris: Boivin, 1931.

Colby, Alice M. *The Portrait in Twelfth-Century French Literature: An Example of the Stylistic Originality of Chrétien de Troyes.* Geneva: Droz, 1965.

Cross, Tom Peete, and William A. Nitze. *Lancelot and Guenevere: A Study on the Origins of Courtly Love.* Chicago: Univ. of Chicago Press, 1930.

Curtius, Ernst-Robert. *European Literature and the Latin Middle Ages.* Trans. W.R. Trask. New York, Evanston, Ill.: Harper and Row, 1963.

Deroy, Jean. "Chrétien de Troies et Godefroy de Leigni, conspirateurs contre la Fin' Amor adultère." *Cultura Neolatina*, 38 (1978), 67-78.

Duby, Georges. *Medieval Marriage: Two Models from Twelfth-Century France.* Trans. Elborg Forster. Baltimore: Johns Hopkins Univ. Press, 1978.

Faral, Edmond. *Les Arts poétiques du XIIe et du XIIIe siècle: Recherches et documents sur la technique littéraire du moyen âge.* Bibliothèque de l'Ecole des Hautes Etudes, 238. Paris: Champion, 1924.

Ferrante, Joan M. "*Cortes' amor* in Medieval Texts." *Speculum*, 55 (1980), 686-95.

Flori, Jean. "Pour une histoire de la chevalerie: L'adoubement dans les romans de Chrétien de Troyes." *Romania*, 100 (1979), 21-53.

Foerster, Wendelin. *Kristian von Troyes: Wörterbuch zu seinen sämtlichen Werken.* Halle, 1914. Rev. by Hermann Breuer. Tübingen: Max Niemeyer, 1964.

Foulet, Alfred. "Guinevere's Enigmatic Words: Chrétien's *Lancelot*, vv. 211-213." In *Jean Misrahi Memorial Volume: Studies in Medieval Literature.* Ed. Hans R. Runte, Henri Niedzielski and William L. Hendrickson. Columbia, S.C.: French Literature Publications Co., 1977, I, 175-80.

———, and Karl D. Uitti. "The Prologue to the *Lais* of Marie de France: A Reconsideration." *Romance Philology*, 35 (1981-1982), 242-49.

Foulon, Charles. "Le Rôle de Gauvain dans *Erec et Enide*." *Annales de Bretagne*, 65 (1958), 147-58.

Fourquet, Jean. "Le Rapport entre l'œuvre et la source chez Chrétien de Troyes et le problème des sources bretonnes." *Romance Philology*, 9 (1955-1956), 298-312.

Fourrier, Anthime. *Le Courant réaliste dans le roman courtois en France au moyen âge.* I: *Les Débuts (XIIe siècle).* Paris: Nizet, 1960.

———. "Encore la chronologie des œuvres de Chrétien de Troyes." *Bulletin Bibliographique de la Société Internationale Arthurienne*, 2 (1950), 69-88.

Franz, Arthur. "Die reflektierte Handlung im *Cliges.*" *Zeitschrift für romanische Philologie,* 47 (1927), 61-86.
Frappier, Jean. "La Brisure du couplet dans *Erec et Enide.*" *Romania,* 86 (1965), 1-21.
―――. *Chrétien de Troyes.* Paris: Hatier, 1968. English trans. Raymond J. Cormier. Athens, Ohio: Ohio Univ. Press, 1982.
―――. "Chrétien de Troyes." In *Arthurian Literature in the Middle Ages.* Ed. Roger Sherman Loomis. Oxford: Clarendon Press, 1959, pp. 157-91.
―――. *Chrétien de Troyes et le mythe du graal: Etude sur* Perceval *ou le* Conte du graal. Paris: S.E.D.E.S., 1972.
―――. "Le Concept de l'amour dans les romans arthuriens." *Bulletin Bibliographique de la Société Internationale Arthurienne,* 22 (1970), 119-36.
―――. "Le *Conte du Graal* est-il une allégorie judéo-chrétienne?" *Romance Philology,* 16 (1962-1963), 179-213; 20 (1966-1967), 1-31.
―――. "'D'amors,' 'par amors.'" *Romania,* 88 (1967), 433-74.
―――. *Etude sur* Yvain, *ou le Chevalier au Lion, de Chrétien de Troyes.* Paris: S.E.D.E.S., 1969.
―――. "Le Graal et ses feux divergeants." *Romance Philology,* 24 (1970-1971), 373-440.
―――. "Le Prologue du *Chevalier de la charrette* et son interprétation." *Romania,* 93 (1972), 337-77.
―――. "Sur la composition du *Conte du Graal.*" *Moyen Age,* 64 (1958), 67-102.
―――. "Sur un procès fait à l'amour courtois." *Romania,* 93 (1972), 145-93.
―――. "Sur la versification de Chrétien de Troyes: L'enjambement dans *Erec et Enide.*" *Research Studies* (Washington State Univ.), 32 (1964), 41-49.
Freeman, Michelle A. "Chrétien's *Cligés*: A Close Reading of the Prologue." *Romanic Review,* 67 (1976), 89-101.
―――. *The Poetics of* Translatio Studii *and* Conjointure: *Chrétien de Troyes's* Cligés. French Forum Monographs, 12. Lexington, Ky.: French Forum, Publishers, 1979.
―――. "Problems in Romance Composition: Ovid, Chrétien de Troyes, and the *Romance of the Rose.*" *Romance Philology,* 30 (1976-1977), 158-68.
―――. "Transpositions structurelles et intertextualité: Le 'Cligés' de Chrétien." *Littérature,* 41 (1981), 50-61.
Gallais, Pierre. "Hexagonal and Spiral Structure in Medieval Narrative." *Yale French Studies,* 51 (1974), 115-32.
―――. *Perceval et l'initiation: Essais sur le dernier roman de Chrétien de Troyes, ses correspondances "orientales" et sa signification anthropologique.* Paris: Editions du Sirac, 1972.

Gier, Albert. "Das Verwandtschaftsverhältnis von afr. *sens* und *sen*." *Romanistisches Jahrbuch*, 28 (1977), 54-72.
Guiette, Robert. "'Li conte de Bretaigne sont si vain et plaisant.'" *Romania*, 88 (1967), 1-12.
———. "Questions de littérature." *Romanica Gandensia*, 8 (1960), 61-66.
Haidu, Peter. *Aesthetic Distance in Chrétien de Troyes: Irony and Comedy in* Cligès *and* Perceval. Geneva: Droz, 1968.
———. *Lion-queue-coupée: L'écart symbolique chez Chrétien de Troyes*. Geneva: Droz, 1972.
Hart, Thomas Elwood. "Chrestien, Macrobius, and Chartrean Science: The Allegorical Robe as Symbol of Textual Design in the Old French *Erec*." *Mediaeval Studies*, 43 (1981), 250-96.
Hofer, Stefan. *Chrétien de Troyes: Leben und Werke des altfranzösischen Epikers*. Graz, Cologne: Böhlaus, 1954.
Hoffman, Stanton de V. "The Structure of the *Conte del Graal*." *Romanic Review*, 52 (1961), 81-98.
Holland, Wilhelm Ludwig. *Chrestien von Troies: Eine literaturgeschichtliche Untersuchung*. Tübingen: L.F. Fues, 1854.
Holmes, Urban T. *Chrétien de Troyes*. New York: Twayne, 1970.
———, and Sister M. Amelia Klenke. *Chrétien, Troyes, and the Grail*. Chapel Hill: Univ. of North Carolina Press, 1959.
Hunt, Tony. "The Emergence of the Knight in France and England 1000-1200." *Forum for Modern Language Studies*, 17 (1981), 93-114.
———. "The Rhetorical Background to the Arthurian Prologue: Tradition and the Old French Vernacular Prologues." *Forum for Modern Language Studies*, 6 (1970), 1-23.
———. "Tradition and Originality in the Prologues of Chrestien de Troyes." *Forum for Modern Language Studies*, 8 (1972), 320-44.
Imbs, Paul. "L'Elément religieux dans le *Conte del Graal* de Chrétien de Troyes." In *Les Romans du Graal dans la littérature des XIIe et XIIIe siècles*. Paris: C.N.R.S., 1956, pp. 31-53.
Javelet, Robert. "L'Amour spirituel face à l'amour courtois." In *Entretiens sur la renaissance du XIIe siècle*. Ed. M. de Gandillac and E. Jeauneau. The Hague, Paris: Mouton, 1968, pp. 309-36.
Johnston, R.C. "The Authorship of the 'Chevalier' and the 'Mule.'" *Modern Language Review*, 73 (1978), 496-98.
Kellermann, Wilhelm. *Aufbaustil und Weltbild Chrestiens von Troyes im Percevalroman*. Beihefte zur Zeitschrift für romanische Philologie, 88. Halle: Niemeyer, 1936; rpt. Darmstadt: Wissenschaftliche Buchgesellschaft, 1967.
Kelly, Douglas. "Courtly Love in Perspective: The Hierarchy of Love in Andreas Capellanus." *Traditio*, 24 (1968), 119-47.

———. "La Forme et le sens de la quête dans l'*Erec et Enide* de Chrétien de Troyes." *Romania*, 92 (1971), 326-58.

———. "Rhetoric in French Literature: Topical Invention in Medieval French Literature." In *Medieval Eloquence: Studies in Theory and Practice of Medieval Rhetoric.* Ed. James J. Murphy. Berkeley, Los Angeles, London: Univ. of California Press, 1978, pp. 231-51.

———. *Sens and Conjointure in the* Chevalier de la Charrette. The Hague, Paris: Mouton, 1966.

———. "The Source and Meaning of *Conjointure* in Chrétien's *Erec* 14." *Viator*, 1 (1970), 179-200.

———. "Theory of Composition in Medieval Narrative Poetry and Geoffrey of Vinsauf's *Poetria Nova.*" *Mediaeval Studies*, 31 (1969), 117-48.

———. "*Translatio Studii*: Translation, Adaptation, and Allegory in Medieval French Literature." *Philological Quarterly*, 57 (1978), 287-310.

Koenig, Daniel. *"Sen"/"sens" et "savoir" et leurs synonymes dans quelques romans courtois du 12e et du début du 13e siècle.* Publications Universitaires Européennes, série 13: Langue et Littérature Françaises, 22. Bern: Herbert Lang, Frankfurt: Peter Lang, 1973.

Köhler, Erich. *Ideal und Wirklichkeit in der höfischen Epik: Studien zur Form des frühen Artus- und Graldichtung.* Beihefte zur Zeitschrift für romanische Philologie, 97. 2nd ed. Tübingen: Niemeyer, 1970. French trans. *L'Aventure chevaleresque: Idéal et réalité dans le roman courtois: Etudes sur la forme des plus anciens poèmes d'Arthur et du Graal.* Trans. Eliane Kaufholz. Paris: Gallimard, 1974.

———. "Literatursoziologische Perspektiven." In *Grundriss der romanischen Literaturen des Mittelalters.* Vol. IV, part 1: *Le Roman jusqu'à la fin du XIIIe siècle.* Heidelberg: Winter, 1978, pp. 82-103.

———. "Le Rôle de la 'coutume' dans les romans de Chrétien de Troyes." *Romania*, 81 (1960), 386-97.

———. "Il sistema sociologico del romanzo francese medievale." *Medioevo Romanzo*, 3 (1976), 321-44.

———. *Trobadorlyrik und höfischer Roman: Aufsätze zur französischen und provenzalischen Literatur des Mittelalters.* Berlin: Rütten & Loening, 1962.

Kramer, Hans-Peter. *Erzählerbemerkungen und Erzählerkommentare in Chrestiens und Hartmanns* Erec *und* Iwain. Göppinger Arbeiten zur Germanistik, 35. Göppingen: Kümmerle, 1971.

Lacy, Norris J. *The Craft of Chrétien de Troyes: An Essay on Narrative Art.* Davis Medieval Texts and Studies, 3. Leiden: E.J. Brill, 1980.

———. "Thematic Analogues in *Erec.*" *L'Esprit Créateur*, 9 (1969), 267-74.

———. "Thematic Structure in the *Charrette.*" *L'Esprit Créateur*, 12 (Spring 1972), 13-18.

Laurie, Helen C.R. "*Enéas* and the *Lancelot* of Chrétien de Troyes." *Medium Aevum*, 37 (1968), 142-56.
Lazar, Moshé. "Lancelot et la *mulier mediatrix*: La quête de soi à travers la femme." *L'Esprit Créateur*, 9 (1969), 243-56.
Lejeune, Rita. "Rôle littéraire d'Aliénor d'Aquitaine et de sa famille." *Cultura Neolatina*, 14 (1954), 1-57.
———. "Le Rôle littéraire de la famille d'Aliénor d'Aquitaine." *Cahiers de Civilisation Médiévale*, 1 (1958), 319-37.
Loomis, Roger Sherman. *Arthurian Tradition and Chrétien de Troyes*. New York: Columbia Univ. Press, 1949.
Luria, Maxwell S. "The Storm-Making Spring and the Meaning of Chrétien's *Yvain*." *Studies in Philology*, 64 (1967), 564-85.
Luttrell, Claude. "The Arthurian Traditionalist's Approach to the Composer of Romance: R.S. Loomis on Chrétien de Troyes." *Oeuvres et Critiques*, 5, No. 2 (1980-1981), 23-30.
———. *The Creation of the First Arthurian Romance: A Quest*. Evanston, Ill.: Northwestern Univ. Press, 1974.
Maddox, Donald. *Structure and Sacring: The Systematic Kingdom in Chrétien's* Erec et Enide. French Forum Monographs, 8. Lexington, Ky.: French Forum, Publishers, 1978.
Mandel, Jerome. "Elements in the *Charrette* World: The Father-Son Relationship." *Modern Philology*, 62 (1964-1965), 97-104.
———. "Proper Behavior in Chrétien's *Charrette*: The Host-Guest Relationship." *French Review*, 48 (1974-1975), 683-89.
Marx, Jean. *La Légende arthurienne et le Graal*. Paris: Presses Universitaires de France, 1952.
———. "La Quête manquée de Gauvain." In *Mélanges offerts à Etienne Gilson*. Toronto: P.I.M.S., 1959, pp. 415-36.
McCash, June Hall Martin. "Marie de Champagne and Eleanor of Aquitaine: A Relationship Reexamined." *Speculum*, 54 (1979), 698-711.
Ménard, Philippe. "Le Chevalier errant dans la littérature arthurienne: Recherches sur les raisons du départ et de l'errance." In *Voyage, quête, pèlerinage dans la littérature et la civilisation médiévales*. Senefiance, 2. Aix-en-Provence: CUER-MA, Paris: Champion, 1976, pp. 289-310.
———. "Note sur la date du *Chevalier de la charrette*." *Romania*, 92 (1971), 118-26.
———. "Le Temps et la durée dans les romans de Chrétien de Troyes." *Moyen Age*, 73 (1967), 375-401.
Micha, Alexandre. "Sur les sources de la *Charrette*." *Romania*, 71 (1950), 345-58.
———. *La Tradition manuscrite des romans de Chrétien de Troyes*. Paris: Droz, 1939; rpt. Geneva: Droz, 1966.

Michener, Richard L. "Courtly Love in Chrétien: The 'Demande d'amour.'" *Studia Neophilologica*, 42 (1970), 353-60.
Mickel, Emanuel, Jr. "The Theme of Honor in Chrétien's *Lancelot*." *Zeitschrift für romanische Philologie*, 91 (1975), 243-72.
Misrahi, Jean. "More Light on the Chronology of Chrétien de Troyes?" *Bulletin Bibliographique de la Société Internationale Arthurienne*, 11 (1959), 89-120.
Nitze, William A. "*Sans* et *matière* dans les œuvres de Chrétien de Troyes." *Romania*, 44 (1915-1917), 14-36.
―――, and Harry F. Williams. *Arthurian Names in the Perceval of Chrétien de Troyes*. Berkeley: Univ. of California Press, 1955.
Nolan, E. Peter. "Mythopoetic Evolution: Chrétien de Troyes' *Erec et Enide*, *Cligés* and *Yvain*." *Symposium*, 25 (1971), 139-61.
Nykrog, Per. "Two Creators of Narrative Form in Twelfth-Century France: Gautier d'Arras―Chrétien de Troyes." *Speculum*, 48 (1973), 258-76.
Ollier, Marie-Louise. "The Author in the Text: The Prologues of Chrétien de Troyes." *Yale French Studies*, 51 (1974), 26-41.
―――. "Modernité de Chrétien de Troyes." *Romanic Review*, 71 (1980), 413-44.
Olschki, Leonardo. *The Grail Castle and Its Mysteries*. Trans. and ed. J.A. Scott. Berkeley, Los Angeles: Univ. of California Press, 1966.
Owen, D.D.R. *The Evolution of the Grail Legend*. Edinburgh, London: Oliver and Boyd, 1968.
―――. "Two More Romances by Chrétien de Troyes?" *Romania*, 92 (1971), 246-60.
Paris, Gaston. "Etudes sur les romans de la Table Ronde. Lancelot du Lac, I. Le *Lanzelet* d'Ulrich de Zatzikhoven; Lancelot du Lac, II. Le *Conte de la Charrette*." *Romania*, 10 (1881), 465-96; 12 (1883), 459-534; 16 (1887), 100-01.
Payen, Jean-Charles. "Lancelot contre Tristan: La conjuration d'un mythe subversif (réflexions sur l'idéologie romanesque au moyen âge)." In *Mélanges Pierre Le Gentil*. Paris: S.E.D.E.S. and C.D.U., 1973, pp. 617-32.
―――. "Les Valeurs humaines chez Chrétien de Troyes." In *Mélanges Rita Lejeune*. 2 vols. Gembloux: Duculot, 1969, II, 1087-1101.
Pickens, Rupert T. "*Estoire*, *Lai* and Romance: Chrétien's *Erec et Enide* and *Cligés*." *Romanic Review*, 66 (1975), 247-62.
―――. "Historical Consciousness in Old French Narrative." *French Forum*, 4 (1979), 168-84.
―――. *The Welsh Knight: Paradoxicality in Chrétien's* Conte del Graal. French Forum Monographs, 6. Lexington, Ky.: French Forum, Publishers, 1977.

Pollman, Leo. *Chrétien de Troyes und der Conte del Graal*. Tübingen: Niemeyer, 1965.
Press, A.R. "Le Comportement d'Erec envers Enide dans le roman de Chrétien de Troyes." *Romania*, 90 (1969), 529-38.
Ribard, Jacques. *Chrétien de Troyes, Le Chevalier de la charrette: Essai d'interprétation symbolique*. Paris: Nizet, 1972.
———. "Ecriture symbolique et visée allégorique dans *Le Conte du Graal*." *Oeuvres et critiques*, 5, No. 2 (1980-1981), 103-09.
———. "Les romans de Chrétien de Troyes sont-ils allégoriques?" *Cahiers de l'Association Internationale des Etudes Françaises*, 28 (1976), 7-20.
Riquer, Martín de. "Perceval y Gauvain en *Li Contes del Graal*." *Filologia Romanza*, 4 (1957), 119-47.
Robertson, D.W., Jr. *A Preface to Chaucer: Studies in Medieval Perspectives*. Princeton: Princeton Univ. Press, 1962.
Roques, Mario. *Le Graal de Chrétien et la demoiselle au Graal*. Geneva: Droz, 1955.
Rychner, Jean. "Le Prologue du *Chevalier de la charrette*." *Vox Romanica*, 26 (1967), 1-23.
———. "Le Sujet et la signification du *Chevalier de la charrette*." *Vox Romanica*, 27 (1968), 50-76.
Ryding, William. *Structure in Medieval Narrative*. The Hague, Paris: Mouton, 1971.
Schmolke-Hasselmann, Beate. *Der arthurische Versroman von Chrestien bis Froissart: Zur Geschichte einer Gattung*. Beihefte zur Zeitschrift für romanische Philologie, 177. Tübingen: Niemeyer, 1980.
———. "Untersuchungen zur Typik des arthurischen Romananfangs." *Germanisch-romanische Monatsschrift*, n. s. 31 (1981), 1-13.
Shippey, T.A. "The Uses of Chivalry: *Erec* and *Gawain*." *Modern Language Review*, 66 (1971), 241-50.
Shirt, David J. "Chrétien de Troyes and the Cart." In *Studies in Medieval Literature in Memory of Frederic Whitehead*. Manchester: Manchester Univ. Press, 1973, pp. 279-301.
———. "*Cligés*: A Twelfth-Century Matrimonial Case-Book?" *Forum for Modern Language Studies*, 18 (1982), 75-89.
———. "Godefroi de Lagny et la composition de la *Charrette*." *Romania*, 96 (1975), 27-52.
———. "How Much of the Lion Can We Put before the Cart? Further Light on the Chronological Relationship of Chrétien de Troyes's *Lancelot* and *Yvain*." *French Studies*, 31 (1977), 1-17.
Southward, Elaine. "The Unity of Chrétien's *Lancelot*." In *Mélanges de linguistique et de littérature romanes offerts à Mario Roques*. Vol. II. Paris: Didier, 1953, pp. 281-90.

Stanger, Mary D. "Literary Patronage at the Medieval Court of Flanders." *French Studies*, 11 (1957), 214-29.
Topsfield, Leslie T. *Chrétien de Troyes: A Study of the Arthurian Romances.* Cambridge: Cambridge Univ. Press, 1981.
Trimpi, Wesley. "The Ancient Hypothesis of Fiction: An Essay on the Origins of Literary Theory." *Traditio*, 27 (1971), 1-78.
―――. "The Quality of Fiction: The Rhetorical Transmission of Literary Theory." *Traditio*, 30 (1974), 1-118.
Uitti, Karl D. "A propos de philologie." *Littérature*, 41 (1981), 30-46.
―――. "The Clerkly Narrator Figure in Old French Hagiography and Romance." *Medioevo Romanzo*, 2 (1975), 394-408.
―――. "Narrative and Commentary: Chrétien's Devious Narrator in *Yvain*." *Romance Philology*, 33 (1979-1980), 160-67.
―――. "Remarks on Old French Narrative: Courtly Love and Poetic Form." *Romance Philology*, 26 (1972-1973), 77-93; 28 (1974-1975), 190-99.
―――. *Story, Myth, and Celebration in Old French Narrative Poetry 1050-1200.* Princeton: Princeton Univ. Press, 1973.
Vinaver, Eugène. *A la recherche d'une poétique médiévale.* Paris: Nizet, 1970.
―――. "Les Deux Pas de Lancelot." In *Mélanges Jean Fourquet*. Paris: Klincksieck, 1969, pp. 355-61.
―――. "Form and Meaning in Medieval Romance." Modern Humanities Research Association Presidential Address. London, 1966.
―――. *The Rise of Romance.* Oxford: Clarendon Press, 1971.
Warning, Rainer. "Formen narrativer Identitätskonstitution im höfischen Roman." In *Grundriss der romanischen Literaturen des Mittelalters.* Vol. IV, part 1: *Le Roman jusqu'à la fin du XIIIe siècle.* Heidelberg: Winter, 1978, pp. 25-59.
Webster, Kenneth G.T. *Guinevere: A Study of Her Abductions.* Milton, Mass.: The Turtle Press, 1951.
Wetherbee, Winthrop. *Platonism and Poetry in the Twelfth Century: The Literary Influence of the School of Chartres.* Princeton: Princeton Univ. Press, 1972.
Wittig, Joseph S. "The Aeneas-Dido Allusion in Chrétien's *Erec et Enide*." *Comparative Literature*, 22 (1970), 237-53.
Zaddy, Z.P. *Chrétien Studies: Problems of Form and Meaning in* Erec, Yvain, Cligés *and the* Charrette. Glasgow: Univ. of Glasgow Press, 1973.
Zink, Michel. "Une Mutation de la conscience littéraire: Le langage romanesque à travers des exemples français du XIIe siècle." *Cahiers de Civilisation Médiévale*, 24 (1981), 3-27.
Zumthor, Paul. *Essai de poétique médiévale.* Paris: Seuil, 1972.

The Edward C. Armstrong Monographs on Medieval Literature

1 *On Editing Old French Texts*. By Alfred Foulet and Mary Blakely Speer. Lawrence: The Regents Press of Kansas, 1979.
2 *Jean Froissart and His* Meliador: *Context, Craft, and Sense*. By Peter F. Dembowski. 1983.
3 *The Romances of Chrétien de Troyes: A Symposium*. Edited by Douglas Kelly. 1985.